COLLEGIUM

VERITAS

MDCCCXL

The Philosophy of Law

THE PHILOSOPHY OF LAW
An Introduction to Jurisprudence

JEFFRIE G. MURPHY
and
JULES L. COLEMAN

ROWMAN & ALLANHELD
PUBLISHERS

ROWMAN & ALLANHELD

Published in the United States of America in 1984
by Rowman & Allanheld, Publishers
(A division of Littlefield, Adams & Company)
81 Adams Drive, Totowa, New Jersey 07512

Library of Congress Cataloging in Publication Data

Murphy, Jeffrie G.
  The philosophy of law.

  Bibliography: p.
  Includes index.
  1. Law—Philosophy. 2. Jurisprudence. I. Coleman,
Jules L. II. Title.
K231.M87 1984   340′.1   84-6870
ISBN 0-8476-6277-2
ISBN 0-8476-6278-0 (pbk.)

Printed in the United States of America

    85 86 / 10 9 8 7 6 5 4 3 2

For Ellen and Mimsie

Contents

List of Figures

Preface and Acknowledgments

All of us live under a legal system and must confront the law in many aspects in our daily lives. The law sometimes presents itself to us in unattractive ways when it requires that we do things we would prefer not to do or that we believe are positively evil to do. At other times the law can appear almost beautiful when it protects us against harm or helps us to do something we very much want to do—e.g., get married or divorced. Under the law we can be discouraged from smoking marijuana, given or deprived of a place in medical school through a program of preferential admissions for minorities, drafted to fight in a war we may regard as evil, allowed or prohibited to seek and obtain an abortion, compensated for injuries sustained through another's negligence, protected against theft and bodily harm, facilitated in the making of a contract, and so on. Depending upon what we think of these various activities and outcomes, we shall be inclined to view the law as either a force for good or evil—though sometimes, we shall no doubt be forced to admit, a necessary evil. One thing we cannot do, however, is *avoid* the law. Like it or not, it is a pervasive feature of our lives and is likely to remain such in any life that would hope to be social, civilized, and predictable.

Given the major and permanent role of the law in our everyday lives, it is both surprising and unfortunate that ignorance of the law has historically been tolerated in undergraduate education. No reputable college or university would think of willingly graduating a person ignorant of basic facts of science or basic skills of language and mathematics, and yet it has been common for these institutions to graduate legal illiterates—persons who know little more about the law than what they pick up from television crime and lawyer dramas. Even if students are forced to take a few law-related courses in political science or sociology, the focus of such courses is likely to be so narrow that the student winds up thinking of law as basically criminal law plus constitutional rights. The complex and important issues of, for example, tort law, contract law, family law, the law of evidence, and legal ethics—just to name a few—have remained largely virgin territory for undergraduates.

In recent years, fortunately, there have been some encouraging signs that this educational apathy toward the law is being challenged. The political turmoil of the sixties put the law at the center of social attention—some seeing it as an oppressive instrument of racism and warmongering imperialism and others seeing it as the only civilized way to oppose these evils. And even more recently crucial legal issues have been among the major news stories of the day and have aroused deep human passions. (Some obvious examples that come to mind are these: equal rights for women and homosexuals, abortion, the teaching of Darwinian evolution in the public schools, forced busing for school integration, capital punishment, the insanity defense, preferential hiring and admissions programs, the resignation—under threat of legal impeachment—of a lawyer president and his lawyer staff for the obstruction of justice, and the general climate of litigiousness—with multimillion dollar settlements and lawyers advertising on television in the manner of used car salesmen—currently characteristic of our society.) Here again some see the law as a force of evil and others as a force of good, but all see it, however vaguely, as somehow at the very center of these issues and disputes. Thus, not surprisingly, undergraduate students have themselves in recent years increasingly demanded more college courses on law and law-related topics. They realize that knowledge of law should not be confined to graduates of professional legal schools and that every citizen who claims to be educated should have greater sophistication about the law than has been common in the past.

Courses in the philosophy of law (or jurisprudence, as it is sometimes called) are one response to this need, and student demand for them and enrollments in them are steadily increasing. Such courses are not concerned primarily with the actual concrete details of particular legal systems, but rather are courses about the general nature and importance of law itself. If properly taught, a course in the philosophy of law functions to provide an indispensable background for more detailed study of particular laws and legal systems later. (If students come to jurisprudence already having such knowledge, it is a great asset for both student and instructor. Such knowledge should never be presupposed at the undergraduate level, however.) Legal philosophy provides clarity, intellectual order and structure, and standards of rational (often moral) criticism and evaluation. It thus gives insight into the relevant questions to ask when laws are being discussed or legal reforms are being proposed, and can help to introduce reason into areas where passion often dominates.

The purpose of this book is to provide an introduction to the philosophy of law. It is aimed primarily at an audience of beginners and is intended as a first text for such an audience—a text that can be followed up by readings of a more complex and sophisticated nature. Since the book addresses beginners in the subject, it will frequently contain general discussions and surveys of ideas. It will not be limited to this, however, and thus is not simply a textbook in the traditional sense. It is the belief of both authors that the general discussions should be focused, whenever possible, on specific issues that can be used as examples to illustrate in some detail the relevance of the general points made. Thus the chapter on moral theory and the law contains an examination of the moral foundations of freedom of speech and press, the chapter on crime and punishment contains an examination of criminalization and of the death penalty, and the chapter on private law contains an examination of no-fault tort systems and schemes whereby contract law can be used to reallocate wealth. These examinations are much more detailed than the general textual material. Though they are written to be accessible to the beginner (who has mastered the preliminary material that precedes them), they also contain ideas and arguments that should be of interest to the specialist as well.

Persons planning to adopt this book as a text in a college or university course may be assured that the book presupposes little or no background in either philosophy or law. It may be used alone or may be used in conjunction with an anthology of readings, e.g., *Readings in Philosophy of Law*, edited by John Arthur and William H. Shaw. It can also be used with such specialized anthologies in legal philosophy as Jeffrie G. Murphy's *Punishment and Rehabilitation* or Richard Wasserstrom's *Morality and the Law*. In an ambitious upper-division, honors, graduate, or law school course, the book could be used to provide background and a framework for discussing some difficult and important contemporary writing in legal philosophy, e.g., Ronald Dworkin's *Taking Rights Seriously* and Marshall Cohen's anthology *Ronald Dworkin and Contemporary Jurisprudence.* The authors have also had success using portions of the text (in manuscript form) in conjunction with various legal casebooks that allow the instructor to demonstrate how philosophical issues grow out of and are relevant to actual legal cases. (Particularly useful here has been *Criminal Law and Its Processes*, edited by Sanford Kadish and Monrad Paulsen, and *Bioethics and the Law*, edited by Michael Shapiro and Roy Spece.) Whether used alone or supplemented by other readings, this book is an introduction to the most basic philosophical questions that can, in the authors' judgment, be asked about the law, and attempts to show how these questions arise in various branches of law—criminal, tort, contract, constitutional, etc. Of course not all important questions or

areas of law can be covered in a single volume, but few would doubt
the centrality of the ones here selected. The text attempts an accurate
though simplified presentation of the various prominent answers that
have been given to these questions and often provides the authors'
own views as well. Its primary purpose, however, is not to give students
facts for memorization or slogans for allegiance. It is rather concerned
to consider *reasons* for and against the various views discussed and is
thus highly *argumentative* in the proper philosophical sense. As such
it should help to provide students with the basic intellectual tools
required to think through for themselves some of the fundamental
questions of legal philosophy and perhaps even to raise other equally
or more important questions.

The book represents a joint effort on the part of the authors in
the sense that they read and discussed each other's ideas and often
attempted to rewrite material in the light of each other's criticisms.
However, being guided by the wisdom of the old saying that "a camel
looks like an animal designed by a committee," no effort was made
to impose an artificial homogeneity on the final result. Each author
would no doubt have made changes in the material prepared by the
other if he had been writing it instead, but final authority was left
to the primary author in each case. Mr. Murphy has primary responsibility for the Preface, Introduction, and Chapters 1, 2, and 3.
Mr. Coleman has primary responsibility for Chapters 4 and 5.

As the reader progresses from the early introductory material to
the material in the final chapter, an increase in the difficulty and
sophistication of the book's contents will be noted. This is intentional
and reflects the belief of both authors that readers should themselves
increase in sophistication as they pass from the beginning of an
introductory book to its conclusion. Many readers may in particular
find the final chapter—the chapter on law and economics—difficult.
This is both because many persons are phobic about economics (because
it reminds them of mathematics) and because some of the ideas really
are difficult and technical. In presenting this chapter, every effort
was made to simplify and to explain technical material in a non-
technical idiom—e.g., no complex mathematics is presupposed. Even
given this, however, the material is not easy. But the material in the
earlier chapters was not easy either; it perhaps just seemed to be.
Thus this is a good point at which to remind the reader that philosophy,
though often mistakenly thought of as a "soft" humanities discipline,
is to be studied with the care and rigor that one would give to the
study of such "hard" disciplines as physics or chemistry. It should be

studied—not read through in a casual way, as one might read a mystery novel, simply to get the "gist" of it.

*   *   *

I want first to thank my teachers: Joel Feinberg, who introduced me to legal philosophy, encouraged my pursuit of unconventional interests in the field and who now, as my colleague and valued friend, continues to support my flights of intellectual fancy; and Guido Calabresi, who taught me torts, introduced me to law and economics, and who through his life and work demonstrated to me that one can be both a "great man" and a great man. I want also to express my gratitude to H. L. A. Hart and Ronald Dworkin: H. L. A. Hart for making legal philosophy respectable and responsible; Ronald Dworkin for elevating it to its current status and for making it profitable.

Jules L. Coleman
Tucson, Arizona

Three teachers have made an enormous difference in my life, and I would like to thank them here: Eleanor Weiherman, who first introduced me to the world of intellectual concerns; Maurice Mandelbaum, who first introduced me to philosophy and started my life-long love affair with the subject; and Lewis W. Beck, who enriched my education and gave me tremendous help and encouragement at the start of my career. May Brodbeck and Gareth Matthews were intellectually and personally supportive of me during the anxious years from graduate school to tenure; and Herbert Morris and Richard Wasserstrom helped me enormously in my study of law and the philosophy of law. Anthony Woozley edited the series in which my first book appeared, and that book as well as much of my subsequent work has been improved through his willingness to read and offer thoughtful (if not always tactful) criticism of it. For setting the ideal to which all of us in legal philosophy aspire (and for his gracious treatment of me when I visited him in Oxford), I also would like to express both gratitude and esteem for H. L. A. Hart. Finally, a very personal note of thanks: Even more than usual, my wife Ellen Canacakos has helped me greatly in this project. Her skills as a lawyer and her willingness and ability to reflect on the larger issues involved in her profession have provided the basis for many fruitful discussions of the issues involved in this book. Her unwillingness to settle for vague philosophical generalities and theories—particularly when they do

The Philosophy of Law: An Introduction to Jurisprudence

violence to the nature and practice of law as she encounters it on a day to day basis—has been infectious and has helped me to see virtues in certain legal theories (e.g., legal realism) that I had previously regarded as utterly bankrupt. I thank her for this—as well as for so many other things—and dedicate my portion of the book to her.

Jeffrie G. Murphy
Tempe, Arizona

The Philosophy of Law

Introduction

What Is the Philosophy of Law?

The philosophy of law (or "jurisprudence" as it is often called in law schools) is the application of the rational techniques of the discipline of philosophy to the subject matter of law. What does this mean? John Austin, a nineteenth-century English philosopher of law, offered an answer that still serves reasonably well today. Austin distinguished between *analytical jurisprudence* and *normative jurisprudence.* Analytical jurisprudence is concerned with the logical analysis of the basic concepts that arise in law—e.g., duty, responsibility, excuse, negligence, and the concept of law itself. Normative jurisprudence is concerned with the rational criticism and evaluation of legal practices. Such criticism is often moral in nature but it can also be economic, psychological, political, etc. The philosopher is here not primarily concerned to give advice about the law from these perspectives but is rather involved in the task of attempting to understand the logical structure of such advice. Thus, the philosopher who is interested in the moral evaluation of the law will be concerned with the nature of moral reasoning and argument and will be concerned to identify where such reasoning has an application within or to the law. A requirement for moral reasoning might, for example, be present within the law as an essential element in analyzing constitutional concepts such as "due process," "equal protection," or "cruel and unusual punishment." Moral reasoning might be applied to the law in, for example, evaluating the justification for the entire practice of criminal punishment. So, too, for other evaluative perspectives. The philosopher concerned with the economic analysis of law will not be giving economic advice but will mainly be concerned to understand the logical structure of such advice and to discover to what degree such analysis illuminates and helps evaluate legal concepts and practices. What this shows is that the primary task of the philosopher is analytical or conceptual, even when the initial concern is with normative matters. Normative discourse is valuable only when it is analytically clear and rationally structured; indeed, it is positively dangerous when it is sloppy and sentimental or dogmatic and authoritarian, in short, when it is anything but rational. (Recall Nazism and its vague and bombastic "moral" rhetoric taken from German Romanticism.) The goal of philosophy, here as elsewhere, is to articulate and maintain the standards of rational criticism and to fight off the darkness that surrounds any practice when it starts being discussed, not in terms of public and objective reasons, but in terms of unexamined feelings, dogmas, faiths, and conventions.

The subject matter of legal philosophy is thus easily characterized: Whenever one raises a question about law that involves either normative issues or issues of conceptual analysis (including questions about how these two might be related), one is raising a philosophical question about the law. Such questions are not raised only by professional philosophers, of course. Lawyers and judges find that they must frequently raise such questions (e.g., how is "negligence" to be understood, and is the death penalty "cruel and unusual" for rape, etc.) and they often do a subtle and impressive job of answering them. Fortunately, much of the record of these answers is preserved, at least in the United States, through the practice of including any judicial opinions that were written into the texts of federal and state cases published. Though judges are more constrained in their approach than philosophers (who can afford the luxury of developing ideal theories about how things ought to be without being constrained by the limitations of an institutional role), they are still involved in a task of a similar nature. Thus, there is a potential for rich interaction between legal philosophy and legal practice—each side can learn from the other. If philosophers have any unique contribution to make, it probably lies in their trained ability to recognize conceptual and normative problems, even when they lie buried and obscured behind apparently factual material, and to bring to bear on the discussion the refinements in thinking about such problems that has developed in their discipline over its nearly 3,000 year old history.

At this point, of course, a skeptical reader might raise the following worry: "If philosophy (even when dealing with normative matters) is centrally concerned with the analysis of concepts, then does it not simply provide an inefficient, windy, and roundabout way of doing something we can do much more easily by just going to a dictionary? If one wants to know what 'negligence' means, why not simply look it up in *Webster's* or, if that definition is too sketchy, in a legal dictionary such as *Black's*?" The long answer to this skeptical question is to read this entire book and see if what one has learned from it could have been grasped more easily from a dictionary. The short answer is this: Dictionary definitions are reports of how people normally use words;

philosophers are concerned with clarifying the *concepts* that these words (sometimes quite misleadingly) designate.

The philosophical analysis of a concept, while by no means indifferent to ordinary usage (which can be a valuable starting point), is concerned to give a *rational account* of such usage. It is concerned, for example, to answer the question: What is there about all cases of negligence that makes us group them under one concept and thus use the same word? The goal, in short, is not an understanding of words alone but also an understanding of the practices in which these words occur and that are designated by them. Sometimes philosophers will find inconsistencies or incoherencies in ordinary usage (including ordinary legal usage). They may conclude from this that the concept being used is confused, and will then perhaps offer a *rational reconstruction* of the concept in question—i.e., a suggestion for a new and more precise analysis. This will normally be accompanied with a suggestion for a new definition for the term that designates the concept.

The philosopher, in short, is not simply a reporter of usage but is also often a *corrector* of usage. The philosopher is concerned with adopting an analysis of a particular legal concept that is as clear as possible, that explains why the concept is used in the way it is, and that meshes in a logically coherent way with other crucial concepts to which the concept in question is systematically related. Consider one simple example: How should we understand the concept of *unusual* as it occurs in the Eighth Amendment's ban on "cruel and unusual punishments"? If we go to *Webster's* we find the word "unusual" defined as "strange, rare, or exceptional." Shall we then accept this as our conceptual analysis? If we do, then note the bizarre consequence: The very punishments clearly intended by the Founding Fathers to be banned by this amendment—torture and mutilation—will become acceptable if we simply begin inflicting them often enough so that they become common rather than rare! How absurd. Nor will we get a final illumination by hunting up an old dictionary to discover if the word had a different meaning two hundred years ago. The drafters of that amendment were clearly trying to get at something substantive— some important value they sought to protect—and this value should be the object of our search. In a philosophical analysis of the concepts of cruel and unusual punishments, we shall want to articulate that value, see if it can be coherently analyzed, determine if the moral background it presupposes is rationally defensible, discover how it relates to other important legal concepts, and understand how it fits into the legal history of the institutions of which it is a part. That is a philosophical analysis. Knowing the dictionary meanings of the terms chosen to designate the value by those persons who drafted the amendment will sometimes be a helpful start in this philosophical task, but it is only a start and a small one at that. (Another problem worth noting is this: Dictionary definitions often define a philosophically puzzling term with terms that are just as puzzling; e.g., *Webster's* defines the term "law" itself as "all the *rules* of conduct *established* and *enforced* by the *authority* . . . of a given . . . *state*".)

General attempts to characterize a discipline of study can quickly and easily become vague and unhelpful. The best way to understand a field of study is to see it at work in detail. In our case, this will involve studying the following chapters. At the close of these, the intelligent and careful reader will either have a clear grasp of the nature of the philosophy of law or the writers will have failed miserably in their task. As an introduction to the chapters, a brief summary of their contents might be helpful.

In Chapter 1, the concept of law itself will be analyzed. How is law to be distinguished from force? From morality? What is the "rule of law" and what does it mean to recommend a "government of laws and not of men"? What is it to apply or interpret law—is this simply the mechanical application of rules or is some element of discretion and creativity essential? (This may be a version of the "strict constructionist" v. "activist" debate.)

In Chapter 2, an attempt will be made to explain the nature of a moral issue or problem (so that one may recognize one when present) and to explore various theoretical answers that have been given to the question of how such problems are rationally to be resolved. The contrast between theories that make promotion of the general welfare morally central and those that make rights morally central will be emphasized. Moral skepticism and relativism (the views that morality is not objective and that it is simply a matter of personal or cultural preference) will be explored and, it is hoped, partially defused. The presence of moral issues in the law and the use of moral theory in helping resolve those issues will be illustrated. As an example, the First Amendment's protection of freedom of speech and press will be explored in some detail.

Chapter 3 deals with the issue of crime and punishment. Punishment is the use of state power in its most brutal form. The threat of punishment (promised whenever conduct is criminalized) keeps people from doing things they would like to do—a clear curtailment of liberty. If some do the things anyway and are caught, they are very likely to be punished, if for no other reason than at least to show, as Justice Holmes said, that "the law keeps its promises." Punishment will often take the form of imprisonment, another clear curtailment of liberty. In any society that values liberty and regards it as a right, punishment will be viewed very seriously, to be imposed only if a very good justification for it can be mounted.

This chapter will explore the various justifications that have been offered for criminalizing conduct and thereby making those who engage in that conduct liable to punishment. (Why criminalize any conduct? Why not treat all rights violations on a tort model—i.e., allow them so long as compensation is paid to anyone who gets harmed?) If one concludes that some practice of punishment is justified, one will still want to raise many questions about the details of that practice: Should the state punish for acts alone or should it take mental states into account? Will some excuses or defenses for criminal conduct be allowed, and if so, what will they be—e.g., will there be an insanity defense? What *procedures* should surround the criminal prosecution and trial—e.g., why should the burden of proof be on the state to prove guilt instead of on the individual to prove innocence? Should we search for alternatives to criminalization and punishment— e.g., preventive detention of potentially dangerous people, therapy for the criminal as a sick and troubled person, or perhaps outright forgiveness and mercy to the criminal as an act of love and charity? Many of these issues will be brought into focus as the chapter closes with a detailed discussion of capital punishment.

Chapter 4 explores philosophical issues in the private law: in particular, torts and contracts. The torts section considers whether in order to be just liability for the costs of accidents must be distributed on the basis of fault. Is a no-fault system incompatible with our ideals of justice? Contract law is quintessentially *private* law. One's duties in contracts are presumably entirely self-imposed. Because of its private nature, the law of contracts is generally thought of as an inappropriate institution for pursuing *social* goals or policies, in particular, for reallocating wealth among parties. In the contracts section, we explore whether, in fact, contract law is a plausible device for pursuing a society's distributional goals.

Chapter 5 concludes with an examination of law and economics. Many writers are skeptical of a direct moralistic approach to law; they find it unclear, rationally unsupportable, and ideological. Seeking a clear, scientific, and value-neutral approach to the understanding and evaluation of law, several influential writers have in recent years drawn on the theories and techniques of modern economics (particularly microeconomics and game theory) in an attempt to gain a new understanding and method of evaluating the law. Some have maintained that this analysis is not opposed to morality but is, indeed, the best way to capture whatever is coherent in a moral oulook on law. These matters will be explored here.

The topics explored in the five chapters of this book do not by any means exhaust the philosophical problems that arise with respect to law, but few would doubt the centrality of the ones here selected. With the optimistic expectation that these chapters will generate further interest and curiosity in the reader, a bibliography of recommended further readings has been added at the end of the book. These readings either expand on the issues discussed in the text or introduce entirely new philosophical problems about law. Bibliographies are commonly ignored by readers and thus rarely repay the authorial efforts expended in their compilation. The authors of the present text hope that this will not be the sad fate of the one they have compiled, or for the notes at the end of each chapter. Though many of these notes simply provide publication details on works discussed in the text, *a significant number of them expand or qualify the argument of the text in significant ways.* It is thus hoped that the reader will not choose to ignore them entirely.

1
The Nature of Law

Law, says the judge as he looks down his nose,
Speaking clearly and most severely,
Law is as I've told you before,
Law is as you know I suppose,
Law is but let me explain it once more,
Law is The Law.

W. H. Auden
From "Law Like Love"

One of the oldest problems in the philosophy of law, and the problem with which most legal philosophy courses commonly begin, is the analysis of the concept of law itself. At the outset, this might strike the reader as puzzling. Why is this such a problem? Why does it matter? A chemistry course does not begin with a tortured discussion on "what is chemistry?". A history course does not usually begin with such a discussion of "what is history?" (given that we all know that history is just one damned thing after another), and so on for most other courses in a college or university catalog. What is there then about the concept of law that makes its analysis sufficiently difficult and important that it must precede all other issues in the philosophy of law?

This question is natural and sensible enough that it requires a careful answer. Probably the best general start toward an answer has been provided by the contemporary English legal philosopher H. L. A. Hart, who has noted certain features about law that make its analysis puzzling:[1]

(1) Law is clearly a device for *social control*—a device for getting people to do things they would be unlikely to do if left to personal inclination alone. But how does a *legal* method of social control differ from other methods of social control with which the legal may easily be confused—e.g., *morality* or mere *force*? There is so much overlap in the language of morality and the language of the law (both talk

of duty, rights, obligation, responsibility, etc.) that it would be easy to confuse the two. And yet, when we reflect and realize that it is possible for certain laws (e.g., clearly some of those of Nazi Germany) to require conduct that is immoral, we realize that law and morality are in some sense different even if closely related. Is one difference between law and morality perhaps that the former is necessarily backed up by *force* or the *threat of force* and the latter is not?

Force is so obviously a large part of every legal system that some identification of law with force might be tempting. But further reflection again shows that such a simple identification would be misleading. Once we move from the domain of criminal law, it is difficult to support the claim that law must involve force. There may, for example, be force present in the laws detailing procedures for making a valid will, but its presence is certainly not obvious. Also, certain instances of force (e.g., a gunman putting a pistol to your head and demanding your money or your life) are clearly not legal in nature. Thus force, though perhaps intimately related to law, cannot be identified with law. What, then, are the relations between the concepts "force," "morality," and "law" if not relations of identity? The vividness of this question provides one reason why the concept of law requires analysis.

(2) The concept of law may be used ambiguously and may thus cause serious moral and intellectual confusion. Sometimes, when people speak of laws, they are speaking of *descriptive* laws—statements of how things, as a matter of fact, regularly do happen. The so-called "law of gravity" is an example of a descriptive law. Other times, when people speak of laws, they are clearly speaking of *prescriptive* laws—authoritative statements about what should or ought to happen or about what should or ought to be permitted to happen. The First Amendment to the United States Constitution ("Congress shall make no law respecting an establishment of religion . . .") is clearly a prescriptive law concerning the enactment of other prescriptive laws. It is not a statement of what Congress has in fact done or a prediction of what Congress will in fact do. It is rather a statement of what Congress, in enacting other prescriptive laws, is permitted and not permitted to do. These sorts of laws and legal systems, prescriptive laws and systems of prescriptive laws, are the object of study in the philosophy of law. Descriptive laws are examined in the philosophy of science.

As clear as the distinction between descriptive laws and prescriptive laws is, the two senses of "law" are still sometimes confused. Some people, for example, are inclined morally to condemn certain sexual practices (e.g., oral or anal copulation) as "contrary to the laws of nature" or simply "unnatural" in order to support their belief that these practices are evil and should be punished by the criminal law. But when they speak here of "contrary to natural law," what in the world can they possibly mean by this phrase? Surely they do not mean that such acts *cannot* happen, that such sexual acts are like acts of changing water into wine, contrary to descriptive laws of nature in the sense that their occurrence would be a *miracle.* Does "contrary to laws of nature" then mean "statistically infrequent"? If so, then the claim is clearly descriptive and one can draw no moral or other evaluative or prescriptive conclusion from it. (Artistic creativity and genius are statistically infrequent. Does that make expression of these traits immoral?) Suppose then that these persons mean something prescriptive when they say "laws of nature." We might then well ask them what authority prescribes to nature; is there perhaps a cosmic legislature? If, as is most likely the case, these people really mean by "contrary to nature" something like "contrary to my religion's inter-pretation of God's commands," then they should simply say this, avoid all the confusing and ambiguous references to laws of nature, and face the resulting problems honestly and squarely—one of the problems in our system being the First Amendment's ban on an establishment of religion.

Not all linkings between descriptive and prescriptive law, however, are as confused as the one noted above. Consider the following problem: Would we say that a certain document—a written constitution per-haps—was really the prescriptive law of the land if nobody ever in fact obeyed it or paid it even the slightest bit of attention? Does not the claim that the United States Constitution is the highest prescriptive law of the land have something to do with the descriptive fact that this document is actually appealed to in deciding legal cases? If, starting tomorrow (because of a revolution perhaps), all citizens, legislators, government executives, and courts started ignoring the Constitution, would it still be the law of the land? At some point would we not be forced to say that it was at most *former* or *previous* law?

Legality is not to be simply identified with descriptive regularity any more than it is to be simply identified with morality or force. As these questions clearly show, however, it must have some important relationship with such regularity. An analysis of the concept of law will perhaps illuminate what this relationship is.

(3) The concept of law strikes up against certain puzzling but important *borderline cases*—cases of practices or institutions that have enough features in common with clear cases of law to tempt us to regard them as law but enough dissimilar features to tempt us in the other direction as well. Is *international law* really law? Is *primitive law*

really law? Some writers who have been inclined to answer no have raised this challenging question: If these practices really are legal (rather than simply quasilegal or prelegal), then where are the legislative bodies to enact their laws, the courts to authoritatively interpret them, and sanctioning bodies to back them up with force? Let us suppose for a moment that these features are indeed absent. Until we first determine the relations of the concepts of legislation, court, and sanction to the concept of law itself, we shall not be in a position to know to what extent, if any, an absence of these features will pose a problem to the classification of international law and primitive law as genuine instances of law.

The point here is not to guarantee the removal of international law and primitive law from the class of borderline cases of law, because they may genuinely be borderline cases. If so, their removal would be arbitrary conceptual legislation or stipulation and would simply achieve, not clarity, but what Hart has called "uniformity at the price of distortion." The point is really to understand precisely the nature of these cases—to determine, if they are borderline, exactly why they are borderline. Only an adequate analysis of the concept of law will allow us to do this.

(4) The final problem worth noting is the following: The concept of law, it will later be discovered, will require analysis in terms of elements that, in themselves, also raise interesting and important philosophical issues. At least some laws, for example, seem to involve, depend upon, or even be *rules*. But what is a rule and what does it mean to say of a rule that it *exists*? Rules are not material objects that can be seen, touched, and pointed to. We cannot hang our hats on them or eat our food off the top of them, and thus they clearly do not exist in the same way in which hatracks and tables exist. And yet there is some point in saying of some rules that they do exist, and of others that they do not. There *really is* a legal rule in our society prohibiting rape. And there *really is not* a legal rule in our society requiring attendance at church. But what does this talk of "exists" and "really is, really is not" actually come to with respect to such queer entities as laws and rules? We have here then a class of *existence* questions, and an adequate analysis of the concept of law will perhaps help us with these questions. We must know what law is, what kind of "thing" it is, before we shall be in a position to know what sense of "exists" applies to it.

We have now considered the main reasons that Hart gives in defense of his claim that the analysis of the concept of law is interesting, difficult, and necessary before proceeding to other questions in the philosophy of law. But in what sense, if any, is the analysis of the concept of law important? Hart's four reasons alone, of course, demonstrate that an inquiry into the concept of law is *philosophically* important. But is this inquiry important in some more "practical" sense—some sense that would commend it to those motivated by concerns other than philosophical curiosity?

I think that the answer to this question is yes, and I would cite two considerations in defense of this answer. First, it is instructive to see how central an understanding of law is to some very profound moral and political concerns. We are, for example, inclined to criticize and perhaps fight states (e.g., Nazi Germany) that depart substantially from our ideal of the "rule of law," and we often like to praise our own system by reciting, even if without full understanding, the venerable slogan that we live under "a government of laws and not of men." Indeed, most of us feel, whether reasonably or not, that we owe some kind of moral duty or allegiance to the law or to our own legal system, and we often call on ourselves and others to respect and obey the law of the land even when we or they do not wholeheartedly approve of what that law requires in a particular case. In short, for most of us the claim "because it is the law" carries some moral force—disobedience being regarded as morally serious (requiring moral justification) and not simply as unwise or imprudent.

We cannot, of course, even understand this claim of moral allegiance to law until we understand the concept of law itself, and, given that rational evaluation presupposes understanding, we cannot evaluate the claims for moral fidelity to law in the absence of such analysis. If, for example, law is simply to be identified with mere force, then it would be hard to mount a persuasive case for a moral obligation to obey the law. I may fear and understandably obey the thug holding a gun to my head, but the thug surely has no moral claim on my obedience. These considerations of moral fidelity and allegiance are surely provocative enough to demonstrate the importance of analyzing the concept of law even to those (their numbers are legion) who do not see philosophical clarity as a good for its own sake.

A second (and related) practical reason for being concerned with an analysis of the concept of law is more strictly *legal* in nature. When, in an everyday context, we seek to have "the law" applied to a controversy in which we are involved, what exactly are we seeking? Those who are naive about the nature of law are inclined to think that it is easy to discover the law that applies to any particular case: one just looks it up in a statute book or pays a lawyer to look it up. In reality, however, the process of discovering the law is often not so simple. Perhaps the statute is vague—e.g., it prohibits driving a vehicle while intoxicated and you, cited for being intoxicated while pedaling your bicycle, believe that the statute does not really cover your action (you believe that a bicycle is not a vehicle). When the court agrees with you and holds that a bicycle is not a vehicle for purposes of this statute,[2] even though in an earlier case it had held that a moped with its engine off is a vehicle,[3] what is actually going on? Is the court really applying a law to new cases or is it simply making it up as it goes along, legislating rather than judging?

If interpreting a simple statute can raise problems about the nature of law, imagine how these problems can be compounded in other more complex sorts of cases. Some cases are only loosely governed by statute or not governed by statute at all. In a common law system such as ours, applying "the law" to a particular case often means, not applying a statute, but rather a present judge applying to the present case the rulings (called "precedents") of previous judges in earlier cases. Since these earlier cases are rarely exactly like the present case, however, the judge will have to depend on analogies, a process that at least seems to leave a great deal of free play for the judge's discretion. Sometimes the decision, though defended by analogy with the past, will transform the law for the future, as when Justice Cardozo, for the first time, interpreted precedents so that automobile manufacturers could be held liable for injuries caused to the driving public by negligent manufacture of their product.[4] What does it mean to talk about "the law" here—was it something Cardozo discovered and applied or did he just invent it, using the talk about precedents simply as a rationalization? Or consider controversial constitutional cases— e.g., the Supreme Court finding that the right to privacy, though never mentioned in the Constitution, is a fundamental constitutional right and then holding that this right encompasses the right of a woman to choose an abortion.[5] The more we consider cases such as these, the more puzzled we become. We started off thinking that, as practical persons, we need only be concerned with *the* law—i.e., with the particular laws that apply to our daily lives. When the issues become even remotely complex, however, we soon discover that *the* law is not so easily determined, and we might at this point begin to find our slogan "a government of laws and not of men" less and less clear. Unless we want simply to adopt the cynical view that the whole legal process is nothing more than a con game, we shall want to distinguish, even in those cases of unpredictable outcome where great discretion seems to be allowed, a judge's being guided by consideration of factors that are clearly nonlegal (e.g., bribes, coin flips, etc.) in contrast to being guided by considerations that, however vague and imprecise they may be, have a proper place in the legal process. But how could we possibly draw this distinction without an examination of the concept of law itself, without an inquiry into the question of what makes a process a legal process in the first place?

Having defended the enterprise of analyzing the concept of law, we are now in a position to begin the enterprise itself in earnest. We shall examine the question "What is law?" and shall start our examination with a consideration of some of the main theories that have been put forth as answers to this question.

NATURAL LAW THEORY

Natural law theories maintain that there is an essential (conceptual, logical, necessary) connection between law and morality. The demands of law and the demands of morality do not just happen to overlap sometimes as a matter of fact; their overlap is not just a contingent matter for empirical discovery. Rather, according to natural law theory, it is part of the very meaning of "law" that it passes a moral test. This does not necessarily mean that there is an equivalence between law and morality, because some natural law theorists are willing to admit that there are many moral obligations that have no place as legal requirements (e.g., private obligations of courtesy and gratitude) and that many legal requirements do not, in content, represent moral obligations (e.g., a legal requirement that certain documents be submitted in triplicate for administrative convenience). What is a necessary truth, however, is that no rule can count as a law unless what it requires is at least morally *permissible*—hence St. Augustine's famous natural law slogan that "an unjust law is no law at all." In short: Moral validity is a logically necessary condition for legal validity. Satisfying certain demands of morality is part of the very *definition* of "law," and therefore the connection between "law" and "morality" is more like the connection between "puppy" and "young" rather than the connection between "puppy" and "difficult to toilet train."

Given what we have already noted in the Introduction concerning the dangers of confusing law and morality, it might seem that what has here been identified as "natural law theory" is too implausible to merit serious study as a philosophical theory on the nature of law. There is perhaps a sense in which this suspicion may be justified, at least for the earliest and simplest versions of the theory. However, because the motivations of the theory were important and because it was groping, however confusedly, toward some genuinely profound insights and because it has been and continues to be influential in some circles, natural law theory merits study in an introduction to legal philosophy. The historical origins of the natural law tradition are very ancient, and this section will examine the traditional or "classical" version of the theory. In a later section of the chapter we shall explore certain contemporary attempts to reformulate natural law theory or to save some of its essential insights from the attacks to which it has been subjected by proponents of other legal theories. Even though some hard and unsympathetic things will be said about natural law theory in this section, the reader should suspend judgment about the ultimate merits of the theory until reading the much more sympathetic closing section.

Classical natural law theory was originally developed by such ancient writers as Plato, Aristotle, and Cicero and attained its most systematic statement in the medieval Christian philosophy of St. Thomas Aquinas.[6] Though the claim that there is an essential connection between law and morality will strike many modern readers as counterintuitive, the theory represented a distinct advance in the history of thought for it grew directly out of the development of a *moral* outlook on social and legal arrangements. Traditionally, people had simply obeyed the law out of custom, habit, or fear of force—the role of the latter being so great that there was even some tendency to identify the law with force. Increasingly, however, reflective people (e.g., Socrates) insisted on raising the question: Why morally *ought* one obey the law?[7] It cannot be morally right to obey the law merely because it is customary to obey it, since obviously customs can be irrational and evil. Just because something is usually done it does not follow that it ought to be done. Similarly with force: The threat of force can certainly provide one with motives (e.g., fear), but this can hardly establish the law's rational claim on our allegiance. Before this can be established, we should first need to present morally sufficient reasons for legal obedience. Thus, the questions: How should a morally serious and reflective person consider the law? When is such a person morally obligated to obey the law?

Now there is one rather simple answer that one might be tempted to give to this question, and the answer forms an essential part of the classical natural law theory. This is: One is obligated to obey the law only if the *content* of the law is itself moral. Should I obey the law against murder?—yes, because murder is wrong in itself (*malum in se*). Should I obey the law requiring that certain forms be filed in triplicate even though contrary filing is not wrong in itself but only wrong because prohibited (*malum prohibitum*)?—yes, if most of the laws under which I live serve moral purposes, because it is reasonable that the law aims at administrative convenience in its efforts to do good and because what is required of me in this case is not morally wrong. Should I obey a law requiring that I kill innocent persons in time of war?—no, because this law is unjust and thus no law at all. If the legal order is viewed as essentially connected with the moral order, then there will be moral reasons justifying allegiance to law and moral reasons justifying disobeying fraudulent imitations of law, and the grounds for legal obedience and disobedience will transcend appeals to mere custom or force.

It seems as though a title such as "moral law theory" would capture the nature of the account thus far given, and so one might wonder why such theories are typically referred to as natural law theories. Where, one might well ask, is the notion of nature or natural that gives these theories their title? The answer to this question is this: Initially, natural law theories involved more than the simple claim that the legal order was to be understood as essentially connected with the moral order; also involved was a certain claim about the *nature of the moral order itself.* On this view, the moral order (or at least that part of it not dependent on divine revelation) was viewed as a part of the order of nature. Nature had fixed a set of ends or purposes (an essence) for human beings in the natural order of things. (In the Christian view, God had implanted these essential purposes in nature.) Moral duty consisted in acting in accord with these purposes, and we thus were supposed to discover the essential purposes of creatures such as ourselves. The virtuous human life consisted in living consistently with our natural (perhaps God-designed) function, and systems of social coercion were properly called "legal" only if consistent with such functions.[8]

To view nature and the place of humans in it in terms of ends, goals, or purposes is called a *teleological* worldview (from the Greek word *telos,* meaning "end" or "purpose"). We now, of course, live in the post-Darwinian world and are accustomed to viewing nature (even human nature) in terms of mechanistic causation, and thus we are generally inclined to view teleological worldviews as quaintly pre-scientific. The modern mind finds it difficult to accept that people have ends or purposes other than those they have set or accepted for themselves. Even if we grant the existence of cosmic purposes, however, any moral theory based on them would still be faced with serious problems. Suppose that I do have a purpose set by God or nature (whatever that might mean). By what logic does it follow that I am ethically required to act in accord with that purpose? It might be imprudent (if God is vengeful) to act contrary to the plans He placed in nature for me, but do I make any kind of *logical* blunder if I adopt the opinion that a moral person will often choose to act contrary to these dictates? If God commands that I sacrifice my eldest son, might I not say, without logical error, that I regard such a command as evil and will not obey it? And suppose that I come to believe that the natural (typical, biological) function of my mouth is to provide an opening for the attainment of nourishment; can this have any rational bearing on answering the question of whether I act permissibly if I choose to use my mouth for erotic or sensual purposes? Is becoming a gourmet "unnatural" and thus obviously evil? Surely not. Indeed, on one plausible view, the very best achievements of human beings result when they learn in a sense to overcome nature (e.g., by being less violent than they are naturally inclined to be).[9]

This view may be incorrect, but it seems to involve no logical incoherence. Neither does there appear to be any logical incoherence in the view that the idea that human beings have a function, far from being the basis of morality, is actually a *degrading* view. Is our moral status simply to be a matter of our having functions or purposes in the way that hammers and other instruments do, or in the way that occupants of social roles (e.g., servants) do? And if it is, what happens to the notion of human dignity then? (How would you like it if someone said to you, "And what are you for?") Different people will answer such questions differently no doubt, but no one answer gets preferred logical status by having the label "natural" attached to it. To use the language of G. E. Moore, it is always an "open question" what morally ought to be done given any statement of what is naturally done or factually the case. To think otherwise is to commit what Moore called "the naturalistic fallacy"—the fallacy of believing that one can derive a theory of what *ought* to be the case from an account of what *is* the case.[10] Thus, because of what is (to put it mildly) a certain logical looseness in any account of natural duty, natural law ethical theory often appears arbitrary and confused—an attempt to explain the obscure (what we ought to do) in terms of the even more obscure (moral duties built into nature). When they do attempt to be clear, natural law theorists often offer clarity at the price of uselessness, as when Aquinas offers the following as the first principle of natural law theory: "Do good and avoid evil."[11] One can hardly quarrel with the sentiment expressed here, but one troubled with a moral problem is going to find this piece of highly general advice of very little use. For all these reasons, it is not surprising that natural law ethical theory has often provoked impatience and even contempt from its critics. For Aristotle and Aquinas, the natural law was viewed as a mechanism for imposing duties and giving guidance for the virtuous life. In the later and much more individualistic "natural rights" formulation developed during the Enlightenment and influential during the French and American Revolutions, the natural law was viewed as establishing certain moral entitlements (e.g., the right to freedom) that all human beings supposedly have simply by virtue of being human. In either form the doctrine is open, according to its critics, to the charge that it must be based either on the dogmatic acceptance of an implausible worldview or on the subjective deliverances of the private conscience of each individual—neither foundation having much to commend it to the rational person. Representative of such critics, Jeremy Bentham called the doctrine "nonsense on stilts" and the Danish legal philosopher Alf Ross wrote of it as follows:

> Like a harlot, natural law is at the disposal of everyone. The ideology does not exist that cannot be defended by an appeal to the law of nature. And, indeed, how can it be otherwise, since the ultimate basis for every natural right lies in a private direct insight, an evident contemplation, an intuition. Cannot my intuition be just as good as yours? Evidence as a criterion of truth explains the utterly arbitrary character of the metaphysical assertions. It raises them up above any force of intersubjective control and opens the door wide to unrestricted invention and dogmatics.[12]

To summarize: Classical natural law theory can be understood as a commitment to the following two claims: (1) Moral validity is a logically necessary condition for legal validity—an unjust or immoral law being no law at all; and (2) The moral order is a part of the natural order—moral duties being in some sense "read off" from essences or purposes fixed (perhaps by God) in nature.

At this point, it is important to note the following: Even if one rejects (2) utterly, one might still consistently subscribe to (1). That is, one might be a natural law theorist in holding that moral validity is a necessary condition for legal validity without subscribing to the particular theory of moral validity (consistency with natural purpose or end) typically conjoined with that view. This possibility forces one to confront the following question: Is an attempt to tie the concept of law to *any* concept of morality doomed to failure, or are the problems with classical natural law theory due solely to the controversial moral theory then adopted?

An examination of this question does not initially raise one's hopes for the viability of natural law theory even so limited or modified. Classical natural law theory typically tied law to a highly controversial moral theory; but, given even the most plausible theory possible about the nature of morality, it still seems initially reasonable to maintain that such a theory should be distinguished from a theory about the nature of law. Careful reflection certainly inclines the rational person to believe that law and morality are simply different and that failing to appreciate this difference is the root mistake and confusion in traditional natural law theory. Consider the definition of "law" offered by Aquinas:

> Law is nothing else than an ordinance of reason for the common good, promulgated by him who has the care of the community. . . . Human law has the nature of law in so far as it partakes of right reason. . . . So far as it deviates from reason, it is called an unjust law and has the nature, not of law, but of violence. . . . Such are acts of violence rather than laws because, as Augustine says, a law that is not just seems to be no law at all.[13]

What seems to be happening here is that the concept of *ideal* or *perfect* or *morally good* law is seen as part of the moral order; from this correct insight, a careless slide is made into identifying law itself with a part of morality—the ideality no longer being regarded as a possible and desirable feature of law but as a part of the very meaning of "law." The phrase "morally acceptable law" is redundant, and the phrase "morally evil law" is contradictory. When Aquinas speaks of "being in accord with reason" and "being for the common good," he seems to be making a comment, not merely (and sensibly) about desirable features of law, but rather as part of the analysis of the concept of law or legality—matters of definition rather than evaluation. If this is the view, then it seems immediately open to some serious and rather obvious objections. There are many rules in any society that are surely laws but are just as surely morally neutral—e.g., some law requiring that one have one's validated registration tag on the auto license plate prior to March 1. Aquinas sensibly admits that such rules are laws, but the degree to which the admission is compatible with the literal wording of his definition is unclear. Such rules, though no doubt consistent with the common good, are not obviously *for* the common good in the sense that laws prohibiting murder are clearly for the common good. However, interpretive charity perhaps requires that we give Aquinas the benefit of the doubt on this one. What does seem noncontroversial and central about Aquinas's theory is that he is committed to the claim that an evil or unjust law is no law at all, that legal requirements must, as a matter of definition, require only conduct that is morally permissible.

A dramatic and decisive counterexample to this view, however, is the obvious existence of legal rules that clear thinking would force us to acknowledge as laws even if we believed them to be morally evil. Suppose, for example, that you believe that it is morally wrong for the state to eliminate all considerations of fault in granting legal divorces. Surely you could not reasonably conclude from this that all those persons in a "no-fault" state who claim to be legally divorced are really not divorced at all but are still legally married. You may think that these laws are unworthy of your respect (because they are, in your judgment, evil or irrational laws), but what is gained in saying that they are not laws at all? The sentence "That law is evil and unjust and I will not, on moral grounds, respect or obey it" does not seem incoherent, and the sentence "That law is just and so I morally admire it" does not seem redundant, as each would if the claims of classical natural law theory were taken literally.

At this point, one might well begin to wonder if classical natural law theory is really saying anything useful at all. Its great value historically was that it brought to light the need for moral criticism of law and got people thinking about obligation rather than force as of the essence of law. But when these insights were built into an attempted analysis or definition of the concept of law itself, the resulting confusions and incoherences became very great indeed. According to one critic, H. L. A. Hart, natural law theory is correct in its attempt to distinguish law from mere force by the use of the concept of obligation—a concept having no home in a world of mere force.[14] What the natural law theorist does not see, however, is that the concept of *legal* obligation is different from the concept of *moral* obligation. One way of being under a legal obligation to perform some act *A* is simply to be required by a legal rule to do *A*. To be under a moral obligation, on the other hand, is to be required to do *A* by the weight of all morally relevant reasons with respect to *A*— e.g., that *A* will promote human welfare, is the just or fair thing to do, etc. Because of the necessary connection with reasons of this nature, we regard moral obligations as necessarily ranging over matters of importance, but this is not necessarily so for legal obligations— e.g., the obligation to have your auto license tab displayed before March 1. Also, moral obligations require only voluntary conduct from us. "I could not help it," if true, is always an excuse in morality, for involuntary conduct is conduct without moral fault. The law, however, can intelligibly (even if not justly) hold people responsible for their involuntary and thus faultless conduct. In the law this is called *strict* or *absolute* liability, but there is no such thing as strict moral responsibility.[15]

Finally, we think of legal obligations as changeable at will in a way that moral obligations are not. A legislature could repeal all laws against libel and slander and thus make it false henceforth that libel and slander are illegal. (Throughout most of the United States, libel and slander have ceased to be criminal offenses, either because of repeal or because of a longstanding refusal to prosecute these acts, thereby forcing individuals to view these injuries as private and seek civil remedies for them.) But what individual or collective act would make it false that libel and slander are immoral? The very idea of a legislature for morality is absurd on its face.[16] Of course a particular legislature or constitutional convention might build a substantial number of its moral beliefs into its legal system. Nobody would deny this. All this would show, however, is that there is, for this system, a *contingent* or *empirical* overlap between law and morality. This is not the kind of necessary connection claimed by natural law theory.

What all of this adds up to is the following: Moral pressure must always involve the *appeal to reason*. The sentence "This is your moral obligation but there is no good reason or justification in favor of your doing it" makes no sense. Substitute the phrase "legal obligation" for the phrase "moral obligation" in the sentence, however, and the resulting sentence, even if not admirable, is perfectly intelligible. Laws and their attached legal obligations should be rationally defensible, but, in contrast to morality, it is not of their very essence that they must be.

As one final attempt to save classical natural law theory, one might throw out this challenge to alternative theories: If we do not identify law and morality in some way, how can we account for a *moral* obligation to obey the law and thereby avoid an appeal to mere force as a ground for fidelity to law? If natural law theory were in fact the only route toward establishing a moral obligation to obey the law, then one might abandon it (if at all) only with very great reluctance—unless, of course, one holds the view that there simply is no moral obligation to obey the law as such. A close consideration of the matter, however, reveals (a) that natural law theory does a very inadequate job of establishing a moral obligation to obey the law, and (b) that there are alternative possible ways of generating such an obligation. If one holds the view that one has a moral obligation to obey the law only when the law is moral in content, one holds a view that stresses the moral obligation to obey the law in just those cases where it is least needed! (Who thinks that an important moral reason against rape and murder is that there are laws prohibiting these acts?) People are often called upon to recognize their moral obligation to obey the law in those cases where they morally disagree with the law—e.g., the law perhaps requires that they fight in a war they regard as evil or requires that they accept a way of life, say racial integration, that they regard as contrary to the common good. It is unclear how natural law theory will illuminate such cases. Such cases may be understood, however, when one realizes that foundations for moral obligation other than morality of content may be possible. Consider promises. My moral obligation to keep my promise is generated by the *act* of promising, not by the content of what I promise. My helping you paint your fence is morally trivial and, by itself, generates no moral requirement for me. If I *promise* to help you paint the fence, however, then my doing it takes on the character of a moral requirement. Is there any important analogy between the obligation to obey the law and the obligation to keep a promise? Social contract theory claims yes, and this shows that it is at least possible that grounds for the moral obligation to obey the law other than those favored by natural law theory might be articulated.[17]

The confusions in classical natural law theory thus seem to run very deep indeed. It forces us to say confused and confusing things (e.g., "an unjust law is not really law") with no obvious gain in analytical or moral power. The important things it supposedly allows us to do (e.g., morally evaluate the law and determine our moral obligations with respect to the law) are actually rendered more difficult by its collapse of the distinction between morality and law. If we really want to think about the law from the moral point of view, it may obscure this task if we see law and morality as essentially linked in some way. Moral criticism and reform of law may be aided by an initial moral skepticism about the law—a frame of mind difficult to adopt unless the concept of law itself is demythologized—and, to put it mildly, natural law theory has not been in the business of demythologizing law. For natural law theory, the term "law" is a morally honorific title; the goals of both intellectual clarity and moral evaluation might better be served by a more neutral analysis.

Is classical natural law theory then a total washout and all of its proponents idiots? The answer to this question is clearly no, and it would be a shame if the reader went away from this section thinking otherwise. The philosophical reflections of every age tacitly presuppose, as unchallenged assumptions, a general worldview and philosophical idiom, and the best philosophers of the age proceed brilliantly and develop profound insights within the confines of that worldview and idiom. When the background worldview comes to seem implausible (or just unfashionable) to a later age, the proper response of that later age is to mine the earlier tradition in order to discover the insights toward which (sometimes quite obliquely) it was groping— insights that can be used and reformulated in the current philosophical idiom. By "rethinking the works of the great philosophers in the idioms of our own age" (to use Peter Strawson's phrase), we are perhaps able to pay homage to the past and learn from it without being trapped by its limitations of thought. It is surely enough that we be trapped by our own limitations of thought.

In this spirit of qualified historical piety, we shall consider in a later section if contemporary reformulations of natural law theory can avoid the charges leveled above against the classical form; it will be suggested that, to some degree, they can. Contemporary natural law theories gain considerable advances in sophistication and plausibility over the classical versions in three ways: (1) They do not appear to depend on controversial or weird metaphysical or theological theories. (2) Some contemporary natural law theorists (e.g., Lon Fuller) argue that the connection between law and morality is necessary only at the level of an entire *system*—that legal systems may, of course, contain particular laws that are unjust or immoral in some other way, but that the system as a whole must satisfy certain moral demands in order to count as legal.[18] (3) Other contemporary theorists (e.g., Ronald Dworkin) argue that too sharp a conceptual separation of law from morality will force us to miss the essential nature of certain central features of judicial deliberation—e.g., deliberation about constitutional rights.

Before exploring these contemporary developments, however, it will be instructive to consider a theory on the nature of law that was developed largely as a reaction against classical natural law theory. This theory is called Legal Positivism, and its starting assumption is that—for all the reasons already explored—a sharp distinction is to be drawn between law and morality.

LEGAL POSITIVISM

John Austin, the nineteenth-century English moral and legal philosopher who gave the theory of legal positivism its first systematic statement,[19] argued that legal philosophy (jurisprudence) has two important but quite different tasks and that a failure to keep these two tasks separate produces both intellectual and moral confusion. He distinguished between *analytical jurisprudence* and *normative jurisprudence.* Analytical jurisprudence is concerned with the analysis of the concepts and structures of "law as it is." Normative jurisprudence involves the evaluative criticism of law and thus represents claims about "law as it ought to be." That Austin draws this distinction clearly shows that his whole conception of legal philosophy involves a repudiation of natural law theory. Austin's contributions to normative jurisprudence mainly involve some interesting attempts to apply the moral theory of utilitarianism to legal issues—a theme to be explored in a later chapter. The contributions for which he is most famous, however, are in the area of analytical jurisprudence—particularly his theory of the nature of law itself, his analysis of the concept of law. ("Law as it is" is called *positive law* because it is set or posited or given its position by human authority, hence the name "Legal Positivism.")

Austin's particular theory is often called "the command theory of law" because he makes the concept of *command* central in his account of law and maintains that all laws are commands, even when they do not take a form that appears imperative in nature. Why does he make such a claim? What does Austin notice about laws that makes him think that the concept of command will illuminate their essential nature? Basically it is this: the *nonoptional* nature of legal requirements. The law is not like one's puritanical Aunt Sophie, giving all sorts of moralistic advice that one may simply ignore with impunity if one does not care to be guided by her. The law is rather a coercive method of social control: it demands both the attention and compliance of those to whom its regulations are directed. According to Austin, the locution "There is a law against X but you may still do X with impunity" is senseless. Such a "law" could not control social behavior, the very point of having laws in the first place.

What is a command? Austin defines a command in terms of two concepts: (1) signification of desire, and (2) ability to inflict evil or harm for the nonsatisfaction of a desire. To command people to do X is simply this: to express to them my desire that they do X and to make it clear to them that it is within my power to inflict some evil or harm on them if they fail to do X. Austin calls this threatened and possible evil a *sanction*. A person so commanded is, according to Austin, *bound*, *obliged*, or *under a duty* to do what is commanded.

Initially, this conception of command and the theory of law based upon it seems rather bizarre. Must I want or desire some outcome in order to command that you act in a certain way? Might not a sergeant, believing that his duty requires it, command a soldier to go on a dangerous patrol while secretly wishing or desiring, because he likes the soldier so much, that the soldier will in fact go AWOL rather than risk his life? Do not legislators sometimes vote out of party loyalty for laws, and thus issue "commands," when they are ignorant of the contents of those laws and thus can have no desire to realize the objective of those laws? It would of course be odd if in general people commanded others to do things in the absence of any desire that those things be done, but the connection between desire and command does not seem strong enough to make the connection between them one of definition. (Perhaps it is a necessary truth that generally people desire what they command, but even that would need to be argued.) Also, it seems odd to maintain that a person has not been commanded or ordered to do something unless there is a real possibility—not just a threat or provision but a real possibility—that the commander can make a harm or evil befall him for noncompliance. Suppose Jones disobeys a command or law and flees to Canada where (let us suppose) he cannot be reached or extradited. Does it follow from this, since no sanction is possible, that he really was not commanded at all, that he really broke no law? This view would have the extremely odd and unfortunate consequence that the more clever a person was at avoiding threatened sanctions the less it would be true that he was commanded and thus under a legal obligation at all. In order to avoid this absurd consequence, the later legal positivist Hans Kelsen suggested that all that is required for an expression of desire to have the status of command or law is that it *stipulate* or *provide* for a sanction—not that there be a significant probability that the sanction will actually be inflicted.[20]

But, even given this weakening of the claim, is it reasonable to regard the concept of sanction as essentially tied to the concept of law? Must all laws, by definition, have sanctions? There are reasons for thinking that the answer to this question is no. If we take criminal law as our paradigm of law, then the sanction theory of law seems reasonably plausible. Criminal laws typically have the purpose of preventing people from doing certain things. The method of prevention here is a price tag (a sanction): Do this and it will cost you your life, liberty, property, etc. But when we move to a consideration of other kinds of laws, the sanction theory seems less plausible. Take the rules of contract law. They exist, not to prevent us from doing certain things, but rather to *allow* us to do certain things in an official way. They take the form "If you want to do X (make this contract valid in this state, say), then you must do Y (put it in writing if the amount is over $500, say). If we fail to follow the rules of contract law, no evil is visited on us. Rather we have simply failed to do what we set out to do, namely, make a valid contract.

If the sanction theory really charms us, we could of course attempt to save it in cases like this by following Kelsen's suggestion that we distinguish between *punitive* and *privative* sanctions. To suffer a punitive sanction is to be punished by the state, as is the case in criminal law. To suffer a privative sanction is simply to be deprived of the enforcement power of the state with respect to our transactions—a way of construing what happens when we fail to follow the legal rules for making a valid contract. The degree to which it would be reasonable to embrace this complexity is a function of the degree to which one thinks it important to preserve the concept of sanction at the center of law. And that issue cannot be decided without further exploration of the theories based on sanction and a comparison of them with theories that do not regard the concept of sanction as legally central.

H. L. A. Hart thinks that he can quickly demolish sanction theories by showing that they involve a fatal confusion between the concept of being *obligated* (or under a duty) to do something and being *obliged* (i.e., forced) to do it.[21] Austin's theory forces us to say that we are obligated or duty-bound to surrender our money to a gunman in a stickup; that consequence, according to Hart, is sufficiently absurd to destroy any theory that entails it. If the gunman desires our money, expresses that desire to us, and makes it clear to us his intention and ability to inflict harm on us if we do not surrender the money, then, by Austin's definition, he has commanded that we give him the money. But, according to Austin, to have a duty just is to be under a command, so it looks as though we are forced to say (what seems absurd) that we are obligated to give the money to the gunman. Hart's criticism thus seems made. But is it? One must always be cautious in claiming to have found a simple error in a thinker of Hart's intellectual power, but it does seem in this case that he has simply begged the question against Austin. We would all of course agree that the gunman places his victim under no *moral* obligation or duty, but Austin, since he clearly wants to draw a sharp distinction between law and morality, will surely immediately grant this point. Austin's theory is about the nature of *legal* obligation, and the nonmoral model of the command is his attempt to provide the locution that will ultimately illuminate legal obligation. Since in a very real sense he wants, as a part of his theory, to identify legal obligation with force (and thereby identify legal obligation with being obliged), it will hardly count as a refutation of his theory to point out, as Hart does, that he is confusing being legally obligated with being obliged. This is not to refute Austin's theory; it is simply to tell Austin what his theory is in slightly different terms. Thus a refutation of the command theory will have to be more systematic and subtle than this.

Hart's point about the gunman, even if it does not totally refute Austin's whole theory, does still raise one serious worry for that theory. Even if we follow Austin in ruling out all moral factors from our analysis of law and legal obligation, it still seems that his theory, as thus far presented, does have one *legally* absurd consequence—namely, that the gunman we have discussed, since he is issuing commands, is making *law*. That does indeed seem absurd.

Fortunately, Austin himself sees the absurdity of this and clarifies (and thus renders much more plausible) his thesis in the following way: Law is not to be identified with any command, it is rather a *species* of command. We of course want to distinguish those commands of the state that represent law from those lawless commands issued by our gunman, and thus, we must now look for those special distinguishing features that will allow us to tell which, of all commands, are the commands that are legal in nature. What must be added to a command to make that command a law?

Austin's answer to this question involves an idea that many philosophers (e.g., Ronald Dworkin) regard as the most original and essential feature of the doctrine of legal positivism—namely, that the legal is distinguished from the nonlegal in terms of *pedigree*. One pedigree test for law and legal validity is simply this: *L* is a law of some system *S* if *L*'s generation or enactment can be traced to a person or body of persons whose actions define legality for *S*. In Austin's terminology, such a person or body of persons is called a *sovereign* and thus Austin's final definition of law is this: A law is a command of the sovereign. True laws have this pedigree. Other commands (e.g., that of the gunman) lack this pedigree, and thus they are not laws.[22]

Is this theory correct? We are not in a position to answer this question until we first attempt to understand the concept of sovereignty itself. What does Austin mean by calling a person or body of persons a "sovereign"? Are there clearly sovereign persons or bodies present in all those systems we would correctly call "legal"? If the doctrine of sovereignty is ultimately incoherent or if it fails to illuminate the character of actual systems of positive law, then Austin's particular version of legal positivism will be of doubtful philosophical value.

Given Austin's strong desire to avoid any confusion between moral and legal matters, he clearly is not going to define sovereignty in terms of even possibly moral or evaluative concepts. He will not, for example, define a sovereign as one who has a *right* to rule or one who rules *legitimately*.[23] Instead he offers a purely *factual* account of sovereignty:

> The essential difference of a positive law (or the difference that severs it from a law which is not positive law) may be stated thus. Every positive law, or every law simply and strictly so called, is set by a sovereign person, or a sovereign body of persons, to a member or members of the independent political society wherein that person or body is sovereign or supreme. Or (changing the expression) it is set by a monarch, or sovereign number, to a person or persons in a state of subjection to its author. Even though it sprung directly from another fountain or source [e.g., custom or morality], it *is* positive law, or a law strictly so called, by the institution of that present sovereign in the character of political superior. . . . The superiority that is styled sovereignty, and the independent political society which sovereignty implies, is distinguished from other superiority, and from other society, by the following marks or characters: 1. The *bulk* of the given society are in a *habit* of obedience or submission to a *determinate* and *common* superior: let that common superior be a certain individual person, or a certain body or aggregate of individual persons. 2. That certain individual, or that certain body

of individuals, is *not* in a habit of obedience to a determinate human superior. . . . If a *determinate* human superior, *not* in a habit of obedience to a like superior, receives habitual obedience from the *bulk* of a given society, that determinate superior is sovereign in that society, and the society (including the superior) is a society political and independent.[24]

Notice how *factual* and *empirical* is this characterization of sovereignty and law. If a person is in fact habitually obeyed by the bulk (over 50 percent?) of the population of a society and in fact does not habitually obey another, then that person is sovereign. If that person in fact expresses desires that things be done and makes a credible threat to inflict harm on those who do not do as he desires, then that person has commanded and, given his status as sovereign, this command is law.

Should we accept this as a correct account of law? There is no doubt something appealing about the elegant simplicity and power of this theory. It seems almost geometrical in its systematic attempt to explain all the very complex features of legal systems in terms of a few primitive locutions—e.g., "habit," "desire," "sanction," etc. For all of its attractions, however, it does on reflection seem not just simple but also simplistic, achieving again what Hart calls "uniformity at the price of distortion." The notion that legal validity (i.e., the status of something, a rule say, as law) is a function of pedigree is a powerful notion that is employed in later theories (e.g., Hart's own) that remain largely positivistic without subscribing to the details of Austin's command and sovereignty version of positivism. For this insight Austin is thus to be greatly credited. Much of the details of his own particular version of positivism will not, however, survive careful criticism. Let us see why this is so.

H. L. A. Hart (again, as always, the most astute critic in legal philosophy) argues persuasively that there are two basic features of legal systems that Austin's sovereign command theory either distorts or for which it cannot account at all. These are "the *continuity* of the authority to make law possessed by a succession of different legislators, and the *persistence* of laws long after their maker and those who rendered him habitual obedience have perished."[25]

To develop his point about continuity, Hart asks that we consider the fable of monarch Rex I who, upon his death, is succeeded by Rex II. Let us suppose that Rex I has issued many commands and, since he was habitually obeyed by the bulk of the population over which he ruled and since he did not habitually obey anyone else (what if he had systematically deferred to his wife?), his commands counted, on Austin's theory, as law during his lifetime. But what happens after his death? It looks as though Austin's theory forces us to say that all law has died with him. Since Rex I is dead (and is not there to be habitually obeyed) he is not sovereign and thus his former commands no longer can count as law. Can Rex II keep his predecessor's commands in their status as law by reissuing them or ratifying them? No, because Rex II has not been around long enough for it to be the case that anyone habitually obeys him, and thus he is not sovereign either. Therefore, this society is without a sovereign and, on Austin's theory, without law. But this is absurd. This theory makes the unusual situation into the typical. Normally there is orderly and lawful succession of power in society and thus continuity of authority and law: the unusual situation is the case of revolution—the case where, when the previous leader is gone, nobody really knows who is now in authority and thus what the law actually is. But on Austin's theory, given that in any transition period there will be nobody who is habitually obeyed, every transition is a revolutionary situation. How very odd.

At this point of course someone might say that we are being unfair to Austin. Surely the habitual obedience is given, not to a person, but to an *office*. This may well be true, but then the question becomes: will Austin's theory allow him to define the concept of an office in a satisfactory way? It seems not. Typically (in those societies that even have an Austinian sovereign), the office of sovereign will be defined in terms of certain legal *rules*. Such rules will typically state the criteria for sovereignty and will provide procedures for legal or rightful succession—e.g., "The sovereign is the oldest living male member of the Dingbat Clan." Such a rule provides authoritative guidance in recognizing the current sovereign and in replacing him in an authoritative way when he dies. But can Austin's theory make room for such a rule? Surely not. For Austin, all laws are commands of the sovereign, but this rule or law, since it defines who shall count as the sovereign, is presupposed by sovereignty and thus cannot be generated by it. Thus, such concepts as "office," "legal right of succession," and "legally legitimate succession" are all without a home in Austin's theory, and he cannot account for continuity of law and legal authority, one of the (thankfully) most salient features of stable legal systems.

So, too, for the fact of persistence of laws. Fortunately, when the head of state dies, those of us who live in typically stable legal systems do not normally develop the worry that perhaps all previous laws are now gone and that our system is perhaps now lawless. We do not wait anxiously to see if the new head of state will reissue all the old commands of his predecessor and thereby guarantee that the laws under which we previously lived will persist into the future. But, on Austin's theory, we would have such a worry. For even if Austin could solve the problem of who will count as the new sovereign after the old one is gone, the commands of the former sovereign would not count as laws unless the present sovereign commanded them again. Austin tries to get around this worry by a concept of *tacit command*— if the new sovereign does not actively repeal the commands of the old sovereign, then he can be said tacitly to command them and thus allow them to retain their status as law. But is there any reason to say such a thing other than a desire to save the philosophical theory that depends on it? It certainly seems an odd way to look at the matter. If certain edicts counted as law because they were enacted in accord with the rules operative in society for making laws, then *that* (i.e., that the proper rules were followed) explains why they were and still are laws. No references to commands, either explicit or tacit, seem needed.

Austin's "law is a command of a sovereign" theory would seem to be in big trouble. Why did it go so far wrong? Hart's answer is this: in our dealing plausibly (in a way that Austin had not) with the problems of continuity and persistence of law and legal authority, it was necessary to make repeated references to *rules*—rules defining offices, rules of succession, rules for making laws, etc. It is the main flaw in Austin's theory that it can make no coherent place for rules or for the concept of rules. In seeking to avoid moral rules in the analysis of legality, Austin went so far as to avoid all rules, even the legal ones necessary for analyzing legally central locutions (even his favorite one of "sovereignty"). Austin, in avoiding all normative concepts (not just the moral ones), is thus forced to attempt to analyze all legal concepts in terms of such empirical *facts* as expressions of desire, habitual obedience, probability of sanction, etc. Clever as this attempt often is, we have now seen ample reasons why it simply will not work as a comprehensive systematic theory of law and legal systems. By focusing on particular laws as instances of individual commands, Austin is blinded to the realization that typically some rule or edict *L* is a law because *L* is a part of some social *system* for generating rules—the system being in part itself defined in terms of rules. Thus, not surprisingly, later legal positivists tended to drop the command theory and the sovereignty theory and sought instead a theory that stressed legal systems (not just particular laws) and legal rules (not just acts of determinate persons). These theories are still positivistic in that they (a) insist on a sharp separation between law and morality (the rules and norms they stress will not be moral in nature), and (b) they will offer a pedigree test for legal validity—e.g., a rule will count as law if, historically, it was *generated* in a certain way (typically, if it was enacted in accord with the rules for generating laws in the society, such as passage by the legislature). We shall shortly explore the most powerful of such positivistic theories—that developed by H. L. A. Hart.

Before moving to this discussion, however, it might be wise to pause for a moment and reflect on why a philosopher of Austin's great knowledge and brilliance could have gone so far wrong in his analysis of law. The answer, I think, is that he succumbed to a temptation that is a common danger in philosophy and often snares even the best minds—namely, the danger of becoming enamoured with too narrow a paradigm or model of what one is studying. If you think of the law around the limited paradigm of statutory criminal law, then you will be inclined to look very favorably upon the idea that law is a set of sanctioned commands. If you think of a legal system around the model of an absolute monarchy, then the idea that sanctioned commands get their status as law by flowing from a sovereign body will also charm you. (How odd that Austin should have been charmed in this way since he lived in a common law country in which the monarchy was radically limited.) But as soon as you open yourself up to the *variety* of laws and legal systems, these charms will begin to disappear. Take a legal system such as that found in the United States. Who or what in Austin's sense is the sovereign here? There is no one supreme power of command, for the legal system essentially involves a balance of power wherein each branch of government has certain legal ways of checking and balancing the other. And each branch is legally limited by certain side constraints laid down in the Constitution. The idea of a *legal limitation* on sovereign power is an obvious feature in a system such as ours, but the whole idea cannot even be regarded as sensible on Austin's theory. Are we then to say that the United States does not really have a legal system after all since it fails to have an unlimited Austinian sovereign? Certainly not. If any society has a legal system, then surely the United States does. That we have a legal system is surely far more obviously true than any abstract theory in legal philosophy, and thus it would be ludicrous to deny the former to save the latter. "Here is my theory of the nature of law, and it has the interesting consequence that England, Germany, France, and the United States do not really have laws" carries its refutation on its face. If the sovereignty theory requires such nonsense, then so much the worse for the sovereignty theory. Of course, at patriotic rallies, we often hear mouthed such platitudes as "In our society, the *people* are sovereign." But what would this mean on Austin's analysis—that we as a people habitually obey ourselves and thus express our desires to ourselves in a threatening way and thereby make law? One surely need not go on in this vein.

If one does not become overly charmed by certain narrow paradigms of law but rather remains open to the variety of law and such salient features as its continuity and persistence, one will seek a theory of law that is much more complex and systematic than the one offered by Austin. It is to such a theory that we shall now turn.

H. L. A. Hart's *The Concept of Law* (Oxford, 1961) is universally regarded as the most significant contribution to legal philosophy of this century. Prior to Hart's book, the philosophy of law was almost never taught in departments of philosophy or was, at most, covered as a kind of perfunctory appendix to courses in social and political philosophy. And the courses called "jurisprudence" in law schools were mainly systematic overviews of actual legal doctrines or concepts that had developed in various branches of law. Hart's book changed all this. By applying the analytical and normative techniques of contemporary philosophy to law, Hart was able to develop a way of thinking about the law that provided both intellectual illumination and a basis for moral criticism. Legal philosophy or jurisprudence was suddenly both transformed and made philosophically respectable again. Today, most departments of philosophy offer at least one course in the philosophy of law and the jurisprudence courses in most law schools are now very influenced by the writings of Hart and other contemporary philosophers of law.

In *The Concept of Law*, Hart gives the theory of legal positivism the most systematic and powerful statement it has ever received and is ever likely to receive. Though in many respects derivative from the work of the Austrian legal positivist Hans Kelsen, Hart's theory manages to preserve most of Kelsen's central insights without surrounding them with Kelsen's complex prose and without preserving the obscurity and ambiguity often found in Kelsen's own development of positivism.[26]

According to Hart, Austin began the development of his command theory of law brilliantly (by the sharp separation of law from morals and by asking many of the most profound philosophical questions about law) but then ultimately wound up with a theory of law that was almost totally unsatisfactory—a theory that, in Hart's language, implausibly makes a legal system nothing more than a "gunman writ large." If we follow Justice Holmes's counsel and "view the law as the bad man views it," then the idea of law as a large bully able to enforce his commands may seem accurate. Most of us, however, do not view the legal system in which we live in this way. This is revealed, according to Hart, in our perception of ourselves as being *obligated* by law—a concept that we would never use with respect to obedience to a gunman or bully.

Why did Austin go so far wrong? We have already noted two reasons: (1) Austin makes no place for the legally central concept of *rule*, and (2) Austin adopts what might be called a criminal law rather than a civil law model of law. He views law primarily in its role as *obstacle*— as a force to keep us from doing things we want to do (just as a bully often does). But substantial parts of the civil law (e.g., the law of contracts) cannot be viewed in this way. Contract law exists, not to prevent our doing things, but rather to facilitate our doing things— to make our agreements binding, regularized, predictable, and stable. Law is here not some kind of necessary evil (as we might think of the criminal law with its mechanisms of punishment) but is rather one of the factors that makes for civilized life and complex institutions. In this loose sense of "civil law," Hart can be said to adopt a civil law model of law. His primary ideological vision of law is as a facilitator, a problem solver, and because of this vision, he is able to do what Austin never was: to see law as a system of rules that impose obligations (not simply a system of commands that inspire fear). Austin was correct to see that a legal system is not simply a system of advice, but that it functions essentially to render certain acts *nonoptional.* But Hart (following Kelsen) argues that legal nonoptionality is normative rather than, as Austin thought, factual. The law (to use a favorite analogy of contemporary positivists) is in this respect like a game: Moving the bishop in chess in any way other than on a diagonal is not an option in chess. This means simply that nondiagonal moves are forbidden by the rules of chess, *not* that someone will hurt you if you move the bishop in the improper way. We have here then an example of a nonoptionality that is normative but not moral—it surely being a matter of moral indifference how the bishop is moved.

Hart characterizes his own positivistic theory with the slogan "law as a union of primary and secondary rules," and he begins the explication and defense of this theory in an interesting narrative way: He asks us to imagine a nonlegal or prelegal system (a social system that we would all agree lacks law) and to note the many problems and pathologies that would characterize such a system. If we then imagine the changes that we would have to make in such a system in order to cure the pathologies, we will find that we have thereby created law. Legality, in short, is a cure for the social pathology or disease that would be present in a prelegal or nonlegal world.[27]

How is a prelegal or nonlegal world (that would still be a human and social world) to be characterized? Since human social behavior is essentially governed by rules—norms telling people how they ought to behave in varous circumstances—even the prelegal world will have to contain rules of some sort. Hart calls the rules that would be present in this world *primary rules.* By a "primary rule" Hart means a rule directed to all individuals in the social group telling them how they ought to act in certain circumstances—i.e., the rule is *to* them and is *about* how they ought to act. In other words, these rules function to impose duties or obligations on people. Some examples of primary rules are: "Do not marry outside the tribe," "Keep off the grass," "Do not drive over 25 miles per hour in a residential area," "Do not touch a taboo object," "Take no medicine unless approved by the poison oracle," "Always give your relatives a decent burial," "Do not steal," etc. These examples, drawn obviously from different kinds of cultures, are purposely a mixed bag, for one important question to be considered is how one tells when such rules are part of the same *system.* Why am I, for example, bound by the one concerned with speed limit and not the one concerned with the poison oracle?

What does it mean to say that primary rules impose obligations? According to Hart, this manifestly does not mean (as Austin thought) that the rules are simply ways of predicting whether or not bad things (sanctions) are likely to befall one. Primary rules impose obligations or duties in the sense that they serve as standards of criticism or justification. A rule providing for a sanction serves as a *reason* that *justifies* imposing the sanction, not a ground for predicting the actual occurrence of the sanction. Certain persons in a society (Holmes's "bad men") may see legal rules as nothing more than devices to predict when the state is likely to harm them.[28] Such persons take what Hart calls an "external" view on rules—i.e., they see the rules not as standards that in part define their own group membership but rather (in the manner of an anthropologist viewing some primitive tribe) as simply a set of behavior patterns of a group that one observes externally and finds alien. In any viable and stable legal order, however, the majority of citizens (and certainly the majority of those involved in some official capacity in enacting or enforcing the rules) must take what Hart calls an "internal" attitude toward the rules of their legal order—i.e., they must see them as standards of criticism and justification.

Let us suppose, then, that we have a society organized by a set of primary rules imposing obligations, and let us further suppose that most or even all members of this society take an internal attitude toward those rules. What serious problems would plague such a society? Why are we inclined to say that the society lacks a legal system? (Hart, of course, sees these two questions as closely related.)

When we imagine such a society, it is immediately obvious that "only a small community closely knit by ties of kinship, common sentiment, and belief, and placed in a stable environment, could live

successfully by such a regime of . . . [primary] rules."²⁹ This is because
the moment we imagine the introduction of certain common complexities into the society, we thereby imagine a set of problems with
which a system of primary rules simply cannot deal. Three such
problems are particularly worth noting. First, there is the problem
of *uncertainty* about the rules. Such uncertainty can be of two sorts.
I can be unsure if there really is a rule that prohibits what I want
to do (is the injunction to take off one's hat in church simply a matter
of commonly accepted etiquette, or is there really a rule that obligates
me to act in this way?) or I can be sure of the existence of rules but
uncertain of what I am obligated to do if these rules are in conflict,
as in any reasonably complex society they are almost certain sometimes
to be. (Recall Antigone's dilemma in Sophocles's play: She accepts
two primary rules, "Give your relatives a proper burial" and "Obey
the King." There is uncertainty about what she is obligated to do
when King Creon, who regards her brother Polynices as a traitor,
forbids his burial after he is killed in battle.) Since the primary rules
are just a collection or aggregate of separate rules, they do not form
a system; there is no authoritative way to distinguish "really is one
of our rules" from "is claimed, perhaps falsely, to be one of our rules"
and no authoritative way to answer the question of priority among
conflicting rules.

Another serious problem that would be generated for our imaginary
society would arise from the *static* character of primary rules. Circumstances (natural and social) can change radically over time, and
rules ideally adapted for one set of circumstances may be radically
inappropriate when those circumstances change. Sometimes one needs
to develop new rules—e.g., rules to help curtail oil consumption when
an oil shortage develops. At other times one needs to get rid of old
rules—e.g., repeal of rules permitting segregated public education
when it is discovered that such forms of education harm children of
racial minorities. But how can one make such needed changes when
there is no mechanism for such changes—only a set of rules of the
"do" and "do not" variety?

Finally, there is the problem of *inefficiency*. Suppose that you and
Jones recognize the same rule for making a binding agreement, but
you believe that the rule has been followed and Jones does not. Is
the agreement made between you and Jones binding or not? Or
suppose that Smith has clearly violated a rule prohibiting an assault
on you. What are you supposed to do to get the controversy between
you and Jones resolved or to get the assault rule enforced against
Smith? Since there are no authorities or officials (because there are
no rules establishing them, only primary rules of obligation), you are

pretty much left to deal with these matters on your own, thereby helping to perpetuate that "state of nature" described by Thomas Hobbes wherein human life is "solitary, nasty, brutish, and short."

A society structured only in terms of primary rules, plagued as it necessarily will be with uncertainty, rigidity, and inefficiency, does indeed look pathologically grim. What is the cure? Hart writes as follows:

> The remedy for each of these three main defects in this simplest form of social structure consists in supplementing the *primary* rules of obligation with *secondary* rules of a different kind. The introduction of the remedy for each defect might, in itself, be considered a step from the pre-legal into the legal world, since each remedy brings with it many elements that permeate law. . . . Though the remedies consist in the introduction of rules which are certainly different from each other, as well as from the primary rules of obligation which they supplement, they have important features in common and are connected in various ways. Thus, they may be said to be on a different level from the primary rules, for they are all *about* such rules; in the sense that while primary rules are concerned with the actions that individuals must or must not do, these secondary rules are all concerned with the primary rules themselves. They specify the ways in which the primary rules may be conclusively ascertained, introduced, eliminated, varied, and the fact of their violation conclusively determined.[30]

According to Hart, there are three basic and intimately related kinds of secondary rules ("rules about rules") that both cure the pathologies of the prelegal society and define the concept of law itself. These are rules of *recognition*, rules of *change*, and rules of *adjudication*. What Hart means by these is, of course, nearly self-explanatory. A rule of recognition allows one to identify or recognize the actual rules of one's society. Such a rule "will specify some feature or features possession of which by a suggested rule is taken as conclusive affirmative indication that it is a rule of the group to be supported by the social pressure it exerts."[31] For groups of minimal complexity, there could simply be one such rule—e.g., "Any rule on the following list is a law and nothing else is" or "The oldest living member of the Dingbat Clan is the King, and whatever the King says is law." Thus, a rule is recognized as a law in terms of the formal property of its having the proper pedigree—a source in a law-defining document or list or in the decisions of the Dingbat King whose rulings define law for this system. (This rule could also serve, not merely to recognize rules, but also to change them and adjudicate controversies about them.)

We might think that we could also formulate some single and simple rule of recognition even for complex societies. Kelsen, for example, thought that every society had one Basic Norm (*Grundnorm*) defining legal validity for that system. We might, of course, as a kind of shorthand, state such a rule for various systems—e.g., "In England whatever the Queen enacts in parliament is a law" or "In America whatever the legislatures enact consistently with the Constitution is a law" or even "The Constitution is the rule of recognition for the American legal system." If we do make such statements for complex societies, however, it is important to remember that they are just shorthand and that the actual situation is much more complex than the simple formula suggests. In a society such as the United States, for example, the pedigree of valid law will not really be traced to one simple rule of recognition but to various rules of recognition all related to each other in subtle and complex ways. (If you want to say it is still one rule, then it will have to be a highly disjunctive one: "Law is made by doing *A*, or *B*, or *C*, or *D*, or etc., and by various complex relations among all these"—hardly a helpful notion of "one rule.") Hart writes:

> In a developed legal system the rules of recognition are of course more complex; instead of identifying rules exclusively by reference to a text or list they do so by reference to some general characteristic possessed by the primary rules. This may be the fact of their having been enacted by a specific body, or their long customary practice, or their relation to judicial decisions. Moreover, where more than one of such general characteristics are treated as identifying criteria, provision may be made for their possible conflict by their arrangement in an order of superiority, as by the common subordination of custom or precedent to statute, the latter being a 'superior source' of law.[32]

Having understood the nature of a rule of recognition as a cure for the problem of uncertainty, we can now see how other sorts of secondary rules will cure the other problems we noted in our prelegal model. Rules of change will establish authoritative mechanisms (e.g., legislatures) for enactment and repeal of rules and will overcome the static character of a system of primary rules. Rules of adjudication will establish mechanisms (e.g., courts) to overcome the problem of inefficiency present when controversy over primary rules exists. And since the rules of change (e.g., through the enactment of statutes) and adjudication (e.g., through the doctrine of judicial precedent) are sources for future primary rules, we can see that the connection between these rules and rules of recognition is quite intimate.

We have now seen what Hart means by "secondary rules": they are rules that create powers and authorities (to validate rules, create rules, and adjudicate controversies about rules), not rules that impose obligations.[33] We have also seen how important such rules are to an understanding of the nature of legal systems. They are, indeed, the factors that give legal systems their character as *systems*. Very simply put, legal rules are all a part of the same legal system if they have the same pedigree—i.e., they can all be traced to the same rule of recognition or set of rules of recognition that define validity for that system. This device also gives us an easy way to answer, at least for the primary rules, the question of what it means to say that these rules *exist*. Some rule R exists as a rule in legal system S if its pedigree can be traced to the rule or rules of recognition defining legality for S. Thus: There exists (for example) a valid law prohibiting driving over 25 miles per hour in a residential area, *even if nobody ever obeys that law*, so long as the law was enacted in the proper law-creating and law-defining way. We can now thus distinguish, as Austin was not able to, the *normative* existence of a legal rule from the *factual* existence of descriptive regularity or predictability of behavior.[34]

But what about a rule of recognition? What does it mean to say that it exists? Its existence cannot be established by tracing its pedigree to a rule defining validity for the system, for it is itself the rule that defines validity for the system. Thus, at this level, talk about existence must mean something else, indeed, it must involve some factual notion of descriptive regularity. For the rule of recognition is itself identified by its being the rule actually appealed to in deciding legal controversies in a legal system. If the Constitution is in some sense the basic rule of recognition (or part of such a rule) for the legal system of the United States, then this is because citizens, legislatures, government executives, and the courts all so regard it *in fact*. If (after a revolution, say) all these persons and agencies started ignoring it, it could no longer be said to exist as a rule of recognition for American society. Kelsen put this by saying that, at the level of the Basic Norm, "legal validity presupposes efficacy." Hart puts the point this way:

> The statement that a [primary] rule exists . . . [is] an internal statement applying an accepted but unstated rule of recognition and meaning (roughly) no more than 'valid given the system's criteria of validity'. In this respect, however, as in others a rule of recognition is unlike other rules of the system. The assertion that it exists can only be an external statement of fact. For whereas a subordinate rule of a system may be valid and in that sense 'exist' even if it is generally disregarded, the rule of recognition exists only as a complex, but normally concordant, practice of the courts, officials, and private persons in identifying the law by reference to certain criteria. Its existence is a matter of fact.[35]

Hart's slogan "law as a system of primary and secondary rules" has now been elucidated, and the theory of which the slogan is a capsule summary has been revealed as one of profound scope and power. So impressive an achievement is it, indeed, that many persons after reading Hart's book believe that the question "What is law?" has now been answered once and for all, that legal philosophers can now move on to other matters. By no means do all legal theorists share this pious view, however. Though nearly all would acknowledge that Hart has given the doctrine of legal positivism the most impressive statement and defense of which it is capable, some critics still maintain that the entire outlook and perspective of legal positivism, even at its best, seriously distorts the nature of law and legal systems, that it only achieves (to use Hart's own phrase against him) "uniformity at the price of distortion." It is to the doubts and theories of such writers that we shall now turn.

LEGAL REALISM

According to Hart, the central concept in terms of which law is to be understood is that of a *rule*. Hart (along with many earlier positivists such as Kelsen) adopts what Ronald Dworkin has called "the model of rules"—the view that law is best understood as a system of rules.[36] Though this view has a certain undeniable appeal to those whose perspective on the law is academic (e.g., philosophy and law professors), it has often seemed misguided to many lawyers, judges, and social scientists doing empirical research on legal behavior—all persons whose contact with the actual workings of legal systems is on a day-to-day basis. Earlier in this century, a group of Americans (loosely led and inspired by the judges Oliver Wendell Holmes and Jerome Frank and by the social scientist Karl Llewellyn) developed something of a movement or school in jurisprudence called "Legal Realism."[37] Declaring that "the life of the law has not been logic," Holmes ridiculed the idea that legal cases are best understood as the application of rules. If this were so, then why do so many cases get litigated (i.e., why don't people just apply the rules the way they do in chess?) and why is it that, in most cases that do get litigated, the outcome could really go either way, something one would not expect for genuinely rule-governed behavior? Perhaps, suggested Holmes, this is because the law is *not* a system of rules waiting there in a strongbox to be taken out by judges and mechanically applied to cases as they arise. The role of the judge is actually much more discretionary and creative than this. Since the "rules" allow the judge considerable free play, he or she can in fact decide the case in a variety of ways, and the way that is in fact adopted will be more of a function of such factors as the judge's psychological temperament, social class, and values than of anything written down and called "rules." It is time, in short, for more realism about the law, where "realism" is understood to mean a scientific examination of why decisions are in fact reached rather than some academic exercise about how decisions could be constructed as logical consequences of rules. Think of the law, said Holmes, as a "prediction of what courts will decide," and base your predictions of what the courts will decide, said Frank, on a good psychoanalytic understanding of judicial temperament and not on some notion of "the rules."

So baldly stated, legal realism seems overly cynical. There is no government of laws—only a government of men (judges) who can do whatever they jolly well feel like subject only to the constraints of their own temperaments and what others in society will tolerate. They may decide cases on whim (e.g., sexual attraction to one of the parties) and, though they may be subject to moral and political criticism for this, they can be subjected to no *legal* criticism. For, since there really are no legal rules, they cannot be criticized for failing to follow such rules. And what else could legal criticism be?

Though there are no doubt some judges who behave like this in some cases, most of us probably believe that they are a minority and would not take their arbitrariness as a model for judicial decisionmaking in general. We would probably describe them as not doing their job of attempting to apply the law (thereby showing that we regard them as open to legal criticism) and would no doubt echo the sentiments expressed by Neil MacCormick:

> In the absence of much good evidence, it seems reasonable to suppose that judges and lawyers are, like all humans, capable of occasional fits of humbug and hypocrisy, or of interpreting rooted prejudices as revealed truths. But equally, they are more commonly honest and honorable, capable of real efforts at, if never total achievement of, impartiality and objectivity; through practice, moreover, they have normally done more to develop habits of impartiality than many of those who are most strident in their denunciation.[38]

Not only does the theory seem overly cynical, it also seems open to easy refutation, at least as a definition or analysis of the concept of law. Consider Holmes's slogan: "Law is a prediction of what courts will decide." Some obvious problems arise for this.[39] (1) How do we tell what a court is? Is that not itself a legal question to be answered by applying rules (what Hart would call rules of recognition)? (2) On this model what is a judge himself really doing in interpreting a law in an actual legal case? According to this theory he is not really involved in deciding or interpreting at all. He is rather involved in an attempt to predict what he will decide! But what can this even mean? (3) On this theory we can draw no distinction between what is legally relevant in judicial decisions (e.g., precedents) and what is legally irrelevant (e.g., bribes); for, simply by being a factor in a particular judge's decision, any factor thereby becomes legally relevant. In short, this theory cannot capture an obvious feature of legal decision—namely, that certain considerations (e.g., precedents) function not merely to explain a judge's decision but also rationally and publicly to *justify* that decision in terms of standards shared by (and thus definitive of) a particular legal community. Just because in hard cases there may not be a unique outcome logically demanded by the rules, it does not follow that just anything goes. (4) Even if there are some hard cases that are radically underdetermined by legal rules, it is important to see that the vast majority of legal matters never even get litigated because, given certain rules, their outcome is almost mechanically obvious. It may be unclear just what constitutes "equal protection under the laws" in an exciting and controversial constitutional case before the Supreme Court, but it is not comparably unclear on what date one is legally required to have one's driver's license renewed in Arizona.[40]

Since lawyers and judges spend much of their time on hard cases (e.g., in law school they read mainly casebooks that contain cases so complex that they are being discussed on appeal), these persons are perhaps inclined to overestimate the underdetermined nature of legal cases and fail to see that the hard and uncertain cases take place against a background of the vast majority of cases that are reasonably clear.

How could thinkers of such obvious intelligence have put forth a theory of law so easily refuted? The answer is that it is a mistake, I think, even to interpret them as attempting to create a general theory of the nature of law of the same type as that found in Austin and Hart, and it is really a cheap shot to take a programmatic remark such as "law is a prediction of what courts will decide" as a theory of this nature. This will make the legal realists open to easy (if unfair) refutation, but it will also cause us to miss some genuine insights that they had about the nature of law and the legal process. The theory of law that seems most plausible to a person is often a function of the *perspective* of that person on the law. Legal realism is, in large measure, the *lawyer's* perspective, and though it is unlikely that this perspective is the whole story, it is almost certain that it is such an important part of the story that any legal theory that leaves it out will be seriously flawed.

The insights of legal realism are mainly negative—a deep skepticism about the model of rules. Such skepticism could still be justified (as a criticism of positivism, say) even if the realists have no plausible theory to put in its place. Indeed, it is perhaps part of the skeptical program of legal realism to be skeptical about the value of *any* general and abstract theory of the law—to suggest instead that we look at the many and varied practices and behaviors we call "legal" and seek, in a somewhat piecemeal way, to build our understanding of law from below in a gradual and accumulative way.

If we do look at the actual practice of judicial decisionmaking, we will surely be forced to admit that it is at least not obvious that in hard cases judges are simply applying rules. And though this may not mean that just anything goes, the apparent presence of judicial discretion in cases where there either are no rules or the rules are vague or conflicting might mean that more than *one* outcome is legally possible—something not compatible with the yes/no, on/off character of rules. There is nothing necessarily cynical about this view; indeed, it might be defended on moral and political grounds as providing an opportunity for an otherwise static legal system to respond to novel cases. Justice Louis Brandeis, for example, believed that in many hard cases judges have to go beyond the rules of the law and decide cases, not on subjective whim or prejudice, but on grounds of good social policy. Thus, judges (so Brandeis claimed) should be aware of the social consequences of their decisions so that they can, where allowed discretion by the underdetermined nature of the rules, make these decisions wisely for the general good. As a lawyer, Brandeis used to present judges with lengthy briefs containing sociological data about probable impacts of various decisions and policies. Such briefs are today still referred to as "Brandeis Briefs." The elaborate argument that won the day for school integration in *Brown* v. *Board of Education*[41] was a Brandeis Brief that developed an empirical case attempting to show that segregation psychologically harmed black children. This was used to argue that segregation is "inherently unequal," thereby denying black children "equal protection of the laws."

If Brandeis was correct in his general view, then those who condemn "judicial activism" and call for a judicial policy of "strict construction" (i.e., to simply "apply the rules") are speaking incoherently, at least for hard cases. These cases are hard just because they are under-determined by rules, and thus some kind of "activism" (i.e., judicial use of discretion) is unavoidable. The debate should thus not be over activism versus nonactivism but rather over what kind of activism (reachings beyond rules) is acceptable. A judge can appeal to perceived intentions of founding fathers, a conception of good social policy, general moral principles built into the common law, or do nothing at all; all of these (even the last) is a kind of activism because all represent ways of doing something other than simply applying rules.

The *perspective* (if not the attempts at theory) of legal realism has now been revealed as important and provocative. If legal positivism is a correct theory of law, it must hold for all law, including hard cases. These cases at least seem nondetermined or underdetermined by rules, and so they seem to constitute a counterexample to the model of rules. Recent critics of Hart and positivism (including Ronald Dworkin who certainly would not call himself a legal realist) regard this objection, first developed by the legal realists, as the most serious objection to positivism, and most contemporary debates about legal positivism now center on the question "Can legal positivism provide a correct theory of adjudication (judicial decision) especially in hard cases?" Even Hart sees this problem, accepts that it is potentially the most serious problem for his theory, and makes efforts to refine his theory in such a way that the problem will be resolved and thus any objections based on it overcome. These are matters we shall explore in the next section.

THE REEMERGENCE OF NATURAL LAW

The theories developed in legal philosophy in recent years have reached such a level of subtlety and sophistication that application to these theories of such traditional labels as "positivism," "realism," or "natural law" is likely to distort as much as clarify the issues involved. All these traditional theories contained some profound insights, and it is thus not surprising that contemporary writers tend to attempt to take the best from each. And this is, of course, as it should be, for the goal of legal philosophy is to attain the most illuminating analysis of law, *not* to make sure that one keeps one's ideological credentials pure in order to merit a certain title for one's theory.

In spite of the above caution, however, it still seems correct to say in a very general way that many contemporary writers are expressing sympathy for certain views that are not too misleadingly called "natural law" in character. These views have no grandiose metaphysical and theological pretensions, are generally free from the kinds of ambiguities and confusions that plagued those of Aquinas, and make no attempt to state a full moral theory and connect that theory to law in all sorts of implausible ways. In this sense, current natural law thinking is much more intellectually modest than the classical variety criticized in an earlier section of this chapter. What makes these current theories in any sense "natural law" theories then? Simply this: the various writers to be discussed in this section all maintain that the connection between law and morality, though not perhaps as pervasive and dominant as was maintained by classical natural law theory, is also not as loose and accidental as claimed by a traditional positivist such as Austin. There are interesting logical or conceptual connections between law and morality, and thus a full analysis of the concept of law will have to make reference to at least some moral concepts.

Even H. L. A. Hart, who still refers to himself as a legal positivist, is prepared to make certain concessions to natural law theory and articulate and defend something that he calls a "minimum content" theory of natural law.[42] It must be acknowledged, says Hart, that law and morality are both major social institutions concerned to regulate human conduct with respect to central human values. Because of this, there will necessarily be some overlap between the content of morality and the content of law—i.e., law and morality will, at least in part, be *about* the same issues and concerned with the same problems. And, since these issues and problems will in a sense be "natural" features of the human condition, it does not seem wrong to refer to the necessary overlap in content between law and morality as a concession, although a minimal one, to natural law theory. Consider these five natural facts about human beings and the world in which they live: (1) Human beings want to live and be secure but are vulnerable to assault and harm from their fellow humans. Unlike crustaceans, for example, they do not have hard exoskeletons. (2) Human beings are approximately equal in strength, ability, and intelligence, and thus, they all can benefit from schemes of cooperation and forbearance. (3) Human beings are limited in their altruism and are thus often motivated merely by self-interest. Because of this, they cannot always be counted on to cooperate and forbear voluntarily. (4) Human beings live in a world of moderate scarcity—a world where resources are too limited for each to have plenty unless cooperative schemes are adopted. (5) Human beings are limited in their knowledge and understanding and in their ability to control themselves solely on the basis of knowledge and understanding even when they do have it.

Surely, argues Hart, if human beings were radically different in these five respects (either by being more or less favored) then the nature of both law and morality would be radically different also for they are just institutional ways of dealing with these basic features of human life. And because of this, much of our moral and legal language depends upon these features as presuppositions of its very intelligibility. Thus, these "natural" facts have more than a merely contingent or empirical connection to our moral and legal concepts. Consider, in this regard, the simple and obvious natural fact that the vast majority of humans desire to live and be secure:

> It is not merely that an overwhelming majority of men do wish to live, even at the cost of hideous misery, but that this is reflected in whole

structures of our thought and language. . . . We could not subtract the general wish to live and leave intact concepts like danger and safety, harm and benefit, need and function, disease and cure; for these are ways of simultaneously describing and appraising things by reference to the contribution they make to survival which is accepted as an aim. . . . We are committed to [these values] as something presupposed by the terms of [moral and legal] discussion; for our concern is with social arrangements for continued existence, not with those of a suicide club.[43]

Thus, according to Hart, there is at least this one necessary overlap between law and morality: they are both institutions concerned, at least in part, with the same problems. Of course different legal systems could employ vastly different techniques and principles for dealing with these problems—e.g., wage labor and slave labor are both ways of dealing with the problem of raising food so that the community will survive in a world of scarcity. Since some of the legal solutions to the basic problems of human existence will be clearly immoral, it should be clear that a legal system can address itself to the "minimum content" of natural law and still be very evil.

Another contemporary writer who has defended a reasonably modest conception of natural law is Lon Fuller.[44] Fuller attempts to show that a plausible version of natural law theory (as a claimed necessary connection between law and morality) can be built from two insights basic to Hart's own positivistic theory: (1) that legal theory should concentrate on legal *systems*, and not particular laws, as the basic unit of analysis; and (2) that legal systems are (at least sometimes) profitably viewed as systems of rules. Of course, agrees Fuller, critics of natural law theory are correct when they point out that particular rules can still be laws even if deeply immoral. But could such rules still be laws if they were a part of an *entire system* that was itself deeply immoral? Fuller says that the answer to this question is no—that a system immoral in certain ways will simply fail to be a legal system because *it will fail to be a system of rules.* For what is it, asks Fuller, to control human behavior through rules? It is at a minimum to control behavior by giving people public advance warning that certain price tags attach to certain bits of their contemplated behavior and then treating them in accord with those warnings. This allows them to avoid paying the price by avoiding the behavior and renders their lives reasonably predictable and stable.

But what if the "rules" were enforced arbitrarily (i.e., like cases were not treated like), or were never published, or were generally applied *ex post facto*, or were changed constantly on a case-by-case basis, or were hopelessly vague and ambiguous, or gave officials such massive discretion that one's treatment at the hands of the state was never predictable? In a case such as this, it would be meaningless to call this control by rules at all; for the world "rule" here would be used as a joke or in some Pickwickian sense. This so-called system of rules would really be nothing more than control by the arbitrary and personal whim of those with power. Nazi Germany, especially in its final years, is used by Fuller as an example of a state controlled largely without rules—e.g., people could be rounded up by the police and detained simply on the personal whim of those in power. A system might have a few individual rules suffering from the above pathologies, but an entire system where the common practice was to act in such a secret and arbitrary way would not be a system of rules at all; and, if Hart is correct in claiming that legal systems are systems of rules, this would not be a legal system either. This account, claims Fuller, explains why we are inclined to say that Nazi Germany, in addition to all its other faults, had the fault of departing from the ideal of "the rule of law."

Why call this a kind of "natural law" account? Because, argues Fuller, a moment of reflection should make us realize that such injunctions as "Treat like cases like," "Don't apply rules after the fact," "Don't keep the rules private," etc. are all clear examples of rules demanding the moral values of *justice* or *fairness*. Probably the most easily recognized examples of injustice, indeed, are cases where a person in authority (e.g., a judge in sentencing) gives favored treatment to one party and harsh treatment to another in the absence of any legally relevant difference between them (e.g., he simply likes the looks or sex or social class of the one more than the other) and thereby treats like cases differently. (What makes two case alike is, of course, specified by the rules.) Thus: In order to be a legal system (because in order to be a system of rules) the system must be such that the vast majority of its rules satisfy certain procedural moral demands of justice or fairness—impartial enforcement, fair notice, etc. These demands, called by Fuller "the internal morality of law" or "the morality that makes law possible," are of course only formal or procedural in nature—i.e., they impose no limitations on the *content* of legal rules. These demands would not, for example, disqualify a rule making all blacks slaves so long as the rule was public, applied to and only to the specified persons, etc. For this reason, writes Hart in commenting on Fuller's views, it should be recognized that the satisfaction of Fuller's moral constraints is still compatible with a great deal of iniquity.[45]

We now come to the contributions made to legal philosophy by Ronald Dworkin, particularly as presented in his important and influential book *Taking Rights Seriously*.[46] As the present text goes to press, there can be no doubt that Dworkin's views now dominate philosophical and legal discussion of the concept of law. Some express deep admiration for his views and seek to apply them in a wide variety of legal contexts; others see these views as open to serious objections and seek to challenge them and minimize their influence. Almost all current writers on legal theory, however, feel the need to build their own views on a discussion, either sympathetic or unsympathetic, of Dworkin's views.

What is there about Dworkin's writings that make them an object of such intense current interest among legal philosophers and legal theorists? There are, I think, three related factors that explain the interest. (1) Much more than most legal philosophers, Dworkin uses discussion of actual legal cases in his philosophical writings. The cases are used to illuminate the philosophy and the philosophy is used to illuminate the cases in an interesting mutual interplay. (Dworkin's insistence that legal philosophy make sense of judicial decisions as revealed in actual cases is a legacy of legal realism.) (2) Dworkin is a subtle and powerful critic of legal positivism as that doctrine is best formulated by H. L. A. Hart, and one's own views become important if they involve good criticisms of other views already regarded as important. Dworkin argues that Hart's model of judicial decision in hard cases is defective because, by overly focusing on rules, it misses the way in which such decisions often *essentially* and *necessarily* involve appeals that have to be recognized as *moral* in nature. (This is, of course, a legacy of natural law theory.) (3) Finally, in stressing the importance of legal history, tradition, and the "moral principles that underlie the community's institutions and laws" as constraints on the permissibility of judicial decisionmaking, Dworkin shows an understanding of the degree to which moral appeals in the law are radically limited. Not just any moral appeal, no matter how commendable, has a necessary place in legal decisions; only those moral appeals that form a part, either explicitly or latently, of the moral traditions of the system in question are legally legitimate. (Thus Dworkin, though not tracing all law to some ultimate rule of recognition, still accepts something analogous to the positivistic notion of *pedigree* as one important element of legal validity—a legacy of positivism present in even this harshest of positivism's critics.)[47] In short: Dworkin, perhaps more than any other writer, has attempted to draw together and synthesize the best insights of previous theories on the nature of law. Since he writes most extensively on the problems of judicial decision and since he stresses that such decisions necessarily involve a moral element, it is not too misleading to see his "natural law" tendencies as dominant in his thinking.[48] They have certainly been the dominant concern of those who have written on Dworkin.

One word of caution should be introduced at this point: Dworkin originally presented his theory in 1967 in a brief and elegant article entitled "The Model of Rules."[49] Since then, the theory has been refined and elaborated in a variety of complex ways. Most of these changes occur in *Taking Rights Seriously* and involve extensive attempts on Dworkin's part to reply to his many critics. It is not always clear whether these changes simply represent explanations of ideas that were latent in his theory from the first or if they are rather new ideas presented in the guise of explaining the old. (It is interesting that this is exactly the main question one wants to ask about many judicial decisions!) It is even the case that many of Dworkin's critics fail to agree on the nature and implications of his views. For these reasons it is very likely that a brief summary of Dworkin's views (to which one is necessarily limited in a text) will distort those views in certain ways, at the very least by making them appear clearer and simpler than they in fact are. It is thus strongly recommended that the reader sample the primary literature here: Dworkin's own writings and the writings of his critics.[50] Advice to "go to the primary sources" is, of course, generally well taken and applies to the thinkers discussed already in this chapter: Aquinas, Austin, Hart, and Fuller. Such advice is more pressing with respect to Dworkin, however, because of the degree to which his views—appearing to evolve in the confines of even one book—are resistant to a capsule summary. (That this is so, by the way, should be taken as neither a virtue nor a vice of those views.) This caution having been given, we may now return to our exploration of the question "what is law?" as this question arises in the context of judicial decision.

As a prelude to a discussion of Dworkin's theory of judicial decision, let us return again briefly to legal positivism; for, since it is Hart's positivistic theory of judicial decision that troubles Dworkin and prompts him to develop an alternative account, a discussion of Hart's view on this is central to an understanding of Dworkin.

It is an acknowledged weakness of Hart's book that it does not contain a well-developed theory of judicial decision; thus, it is not clear if what he does say really represents his full view of the matter. We (and Dworkin) are limited, of course, to what Hart has actually written, and a fair (it is hoped) summary of the doctrine presented is this: Law is a system of rules. Therefore, judges are often involved in simply applying rules in a rather mechanical way. Some rules, however, contain terms that are "open-textured"—i.e., terms clearly applying to certain cases but unclear in the degree to which they apply to various "borderline" cases. Consider the term "vehicle" as it occurs in a statute forbidding the operation of a vehicle while intoxicated. It is clear that cars, trucks, and buses are "vehicles" for purposes of this statute, but what about a moped, or a bicycle, or a pair of roller skates? Here the rule is simply vague and gives the judge considerable discretion in how it will be applied. Since the rule itself does not answer these questions, the judge cannot be said to be simply applying a rule when he or she answers them. What then is the judge doing? According to Hart, in these cases the judge is *legislating* and there is no reason to pretend otherwise. Since legislators have no way of anticipating all possible fact situations that might arise (e.g., the invention of mopeds) and since they (like the rest of us) can only be generally and reasonably clear about their aims or values, there is no way that they could draft rules that would never contain any elements of vagueness or uncertainty. The creative discretion of the courts as deputy legislators is a vital way of filling in these gaps as they arise. Hart writes:

> In fact all systems, in different ways, compromise between two social needs: the need for certain rules which can, over great areas of conduct, safely be applied by private individuals to themselves without fresh official guidance or weighing up of social issues, and the need to leave open, for later settlement by an informed, official choice, issues which can only be properly appreciated and settled when they arise in a concrete case. . . . [When applying a vague concept], we confront the issues at stake and can then settle the question by choosing between the competing interests in the way which best satisfies us. In doing so we shall have rendered more determinate our initial aim, and shall incidentally have settled a question as to the meaning, for the purposes of this rule, of a general word. . . . The open texture of law means that there are, indeed, areas of conduct where much must be left to be developed by courts or officials striking a balance, in the light of circumstances, between competing interests which vary in weight from case to case. None the less, the life of the law consists to a very large extent in the guidance both of officials and private individuals by determinate rules which, unlike the applications of variable standards, do *not* require from them a fresh judgment from case to case.[51]

According to Dworkin, the way to test a model such as Hart's is to examine actual legal cases and see if it illuminates or distorts those cases. Dworkin's view is that it mainly distorts. It is, he argues, far too simplistic to maintain the dichotomy that judges are either applying and intepreting rules *or* they are legislating. The legal institutions of which they are a part are in some respects too rich and in other respects too limited to support this "model of rules" that Hart offers. They are too rich in that they offer, not simply rules, but a variety of other legal standards for use in decisionmaking—some of these obviously moral in nature. They are too limited in that they simply do not give judges the kind of legislative discretion of which Hart speaks. Hart's theory of judicial decision is thus a failure and the consequences of this failure for the general program of legal positivism are enormous for reasons to be outlined later.

In order to establish his criticisms of Hart's "model of rules," Dworkin invites us to consider two legal cases (cases he takes to be representative of "hard cases"). In *Riggs* v. *Palmer*,[52] the court had to decide whether an heir named in the will of his grandfather could inherit under that will, even though he had murdered his grandfather to do so. The court admitted that all statutes with respect to wills (the "rules") had been clearly and literally satisfied. There was nothing vague or open-textured in any of the language. These rules, "if their force and effect can in no way and under no circumstances be controlled or modified, give this property to the murderer." In spite of this, however, the court did not award the inheritance to the murderer. It found something to "control or modify" the rule and stated the rationale in this way: "All laws as well as contracts may be controlled in their operation and effect by general, fundamental maxims of the common law. No one shall be permitted to profit by his own fraud, or to take advantage of his own wrong, or to found any claim upon his own iniquity, or to acquire property by his own crime." This was not the application of a rule but was rather the setting aside of a rule on the basis of other sorts of considerations.

Or consider *Henningsen* v. *Bloomfield Motors Inc.*[53] In this case Henningsen had bought a car and had signed a contract which said that the manufacturer's liability was limited to replacement of defective parts. Henningsen was injured because of a defect in the car and argued that the manufacturer ought to be liable for his medical and other expenses in spite of the contract he had signed accepting a limitation of its liability. No settled or established rule of law could be cited by Henningsen that prevented the manufacturer from standing on the terms of the contract, but the court sided with Henningsen anyway. Though stressing the importance of the principle that in the absence of fraud, "one who does not choose to read a contract before signing it cannot later relieve himself of its burdens" (a principle supporting the manufacturer's case), the court insisted that other factors were also relevant: (1) the "freedom of competent parties to contract is a factor of importance," (2) "freedom of contract is not such an immutable doctrine as to admit of no qualification in the area in which we are concerned," (3) there is a "special obligation" that arises in a complex and impersonal society when one manufactures a widely used, complex, essential, and potentially dangerous item such as a car, (4) "the basic doctrine that the courts will not allow themselves to be used as instruments of inequity and injustice," and (5) "the courts generally refuse to lend themselves to the enforcement of a 'bargain' in which one party has unjustly taken advantage of the economic necessities of the other." Thus: the manufacturer will be held liable, in spite of a contract limiting liability, because it takes unfair advantage of the public if its members are allowed to purchase an essential item such as a car only if they sign a contract that in effect offers them no real protection against harm.

What is most interesting about these cases, according to Dworkin, is that they do not involve appeals to rules—indeed may even involve, as in *Riggs*, an explicit override of the relevant rules. Are they then simply pieces of *legislation* as Hart would argue—uses of discretionary power to weigh social costs and benefits much in the same way that a legislature would? Dworkin answers no to this question. In these cases, the judges are certainly appealing to values; but they are not free, as a legislator would be, to appeal to simply any value. If a Marxist legislator were elected to Congress, he could, with a perfectly coherent understanding of his institutional role, vote to eliminate schemes of private property and publicly cite as his reason his belief—perhaps also the belief of his constituents—that private property is evil, a form of theft. A judge has no comparable freedom. It would clearly involve an incoherent conception of his role for a judge to side with Henningsen and give as his reason his moral belief that capitalism should be brought to its knees and that making large corporations pay heavy damage settlements is a good step in this direction.

This kind of "legislative" discretion the judge clearly does not have.[54] The judge legitimately appeals to values, but these must be the values that in some sense inhere in or ground the system of law in which he is an official. The judges will often speak, for example, of what "the common law" teaches and will usually cite as that teaching some general standard of justice or fairness. These are moral standards, certainly; but, though they are not to be identified with the conventional practices of a particular society, they are not to be regarded as utterly divorced from those practices either. In this way they differ from the abstract and ideal moral theorizing of philosophers such as Plato and Marx who condemn the entire moral fabric of their societies as evil, from theological pronouncements of religious teachers (e.g., Jesus) who condemn their societies as sinful, and from moral visions drawn from radically different cultures (e.g., Africa or the Orient). Though not necessarily endorsing each moral prescription of his society, the judge in his proper role must be drawing upon the general moral fabric of the society in which he lives and must give reasons the relevance (if not the weight) of which would be granted by all reflective members of that society.[55]

Dworkin calls these appeals to general standards of justice or fairness appeals to *principles,* and he argues that principles differ from rules in important respects.[56] Rules, he says, are applicable in an "all-or-nothing" fashion. Consider the rules of a game such as baseball. There is a rule stating that a batter is out after three strikes. If the batter has three strikes, then he is simply out—no controversy possible. (Of course he is not out unless tagged or thrown out if the catcher drops the third strike, but a full statement of the rule would include this complexity.) An analogous rule in law would be the rule that in a particular state a valid will requires three witnesses. If there are three, it is validly witnessed. If there are less, it is not validly witnessed—no controversy. (Again, as in the baseball example, if there are exceptions allowed, then a complete statement of the rule would contain them.) And what if the rule in question conflicts with another rule? Then, because of the "all-or-nothing" character of rules, one of them has to go either by being dropped entirely, modified to allow an exception, or officially regarded as always overridden by the other in cases of conflict. If a state has the rule "no person may be denied a job because of his or her place of residence" and another rule "members of city police departments may be required to be residents of the city in which they work," then one of these rules must be invalid as it stands. One must be either dropped or modified to make an exception for the case of conflict—e.g., the first rule could be rewritten as "no person engaged in any employment other than law enforcement may be denied a job because of his or her place of residence."

The application of principles, Dworkin argues, proceeds by a very different logic. Principles are not all-or-nothing, yes/no or on/off switches. They can be relevantly brought to bear and can be in conflict with each other on the same case. This does not mean, however, that any one must control the outcome of the case and that the ones that do not must be dropped or modified. An unmodified statement of principle may be relevant over a wide range of cases but be decisive (i.e., carry the day) in only some of them. Dworkin calls this the property (essential to principles but not present in rules) of having *weight.* For example: It is sometimes allowed that a person will profit from his own wrongdoing—e.g., the doctrine of adverse possession says that if I wrongfully walk on your land long enough I will acquire a right to walk on your land. Does this mean that the principle "no person should profit from his own wrongdoing" must be dropped or modified? No. All it means is that the principle was overridden or *outweighed by other principles* in the one case but not in the other. (Perhaps a principle relevant in adverse possession is that a person's life should not be disrupted by abruptly denying him the right to do something he had been encouraged to expect that he might freely do.) Thus: Several principles may be in conflict in a particular case. It may be controversial which has greatest weight in the case, but it should not be a matter of controversy that each is relevant and should have its claims considered. Those principles that lose out in this case (unlike a rule that might lose out) do not get dropped or modified, for the relevance of each remains intact even when it is, in a particular case, outweighed by another.

Each principle—winners and losers alike—may thus "return to fight another day" intact and unmodified. Principles are *reasons,* and a reason does not cease to be a reason, even a good reason, just because, in a particular case, some other reason was even more compelling. Showing concern for the feelings of others is a relevant reason—i.e., something any decent person should take account of—in assessing the permissibility of contemplated actions. But pursuing my own happiness in those cases where I have a right to is also a relevant reason and goes toward justifying my marrying Sophie when I want to even if I know that this will break Mary's heart. Suppose I decide to marry Sophie and regard this as justified, all things considered—i.e., in this case, especially since I never led Mary on, I conclude that my rights outweigh damage to her feelings. Does this mean that concern for others' feelings is less of a relevant or good reason in future cases— or even that it was not relevant in the case where it was outweighed?

There has been great controversy over whether or not Dworkin has succeeded in making his contrast between rules and principles clear.[57] Let us suppose for a moment that he has. We might still ask why it all *matters*. Hart says that in hard cases judges weigh values in a quasilegislative manner in order to interpret vague rules. Dworkin says that in hard cases judges go beyond rules and weigh various principles. To what degree, one might ask, is this disagreement more than merely verbal? Both Hart and Dworkin agree that in hard cases judges go beyond rules and consider values. Why should it matter (except to those concerned with linguistic purity) whether we call this appeal to values a legal appeal to principles or a legislative act?

There are two reasons why the difference does matter. First, for reasons already noted, a legislative model does not capture the degree to which judges are limited—by the logic of their role as judges in a particular system of law—to consider only certain values. Recall that Hart does not actually say that judges are free to consider *any* value or aim. He rather says that they are to "render more determinate [the] initial aim." Thus, his model is perhaps not quite as "legislative" as it seems or even as he thinks it is. Legislatures do indeed have discretion in a strong sense—i.e., they are free (even if not always wise) to regard any issue as open for total rediscussion and change. Not so with judges. Because they are bound by the principles of the system in which they play a role, their decisionmaking process is always limited and structured by those principles. They exercise discretion only in the weak sense that they must use their judgment to do the best job they can of understanding and weighing the relevant principles.

This leads us to the second reason why the distinction between the legislative (or strong discretion) model and the principle (or weak discretion) model is important. Depending upon which model we adopt, we will hold a very different view concerning what a litigant is requesting when going before the court in a hard case. On the legislative model, the litigant is asking that the court, in considering his case, base its decision on its conception of what would represent the best policy for the good of the society as a whole. (Since the rules are too unclear to give him any rights, his role before the court must be mainly to alert the court to the need for some judicial legislation in the *hope* that the legislation will benefit him by allowing him to win his case.) On the principle model, on the other hand, the litigant is asking that the court protect a *right* that he or she has. Though there may be no decision procedure to yield a noncontroversial answer to the question "Given the weight of all relevant principles, does the litigant have a right?" the principle model claims that such a question should guide the deliberations of the court. On Hart's view, the claim "I had a right to win" makes no sense when a hard case has been lost; for rights and obligations, according to Hart, are simply entailments of legal rules. And the mark of a hard case, of course, is that it is underdetermined by such rules.

On Dworkin's view, however, the claim makes perfectly good sense if it purports to involve a marshalling and weighing of principles that is more persuasive than that performed by the court. Dissenting judges, appeals judges who overrule lower courts, and appeals lawyers make (or at least think they make) such cases all the time; thus, Dworkin's model should surely appeal to them. These persons at least claim to be appealing and dissenting on *the law* and do not speak and write as though they think their task is merely the political one of balancing (or persuading a judge to balance) a whole range of social interests. They maintain that a certain client has a *right* to win, not simply that it would be good for that client to win. Are they deluded or does their practice rather constitute an important counterexample to Hart's legislative model of strong discretion?[58]

If Dworkin's general attack on "the model of rules" is well-founded, what general implications does this have for the program of legal positivism? There are mainly two. First, it appears that postivism's sharp separation of law and morality may be threatened, for Dworkin seems to show that principled appeals that we would all regard as moral are a central part of judicial decisionmaking. (Dworkin's examples are all drawn from Anglo-American law, and so it is unclear whether he thinks that the law-morality union is a feature simply of our legal system or will be present, in some form, in any legal system. Positivism could, of course, happily grant the former.)[59] Second, the general principles of law that Dworkin regards as central cannot be validated, as can rules, by having their pedigrees traced to some "rule of recognition." They have a kind of pedigree in their character as arguably present in the moral foundation of one legal system rather than in another, but this is a much looser notion of pedigree than that found in Hart and other positivists.

Some writers (e.g., Joseph Raz and Rolf Sartorius) attempt to "save" Hart by suggesting that we should not insist on a rigid and simple formal statement of the rule of recognition but should rather see it as flexible—either "open textured" or incompletely specified. If the rule of recognition is so characterized, Dworkin's legal principles might be traced to or be a part of a rule of recognition after all. As Dworkin points out, however, to the degree that the rule of recognition is uncertain then to that same degree will it fail to do the job of clearly identifying valid law—the main attraction and selling point of legal positivism.[60]

We have concentrated thus far mainly on Dworkin's attack on the legal positivist's model of rules and have considered his positive views only in so far as they are a part of this negative case. Before closing our discussion, however, we should explore Dworkin's own theory of law in more detail, specifically his theory of judicial decision in hard cases. He calls this theory "The Rights Thesis," and it is to this thesis that we shall now turn.

Simply stated, Dworkin's "rights thesis" is this: Even in hard cases, judicial decisions enforce *rights* on principle.[61] Indeed (to define "principle" a bit more carefully than previously), we can say that an appeal to principle just is "an argument [that] . . . a decision respects or secures some individual or group right." What is a right? It is not, as some metaphysically or theologically inclined writers of the past have suggested, some spooky charm embedded in one's soul for the purpose of warding off the threat of secular tyranny—i.e., it is not what Bentham meant to condemn when he described natural rights as "nonsense on stilts." A right is simply a moral claim of a particular logical character. To understand this character, Dworkin suggests that we contrast rights appeals with appeals of another sort—appeals to what he calls considerations of "policy." An argument of policy (appropriately found in a truly legislative body) is an argument that some decision is justified because it advances some collective goal (e.g., general welfare) of the community—a goal established by an attempt to discover the various preferences and interests that should be taken into account. A decision to pursue a certain policy (e.g., internment of Japanese Americans after the attack on Pearl Harbor)[62] on the basis of a belief that this would promote national security and thus the general welfare would be a decision of policy in this sense, though perhaps not a rational one. Understanding what a policy or collective goal argument is, we can now see a rights argument as an argument that an individual or group must be respected or protected in a certain way on the basis of considerations other than considerations of policy. Dworkin writes (p. xi): "Individual rights are political trumps held by individuals. Individuals have rights when, for some reason, a collective goal is not a sufficient justification for imposing some loss or injury upon them." If one had argued against the internment of the Japanese Americans after 1941 on the ground that it is wrong, even if it furthers some desirable collective goal, to incarcerate persons who have not been convicted of any criminal offense, then one would have been offering an argument of principle—an argument that these citizens had a *right* not to be interred.[63] One might even call such a right "natural" in a harmless sense if all one means by this designation is that it is a right that, even if not currently recognized in the law, *should* be so recognized, perhaps because it is presupposed by the moral values upon which our legal order is generally based.[64]

As Dworkin develops it, the rights thesis has an interesting corollary—a thesis that might be called the "right answer" thesis. When rights are at stake, whether these are constitutional rights or a right to recover in a damage suit, there is always a right or correct answer to the question "Who has a right to win?" We are inclined to doubt this claim because there is no mechanical decisionmaking procedure that will let us know for sure if the right answer has been reached, but the absence of such a procedure for determining the right answer surely does not prove that there is no right answer. Suppose that the technology for inventing and developing microscopes never arose and could never arise because of some limitation of optics. Would this mean—just because we could never discover it—that there is no correct answer to the question "Are there organisms so small that they cannot be seen by the naked eye?" Or, more analogously perhaps, suppose that the completeness proof for the propositional calculus in logic had never been developed and never would be developed because of some limitation in the human intellect. Would it follow from this— just because we could never know—that there is no correct answer to the question "Is the propositional calculus complete?"

At the very least, Dworkin argues, the only acceptable model of judicial decision is one in which judges conceive of themselves to be searching for the right answer to the question "Who has the right?" This is their institutional role and is the main way in which they differ from legislators who may properly base decisions on a conception of collective good. The role of the courts in a democracy is not to provide one more legislative body to enact majoritarian preference; it is rather to identify and protect rights and thereby often check or limit majoritarian preference. Even the traditional and proper conception of a judge as one who gives great weight to precedent in decisionmaking only makes sense, according to Dworkin, on the basis of a principle of right—namely, the principle that it is unfair or unjust to thwart the legitimate expectations that a person developed because of previous judicial decisions in similar cases. This principle must be given weight in those cases where it is relevant; indeed, a litigant has a *right* that it be given weight. But how much weight? There is, of course, no easy answer to this question, but there is, according to Dworkin, a right answer. And it is the job of the judge to search out and articulate that answer.

We have then a model of an ideal or "philosophical" judge whose task is to search out in each hard case the right answer to the question "Who has the right to win?" This will involve a careful analysis and weighing of competing rights claims and also an articulation of a general theoretical account of rights—a theory of law—in which this case both illuminates and is illuminated by other cases. Small wonder that Dworkin calls such a judge "Hercules."[65]

Suppose we accept this general model. We agree that a judge should view himself or herself as involved in principled decisionmaking—i.e., decisionmaking that involves a search for an articulate statement and defense of rights in order that the correct answer to the question "Who has a right to win in this case?" will emerge. How will the judge do this? What intellectual goal should the judge set and what rational techniques will advance that goal? We know that an undefended and intuitive statement of rights ("Here they are—I have it by revelation!") will not do. What we want instead is some kind of *theory* of rights in which particular rights controversies can be embedded and thus resolved. But what is it to articulate and defend such a theory?

It seems that Dworkin's answer to this question, or at least the expression and emphasis of that answer, has changed in the years since his 1967 article. At that time Dworkin emphasized that the discovery and defense of legal principles would proceed primarily by an examination of the legal history, traditions, and conventions at the heart of a particular legal system. He wrote: "The origin of . . . legal principles lies not in a particular decision of some legislature or court, but in a sense of *appropriateness* developed in the public and [legal] profession over time. Their continued power depends upon this sense of appropriateness being sustained."[66] This appeal, though perhaps not to be identified with an appeal to convention, is closely linked to convention—close enough, at any rate, to make the task of the judge clearly different from that of the moral philosopher. Here the task of the judge looks hard, but perhaps not yet Herculean. (Also, and not surprisingly, this way of expressing the view led many of Dworkin's critics to suspect that his differences from such positivists as Hart were not actually as great as Dworkin had suggested.)

As Dworkin now expresses his view (and this may have been the view all along) he makes the judge's task begin to look very philosophical indeed. In fact, he makes the law appear to be a kind of institutionalized moral philosophy. Dworkin now speaks of judges' responsibility "to fit the particular judgments on which they act into a *coherent* program of action,"[67] of the search for "moral principles that *underlie* the community's institutions,"[68] and even of the search for the "*soundest theory* of law . . . that will *justify* the settled rules"—a search that, by Dworkin's explicit admission, "must carry the lawyer very deep into political and moral theory."[69] Explicitly identifying himself with "naturalism" (i.e., natural law theory), Dworkin writes:

> According to naturalism, judges should decide hard cases by interpreting the political structure of their community in the following perhaps special way: by trying to find the best *justification* they can find, in principles of political morality, for the structure as a whole, from the most profound constitutional rules and arrangements to the details of, for example, the private law of tort or contract.[70]

While there is still an important link to the conventions of a particular society, the task of the judge begins to look more and more like the task of the moral philosopher—a task of not simply finding the institutionally relevant principles but also, in some sense, of rationally justifying those principles in terms of the best possible theory of justification. Even moral philosophers, in spite of their frequent

pretenses to the contrary, do not operate in total independence of
the actual conventions and beliefs of the societies in which they live,
for their moral theories are typically a rational reconstruction of those
conventions and beliefs. (They sometimes, of course, offer us the
fiction that their theories transcend all conventions and are deliverances
of pure reason.) Such philosophers will often criticize and reject
particular moral beliefs current in their culture as rationally unjustified,
but they will not regard *all* of them as unjustified; for it is the value
structure lying behind the majority of beliefs that tells us what our
true values really are and allows us to criticize certain of our beliefs
as inconsistent with the dominant thrust of our dominant morality.
For example: John Rawls, one of the most important moral theorists
of recent years, argues that a moral principle is rationally justified if
it puts "us" into a state of "reflective equilibrium" with respect to
the largest set of "our" pretheoretical moral convictions—i.e., if it
orders and systematizes and rationalizes those convictions for "us" in
a satisfying way. But what are these references to "us" and "our" if
not to persons very like us, or idealized versions of us, with conventions
and beliefs rather like our own? (Would the moral theory of a Harvard
philosophy professor be likely to put a morally sensitive citizen of
China or India or Japan in a state of "reflective equilibrium"—or
even members of all social classes in our own society?)[71] The "rational
morality"/"conventional morality" contrast begins to lose its clarity.

Another contrast that begins to lose its clarity is that between
contemporary legal theory (as practiced by Dworkin) and contemporary
moral theory (as practiced by Rawls, say). A blurring of this distinction
is part of Dworkin's purpose, of course, because he seeks to challenge
"the orthodox idea that legal standards can be distinguished as a
group from moral or political standards."[72] One thing, however, is
clear: To the degree that the rights thesis and the right answer thesis
both depend on moral theory, then to that same degree will they be
rendered suspect if moral theory is suspect. That is, if there are no
right answers in morality, this may make the search for such answers
in law a vain one. In criticizing Dworkin, the philosopher Alasdair
MacIntyre makes just this point. He writes:

> Moral philosophy, as it is dominantly understood, reflects the debates
> and disagreements of the culture so faithfully that its controversies turn
> out to be unsettlable in just the way that the political and moral debates
> themselves are. . . . Important conclusions follow for constitutional
> theory. Liberal writers such as Ronald Dworkin invite us to see the
> Supreme Court's function as that of invoking a set of consistent principles,
> most and perhaps all of them of moral import, in the light of which
> particular laws and particular decisions are to be evaluated. [Dworkin

suggests that we should view the *Bakke* case in this way, criticizes the court for the degree to which it politicized the decision rather than making it one of pure and consistent principle, and attempts to articulate the principles the court should have used.] But even to make such an attempt is to miss the point. The Supreme Court in *Bakke*, as on occasion in other cases, played the role of a peacekeeping or trucekeeping body by negotiating its way through an impasse of conflict, not by invoking our shared moral first principles. For our society as a whole has none.[73]

We have now reached a point where we can neither understand nor evaluate Dworkin's fully developed theory without a detailed exploration of moral philosophy and its application to law. Dworkin's theory that legal reasoning is often moral reasoning cannot be understood simply in terms of a few vague and high-sounding remarks about rights and principles coupled with a set of arguments showing where a positivistic theory goes wrong. Hart's positivistic model of quasilegislative discretion was tested by Dworkin through an examination of some representative legal cases (*Riggs* and *Henningsen*) and his own theory needs to be subjected to a comparable test to see if his moral reasoning model illuminates or obscures the legal issues involved. Some of Dworkin's best case studies occur in the area of constitutional law—perhaps the most obviously moralized branch of law in our society. (It is sometimes said of Dworkin that he is not, like Hart, offering a philosophical theory of law that would hold for all cultures but is really offering a philosophical theory or reconstruction of United States constitutional law.)[74]

Thus, both to understand and assess Dworkin it will be useful to examine moral theory and its application to law, especially constitutional law. The legal value of the study of moral theory is not, however, limited to those with an interest in Dworkin. Even those legal positivists who are in total disagreement with Dworkin should also find this project worthwhile; for, even though they do not think that morality is in any sense to be identified with law (and thus has no role in analytical jurisprudence), they will surely be concerned with the moral evaluation and criticism of law, i.e., with normative jurisprudence.[75] Neither is the importance of moral theory limited to constitutional law, for it is hard to imagine any area of law that does not generate problems of moral analysis and evaluation.

We shall thus begin, in the following chapter, an examination of moral theory and attempt to answer these questions: What is moral reasoning? Can such reasoning be put on an objective foundation or is it ultimately a matter of subjective or culture-relative opinion and preference? What is the proper role, if any, for systematic theories in morality? How, if at all, can such reasoning and theories be properly applied either within or to the law? It is to these questions that we shall now turn.[76]

NOTES

1. H. L. A. Hart, *The Concept of Law* (Oxford: Oxford University Press, 1961), chap. 1 (hereinafter cited as *CL*).
2. *Clingenpeel* v. *Municipal Court*, 108 Cal. App. 3d 394, 166 Cal. Rptr. 573 (1980).
3. *People* v. *Jordan*, 75 Cal. App. Supp. 2d 1, 142 Cal. Rptr. (1977).
4. *McPherson* v. *Buick*, 217 N.Y. 382, 111 N.E. 1050 (N.Y., 1916).
5. The basic right to privacy case is *Griswold* v. *Connecticut*, 381 U.S. 479 (1965). The basic abortion case is *Roe* v. *Wade*, 410 U.S. 113 (1973). Specifically the Supreme Court held that a woman's right to privacy encompasses the right to have an abortion during the first trimester of her pregnancy subject only to her ability to find a licensed physician willing to perform it. (The woman's right to privacy does not require forcing a doctor to perform an abortion nor does it require that the state pay for the abortion— only that her seeking the abortion not be actively inhibited by the state. See *Maher* v. *Roe*, 432 U.S. 434 [1977]). After the first trimester, the Court held, the state may regulate abortions because of an interest in protecting the mother's health (starting with the second trimester) or, because of the interest in the fetus as future human life, ban abortions entirely beginning with the third trimester.
6. See Thomas Aquinas, "The Essence of Law," in *Introduction to St. Thomas Aquinas*, ed. Anton C. Pegis (New York: Random House, 1948), 609–50. For a discussion of the various forms taken by classical natural law theory, see A. P. d'Entreves, *Natural Law* (London: Hutchinson, 1951). For a discussion of the influence in England and America of the natural law tradition—particularly the "natural rights" formulation that arose during the Enlightenment, see Sir Ernest Baker, *Traditions of Civility* (London: Cambridge University Press, 1948). The natural rights moral tradition will be discussed in Chapter 2.
7. The first sustained philosophical discussion in our civilization of the moral obligation to obey the law occurs in the Platonic dialogues *Euthyphro, Apology,* and *Crito.* (In these dialogues Plato reports teachings of his teacher Socrates.) For an excellent discussion of these dialogues, see A. D. Woozley, *Law and Obedience* (London: Duckworth, 1979). See also "Violence and the Socratic Theory of Legal Fidelity," in Jeffrie G. Murphy, *Retribution, Justice, and Therapy: Essays in the Philosophy of Law* (Dordrecht and Boston: D. Reidel, 1979). Socrates presents an early statement of what has come to be called a "social contract" justification for moral allegiance to government—i.e., for a prima facie moral obligation to obey the law. It should not simply be assumed, of course, that there is such a prima facie obligation. Common as is the view that moral allegiance is owed to the law itself (i.e., that "because it is the law" is always a morally relevant reason in favor of action), this view may be (as is the case with many commonly accepted views) so much superstitious claptrap. For a sustained defense of the skeptical view, see M. B. E. Smith, "Is There a Prima Facie Obligation to Obey the Law?," *Yale Law Journal* 83 (1974):950. It is important to realize that those who argue against a prima facie obligation to obey the law are not denying that people often (perhaps most of the time) have good moral reasons for obeying the law, but simply that "because it is the law" is not among those reasons.
8. For Aristotle, all moral requirements are discoverable by reason's study of the law of nature. For Aquinas, certain moral requirements have to be learned through revelation. Since God's natural law will never be inconsistent with His revelation, however, the natural law can be used as a moral test for human law. The relevance of nature (e.g., biology) to ethics is explored at an elementary level in Jeffrie G. Murphy, *Evolution, Morality, and the Meaning of Life* (Totowa, N.J.: Rowman and Littlefield, 1982). Some of the discussion in this section draws on this book.
9. Aquinas does not say that the law of nature requires that a person act in accord with all common and frequent (and in that sense "natural") temptations—e.g., the

temptation to be violent or to engage in "perverted" sexual activity. When Aquinas speaks favorably of the "natural inclinations" of human beings, he means those inclinations that are, in his view, "proper." The problem with this, of course, is that to the degree that "natural" means "proper," then to that same degree is natural law theory merely restating moral beliefs rather than giving any independent reasons for those beliefs. "It is wrong because it is unnatural" begins to sound suspiciously like "It is wrong because it is wrong (improper)." Aquinas's own condemnation of homosexuality as a crime against nature seems to involve such circularity, and it may get what plausibility it has simply because it restates (rather than argues for) a commonly held conventional moral prejudice. (Those who are eloquent spokesmen for our own prejudices always strike us as wise.) For a clear example where natural law talk seems to do just this, consider this remark by St. Paul: "Judge it yourselves: is it comely that a woman pray unto God uncovered? Doth not even nature itself teach you, that, if a man have long hair, it is a shame unto him? But if a woman have long hair it is a glory to her: for her hair is given to her for a covering." It is a possibility, of course, that all moral recommendations are ultimately nothing more than ways of expressing shared conventional beliefs and feelings. Natural law theory certainly maintains that it is doing more than this, however.

10. G. E. Moore, *Principia Ethica* (Cambridge: Cambridge University Press, 1903). Even if Moore is correct in claiming that one may not *derive* values from facts, it does not follow from this (as the later discussion of Hart's "minimum natural law" theory will show) that there are no interesting conceptual or logical connections between facts and values.

11. Aquinas, "The Essence of Law," 637. Aquinas writes as follows: "This is the first precept of law, that good is to be done and promoted, and evil is to be avoided. All other precepts of the natural law are based upon this."

12. Alf Ross, *On Law and Justice* (London: Stevens, 1958), 261.

13. Aquinas, "The Essence of Law," 615, 633, 649.

14. The following discussion of the differences between moral and legal obligation is drawn from Hart, *CL*, 169 ff. See also his "Legal Positivism and the Separation of Law and Morals," *Harvard Law Review* 71 (1958):593. As the later discussion of Ronald Dworkin will reveal, the whole issue may turn out to be a bit more complex than Hart suggests; for Dworkin will argue that the distinction between moral and legal obligation is ultimately not as sharp as it initially seems—a claim that will reveal Dworkin as in some sense a contemporary defender of natural law theory. Other critics of a very different persuasion will suggest that it is misleading even to use the concept of legal obligation because of its misleading moral overtones. They will suggest replacing talk of legal obligations with talk about legal *requirements* (as opposed to legal permissions) and will argue that references to legal obligations are simply misleadingly redundant ways of making this simple point—i.e., that "there is a legal requirement that *P*" is not a reason in support of the claim "there is a legal obligation that *P*" but just another way of saying the same thing. Some would also regard Hart's characterization of morality as controversial (e.g., see note 15 below).

15. What about cultures such as the one present (according to Sophocles in *Oedipus Rex*) in ancient Thebes—a culture that condemned Oedipus as vile even though he acted in nonculpable ignorance when he killed his father and had sexual relations with his mother? Is this not a notion of strict or absolute moral responsibility? Perhaps, though the issue is complex. Some writers have suggested that the culture described had standards of conduct that were not really moral in nature but are to be understood under some different model—e.g., a *shame* (and thus quasi-aesthetic) model or a *disease* model (a model where the person who acts contrary to rules must be exiled as "polluted" or "unclean" much as we once quarantined persons with tuberculosis).

16. As John Rawls has argued, a legislative body produces a directive to be acted upon, not a proposition to be believed. The remark "The legislature directed this but I believe it is wrong" makes perfectly good sense in the way that the remark "This is immoral but I don't believe it" does not. See John Rawls, "Legal Obligation and

the Duty of Fair Play," in *Law and Philosophy*, ed. Sidney Hook (New York: New York University Press, 1964).

17. In an early essay (*supra* note 16) John Rawls argued for the moral obligation to obey the law in this way: I can have a moral obligation to obey rule *R*, even if I disagree with the moral content of *R*, if I accept, on moral grounds, a *procedure* for controversy resolution (i.e., a procedure for generating laws) and *R* flows from that procedure. Suppose I subscribe to the principle of majority rule as a procedure that, in the long-run, promotes both utility and fairness. I realize that the procedure will work—i.e., will produce its benefits—only if people defer to its results even in cases where they disagree (even on moral grounds) with the results. I expect others to do this and thus it is only "fair play" that I do likewise. This obligation of fairness is only prima facie, of course, because it could be overridden if *R* is sufficiently evil—e.g., if it mandates genocide. Of course if the rules generated by the procedure are generally or typically immoral, then there would be little reason for giving that procedure allegiance in the first place. For various reasons, Rawls has now abandoned this account and offers a different theoretical foundation for moral allegiance to law, based on the idea that we have a "natural duty" to support just institutions, in his *A Theory of Justice* (Cambridge: Harvard University Press, 1972). For a powerful attack on all attempts to provide a moral foundation for allegiance to law, see Robert Paul Wolff, *In Defense of Anarchism* (New York: Harper and Row, 1970).

18. Aquinas occasionally says things that suggest that it might be possible sympathetically to reinterpret or reconstruct his theory as applicable to systems rather than particular laws. See, for example, the section "Whether Every Law is Derived from the Eternal Law" at pp. 632 ff., *supra* note 6. It may be that, in spite of all the problems noted, Aquinas has succeeded in establishing one logical or conceptual connection between law and morality. Let us assume that Aquinas has given us only a theory of the ideal, or perfect, or paradigm case of law (a paradigm exemplification of the rule of law) and let us suppose that he has demonstrated that, at least for such a case, the satisfaction of moral requirements must enter into the analysis. This would show a conceptual connection between law and morality, because it is not the case that the ideal or perfect or paradigm instance of every institutional human activity has a moral dimension—i.e., not all perfection is moral perfection. Some ideal cases (e.g., the paradigm ballet) will involve aesthetic perfection. This possible way of establishing a conceptual connection between law and morality occurred to me after conversations with my colleague Michael White, and I am grateful to him for discussing these matters with me. Three persons whose opinion I greatly value—Merrilee Salmon, Michael White, and A. D. Woozley—took me to task for my treatment of classical natural law theory in an earlier draft where, in their view, I took too many cheap shots at a theory with which I obviously have little sympathy. I recast this section under the influence of their criticisms and, though I know that I have not gone as far toward sympathy as they would like, I hope that they will agree that the shots are now at least a bit more expensive.

19. John Austin, *The Province of Jurisprudence Determined*, 1832. This is most easily available in the edition edited by H. L. A. Hart, published in London by Weidenfeld and Nicolson in 1954. Also important are the *Lectures on Jurisprudence*, 1885.

20. See the discussion of Kelsen at note 26 below.

21. This discussion occurs in Hart, *CL*, 80 ff.

22. According to Austin, the sovereign commands that constitute laws must also be *general*—i.e., ranging over *kinds* of people and *kinds* of acts. (This is Austin's sole notion of a "rule.") See Ronald Dworkin, *Taking Rights Seriously* (Cambridge: Harvard University Press, 1977), 17 for the claim that a pedigree test defines legal positivism. Some writers have argued that the concept of pedigree is too narrow to capture the positivistic test for law—that what is essential is that the test be formal (i.e., independent of content) and that a pedigree test (with its emphasis on historical ancestry) is simply one kind of formal test. For example: "All the rules written on that wall over there are law and nothing else is" is a formal test, but not a pedigree test. According to other theorists, the essence of positivism is simply that there is a test for law that is a conventional

social rule (what H. L. A. Hart, as will be discussed later, calls a "rule of recognition"). For a detailed discussion of the controversy concerning the essential nature of legal positivism, see Jules Coleman, "Negative and Positive Positivism," *The Journal of Legal Studies* 11 (January 1982):139–64.

23. The history of political philosophy is filled with competing tests for sovereignty. One of the most memorable occurs in the film *Monty Python and the Holy Grail:*

> *Peasant 1:* "There goes the king."
> *Peasant 2:* "How do you know he's the king?"
> *Peasant 1:* "He's the only one who isn't covered with shit."

(Query: Is this a semantic criterion for characterizing the sovereign, or simply an epistemological test for discovering the sovereign?)

24. Austin, *Province*, Lecture VI.

25. Hart, *CL*, 50.

26. Though difficult and often obscure, the writings of the Austrian Hans Kelsen are monumental works of twentieth-century jurisprudence. It is thus regrettable that limitations of space do not permit an extended discussion of his views here. His major works are *Reine Rechtslehre*, 1934, published in English translation as *Pure Theory of Law* (Berkeley: University of California Press, 1967) and *General Theory of Law and State* (New York: Russell and Russell, 1961). For a summary and critical discussion of some of Kelsen's views, see Martin Golding, "Kelsen and the Concept of 'Legal System,'" in *More Essays in Legal Philosophy*, ed. by Robert S. Summers (Berkeley: University of California Press, 1971).

27. Hart, *CL*, chap. V.

28. It is misleading to call all such persons "bad," because some of them might view the legal system in which they live (e.g., Nazi Germany) in this way because they regard it as morally deplorable. Persons who view the laws under which they live in a purely external way are perhaps better thought of as *alienated;* and there is a whole spectrum of reasons why a person might be alienated from the system in which he or she lives—reasons all the way from being evil or a psychopath (a bad person) to being a saintlike moral critic.

29. Hart, *CL*, 89.

30. Ibid., 91 ff.

31. Ibid., 92.

32. Ibid., 92–93.

33. Hart writes: "Many of the features which puzzle us in the institutions of contract or property are clarified by thinking of the operations of making a contract or transferring property as the exercise of limited legislative powers by individuals" (ibid., 94). Thus, secondary rules are not simply rules that illuminate the conduct of officials; they can illuminate the legal conduct of private persons as well. The citizen's relations to the law is not simply that of being under duties; the law also gives citizens authoritative *powers*.

34. These matters are discussed by Hart in chapter VI of *CL*. Hart has provided a way of showing what it means to say that a particular rule exists as a legal rule in a system even if it is never obeyed. He acknowledges, however, that such cases must necessarily constitute a minority. If all or most of the rules were ignored, there would be no system of rules at all. Thus: "This is a law and it is generally obeyed" is not a necessary truth, but "Most of the laws of the system are regularly obeyed" is a necessary truth. For a sophisticated discussion of these matters, see A. D. Woozley, "The Existence of Rules," *Nous* 1 (March 1967):63–79.

An interesting puzzle is posed by the fact that courts are normally very reluctant to enforce rules that have gone unenforced for a very long time (the problem of *desuetudo*). Is this because the rules have ceased to count as laws? But if so, why? This is a troublesome question for Hart if these rules do satisfy the pedigree test of traceability to a rule of recognition. It is, of course, often *unfair* to suddenly apply a rule to persons who had been led to expect that the rule was dead. But is this simply a moral criticism of applying such laws (a ground why legislatures might explicitly repeal them) or is it a legal criticism (a ground a judge might properly use to void new attempts at enforcement)? These questions may be illuminated in the discussion of Ronald Dworkin later in this chapter.

35. Hart, *CL*, 107. As Hart sometimes puts it: at the level of the rules of recognition, "the only thing that succeeds is success."

36. Ronald Dworkin, "The Model of Rules," *University of Chicago Law Review* 35 (1967):14.

37. For a good general discussion of legal realism, see Chapter 5 of Edward A. Purcell, Jr., *The Crisis of Democratic Theory: Scientific Naturalism and the Problem of Value* (Lexington, Ky.: University Press of Kentucky, 1973). For a powerful statement and defense of a generally realist outlook ("The function of a judge is not mainly to declare the law, but to maintain the peace by deciding controversies") see John Chipman Gray, *The Nature and Sources of the Law* (New York: Macmillan, 1921).

38. Neil MacCormick, *Legal Reasoning and Legal Theory* (Oxford: Clarendon Press, 1978), 17.

39. This attack on legal realism is adapted from Hart's in Chapter 7 of *CL*. It will later be suggested that the attack may involve a few cheap shots.

40. This is a matter of degree, of course. As was noted in the earlier discussion of the rule that one may not drive a vehicle while intoxicated, a rationally cautious person will not adopt an attitude of absolute certainty with respect to any legal rule that there can be no problems in its meaning or application.

41. 347 US 483 (1954).

42. Hart, *CL*, 189 ff.

43. Ibid., 188.

44. Lon Fuller, *The Morality of Law* (New Haven: Yale University Press, 1964).

45. Hart, *CL*, 202.

46. Ronald Dworkin, *Taking Rights Seriously* (Cambridge: Harvard University Press, 1977), hereinafter cited as *TRS*. The paperback edition of this book (Cambridge: Harvard University Press, 1978) contains as a valuable Appendix an extensive reply by Dworkin to several of his critics.

47. I am not at all sure that Dworkin himself would agree with the claim that his theory contains anything even remotely like a pedigree test—or even a formal test as characterized in note 22. Many of his critics have read him as offering such a test (though a much weaker one than that offered by Hart), and Dworkin insists that they have interpreted him incorrectly. Let the following count as a summary of the kind of test Dworkin often seems to offer: the legal validity of a principle will sometimes not depend solely upon the content of that principle but will also require a *location* of that principle in an external context—typically a legal tradition. It is in this very weak sense that I suggest that Dworkin has something like a formal or pedigree test. The legal status of a principle will be formal in the sense that it will not depend solely on its content but will also depend on a certain kind of institutional support—i.e., the degree to which it is entrenched in authoritative legal doctrines (the degree of its weight being a function of its degree of entrenchment). The term "entrenchment" is drawn from Rolf Sartorious; see note 57. Since entrenchment will typically involve tradition or history, something like pedigree also seems involved. For an argument that Dworkin's essential insights are more compatible with positivism than he realizes, see Coleman, *supra* note 22.

48. See Ronald Dworkin, "'Natural' Law Revisited," *University of Florida Law Review* 34 (1982):165.

49. *Supra* note 36.

50. In addition to the works already cited, see Ronald Dworkin, "No Right Answer?" *Law, Morality, and Society*, eds. P. M. S. Hacker and J. Raz (Oxford: Clarendon Press, 1977). For a collection of commentaries on Dworkin, see Marshall Cohen, ed., *Ronald Dworkin and Contemporary Jurisprudence* (Totowa, N.J.: Rowman and Allanheld, 1984).

51. Hart, *CL*, 127. The existence of rules with "open-textured" concepts provides only one argument for judicial discretion. Another argument is provided by the fact that any body of rules is *finite*—i.e., there will be *gaps* in the law. See Jules Coleman's review of *TRS* in *California Law Review* 66 (1978):885.

52. 115 N.Y. 506, 22 N.E. 188 (1889).

53. 32 N.J. 358, 161 A. 2d 69 (1960).

54. The point here is a logical one, not a factual one. Of course a judge can sometimes, in fact, get away with just about anything—i.e., the judge has factual freedom. The issue of concern to Dworkin is to what degree the judge is *logically* free to decide a case in a given way—i.e., at what point will his or her decision cease to count as enforcing the *law* and thus reveal a mistaken or even incoherent conception of the judicial role—will reveal that the judge is trying to make law instead of find law, create rights instead of enforce rights? Dworkin is deeply interested in a question of political philosophy: What is the nature of the judiciary and what constitutes the *integrity* of that governmental branch? If the judicial role is merely legislative, then why have such a body at all—especially since judges are not nearly as accountable as are ordinary legislators?

No matter how much they may pretend otherwise, philosophers are not immune to the social concerns of their day, and their theories often reflect those concerns. Why, one might well ask, did Dworkin succeed in accomplishing what the legal realists never could accomplish in spite of all their efforts—namely, to focus the attention of legal philosophy on the problems of judicial decision and thus make the theory of adjudication the central issue of the discipline? At least part of the answer lies in this: During the fifties and sixties, the courts seemed to be the only hope for protecting civil rights (particularly those of racial minorities) against what was often seen as the bigotry and stupidity of legislative bodies. Part of the appeal of Dworkin, then, lies in his articulate and principled (and élitist!) championing of an institution—the judiciary— that often has as one of its functions the antimajoritarian or antidemocratic role of thwarting the will of legislatures, at least in those cases where legislatures would presume to invade fundamental rights. The considerable virtues of this approach are, of course, obvious; for we are, as a society, always in need of a reminder that we live in a constitutionally limited democracy (not a pure democracy) and that there are therefore other important values at work in our system besides "the will of the people." Sometimes the people simply may not have their collective will enforced if such enforcement would seriously encumber fundamental rights. It is not always clear, however, that Dworkin fully realizes that his approach has serious limitations as well. A complete theory of law would surely contain a theory of legislation, and such a theory would surely be more subtle and complex than Dworkin's offhand suggestion that legislatures simply add up preferences to produce beneficial policies and that principles are the business of the courts. Dworkin rejects Hart's model of strong legislative discretion for the courts but seems to endorse it as a theory of legislation. This may be too quick. Thus Dworkin, in rightly insisting that adjudication has been treated too superficially in legal philosophy, may invite us to treat legislation too superficially. We surely must fear legislative tyranny (the "tyranny of the majority"), but we should perhaps fear judicial tyranny as well. Such a fear is socially important but it is not at all encouraged by Dworkin's sometimes uncritical admiration for the judiciary.

55. Imagine a freedom of expression case where the government attempted to stifle a certain kind of speech as a threat to national security (e.g., publishing a recipe to instruct people on how to make atomic bombs at home from simple ingredients). Different judges might give different weights to the national security claim presented by the government, but each judge would surely have to regard that claim as *relevant* to deciding the case. There could surely be no controversy here. For an actual case that is similar (though somewhat less dramatic) see *U.S.* v. *Progressive Inc.*, 486 F. Supp. 5 (W. D. Wisc, 1979).

56. Dworkin, *TRS*, 22 ff. At this point (Chapter 2, a reprint of "The Model of Rules"), Dworkin calls any nonrule appeal, whether to fairness or social policy, an appeal to "principle." In Chapter 4 he restricts the term "principle" to those appeals that involve rights, justice, or fairness.

57. See Dworkin, *TRS*, 71 ff. Some of the more interesting criticisms of Dworkin on this and related issues have been developed by Rolf Sartorious, "Social Policy and Judicial Legislation," *American Philosophical Quarterly* 8 (1971):151, and Joseph Raz,

"Legal Principles and the Limits of Law," *Yale Law Journal* 81 (1972):823. Another useful study is that presented by George Christie, "The Model of Principles," *Duke Law Journal* (1968):649.

Recall that Dworkin uses the game of baseball as an example of a practice that truly is, unlike law, governed by rules. Judges must appeal to moral principles of justice or even policy in order to decide hard cases, but the officials of baseball have only easy cases—i.e., cases where they simply apply existing rules. (Any "hardness" is not with respect to the rules but is only the observational problem of seeing if the conduct covered by the rules—e.g., a tag applied—really occurred.) These rules are like yes/no or on/off switches in that they allow no *interpretive* controversy (though plenty of observational controversy!); for, once the rule is completely specified, it is always clear what is required. That this is an overly simplistic view of a complex game such as baseball has recently been dramatized by the "pine-tar feud" case in the American League. (See Russell Baker, "Batgate: Baseball's Pine-Tar Feud Reflects Justice vs. Law Conflict," *Arizona Republic*, August 6, 1983.) The case is now quite well known: On July 24, 1983, George Brett of the Kansas City Royals (behind 4–3 with two outs and one man on base) hit a homerun off New York Yankee pitcher Rich Gossage in the top of the ninth inning that put the Royals ahead 5–4—or so Brett thought. After the homerun, Yankee manager Billy Martin protested that Brett's bat was illegal because it had pine tar spread beyond the 18 inch limit allowed by American League rules. The umpires measured the pine tar on the bat, agreed it exceeded 18 inches, disallowed Brett's homerun, declared him out, and thus gave the win to the Yankees. The Royals, of course, appealed to Lee MacPhail, President of the American League. MacPhail, acting the role of a Supreme Court justice and talking like a proponent of natural law, upheld the appeal, gave the homerun back to Brett, and ordered the game to be continued with the score now 5–4 in favor of the Royals. He reasoned that the point and integrity of baseball required that the rules be interpreted in terms of their overall rational justification. The pine-tar rule, he asserted, exists to keep balls from getting dirty, not because it is believed that the use of the substance gives the hitter an unfair advantage in propelling the ball. Only if this latter were the case would it be proper to apply a rule to disallow a hit. Given the principle behind the pine-tar rule, the only proper sanction for its violation would be the removal of the bat from play until it is cleaned. It is perhaps unclear if this case shows that the rule/principle contrast is not as obvious as Dworkin thinks or if it simply shows (as I am inclined to believe) that baseball is a more principled and lawlike activity than Dworkin realizes. At any rate, it raises some interesting problems that would bear further reflection by fans of either baseball or law. (Dworkin's illuminating discussion of chess in Chapter 4 of *TRS*—pp. 102 ff.—shows that he is actually much more aware of the interpretive complexity of games than his remarks in Chapter 2 lead one to suspect.)

58. Recall again (*supra* note 54) that Dworkin is deeply concerned with the question of the integrity of the judiciary. Do we, as potential litigants, really want to go before a judge simply to present him with the exciting opportunity of a lifetime to use our case to pursue his conception of the good? Don't we rather want our rights enforced? (It is possible, of course, that the truth lies in some combination of Hart and Dworkin here. It may not always be, as Hart would maintain, that judges are either applying rules or legislating. Dworkin may be right in saying that sometimes—perhaps a great deal of the time—they are applying principles. But perhaps not all of the time—i.e., perhaps there really is some legislating that is necessary and proper.)

59. I think that Dworkin wants his model to hold for all legal systems, not just Anglo-American law. Take even a rigid system of statutory rules. How are judges to apply these, asks Dworkin, if not in accord with the moral *principle* that like cases should be treated like? There are obvious similarities with Fuller here.

60. Dworkin, *TRS*, 62.

61. Ibid., 81 ff.

62. *Korematsu* v. *U.S.*, 323 U.S. 214 (1944).

63. The recognition of a right does not mean that it is never justified for the state to act contrary to that right—only that the state must have a better reason than mere

net gain in general welfare. In the *Korematsu* case (*supra* note 62), the Court held that the government had the burden of showing that it was pursuing a "compelling" (and not merely a desirable) interest and that it was pursuing that interest in the "least restrictive way" before it could justify encumbering the rights of the Japanese Americans by internment. The Court (unfortunately, in my judgment) held that the government had satisfied this burden of proof. These matters will be discussed in more detail in the next chapter where an analysis of such concepts as "compelling state interest" and "fundamental right" will be offered.

64. See H. L. A. Hart, "Are There Any Natural Rights?" *Philosophical Review* 64 (1955). The relationship between rights and policy (and Dworkin's view about that relationship) is actually more complex than this brief discussion suggests. Some rights, for example, are created by the policy decisions of legislatures. Persons of a certain age and retirement status, for example, have a right to Social Security payments because this governmental program was established for policy reasons. These matters will be discussed in considerably more detail in Chapter 2. For present purposes, however, this observation will do: According to Dworkin, courts may consider policy to settle on rights (e.g., how much of a threat to national security must be involved before aliens may be interred?) but *not* to create rights.

65. In Chapter 4 of *TRS* ("Hard Cases"), Dworkin imagines an ideal judge and names him Hercules. Hercules must construct a *theory* of the body of law in order to decide hard cases. Consider an analogy (often used by Dworkin) with the task of a literary critic, and take this as a sample question that one might ask of such a critic: Did David Copperfield (in Dicken's novel) have a homosexual affair? Some (the positivists of literature) would simply say that there is no right answer to this question because the written text (the novel's body of "rules") is silent on the point. But surely, Dworkin would say, the book as a whole might be rendered more or less coherent depending on the answer we give to the question. Thus, we need a *theory* of the book—a view that renders the whole work most coherent. This coherence argument will determine which answer to our question is the right answer. So, too, with the law. According to Dworkin, there are right answers in all legal cases and these answers enforce preexisting rights. The positivist denies this because the positivist argues that it makes no sense to say that preexisting rights are being enforced if there is no way of telling and, in the absence of rules from which answers can be deduced (the defining feature of a hard case), there is no way of telling. But there is a way of telling, claims Dworkin. We are not limited to deduction but also have coherence arguments at our disposal when deduction breaks down. A hard case is one where a right is not derivable from rules, but there still is a right; it just has to come from theory-based coherence arguments. (There is a problem with this, of course: A coherence argument can normally do a much more convincing job of showing that some answers are clearly wrong than that one answer is uniquely right. It seems at least possible that more than one theory of the body of law or a work of literature could produce the same level of coherence.) For more on the analogies between legal reasoning and literary criticism, see Ronald Dworkin, "Law as Interpretation," *Critical Inquiry* 9 (September 1982):179–200.

66. Dworkin, *TRS*, 40. The more the "later" Dworkin moves from this test, the more serious do his departures from legal positivism seem.

67. Ibid., 160, emphasis added.

68. Ibid., 79, emphasis added.

69. Ibid., 66–67, emphasis added.

70. *Supra* note 48, p. 165.

71. Rawls's theory of "reflective equilibrium" is presented in John Rawls, *A Theory of Justice* (Cambridge: Harvard University Press, 1971), chap. 1.

72. Dworkin, *TRS*, 60.

73. Alasdair MacIntyre, *After Virtue* (Notre Dame: University of Notre Dame Press, 1981), 235.

74. As indicated earlier (*supra* note 59) I think Dworkin has broader visions than this. His case discussion is limited neither to American cases nor to constitutional cases. (See, for example, his discussion of the English case *Spartan Steel and Alloys Ltd.* v.

Martin and Co., 1973, 1 Q.B. 27, at 83 ff. of *TRS*. Also recall that *Riggs* and *Henningsen* are not constitutional cases.) Simply a good moral theory of U.S. constitutional law, however, would be no mean achievement.

75. Dworkin, of course, seeks to break down the normative jurisprudence/analytical jurisprudence dichotomy.

76. Merrilee Salmon, Roy Spece, Michael White, and A. D. Woozley were kind enough to comment on an earlier draft of this chapter. Their recommendations, though not always followed, were always valued and appreciated.

2

Moral Theory and Its Application to Law

> As things now stand, everything is up for grabs.
> Nevertheless:
> Napalming babies is bad.
> Starving the poor is wicked.
> Buying and selling each other is depraved.
> Those who stood up to and died resisting
> Hitler, Stalin, Amin, and Pol Pot—and General
> Custer too—have earned salvation.
> Those who acquiesced deserve to be damned.
> There is in the world such a thing as evil.
> [All together now:] Sez who?
> God help us.
>
> Arthur Leff[1]

John Austin called the task of morally evaluating law "normative jurisprudence." This task, as he envisioned it, consists in understanding law as it is (positive law) and then developing a rational theory about what that law *ought* to be. If Dworkin's theory of law (as presented in Chapter 1) is correct, normative jurisprudence will also have another task—namely, theoretically illuminating the moral content found in the law itself. In this chapter we shall explore both possibilities. Following a general discussion of moral philosophy and moral theory, we shall illustrate some of the legal implications of such theory by discussing as an example the morality of an issue of considerable constitutional importance: freedom of speech and press.

As a prelude to applying moral theory to or within law, it will be useful to develop at least a brief outline of moral philosphy itself—its basic questions and its basic techniques for attempting to resolve those questions. Such a brief summary of a complex discipline will necessarily be somewhat superficial, but it will perhaps be possible to provide enough of an introduction to the subject to give the reader a framework for organizing his or her thinking about the issues of normative jurisprudence.

THE NATURE OF MORALITY

The first question of moral philosophy (also sometimes called "ethics") is this: What is a moral problem? Moral philosophy is supposed to provide us with some help in rationally organizing our thinking about moral problems; but, unless we know what a moral problem is, we shall not know when such philosophical theorizing is applicable. In short: What is morality about?

By now it should come as no surprise to discover that philosophers can be in deep disagreement about how to answer even so basic and preliminary a question as this. Some philosophers, often called "formalists," argue that there is no theoretically defensible answer to the question of what morality is about—that any issue at all can be a moral issue, and any problem at all can be a moral problem. According to these thinkers, morality is more a matter of the attitude that a person takes up to a problem than a matter of any intrinsic characteristic of the problem itself. The philosopher R. M. Hare, for example, argues that we can identify a person's moral judgments in total independence of their content—i.e., in total independence of what they are about.[2] According to Hare, a person has made a moral judgment about some matter if that judgment manifests three formal (i.e., content neutral) characteristics: (1) it is *prescriptive*—i.e., it constitutes a recommendation for one's self and others about how to act; (2) it is *universalizable*—i.e., it is intended to apply not merely to the case in which it is made but also to all similar cases; and (3) it is *overriding*—i.e., it takes precedence over all other judgments in cases of conflict. Thus: If I prescribe "Let there be a blending of red and green in the world," then my judgment, weird as it is, constitutes part of my morality (and not merely part of my aesthetic preferences, say) if I regard it as overriding other values (e.g., I regard it as justified to slaughter people on lawns in order to get the effect) and if I agree to its universal application (e.g., I am willing to support the slaughter even if the victim is myself or someone I care about). This is not a very nice or welcome morality, certainly, but it is *my* morality if the stated formal conditions are satisfied.

The reader has perhaps noticed that there are interesting logical analogies between formalism on the definition of "morality" and positivism on the definition of "law." And, just as the content neutrality of legal positivism provoked a sharp critical response—even the reemergence of a kind of natural law theory—so has the formalism of a theory such as Hare's provoked a comparable response. G. J. Warnock, for example, has argued that Hare's characterization of morality makes it too personal and subjective a matter and thus fails to capture the essence of morality as a social institution.[3] (H. L. A. Hart, in his writings on ethics, has summarized a similar criticism of Hare's theory by calling the theory "too Protestant.")[4] Warnock and other critics of formalism invite us to see morality as a social artifact that has evolved to deal with certain recurring problems occasioned by the human condition—problems that generate a certain essential content for morality. (Recall the discussion, in Chapter 1, of Hart's "mimimum content" theory of natural law where he argues that law and morality necessarily have some overlap in content, are necessarily about some of the same issues, and address some of the same problems.) The fact that we are selfish, vulnerable, limited creatures living in a hostile world of moderate scarcity forces us to confront, as conditions of our very survival, problems of social living. Humans need to work out ways in which they can live amicably together and thereby gain, through schemes of mutual deference (and sometimes cooperation), a greater probability of surviving and securing the things they value than would be possible in isolated competition. The techniques we develop for human coexistence constitute our morality, or at least that part of it with a social dimension.

Given this "content theory" approach to the definition of morality, moral problems—or at least a large and important set of such problems—will be problems about the conditions of acceptable social life: the reduction and control of interpersonal violence, the distribution of resources, principles of property and ownership, etc. A moral problem will be a problem that involves, in some important way, those vital interests and concerns that human beings have (or should have) as social creatures, and a moral reason will be a reason that links up a given act or practice to those interests and concerns. Thus, on this kind of theory, "it will produce a balance of red and green" cannot be a *moral* reason in favor of slaughtering people on the lawn because bringing about that aesthetic effect is not (at least as humans are now constituted) a step toward advancing the interests of human beings as social beings. "It will hurt, kill, and terrify people," however, is on this theory necessarily a moral reason against the slaughter. In short: Even if it should turn out that there are no objective solutions to moral problems, there is an objective answer to the question of what a moral problem is and what kinds of reasons are relevantly brought to bear in discussing such problems.

Fortunately, present purposes do not require that we enter into the details of the dispute between formalists and antiformalists on the issue of defining morality. The reason for this is that only insofar as morality is conceived as having a necessary social dimension (i.e., only insofar as the content theorists are correct) will it be the case that there are interesting and important linkups between morality and the law. Only then will normative jurisprudence have an interesting and important subject matter. Thus, for our purposes, we may provisionally accept the following: Moral principles are principles concerned with establishing and maintaining proper social relations among persons with respect to issues or interests typically vital to such persons (e.g., life and death); and law will be judged morally acceptable only to the extent that it is judged to be consistent with these principles.

At this point, of course, a certain worry becomes obvious. Many different principles have been offered and many different principles are still held concerning proper social interaction. Both within and between cultures, diversity and not unanimity has been one of the most salient features of moralizing. Every advocate for a particular value (e.g., liberty) can be met by an equally persuasive and articulate advocate for a competing value (e.g., tradition and social stability), and it is by no means clear that there is any simple test for resolving the many disputes of this nature. Because of the seemingly irresolvable nature of moral disagreement and argument, moral claims can easily appear to lack objectivity and be nothing more than expressions of personal or cultural or class prejudice. Such skeptical worries seem particularly dramatic in our present age for reasons clearly highlighted in the quotation from Arthur Leff that opened this chapter. Most of us desire to preserve certain basic moral values of the Judeo-Christian tradition in a world that appears no longer to contain the presuppositions for the intelligibility of those values—neither the metaphysical beliefs nor any sense of community and shared commitments. We like to congratulate ourselves on the tolerant "pluralism" that characterizes our society without seeing that this pluralism may not be cost-free— that it may preclude our taking seriously any absolute moral stance in defense of any value (including tolerance itself).

This is, perhaps, the moral paradox of the modern world: the desire to express absolute condemnation of certain evils (racism, sexism, torture, oppression) coupled with the belief (or fear) that all the traditional grounds for such condemnation have been exposed as illusion and superstition. Moral skepticism and righteous indignation do not sit well together, but they have been bedfellows in our culture for some time now and the tensions are beginning to show. It is in addressing this paradox and the resulting tensions that modern moral philosophy enters the picture.[5] In seeking to articulate a rational and secular foundation for ethics, modern moral philosophy seeks to overcome moral skepticism through the application of models of evidence and rational choice, thereby producing a secular replacement for the traditional and now unacceptable appeals to faith and authority. The basic question of ethics thus becomes this: Is there some rational mechanism for the resolution of moral controversy? This is the main question that now provokes the enterprise of moral philosophy. We cannot evaluate its success in answering this question, of course, until we have a more detailed understanding of the theories that have been developed. It is to this issue that we shall now turn.

THE NATURE OF MORAL PHILOSOPHY AND MORAL THEORY

Historically, modern moral philosophy has been the search for a rational (i.e., interpersonally objective) mechanism for the resolution of moral controversy. The search has been for a theory that would establish the *right answer* to each moral question and transform moral opinion into moral knowledge (or at least reasonable moral belief). We might think of *positive morality* as the moral beliefs actually held by a particular group of people and *critical morality* as the moral beliefs that these people would hold after a process of rational evaluation and criticism. Moral philosophy is the attempt to develop the standards of rational evaluation and criticism that will allow us to transform positive morality into critical morality, and an articulated, systematic, and defended proposal of such standards is a *moral theory*.

What are the various plausible moral theories (i.e., proposed standards for rational moral evaluation) and how does one make a rational choice among the competing theories? It should be obvious that there is no obvious answer to these questions. Even if morality is necessarily "about" vital human interests as they present themselves in a social context, there is striking philosophical disagreement about what makes any interest vital or central or basic, and even disagreement about what is and is not social in nature. Some moral philosophers regard human freedom or autonomy as central and will evaluate social and legal arrangements in terms of their impact on interests of this nature. Other moral philosophers see human happiness or well-being as basic and might see interferences with freedom as trivial (or at least not as matters of vital importance) unless those interferences have some impact on happiness or well-being. And what seems private to one person may seem to another to be a matter of important social concern—e.g., is abortion the morally trivial decision to remove a bit of one's bodily tissue or is it the intentional murder of a human person?

With a courage (or foolhardiness) prompted by the demands of brevity, we shall, from the many moral theories that have been put forth in the history of our culture, simply pick two as the best representatives of the tensions that are characteristic of our moral life. These theories are utilitarianism and Kantianism. Utilitarianism is, very generally, the view that the rational choice in morality is always the choice that will maximize human happiness or well-being. Kantianism, again very generally, is the view that the rational choice in ethics is always the choice that respects the rights of autonomous persons freely to determine their own destinies, even if this respect is bought at the cost of a loss of happiness or well-being.[6] Utilitarianism looks primarily to the promotion of desirable future consequences; Kantianism seeks primarily to constrain the means by which those consequences may be promoted. It is, of course, possible that these views are more consistent than they originally appear, but the conflict between utilitarianism and Kantianism seems to illustrate at the broad theoretical level the kinds of conflicts between policy and principle that were discussed in the previous chapter. Utilitarianism and Kantianism may be seen as representing theoretical defenses of the two moral values—policies promoting social welfare and principles securing rights—that have been most influential in the moral development and criticism of our own legal institutions.[7] For this reason, plus the intrinsic interest and appeal of each of the two theories, the application of moral theory to the law can best be studied, at least initially, in the context provided by the conflict between utilitarianism and Kantianism.

UTILITARIANISM AND SOCIAL POLICY

The moral theory of utilitarianism has a long history in philosophy, but it was given its most articulate and persuasive statement and defense by the English moral philosophers Jeremy Bentham and John Stuart Mill.[8] Bentham summed up the essence of the theory in the slogan "The greatest happiness for the greatest number." The basic idea here is that human actions and practices should be evaluated ultimately in terms of their tendencies to advance the general welfare or social good—i.e., to produce as a consequence the happiness or well-being or satisfaction of a majority of persons. The more persons likely to be made better off by an act or practice, then the better that act or practice from the moral point of view. "Look to the future and promote human welfare"—this is the basic utilitarian advice in ethics, advice formally expressed in the Principle of Utility: "Of all the possible actions open to you, perform that action with the greatest tendency to bring about the greatest balance of happiness over misery for mankind as a whole."

Presented so generally, the utilitarian theory has certain undeniable attractions. First of all, who would really deny that human happiness is a good? A world in which as many people as possible get their preferences satisfied and become happy seems clearly preferable to a world in which those same people are unsatisfied and unfulfilled. Who would quarrel with this? A second attractive feature of utilitarianism is that it at least gives the appearance of rendering ethical choice easy—almost a mechanical or quantitative matter. Simply consult and add up people's preferences, discount any preferences that you have good reason to believe will not produce happiness if satisfied (e.g., preferences based on false causal beliefs), and then seek to satisfy as many or thwart as few of those preferences as possible. This is the ethical way to proceed in deciding what acts to perform and what social policies to adopt, a procedure that intuitively seems both correct and easy. The uncertainty and anxiety goes out of ethics—a cause for celebration all around.

But is it? Attractive as the initial utilitarian picture seems, closer reflection upon its implications may cause one to develop some serious doubts. The worry might be put this way: Are future consequences really *all* that matter in ethics? Are there not other moral goods (e.g., respect for free choice) that we should be concerned with? And do we not sometimes properly feel a kind of moral loyalty to the past— e.g., when showing gratitude for benefits or demanding punishment for those who have done wrong—without calculating future consequences? And even when we go forth to pursue good future consequences, are there not limits or constraints on the permissible *means* that we may legitimately use in our earnest efforts to do good and make people happy? Is there not some sense in the idea that people have *rights* or claims based on *justice* to be treated in certain ways even if our efforts at doing good will be inhibited if we respect those rights? And does not each of us have some kind of right simply to be left alone and free from the claims and desires of others—i.e., does not each of us have the right to perform certain personally desired actions without being required to consider if the general welfare would be maximized if we performed some other action instead? (Do I act wrongly in going to the movies tonight because there is some alternative action I could do instead that would be more productive of social utility—e.g., doing volunteer work at a local hospital?)

The most dramatic way to raise the doubts expressed above is through a discussion of some of the "scapegoat" counterexamples that have often been raised against utilitarianism by its critics. These examples typically involve a thought experiment in which we imagine a person or small class of persons being treated in some absolutely horrendous way, imagine that the majority benefits enormously by victimizing these people, and then argue that in consistency the utilitarian is forced to do something that no morally sane person would do—namely, approve of the victimization described. For example: Suppose that cancer and all other major diseases could be cured and the vast majority of human beings thus rendered much more happy and secure by rounding up a few persons against their wills and subjecting them to painful and ultimately fatal medical experiments. (To avoid any complexities that might be raised by the suggestion that we search for volunteers, let us suppose that the experiments require a certain enzyme secreted by the brain only when persons are aware that they are being coerced, hurt, and threatened with death.) Intuitively, most of us would be inclined to say that— even given the general good consequences that would flow from this experimental process—adopting the process would still be deeply immoral. We might say that it is *unjust* to treat people in this way or that they have a *right* not to be treated in this way and say that if utilitarianism cannot accommodate such rights (and thus agree with us in condemning the practice) then so much the worse for utilitarianism. But how can utilitarianism accommodate a respect for rights and justice and thus condemn the practice? Does not its commitment to "the greatest good for the greatest number" require that it approve of treating people in this awful way if the general welfare will be promoted, if happiness will be maximized? The moral then is clear: it *is* so much the worse for utilitarianism, and all morally sensitive people will thus reject it as an ethical theory.

Though the above argument contains the germ of an important criticism against utilitarianism, it will not at this superficial level serve to refute the utilitarian theory. For a utilitarian theory can be constructed that not only will condemn scapegoating and victimizing but will defend the claim that persons have a right not to be victimized. This will render the theory much less counterintuitive.

Basically, the kind of utilitarian theory that we will now consider will depend upon two important distinctions: (1) a distinction between things that are valuable for their own sake (intrinsically valuable) and things that are instrumentally valuable because they lead to things that are intrinsically valuable; and (2) a distinction between applying the Principle of Utility ("the greatest good for the greatest number") in choosing each particular *act* that one performs and applying that principle in choosing various social *rules* or *practices* (particular acts now to be dictated by whatever is required by the rules or practices).[9]

The upshot will be this: We might, as utilitarians, approve of certain general rules or practices that assign certain rights to persons—e.g., the right not to be experimented on without one's consent. We might even build this rule into law—i.e., make a legal rule (a statute) that forbids such experimentation. The reason we adopt this rule or practice, however, is because of our belief that the majority of people will be happier in the long run living in a society having a rule (conferring a right) of this nature. For if citizens had no protection against simply being used by the state whenever the state believed that general welfare could be promoted by such use, then they would never be secure, would never be able to live lives of stability and predictability, and thus could not be happy. Whatever the short-run gains of performing a particular act of victimization, the long-run disutility of allowing the state to act in this way would be enormous. Thus there sometimes are good grounds for refusing to perform such acts because such acts are condemned by social rules or practices that are themselves good to adopt because having them (and the rights they assign) promote the general welfare in the long run—i.e., a society that accords its citizens such rights as the right to refuse being experimented on without consent is likely to be a much happier society than a society that does not accord such rights. Rights are therefore justified for instrumental reasons. No rational person goes to a dentist because he finds the experience valuable for its own sake but instead because he sees the trip as instrumental to something that is good in itself—health and ultimately happiness. So, too, for rights. They are not ultimate or final goods; they are rather derivative goods—protections and guarantees that are valuable because of what they lead to, because the societies that accord them will be happier societies.

To summarize: It is a mistake, indeed a caricature, to claim, as some critics have, that utilitarians can make no place for such important moral concepts as justice, fairness, rights, merit, or desert. They can (and often do) make a place for such concepts—as when, for example, John Stuart Mill defines a right in this way: "To have a right then is, I conceive, to have something that society ought to defend me in the possession of."[10] What the utilitarian cannot do (does not *want* to do, indeed) is regard rights as having ultimate or primary or fundamental value; only utility (the promotion of general welfare) can have that. Rights thus have only instrumental value, which is why Mill immediately follows the above sentence with this sentence: "If the objector goes on to ask me why [society ought to accord me rights], I can give him no other reason than general utility." Thus utilitarianism may not be nearly as counterintuitive as it initially seemed; for much that we traditionally respect and value (liberty, autonomy, rights, justice, even the past and tradition itself) might well be preserved if it can be shown that such preservation would, as a practice, have the instrumental value of promoting the general welfare.

The quarrel between utilitarians and their critics is thus badly represented by the claim that "utilitarians do not respect rights and justice and antiutilitarians (e.g., Kantians) do respect rights and justice." As the above discussion shows, the differences, though profound and important, are much more subtle than the standard clichés of introductory ethics textbooks would have us believe. The basic difference between utilitarians and Kantians is on the question of *why* (and with what priority) they value rights. Kantians will attempt to make the case that, though some rights may simply be socially useful conventions, not all rights are to be analyzed this way. The most important human rights are not simply conventions that we adopt for instrumental or consequential reasons (e.g., to promote the general happiness) but rather are ways of expressing and respecting the status of each person as precious, as an object of intrinsic value. Since, according to Kantianism, not all rights are grounded in utility, there is on this view the possibility of ultimate conflicts between utility and (at least some) rights—a possibility that is logically ruled out by the utilitarian analysis, which regards all legitimate rights simply as derivative from utilitarian values. It is a central tenet of the Kantian view that when basic human rights (rights based on the intrinsic value of persons) conflict with claims based on utility, the basic rights have priority. What does all of this mean and why do Kantians think it is the correct moral outlook? These are the questions we shall now consider.

KANTIANISM, RIGHTS, AND
RESPECT FOR PERSONS

A basic presupposition of any ethical theory is a view about what properties must be possessed by an object to make it a *morally relevant object*—i.e., a proper object of moral judgment and concern. (Rocks are clearly not relevant objects for moral concern and normal adult human beings clearly are; for other objects—e.g., fetuses—we are not so sure.) If human beings merit concern from the moral point of view, this must be because of some property or characteristic they bear that qualifies them for such concern. Thus the following question becomes basic: Of all the charcteristics of human beings, which of these qualifies them for moral concern? A theory that addresses this question may be thought of as a theory of *human nature;* and the differences between different ethical theories can often be traced to different theories of human nature that lie at their foundations.

Many characteristics of human beings—e.g., the property of having a certain amount of hair—would be highly implausible as characteristics of moral relevance. But what about this property: *sentience*, the capacity to feel pleasure and pain? This property is characteristic of humans (though not uniquely characteristic of them) and it does seem to most of us to be of obvious moral relevance—i.e., other things being equal, most of us believe it is wrong to cause pain to a human being (or, indeed, to any other sentient creature). The point is not that it is always wrong under all circumstances to hurt a sentient creature (or always right to give pleasure to a sentient creature) but rather this: the causing of pain is always a relevant moral point against what we do (and thus must be justified) and the causing of pleasure is always a relevant point in favor of what we do.

This account of human nature is fundamental to utilitarianism. According to the utilitarian, what makes a human being a morally relevant object is that creature's ability to feel pleasure and pain. Morality is thus about the promotion of pleasure and the avoidance of pain, and thus the basic principle of ethics will be one that seeks the maximization of pleasure and the minimization of pain. We might think of this as a "consumer" model of human nature. We humans are to be viewed as creatures who go through the supermarket of life seeking to grab as many objects of desire as possible and have as few of our desires thwarted as possible. On this view, the goal of ethics is to articulate principles that will encourage maximum success in this consumer project for as many people as possible. Given the not implausible assumption that each person is likely to be the best judge of what will make him or her happy or pleased, the practical procedure for ethics from the utilitarian point of view is this: find out what people's preferences are and seek to satisfy as many (and thwart as few) of those preferences as possible. Ethics is about preference satisfaction, and the basic requirement is that preference satisfaction be maximized.

In addition to the idea that ethics is essentially concerned with preference satisfaction, utilitarianism also is built around a certain conception of reason or rational choice. On this view, a rational person will seek a rational preference ordering in his or her own life—i.e., to arrange and give priority ranking to his or her various competing preferences or desires in order to insure that as many preferences as possible get satisfied and, in cases of choice, that the strongest preferences get satisfied. According to the utilitarian, something comparable should be the moral goal of society as a whole—a feature of utilitarianism that has made it appealing to and influential on many economists.[11]

Just as an individual should seek for an individual preference ordering that will most efficiently balance his or her own psychological "budget," so should society (treating the claims of each individual in the same way that an individual treats the competing claims within his or her own nature) seek to balance these claims against each other in order that preference satisfaction will be maximized. Some individuals will, of course, have their preferences thwarted—perhaps because there are fewer of them, their preferences are idiosyncratic, or their preferences are perceived to be not as strong as the preferences of others. According to the utilitarian, this result—though unfortunate for those who must face it—will be acceptable (indeed required) if the majority of persons benefit more from the policy that produced the result than they would from any policy that would prevent the result. In a world of choice and conflict, there will inevitably be losers, and the best we can do in ethics is to adopt policies that will produce as few of them as possible. "We have all won and we shall all have prizes" only works in the fantasy world of *Alice in Wonderland*. In the real world the best we can hope for is that the *majority* will win and have prizes.

In order to understand Kantianism in ethics, one must see it at its foundation as in ultimate and violent revolt against the above consumer model of human nature and efficiency model of rational choice that informs utilitarianism. It is not sentience that makes us morally relevant objects, claims Kant and his followers, but something else: our status as free and autonomous creatures with the capacity to make choices that are rational in a special sense. Kant's concept of rationality is highly complex and impossible to summarize in a brief space. It is clearly *not* a concept limited to efficient maximization of one's individual utilities, however, but is rather something more like this: the ability to appreciate morally relevant differences and similarities in people, actions, and states of affairs and to choose to act consistently on the basis of an appreciation of those differences and similarities.[12]

According to Kantianism, ethics is not primarily about preference satisfaction or indeed about any other positive sort of welfare promotion; it is rather about how to respect the freedom of rational beings—where respect is mainly concerned with the negative counsel to leave such beings alone in what Robert Nozick calls their own "moral space" to control their own destinies by their own choices even if this tends to produce social and individual unhappiness.[13] Each autonomous person is to be viewed as something more than simply a unit to be weighed or balanced in some great social equation. For an autonomous person to suppress one of his desires in order to satisfy his other desires is one thing; for a group of autonomous persons to suppress another autonomous person so that they can get their desires satisfied at his expense is something quite different. If utilitarians cannot see this—if they really think that society may legitimately balance people the way people balance their own desires or preferences—then they are, according to Kantians, morally degenerate. The world will indeed inevitably contain losers, but it will never count as a justification for their unfortunate position that their losses were required in order that others (even the vast majority) could be gainers. It is one thing if I suffer a loss because I brought it upon myself through my own free choices; it is something quite different (and quite unacceptable) if I suffer a loss because others brought it on me for their benefit. Respect for autonomy demands considerably more than this latter sort of justification.

What do Kantians mean by this high-sounding talk of such things as "autonomy" and why do they think it has something to do with the foundations of ethics? A helpful first step in answering this question is to see why they reject the utilitarian consumer model, why they will not accept sentience as the property that confers moral relevance on human beings.

It has often been said that Kant's ethics was an attempt to pursue Christianity by secular means, and there is considerable truth in this observation. A core claim of Christian ethics—a claim accepted by Kant—is that there is something uniquely precious about human beings from the moral point of view. There are, for example, certain special moral requirements (rights) that attach to human beings that do not attach to any other animal—e.g., the requirement that we not kill and eat them for food, or hunt them for sport, or experiment on them for medical science.[14] They are, in short, owed a special kind of respect simply because they are people. But what is the basis for this? Not mere species membership, surely, since that property alone could hardly be morally relevant.[15] What is needed on this view is some obviously important characteristic or property possessed by and only by members of the human species, a property that confers moral uniqueness on human beings and thus qualifies them for the special respect that morally separates them from all other animals and grounds those special rights that protect them in a way that other animals are not protected. Could sentience, the basis of the utilitarian model, do this? Of course not, since the capacity to feel pleasure and pain is a property we share with other animals, not something that separates us from them and makes us morally unique. Thus utilitarianism fails in large measure because it cannot capture the special respect that, according to Christianity and to Kant, is owed to human beings because of their special moral status.[16]

Though Kant agrees with the Christian tradition in claiming that human beings are morally special (precious, sacred, uniquely valuable) and merit a special kind of respect, concern, and protection because of that status, he parts company with that tradition in the answer he gives to the question of exactly what it is that does (in a way that sentience does not) constitute the essence of human uniqueness. Christianity seeks to ground the morally special status of persons in the doctrine of *ensoulment.* Human beings are special (and thus have rights that no other animal has) because they all have been given immortal souls by God, something members of no other species have. We human beings are precious because we all, as it were, carry around within us a precious jewel (the immortal soul). *We* are specially valuable because *it* is specially valuable.

If the goal of ethics is to find a foundation for morality that will have rational appeal, then the above doctrine seems useless. If ethics rests upon something metaphysically mysterious—something at worst incoherent and at best resting on faith because it lies beyond any evidence or proof—then ethics is fragile indeed. Small wonder, them, that Kant should have searched for some *secular equivalent* to the religious doctrine of ensoulment, some attribute of human beings (and only human beings) that (a) would confer upon them a morally exalted status but (b) would not require a highly dubious metaphysical foundation. Kant believed that he found such an attribute in the human capacity for rational choice. Kant labeled as "autonomous" those creatures who possessed the capacity for rational choice and argued that autonomous creatures are morally special. They have a moral status that Kant labeled "dignity" and he built his entire moral theory around the idea that this status is to be respected and protected. This does seem to carve out an area of special moral protection for human beings, because it does seem obvious that human beings (at least most of them) do have a capacity for rational deliberation and choice that other animals do not have. Thus: I must consult with and obtain consent from a person before subjecting that person to medical treatment or experimentation; I am not, however, required to do this with a cat.

One obvious but very profound reason for this differential treatment is that the concepts of "consult" and "consent" make sense only when applied to a rational creature such as a human being. (We do not even know what it would mean to seek a cat's informed consent to a medical procedure.) On this theory, then, some human rights (e.g., the right that informed consent be secured before medical procedures are instituted) function not merely to produce beneficial social con-sequences (e.g., freedom from fear or insecurity about what the medical profession might do) but primarily to insure that the special status of persons as rational choosers be respected. "Always act," wrote Kant, "so that you treat rational persons as ends in themselves and never as means only." Put in a more contemporary idiom, this surely comes to the following: "All rational persons have a right not to be used without their consent even for the benefit of others."[17]

At this point, the reader might still wonder if the differences between Kantians and utilitarians have any practical significance. We now know that Kantians believe that human beings have rights. But, as was noted in the previous section, most utilitarians also believe that human beings have rights. So what if each tradition gets to this result via a different route? Does this really matter given that the result is the same?

This understandable worry requires a complex response. There will, of course, be enormous areas of agreement in outcome between utilitarians and Kantians, and the differences between the two traditions will often seem to be merely a matter of emphasis. This should not be surprising. For if the two traditions disagreed on all outcomes, then at least one of them would probably strike us as too implausible to take seriously. (If utilitariansm came out in favor of murder, rape, assault, and theft and Kantianism condemned these acts, then surely we would no longer give utilitarianism the time of day.) But both traditions do, I think, seem highly plausible to most of us. We are inclined to think that each has an important perspective to offer on ethics, even if we are unsure of just how to integrate them both into one coherent overall moral vision.

General agreement on outcomes in the obvious cases (e.g., murder is wrong), however, does not mean that agreement will be present in all cases, particularly in the difficult ones where we do not start with a clear intuition about what the outcome ought to be. (Rational persons are probably initially in this position about abortion. Murder is wrong surely, but is abortion—morally speaking—the same thing as murder? Are fetuses sentient? Rational? Is it one of these questions that will make the moral difference? Is it clear that Kantian and utilitarian concerns will necessarily converge on this issue?) Thus an understanding of why Kantians and utilitarians sometimes agree on the result but not on the justification (sometimes concur in the judgment but not in the rationale, to borrow from legal language) will perhaps reveal that the disagreements between them are deep after all and that there are some results on which they cannot agree.

Recall that John Stuart Mill (in company with all other utilitarians who embrace human rights) argued that rights exist because a society that did not grant such rights would be insecure and fearful and thus unhappy. My rights are, then, simply a function of how uncomfortable it would make others if my rights were violated. According to the Kantian, this is the wrong reason for respecting rights and, because it is the wrong reason, it can lead to a failure to protect rights in cases where the Kantian would want to protect them. Consider certain obvious claims of right: the right not to be made a slave, the right not to be punished if I am innocent, and the right not to be experimented on without my consent. These are all rights that would be defended by the utilitarian. Why? Because societies that do not grant these rights are likely to be more fearful, insecure, and thus unhappy than societies that do grant these rights. Is this really the correct reason? A persuasive case that it is *not* the correct reason has been made by the contemporary Kantian John Rawls.[18] Take slavery. According to Rawls, there is something perverse from the moral point of view in thinking that we must suspend judgment on the morality of slavery until we find out if the benefits to the slaveholders do or do not outweigh the burdens placed on the slaves. This is because there is a prior question of right here that the utilitarian overlooks— namely, does the slaveholder have a right to any of the benefits that he derives from the unjust exploitation of his fellow human beings? Rawls thinks that anyone who truly values the rights and dignity of persons will answer no to this question and will thus argue that the benefits to the slaveholders should never be counted in the first place and that the utilitarian calculation (do the benefits outweigh the burdens?) will never be allowed to get off the ground. Slavery is wrong because it allows some to benefit through their unjust exploitation of others (through violating a right against unjust exploitation) and *not* because a system that allowed them such exploitation would be unlikely to promote the general welfare. On the Kant-Rawls view, slavery would be wrong even if it *did* promote the general welfare.

The utilitarian might be able to explain in part why it would be wrong to make *general* and *widespread* the exploitive practice of slavery (or any other kind of victimization) because such a practice (given the meanings of "general" and "widespread") would almost certainly undercut social utility. But there are two ways one could go from this insight: (1) argue that all persons ought to be granted an absolute right against such victimization, or (2) argue that when victimization is practiced it should be sharply confined to some small, powerless, easily identifiable minority so that the majority will not be alarmed and rendered fearful that something comparable might happen to them. Kantians, valuing the sanctity of each person, will clearly opt for protection by an absolute right; for on their view it is a grave injustice or rights violation if even one person is sacrificed in the ways described and no matter how much all others may be honestly assured that they need have no fear that such violations will happen to them. (Was there any reason for southern whites to fear their legal system because of the way black rape defendents were treated? Was not such treatment clearly wrong regardless of the answer to that question?)

It is unclear that utilitarians can give any reason for preferring (1) over (2), however, and thus we may have reached a genuine disagreement in result between utilitarians—even sophisticated rule utilitarians—and Kantians. The Kantian will say it is *always* wrong to victimize and that each human being has an absolute right to be protected against such victimization. The strongest claim that the utilitarian can make is that a right against victimization should be granted only to the degree that this will advance social utility. Since, for all the reasons noted, there is no reason to suppose that arguments of social utility would support the strong claim of absolute right that would be defended by Kantians, the conclusion seems obvious: Though both Kantians and utilitarians will defend a "right against victimization" (and many other rights), they will not mean the same thing by the phrase and thus will not advocate the same level of protection.

This failure of concurrence in rationale or justification, then, produces an ultimate failure of concurrence in result or outcome. Ronald Dworkin, in the spirit of Kant, defines a right in this way: "Individual rights are . . . trumps held by individuals. Individuals have rights when, for some reason, a collective goal is not a sufficient justification for denying them what they wish, as individuals, to have or to do, or not a sufficient justification for imposing some loss or injury upon them."[19] This definition could never be embraced by a utilitarian (compare it to Mill's given earlier) and, as I have argued, this difference of analysis can lead to serious practical differences— differences in approved outcomes. On the Kantian view, some rights are simply not expressions of social utility; they are rather (to use the language of the philosopher Robert Nozick) absolute *side-constraints* on the pursuit of social utility—i.e., moral protections of individuals that must be unconditionally respected as one sets out to do social good, protections that preclude their being sacrificed for that social good.[20] Thus, at some ultimate level, a choice between utilitarianism and Kantianism will have to be made. The rosy view that they are just two different ways of saying the same thing simply will not wash.

How does one make a choice of this nature? Is there some rational mechanism—some decision procedure—that will *prove* the preferability of one of these theories over the other? Or is the matter all subjective and arbitrary, to be decided by personal preference, existential leaps of faith, or even coin flipping?[21] This is a profound question and will occupy our attention in the final section of this chapter. Prior to a discussion of that issue, however, I think it would be beneficial if we moved our discussion of rights from the present level of abstraction into a concrete legal context so that we can explore an example of how these moral disputes can illuminate the law. The context I have chosen is constitutional law, and I have chosen for my particular example the issue of freedom of expression, particularly the rights granted in the First Amendment of freedom of *speech* and freedom of the *press.* These are legal rights and most of us, I think, believe that these rights enshrine and protect some important moral values. To understand these values and the nature of the constitutional protections involved, it might make a difference if these rights are analyzed from a utilitarian perspective (we accord these rights because it is socially useful to do so) or from a Kant-Rawls-Nozick-Dworkin perspective (we accord these rights as a way of respecting and protecting the special status of autonomous persons). This is the issue to which we shall now turn.

MORAL PHILOSOPHY AND CONSTITUTIONAL LAW: FREEDOM OF SPEECH AND PRESS

Congress shall make no law respecting an establishment of religion, or prohibiting the free exercise thereof; or abridging the freedom of speech, or of the press; or the right of the people peaceably to assemble, and to petition the Government for a redress of grievances.

First Amendment
Constitution of the United
States of America

At a minimum, to say that an individual A has a *right* either to do or have a certain thing T is to say that at least one other person B has an *obligation* either to provide A with T or at least not to interfere with A in his attainment and enjoyment of T.[22] If Jones promises Smith to give him a book at a certain time, then Smith has a right to be given the book at that time and Jones has an obligation to give him the book at that time. If Jones has a right to life, this means at a minimum that all other persons have an obligation not to kill Jones and perhaps (though this is highly dubious) an obligation to help Jones stay alive. (If the former is all that is really defensible, then we should speak more accurately if we spoke of a right not to be killed instead of a right to life.) If children have a right to a basic education, this presumably means that the government has an obligation to provide at state expense a certain level of schooling for all children in its jurisdiction. These few examples are sufficient to show that claims of right are extremely diverse and that with respect to any claim of right we must ask three basic questions of analysis before exploring any questions of justification: (1)What person or class of persons has the right? (2) To what is it a right (a liberty against interference or positive assistance)? (3) Against whom is the right claimed—i.e., what person or body of persons has the obligation to respect the right?

The first ten amendments (the "Bill of Rights") of the United States Constitution grant certain rights to all citizens in order to protect them against certain kinds of interferences from their own government.[23] One citizen cannot violate the constitutional rights of another citizen for the purely logical reason that constitutional rights are rights against the government, not rights against other individuals. The phrase in the First Amendment that "*Congress* shall make no law . . ." clearly makes the point that it is the government that is obligated to respect religion, speech, press and assembly; thus, from a purely constitutional perspective, the private individual seems left free to be as contemptuous and intrusive in his behavior with respect to these values as he sees fit.

The matter is actually not quite this simple. The developed constitutional doctrine is that constitutional rights protect the citizen, not merely against intrusive enactments of Congress, but against any *state action* that might be intrusive of these rights. Since courts have held that state action may be present in a variety of contexts, the net of constitutional protection spreads wider than it initially appears. For example: If the enforcement power of a court in validating a contract or in awarding damages is characterized as state action, then constitutional rights might be protected in contexts that initially seem private and merely involve the dealings of one citizen with another. For example, the Supreme Court has held that covenants signed by neighbors to restrict certain racial or ethnic minorities from the neighborhood are unconstitutional.[24] The underlying idea in this decision is that if the state lends its enforcement power to private attacks on rights, then this is tantamount to the state itself acting against those rights. Highly relevant in the free speech/free press area is the Supreme Court's willingness to find state action in a trial court's decision to award damages against newspapers in libel cases.[25] Though this seems private—a private business libeling a private individual—the Court's finding of state action in such cases makes the private law of libel (part of the private law of torts) open to constitutional review.

Though philosophers like to talk in general terms of a right to free expression, it is initially helpful to limit constitutional discussion to the kinds of expression explicitly protected by the First Amendment. Though there is a sense in which I may express myself (even in a very profound way) when I engage in sexual intercourse, this is clearly not the kind of expression that the First Amendment is primarily concerned to protect. For that amendment, as its language of "speech" and "press" and "petition" makes clear, is concerned primarily with expression as *cognitive communication*—i.e., the attempt of people to convey ideas and information to each other.[26] Throughout history, governments have made, and still make, a concerted effort to silence their citizens, particularly those citizens who attempt to convey ideas that are controversial or offensive or potentially productive of political change. The First Amendment explicitly opposes this common historical tendency. By establishing a right of free speech (which includes the freedom to write, circulate, and publish ideas and information), this amendment imposes upon the state what appears to be a nearly absolute obligation to avoid interferences in these areas.

The actual constitutional doctrine with respect to protected speech is highly complex. The right to freedom of speech has been identified by the Supreme Court as "fundamental."[27] Speaking generally, the designation of a right as fundamental means that the Court has decided either (1) that the right is *politically* essential to the existence of our society as a "system of ordered liberty," or (2) that the right is essential to *individuals* if they are to be respected as human beings and allowed to lead the kinds of meaningful lives that our system is supposed to cherish. (It is not uncommon, of course, that a particular right will have both a political and an individual value.) There are thus two often overlapping sorts of fundamental rights—those based on social policy considerations (e.g., we must secure this right as a means to the health of our political institutions) or Kantian considerations (e.g., we must secure this right in order to take people seriously as people). The right to petition for a redress of grievances seems mainly in the former camp; the right to privacy seems mainly in the latter camp.[28]

Since the politically based rights are valued for instrumental reasons—i.e., in terms of the good social consequences they are thought to produce—it would be natural to see them as solely utilitarian in nature. The matter is a bit more complicated than this, however, because at least a part of the consequential or instrumental justification for these rights might involve what Robert Nozick has called a "teleology of rights," an argument that certain rights should be adopted not merely because they promote utility (general happiness or welfare) but because they promote a system that increases the probability that rights of the more basic Kantian sort will be respected.[29] A teleology of rights does bear this striking moral similarity to utilitarianism, however: it would allow rights violations of some if such violations would have the tendency to expand rights protection for the majority. It is thus still an attempt to base rights protection on considerations of social policy, the main difference between it and utilitarianism being that it has a richer concept of desirable social policy (i.e., includes rights maximization along with happiness maximization).

The Kantian, of course, is unwilling to approve even a single instance of violating those rights of an individual that are part of what is meant by respecting that individual as a person, even where such violation would advance rights enjoyment for the majority. The objection here would be that this would still be using the individual as a mere means. Thus the Kantian will oppose teleology of rights arguments when they require treating any individual with less than the full respect that individual is owed as a person. When solely teleological considerations are at stake, however, the Kantian will clearly regard rights teleology as of greater moral importance than utility teleology. The degree to which all of this can be rationally defended is, of course, a matter of some controversy. It will be explored in the final section of the chapter.

When a right identified as fundamental is encumbered by state action, this triggers what is called the doctrine of "strict judicial scrutiny." In judicial review, the application of strict scrutiny to the encumberance of a right involves the application by the court of a two-pronged test that places a very heavy burden of justification on the state. In order to justify encumbering a fundamental right, the state must show (1) that the right must be encumbered in order to accomplish a *compelling* (and not merely rationally desirable) state goal or interest, and (2) that in accomplishing its compelling interest, the state is employing the least restrictive means possible—i.e., it is encumbering the right only to the degree actually necessary to attain its compelling goal.[30]

There are, of course, various ways that the state can seek to encumber speech: censorship or prior restraint, criminal penalties for publication, or enforcement of liability and damage judgments for publication, to name the three most common. Censorship or prior restraint, for example, is viewed as the most intrusive action that the state can take against speech.[31] The developed doctrine in this area is that courts must give such threats to free speech the strictest scrutiny; only one state interest—the prevention of immediate, irreversible, and serious harm to the nation—has been held to survive scrutiny at this level and thus serve to justify the state's most coercive encumbrances of free speech. Freedom from prior restraint of speech is very nearly an absolute right, a genuine "trump" to play against almost any state interest that might be cited as a ground for restriction. Putting it simply, in the absence of the kind of threat to national security noted above, there simply is no legitimate state censorship or prior restraint of speech in our society.[32]

The question of interest to the philospher in all of this, of course, is this: why this strong protection of speech and publication? Is this rational? What is so special about speech and writing—about the conveying of ideas and information—that it merits protection at this extreme level? Why is it even the case that the burden is on the state in justifying the suppression of speech and not on the individual to justify speaking? What, in short, is the *moral* status of speech and the freedom of speech? What is *morally* at stake when freedom of speech is defended as a right?

The moral justification of a right of free speech is a problem of considerable difficulty and complexity. The problem becomes even more difficult and complex, however, when we try to make sense of the phrase to which the right of free speech is constitutionally linked: the right of "freedom of the *press.*"[33] Is freedom of the press redundant (only another way of saying freedom of speech or emphasizing the obvious point that speech includes writing and publication) or is it the case that members of the professional press are given special constitutional protections unavailable to the ordinary citizen? Constitutional rights are normally rights of individual citizens; is freedom of the press to be the one case where a private business gets constitutional protection? Some of the Supreme Court's language in the 1974 *Gertz* case suggested that it was at least toying with the latter view that at least one private business may have constitutional rights. This view has been explicitly defended by Justice Stewart.[34]

Only if we have an understanding of the above questions and have in effect a philosophical theory of free expression will we be able intelligently to come to grips with what is perhaps the most basic question of all: are all the demands currently being made by the press (for privileges of confidentiality, freedom from liability for libel, etc.) simply claims for things that the press would *like* or *desire* to have, or are they claims for things to which the press has a *right?* And if the latter, what kind of right is it—one based in utility, political desirability, or the moral rights to personal respect of which Kant spoke? This is a matter of some consequence since we may consistently with justice thwart people's desires in a way we may not consistently with justice fail to accord them their rights. Deciding what is a matter of desire and what is a matter of right is one of the basic questions of moral and political philosophy, of course, and thus large and profound issues are necessarily raised by the topics of free speech and free press.

As an initial step toward clarifying these topics and answering some of the questions I have raised about them, let me briefly explore again the question of what it is to have a right (any right) and what is involved in justifying the claim that persons have or ought to have rights of a certain sort. As previously suggested, there are basically two kinds of rights and two corresponding justifications for those rights. I shall call these *respect-based* rights and *policy-based* rights. (Using the somewhat misleading language of an older tradition, we might call these *natural rights* and *conventional rights*.)[35] A natural or respect-based right is a certain mandatory way in which persons must be treated if their essential humanity is to be respected and preserved. Such rights will typically be claims against certain kinds of interferences—e.g., the right not to be killed, assaulted, deceived, etc. If one violates these rights in a person one thereby shows that one fails to respect that person as a person, that one is willing to use that person as a mere resource or commodity for one's own ends just as one might use some inferior object or being. To violate a person's natural rights is to degrade that person in a basic way—to treat him, in Kant's language, merely as a means or instrument and not as an end in himself. As already noted, some of the rights that the Supreme Court has identified as fundamental seem to have this nature: they protect the special moral status of persons and secure for them at least the minimum of respect required for citizenship in a decent and just society. So conceived, some fundamental rights are in part ways of building into the law, through the mechanism of a constitution, respect for natural rights.

Conventional or policy-based rights, however, are quite different. They give certain people certain powers or liberties against interference, of course, but not because these people would be diminished as people if they lacked those powers or liberties. It is rather and simply that the social good—e.g., the general welfare or health of our political institutions—is judged to be better promoted on the whole if these persons are accorded these rights. Some examples here are the right of a police officer (and nobody else) to carry a concealed weapon, or the right of a physician (and nobody else) to perform surgery, or the right of a lawyer (and nobody else) to represent a client in court. For reasons good or ill, we as a society have decided as a matter of policy to create these social roles and assign certain rights to the occupants of those roles. This is what it means—and *all* that it means—to speak of rights in such a setting. If we decided to rethink some of these roles—eliminate them or change the rights assigned to their occupants—our decision might be criticized as unwise, but it could not be criticized as a fundamental affront to the respect that is owed to persons, as a practice wherein persons were treated as less than fully human. For these special rights that these persons had were never assigned to them because of their status as people (if so, all people would have them) but rather because of a social decision to create, for social purposes, a special role with certain special rights and privileges. To use Ronald Dworkin's terminology: we respect the right of a person not to be killed as a matter of *principle;* we respect the right of a police officer to carry a concealed weapon as a matter of social *policy.*

The practical upshot of the distinction is this: If a right is respected on principle, then it may be overridden—if at all—only for very compelling reasons. (The fact that the majority would like to do so is not such a reason, nor is the mere fact that some net gain in social utility would result. We might allow the state to kill, e.g., in capital punishment, but the reason will have to be more compelling than a mere net gain in utility.) When a right exists merely as a matter of social policy, however, we are free to do a kind of cost-benefit analysis and decide to modify or drop the right simply because of some slight net gain in pursuit of other social policies. This is a way of thinking we would never allow for respect-based or natural rights. If overall social policy considerations dictate that police officers will no longer have the right to carry concealed weapons, we may deprive them of this right without worrying that we are failing to respect their status as persons. They may complain that what we are doing is unwise or even seek other jobs, but they may not coherently argue that we are denying them the basic rights proper to all persons as minimal conditions of self-respect or for life in a just society. A person designated for death for policy reasons, however, would have such a complaint. This is, after all, why Nazi death camps were wrong in principle and not just bad social policy.

What about the freedoms protected by right in the First Amendment, specifically freedom of speech and freedom of the press? Are they to be viewed as natural or respect-based rights (and thus protected on principle even against good social policy arguments) or are they rights simply assigned by convention (presumptively good policies waiting to be overridden if a better policy comes along)? I suggest that free speech should be viewed as a natural or respect-based right and that freedom of the press, insofar as it is roughly equivalent to free speech, should be viewed accordingly.[36] (Recall that "free speech" is shorthand for "freedom to speak, write, and publish.") In constitutional terms, this right may thus be regarded as a "fundamental right" in what I previously characterized as the *individual* sense of that phrase. To the degree that freedom of the press means anything more than free speech, however, I suggest that it involves rights that are conventional and policy-based and thus rights that may properly be balanced against (and thus perhaps sometimes overridden by) other policy considerations. It is important to note, however, that the policy considerations here are of a type particularly important to our system of government. (They involve not mere utility but what I earlier called a "teleology of rights.") Because of this, it seems reasonable to claim that special press rights, though conventional, are more worthy of protection than rights based in a policy of mere social utility (e.g., general happiness or welfare) and thus have some claim to be characterized as "fundamental" constitutional rights in what I previously called the *political* sense of that term. I shall thus propose a threefold classification of rights: (1) respect-based rights such as privacy, freedom of religious worship, and freedom of speech (fundamental constitutional rights$_1$), (2) rights assigned to maintain the integrity of our political system such as freedom of assembly and press (fundamental constitutional rights$_2$), and (3) rights based on ordinary social utility such as the right of the police to carry weapons (rights without significant constitutional status). It is reasonable, I think, to maintain that these rights are here ranked in their order of priority, but arguing for that would require more space than the present context allows.[37] Given this general framework, let me now say a bit more about the rights of speech and press.

Freedom of speech is perhaps the most obvious example of a right that could be given to illustrate those rights I have called respect-based or natural. What is more natural—more essentially human about us—than that we are communicative creatures who value expressing ourselves and forming our opinions and life plans through rational dialogue with others? To thwart such expression is to thwart the essential humanity of a person, to fail to respect one of the most essentially human things about a person. For it is through discourse, dialogue, and argument that we reveal ourselves as thinking, rational, and (in Kant's sense) autonomous beings. Small wonder, then, that many writers such as the late Justice Black have regarded freedom of speech as an absolute: a right not to be encumbered by the state at all or, at most, to be encumbered when only the most compelling reasons (e.g., immediate threat to national security) so dictate. Free speech also, of course, has great social and political value: it fosters the marketplace of ideas as a means to truth—a model favored by both John Stuart Mill[38] and Justice Holmes[39]—and, perhaps even more important, it provides the intelligent dialogue essential for meaningful self-government. It also serves as a mechanism that helps secure other rights—e.g., the right to a fair trial.[40] These social and political considerations would certainly justify making free speech a strong conventional right (much stronger than the right of a police officer to carry a concealed weapon) even if free speech did not have what I have called a natural status in self-respect. But the right does have that status, and thus its value is a function, not merely of the good it does for society or the body politic, but also and primarily of the good it does for the individual who exercises it as an expression of his or her essential humanity. All these arguments also apply as a kind of corollary, I think, to what might be called a "right to listen." I form my own life plans through discourse and dialogue with others, and this requires not merely that I talk to them but also that I get to hear what they want to tell me. Like the right to speak, then, the right to listen has a fundamental individual value as well as its considerable social value. It is properly identified as a fundamental right$_1$.

What about freedom of the press in this context? Clearly much that is claimed under the heading "freedom of the press" fits under the above model very nicely. Journalists are people and citizens, after all, and their self-expression is just as worthy of respect as that of anyone else. And thus the most important demands they make for constitutional protection—e.g., freedom from censorship or prior restraint—are easily justified with traditional free speech arguments.

Most of the issues litigated in recent years under the banner of "freedom of the press," however, have not been simple free speech issues of a traditional nature. The press has often argued (or at least appeared to be arguing) that journalists should enjoy special constitutional protection not necessarily enjoyed by the ordinary citizen. The following claims of right, for example, have in recent years been argued for as a part of freedom of the press: the right to protect and shield confidentiality of sources;[41] the right to be protected against liability for defamation (libel and slander);[42] the right to attend criminal trials and gain information about them even when the defense, the prosecution, or the trial judge believes that this is incompatible with a fair trial;[43] and the right to seek and publish information that at least appears to violate the privacy of persons.[44]

What are we to say of such claims of right? To the degree that they represent claims of right other than those enjoyed by ordinary citizens, they must represent what I have called conventional or policy-based rights—i.e., rights granted to a certain group (in this case the journalistic profession) because of the belief that certain important social policy goals are best served by granting such rights. And it should be fairly obvious what those goals must be: those of securing an informed citizenry in order for our system of constitutional democracy to work in an intelligent and meaningful way. To the degree that maintaining our democratic system of government is valuable, not merely because it promotes utility, but because it is protective of basic human rights, then to that same degree do we have a nonutilitarian policy argument (a teleology of rights argument) that freedom of the press, even when more broadly conceived than free speech, merits some level of constitutional protection. Even if special press rights do not function directly to insure that the basic integrity of persons will be respected (and thus fail to be fundamental rights$_1$), an argument that these rights are indeed essential to our "system of ordered liberty" would function to qualify them for fundamental rights$_2$ status—i.e., for protection at a lesser level than the right of free speech but at a considerably greater level than the right of a police officer to carry a concealed weapon.

Some kind of "intermediate" standard of review (something between strict judicial scrutiny and a mere rational basis test) might thus be in order here.[45] Since these rights are policy-based, they must be open to a cost-benefit analysis and modified or overridden if such an analysis so dictates. Because of the special political status of these rights, however, it might be proper to demand that the costs and benefits be analyzed in terms of a rights teleology and not in terms of mere utility. Thus keeping the press out of pretrial hearings would not be justified on the economic ground that so doing would save the state the costs of providing places for them to sit. Such exclusion might be justified, however, if it could be shown that the integrity of the judicial process would be maximized if the press right were curtailed in this way. This would, at any rate, be a reason of the right sort.

Suppose that we agree that an informed citizenry is important because it is essentially linked to a goal of moral importance: the maintainance of the just institutions of a constitutional democracy. This would explain (1) why we might regard a policy that promotes an informed citizenry (by assigning special press rights perhaps) to be overriding of other policies that promote social utility in a more ordinary sense, but also (2) why we might accept limitations on the policy of an informed citizenry if the limitations were based on a policy that did even more toward maintaining or advancing the just institutions of a constitutional democracy. Thus in addition to the kind of "balancing" test often used by legislatures where the interests of some citizens are weighed against the interests of others (e.g., manufacturers versus consumers), we now have a balancing test to be analyzed in terms of a teleology of rights: policies that advance some rights versus policies that advance other rights. There is much here for the judiciary to consider, much to balance and weigh.

There is perhaps one point, however, where the balancing metaphor may be terribly misleading as an account of proper judicial behavior: the case where the pursuit of a desirable social policy (on either a utility or rights teleology) requires the active encumberance of a particular individual's respect-based rights. The issue here is not to limit some policy-based rights in order to advance other policy-based rights (a case where rights balance seems reasonable) but rather to curtail the respect owed to an individual in order to advance some social policy goal. Some examples of this sort of problem might be the following: denying black children equal education in order to keep the peace in certain states, punishing persons out of all reasonable proportion to the gravity of their offenses in order to make an example of them and thus deter others from crime, or (immediately germane to our present purposes) compromising the right of an individual to a fair trial in order that the press can gain access to information (or shield the sources of their information) and thereby promote an informed citizenry.

On issues of this nature, it could be persuasively argued that the function of the courts in such cases is not to balance one set of claims against the others to see on which side lies the net gain; it is rather to come out actively and aggressively as an adversary of those who would threaten respect-based rights of this fundamental nature. This is, after all, one of the courts' primary functions in a constitutional democracy, which is in this way profoundly different from a pure democracy. The will of the people is a wonderful thing and, when channeled through the legislative branch of government, produces those social policies that allow a citizenry to articulate and live under their own collective conception of the good. But there are limits. No matter how much the majority might want a given outcome or how much better off (as a matter of either utility or rights-maximizing social policy) they might be if they had that outcome, they sometimes simply *may not have it* if its accomplishment would require the violation of fundamental rights₁ as protected by the Constitution's Bill of Rights.

The courts, as the fundamental rights enforcers (and not good doers) of society, are thus obligated to be in a sense *antidemocratic* and thus properly ignore what the people want or what would be good for the people if the only way for the people to get this is through the violations of someone's respect-based rights—e.g., the right to a fair trial. If the right to a fair trial really is compromised by a certain press practice, it is not at all clear that courts should "balance" the social value of the press practice against the right. Perhaps they should rather simply veto the practice out of respect for the right—as they have historically vetoed prior restraint against speech and the press even when those representing the democratic majority wanted such restraint. The upshot is this: to the degree that the special rights of the press rest upon the social desirability of an informed citizenry, then they rest mainly upon the desirability of furthering the democratic process. Courts, as properly antidemocratic in the principled sense I have specified, will sometimes necessarily be antipress in the same sense.

Thus, in summary, I am suggesting this: Though there may be good social policy reasons (reasons that might generate legislative statutes) for allowing journalists certain conventional rights (e.g., to shield sources), it is extreme to maintain that these rights, important as they are, have fundamental rights$_1$ status. It is, for example, ludicrous to maintain that there is a right to shield sources that has First Amendment status at all comparable to free speech. Such a claim would cheapen the whole First Amendment and make it look as though the whole amendment might be thrown up for grabs to the cost-benefit thinking of social policy—a picture probably not in the ultimate interest of any of us. Thus though there may be good social policy reasons for allowing reporters a rather wide conventional right to shield sources, there are other important social policies against which this conventional right might reasonably be balanced and perhaps certain instances where respect for the basic rights of individuals (e.g., to a fair trial) might mandate forced disclosure. To the degree that the law does not move in this direction, it is—in my view—simply moving in the wrong direction. (This is true in Arizona, for example, where a shield statute, probably unconstitutional, gives reporters an absolute privilege of confidentiality with respect to their sources.)[46] It simply does not seem reasonable that the courts should view a right to shield sources as of the same kind or on a par with the right to speak freely, to worship freely, or to have a fair trial.

Other issues are, of course, more complex—e.g., the libel cases. Let us suppose that in *Gertz* the court seriously meant all its language about "media," "newspapers," and "broadcasters"—i.e., that it really meant to carve out certain special rights for the press that are not necessarily to be enjoyed by all citizens. (In this case, the court held that journalists have a right to be protected against liability for defaming a public official or a public figure unless the defamation is the result of actual malice—i.e., publication in the knowledge that the story is false or in the knowledge that the story is very likely false.) As I have argued, rights such as this would have to be conventional or policy-based—justified mainly by the social and political desirability of having an informed citizenry. Giving such protection to the press on policy grounds would, of course, have one negative feature: increased vulnerability of individuals to having their reputations ruined through defamation. But what kind of right is the right to a good (or accurate) reputation—natural and respect-based or policy-based and conventional? The matter is difficult, but a case could be made that it is the latter. (It is perhaps significant here that reputation is protected in tort law and there is no stated constitutional right against being defamed.) Perhaps here we really do have an issue where some balancing test—some cost-benefit policy analysis—might be in order. The court, in striking the balance in favor of the press and the desirability of the public being informed, is probably striking this balance (informed citizenry versus good reputations) in the right direction, though maybe going a bit far in this direction. (One could still, for example, strike the balance in this direction without going all the way to an actual malice standard—e.g., one could drop or limit punitive damages and have something like gross negligence be the standard.)

In summary: Freedom of the press, as I analyze it, means either (1) the fundamental right$_1$ (i.e., respect-based right) to speak and write freely (and, as such, subject like the right to a fair trial to nearly absolute protection) or (2) a collection of conventional or policy-based rights that allow the press to be free from some of the requirements (e.g., cooperating in certain investigations) binding on the ordinary citizen. To the degree that any of the latter rights are justified, they are justified in terms of the desirable social policy of producing an informed citizenry through a protected press. This means that at most these rights may have fundamental rights$_2$ status. When rights of this latter conventional sort conflict with rights of the former respect-based sort, it seems proper that the courts give priority to the former; for it would seem that even things of high social and political desirability—e.g., the desirability that citizens have the knowledge necessary for citizenship—should not be bought at the price of respecting individuals.

Now some of those who defend an absolute protection of the press (but who see the fragility of basing those protections on the shifting sands of social policy arguments) seek to have the philosophical or at least rhetorical power of a natural or respect-based rights argument on their side as well. That being the case, they like to speak of each citizen's "right to know" as a basic right that the courts ought to be willing to protect with the same vigor they protect other individual rights, such as the right to a fair trial. The press should be protected not so much because the press is special as because, without such protection, the citizen's fundamental right to know will be compromised.

I think that this talk of a "right to know" is confused and unfortunate, and I will close this section by saying why I think this. The basic point I would make is this: Though it is certainly *desirable* that citizens have knowledge, it takes more than desirability of an outcome to establish that anyone has a right (in a strong sense of right) to that outcome. Fundamental rights$_1$ talk is the heavy artillery of our moral and legal vocabulary, and it simply cheapens the currency of such talk if we talk this way about everything we happen to think, on balance, to be good. When all good or desirable things become a matter of rights, then nothing is really a right any more. If I really have (as citizen) a right to know or to the truth (or even whatever interests me), this presumably means that it is mandatory (i.e., someone's obligation) that this knowledge or information be provided to me. But note the ludicrous consequences of this view by recalling the Farber case. Farber was a *New York Times* reporter who refused to turn over the portion of his files relevant to the defense in a criminal case. Many who defended Farber's decision did so by saying that if reporters such as Farber did not shield sources they would be inhibited in gathering the news and the public's "right to know" would be encumbered. But if the public really has a right to know, then surely Farber is *obligated* to turn over everything to them that they want—it is their *right* after all. The press should certainly not welcome this implication for all the reasons pointed out by Ronald Dworkin:

> It is [simply] wrong to suppose that individual members of the community have, in any strong sense, a right to learn what reporters might wish to discover. No citizen's equality or independence or integrity would have been denied had Farber, for example, chosen not to write any of his stories about the matter in question, and no citizen could have sued Farber requiring him to do so, or seeking damages for his failure to write. It may be that the average citizen would have been worse off if the stories had not been written, but that is a matter of the general welfare, not of any individual right.[47]

Thus if individuals do not have this strong "right to know," then who does?—the group or the whole community or the society or the public? But of course the whole idea of group rights is a moral, intellectual and legal quagmire. And how are we to talk here? Are we to say that when the community decides (through its legislature) to exempt something—e.g., medical records—from its Freedom of Information Act that this compromises its own right to know? What a confused and confusing way to dress up a claim that can be made much more clearly and modestly simply in this way: It is highly desirable, as a matter of policy, that the public have wide access to information relevant to their social lives as citizens. The rights talk adds nothing but confusion to this claim, at least if the talk is in terms of some totally general right to know or right to information. Some other attempts to generate a rights claim here—e.g., in terms of a right to *listen* to what others want to tell you—might fare better, but space does not allow exploration of this interesting possibility. (It is surely a right to listen and not a right to know, for example, that is involved in court decisions allowing citizens to receive mailings from foreign authors.)

Also worth exploring, if space allowed, would be what might be called a right of *access*—a right, not to know, but to be free of unjustified restrictions in one's attempt to find out. And even talk of a right to know might make some sense if the right is viewed as *limited* to information possessed by the government, which is our servant, after all, in a way that other human beings are not. (This right could not, of course, be a right to *all* the information possessed by the government, since release of some of this information would violate privacy rights of individuals.) There are complex and interesting issues here that require further detailed thought—something not likely to be facilitated by the high-sounding and unqualified rhetoric of the slogan: "we all have a right to know."

This draws to a close my discussion of the moral status of the constitutional rights of freedom of speech and freedom of the press. The discussion has really only scratched the surface of a highly complex area of morality and law, and its thrust has been admittedly controversial—more likely to provoke rather than settle discussion. Its primary purpose, however, was not to present the final truth on these matters but was rather simply to illustrate how the various analytical distinctions and normative theories from moral philosophy could be brought to bear in a consideration of a constitutional issue. We have seen at work on the same issue Kantian arguments from respect for persons, social policy arguments grounded in utility, and social policy arguments grounded in rights teleology. All of these should have emerged as telling, if not the whole story, at least an important part of the story on the values of free speech and free press. Though I have tried to present all perspectives fairly, it is probably obvious to the reader that I intuitively tend to favor a Kantian approach (i.e., an approach that gives respect-based rights priority). Many readers no doubt share this intuition, and many others very likely do not. Thus we might all well wonder if such matters must ultimately be left at the level of mere intuitions or if something like a proof for preferring one moral outlook (and one constitutional interpretation) over another can be given. It is to this problem that we shall now turn.

MORAL SKEPTICISM AND THE LIMITATIONS OF CONSTITUTIONAL ANALYSIS

Suppose, following Dworkin, we regard the correct answer to a question of constitutional right (or any legal question of right) to be the answer (i.e., the assignment of right) that fits most coherently with the most rationally defensible general theory of that body of law. What does "rationally defensible theory" mean in this context? Presumably, at a minimum, it means the theory that does the best job of placing into systematic order our considered judgments in this area of law—e.g., our judgment that the right of free speech is of more ultimate constitutional importance than is the right of a police officer to carry a concealed weapon. In short, the correct assignment of right is the assignment that is most coherent with a theory that it itself defended by a coherence argument.

Some of the problems with such an account have already been noted—e.g., (a) the problem (noted by Alasdair MacIntyre)[48] that our considered judgments of right may not in fact be coherent but may form an inconsistent set, or (b) the problem that coherence arguments can at best rule out certain answers but cannot guarantee one uniquely correct answer (because more than one theory may be consistent with the "data" represented by our considered judgments).[49] If constitutional arguments are, at least in the hard cases, necessarily theory-based coherence arguments, then their ultimate rational persuasiveness (their "objectivity," if you like) will be limited to the degree that coherence is either impossible to achieve or too easy to achieve (as will be the case if there are several equally coherent theories unifying a particular body of law).

Let us imagine, for a moment, that the above difficulties could be overcome. Suppose that there is indeed one and only one theory that renders coherent a certain body of law. This by itself would not yield the *moral* dimension that Dworkin and others claim to find in constitutional analysis. (It is perhaps possible, for example, that something as morally vile as Nazi law may have rested on a coherent theoretical base.) To get a moral dimension, therefore, we need something more than mere coherence—namely, that the theory rendering the body of law coherent must be itself, in part, a *moral* theory and that it be an *objectively correct* or *rationally defensible* moral theory. (Dworkin would not, I think, be thrilled to discover that the only theory that renders coherent the body of constitutional law is a nonmoral theory of economic efficiency or to discover that the only moral theory producing coherence is the one taught by some crackpot religion.)[50] Thus: if our theory of the body of constitutional law is to ground the kind of moral interpretation suggested by Dworkin, it must rest on a *correct* moral theory. If, for example, the most coherent constitutional theory involves a kind of Kantianism—i.e., bases constitutional rights primarily on respect for persons—then Kantianism or some similar respect-based theory must be the correct moral theory or, at the very least, rationally preferable to any alternative theory, such as utilitarianism.

But how does one show that there is a correct moral theory or that one moral theory is rationally preferable to another? There is, after all, a powerful philosophical tradition of moral skepticism that cannot simply be ignored.[51] Moral skepticism is the view that we can never know (or even have good reasons for believing) that there are objective, interpersonally valid, or rationally demonstrable standards of ethics. According to the skeptic, moral judgments for all we know could simply be matters of subjective or cultural preference, each to be regarded as relativized to a private or local standard.

The issues raised by moral skepticism are complex and are the most profound in moral philosophy. Thus it is hardly to be expected that we can provide a definitive treatment of them in our present limited context. As is the case with so many other issues in this book, we can hope only to scratch the surface and present a framework that will structure, in what it is hoped will be a useful way, the reader's further thinking in the area.

Are there objective moral standards? The initial question that must be addressed in dealing with this problem is this: who has the burden of proof on the matter? If the skeptic has the burden of proof, this means that the reasonable starting assumption is that we do have objective moral knowledge and that it is the skeptic who must present arguments to attempt to persuade us out of our original bias. The defender of objective morality now has simply the negative task of attempting to undermine all the skeptic's arguments; for, if the undermining is successful, then we may remain confident in our initial assumption of moral objectivity.

Many moral philosophers believe that the burden of proof is on the skeptic—that our belief in the objectivity of (at least some) moral judgments is so compelling that we would be irrational to give it up in the absence of very powerful skeptical arguments to the contrary. The philosopher William Gass goes even further. He maintains that some of our moral beliefs are more obvious than could be any of the premises in any argument that anyone might mount to make us doubt those beliefs. He writes:

> Imagine I approach a stranger on the street and say to him, "If you please, sir, I desire to perform an experiment with your aid." The stranger is obliging, and I lead him away. In a dark place conveniently by, I strike his head with the broad of an axe and cart him home. I place him, buttered and trussed, in an ample electric oven. The thermostat reads 450 degrees F. Thereupon I go off to play poker with friends and forget all about the obliging stranger in the stove. When I return, I realize I have overbaked my specimen, and the experiment, alas, is ruined. . . . Any ethic that does not roundly condemn my action is vicious. It is interesting that none is vicious for this reason. It is also interesting that no more convincing refutation of any ethic could be given than by showing that it approved of my baking the obliging stranger.[52]

What Gass has rightly noted is that we will reject any ethical theory that does not accord with our most fundamental intuitions about ethical matters. Thus if the fundamental business of ethics is to provide the best theory to render our intuitions coherent, then it would seem that we can indeed attain a kind of objectivity.[53] But this is hardly the kind of objectivity that would be of interest to the skeptic. For (so the skeptic might argue) who is the "we" here who have "our" intuitions formulated into a coherent system that will satisfy "us"? This surely cannot mean every member of the human race, since it is ludicrous to suppose that all the various moral intuitions in the world come even close to forming a consistent set.

Most readers of this book (having as they very likely do very similar upbringings) no doubt share Gass's shock at the very idea of baking an obliging stranger and would also reject any ethical theory that did not condemn such baking. Persons who have been subjected to radically different socialization, however, might not share the repulsion. What might repel them and thus condition their acceptance of a moral theory might be some judgment that those of "us" who are "enlightened" would find repulsive—e.g., a judgment that it is OK to bake members of some despised racial or social class or the judgment that it is fundamentally evil even to consider tolerating homosexuals. I, and no doubt most of my readers, want firmly to reject judgments of this latter sort, but what qualifies us to rule such judgments out of the domain of those that moral theory must account for? Not the strength with which the judgment is held, surely, since I suspect that those persons I regard as superstitious bigots hold their judgments just as strongly as I (regarded by myself as reasonable) hold mine. Is it then the degree to which the belief is *widely* held? Surely this will not do either, for I am not prepared to concede that idiocy ceases to be idiocy simply by attaining a large following. Is perhaps what we are seeking then agreement simply among those who are genuinely enlightened? Is it their intuitions that are to be systematized? This also seems hopeless as an approach to objectivity, for how are we to characterize those who will count as enlightened in a nonquestion-begging way? (Are they to be those who start out agreeing with us?)

From this brief discussion, we can see why the moral skeptic believes that the burden of proof lies, not on the skeptic, but upon the defender of moral objectivity. Look, the skeptic will argue, at the nature of moral disagreement, argument, and conflict. Do you see it resolved in an orderly and systematic way by an agreed methodology—e.g., as we see in empirical science? Certainly not. Radical moral disagreement is common (the most obvious feature of ethics, indeed) and it seems to involve, not resolution through proof or argument, but either no resolution at all or resolution through means of emotional (not rational) persuasion.[54] The ethical skeptic thus holds out this challenge: If there is some method for the objective, interpersonal, intercultural, or rational resolution of ethical controversy, then where is it? Even a superficial acquaintance with ethical discourse makes it plausible to suppose that ethical disagreement lies beyond the scope of rational resolution. This is the way it looks to the unbiased mind—i.e., the mind not already committed to ethical objectivity. Thus, if this skeptical picture is wrong, the burden of proof is surely upon the ethical objectivist to prove (or at least give some persuasive arguments) that it is wrong. In the absence of such arguments, then surely moral skepticism seems the reasonable posture to adopt.

Since assignment of the burden of proof, whether in law or in philosophy, is often determinative of the outcome of a controversy, the ethical objectivist is not going to accept without challenge the above pattern of skeptical reasoning. Two points that the objectivist will surely want to make, for example, are the following: (1) Differences over particular moral beliefs are not sufficient to demonstrate that there is the kind of ultimate ethical disagreement that the skeptic trades on. Very likely the person who regards it as permissable to bake a member of some racial minority will not quarrel with our principle that it is wrong to bake people. Rather our baker will very likely agree with that principle and argue that it does not apply to the present case because members of this particular minority are not really people but are rather subhuman animals. Very likely this claim will be supported by some crackpot pseudoscientific *empirical* claim about the supposed natures of such individuals—e.g., that they are not rational beings.

(2) Though the methodology of proof in ethics may not be as compelling as that found in science, it does not follow from this that just *anything* goes in ethical argument.[55] If, for example, there is indeed the kind of total lack of agreement on how to proceed and argue in ethics that MacIntyre claims, then it is unclear why he and others like him bother to write their books at all. Do they write simply for those who already agree with them? That hardly seems worthwhile. Do they then write in an attempt to persuade those who initially disagree with them? But how is this possible if there is no common style of reasoning that unites the parties to the controversy?[56]

The moral skeptic thus must be careful not to set the standard of acceptable argument so high that no theoretical account, including empirical science and the case for skepticism itself, can meet the standard. For there is no rational human activity that does not at some point simply rest on the fact that there is widespread agreement on how to proceed, on what counts as relevant, on what counts as evidence, on what counts as a sound argument. This admission is, of course, disquieting for it is sobering to realize that we cannot find a perspective that transcends all our concepts and practices and from which we can justify all at once those concepts and practices. This disquiet, however, should not prompt the hysterical reaction that no relevant distinctions can be drawn between what is and what is not reasonable in ethics—that "I like ice cream" is exactly on a par with "I disapprove of baking obliging strangers" in that both are simply rationally unsupportable expressions of preference. Surely the fact that the latter judgment forms (in a way that the former does not) a coherent part of a system of judgments that defines civilized life, while not a skeptic-destroying proof of that judgment, is not rationally irrelevant to it either.

These are large issues that can easily overwhelm several advanced courses and seminars in ethics, and it is hardly to be hoped that one can say much toward their resolution in simply discussing their impact on the philosophy of law. One thing here can be said with confidence, however: Too much is at stake—for morality, for the law, for civilized life as we understand it—for us simply to throw away all notions of moral objectivity as though the matter had already been settled. The matter is emphatically not settled, and it requires continuous thought and discussion—a process that this brief section has, it is hoped, helped to further. Dworkin may be overly optimistic in his view that good moral analysis will yield correct answers to all disputes over legal rights. Scaling down Dworkin's claim to more modest proportions thus might be in order. What is clearly not in order, however, is claiming that morality is now known to be a crock and thus recommending that judges should (on what theory of "should" one wonders) avoid all moral analysis in adjudication over legal rights.[57]

NOTES

1. Arthur Leff, "Unspeakable Ethics, Unnatural Law," *Duke Law Journal* 1979 (1979):1229, 1249.

2. See especially R. M. Hare, *The Language of Morals* (Oxford: Oxford University Press, 1952), and idem, *Freedom and Reason* (Oxford: Oxford University Press, 1963).

3. G. J. Warnock, *The Object of Morality* (Oxford: Oxford University Press, 1971).

4. H. L. A. Hart, "Legal and Moral Obligation," in *Essays in Moral Philosophy*, ed. A. I. Melden (Seattle: Washington University Press, 1958).

5. By "modern" moral philosophy I mean moral philosophy that is centrally concerned to answer the moral skeptic—to present a rational defense of ethics against such a skeptic. Kant is a paradigm of modern moral philosophy in this sense. Such earlier writers as Aristotle, however, saw no such problem. They took for granted the existence of moral reality and sought solely to give it an articulate and systematic statement—which in Aristotle's case largely meant the articulate and systematic statement of certain shared *conventions* characteristic of upper class Greeks. Thus it is not surprising that those philosophers—e.g., Alasdair MacIntyre—who believe that the case of the skeptic cannot be met by reason will express nostalgia for a time when shared conventional agreement was more common than it is today, for they see no hope for ethics except in a retreat to such agreement. For an extremely sensitive discussion of these matters, see Alasdair MacIntyre, *After Virtue* (Notre Dame: University of Notre Dame Press, 1981). As MacIntyre also notes, another characteristic of modern moral philosophy is a shift away from the Greek concern with *virtue* (excellence of the human person) as the basic issue of ethics and the replacement of that issue with a concern about duty or obligation (about how others are to be treated).

6. What will be called "Kantianism" in this text is in no sense attempted to be a literal presentation of the views of Immanuel Kant (1724–1804); it is rather the presentation of a kind of moral view that is highly Kantian in spirit. For a discussion of the details of Kant's actual views, see Jeffrie G. Murphy, *Kant: The Philosophy of Right* (London: Macmillan, 1970).

7. I see Kant as summing up the best of what is generally called the "natural rights" tradition or what might better be called the "liberal" tradition. It is that general tradition (and not Kant himself) that has exercised powerful influences on American constitutional law. Kant simply strikes me as the best at stating and defending the general ideology—individualistic liberalism—that our own traditon tends to associate with such writers as John Locke and Thomas Jefferson.

8. See Jeremy Bentham, *Principles of Morals and Legislation* (1789), and John Stuart Mill, *Utilitarianism* (1863), for classic statements and defenses of the utilitarian position. For a contemporary statement and defense of a utilitarian position that is sophisticated but still open to the beginning reader, see Rolf Sartorius, *Individual Conduct and Social Norms* (Belmont: Wadsworth, 1975). See also J. J. C. Smart and Bernard Williams, *Utilitarianism: For and Against* (Cambridge: Cambridge University Press, 1973).

9. The view that the Principle of Utility should be applied to each contemplated action is called "act utilitarianism." The view that acts should be dictated by rules and that the Principle of Utility should be applied to select the proper rules is called "rule utilitarianism." For a powerful development of a rule utilitarian view, see John Rawls, "Two Concepts of Rules," *The Philosophical Review* 64 (1955). Some writers—e.g., Sartorius and Smart, *supra* note 8—do not find rule utilitarianism clearly distinguishable from or clearly an advance over act utilitarianism.

10. Mill, *Utilitarianism*, chap. 5. In this chapter, Mill does a nice job of explaining all the different moral concerns that tend to be grouped under the heading "justice." For our purposes, we may think of the demands of justice in a legal order as either

procedural or *substantive*. Speaking *very* generally, procedural justice demands that the rights assigned by the law be respected—that like cases be treated like. Substantive justice demands that the original assignment of rights be morally appropriate. Different moral theories will, of course, have different accounts of what makes the initial rights assignment morally appropriate.

11. Some economists are troubled by classical utilitarianism and have developed devices—e.g., Pareto optimality as a test for social rationality—that allow them to articulate and defend a more complex view of social choice. For a discussion of this and certain other problems generated by utilitarianism (e.g., the problem of the interpersonal comparison of utilities), see Chapter 5.

12. In my book on Kant (*supra* note 6, 77ff.), I suggested that Kant's Categorical Imperative (his supreme principle of morals) was a moral instantiation of Leibniz's Principle of Sufficient Reason. Very generally, this principle—taken by Leibniz to be a defining feature of rationality—is the principle that a rational being will not prefer one state of affairs A over another state of affairs B unless that being can cite some relevant respect in which A differs from B—a respect that justifies (provides a sufficient reason for) the perference. (A rational being treats like [or relevantly similar] cases in like ways, and treats different cases differently.) Kant's Categorical Imperative (first formulation) goes: "Act only on that principle that you can will to be a law of nature." I read this to mean: "Claim for yourself only a liberty in action that you could—as a rational being—extend to all relevantly similar agents in relevantly similar circumstances." If you claimed for yourself a liberty you could not (or would not) extend to relevantly similar others (which would be to treat them as means only, something prohibited by Kant's second formulation of the Categorical Imperative), you would be preferring yourself over others without being able to cite a sufficient reason for the preference— something no rational being would do. In this sense, at least, being moral is a part of being rational.

There is, of course, one serious problem with all of this: can one specify, in a rationally compelling way that does not beg any moral questions, those similarities that are morally relevant similarities and those differences that are morally relevant differences? For example: Putting Jones in jail because he is guilty of a crime (while the innocent stay free) seems to be a decision based on a relevant difference in a way that putting Jones in jail because he is black (while whites stay free) seems based on an irrelevant factor. Can we develop a *theory* of moral relevance to explain the difference, or is all to be left at the level of intuition? Is guilt of moral relevance because it results from autonomous choice in a way that race does not? But then why place such heavy moral weight on autonomy? Does such weighting leave some—e.g., the retarded or the senile—out of the moral domain? If so, is this OK? These questions are not self-answering. If one wants to read Kant himself on these matters, the best place to start is with his *Foundations of the Metaphysics of Morals*, trans. L. W. Beck (Indianapolis: Bobbs-Merrill, 1959).

13. See Robert Nozick, *Anarchy, State and Utopia* (New York: Basic Books, 1974).

14. This moral bias in favor of members of our own species, though common, may not survive careful analysis. If it does not, then the Kantian assumption that there must be some factor present in humans that makes them count more than any other creatures will simply be what Peter Singer has called "speciesism"—an undefended preference for one's own kind comparable to racism and sexism. See Peter Singer, "Animal Liberation," *New York Review of Books*, 5 April 1973; and Tom Regan, *The Case for Animal Rights* (Berkeley: University of California Press, 1983).

15. In his "About Mammals and People," *New York Times Book Review*, 27 November 1983, Robert Nozick appears to disagree with this and suggests either that species membership may be no more or less arbitrary than any other single characteristic on which to base moral respect or that we should stop thinking of moral respect as something that grows out of one single characteristic—even something as impressive as Kantian autonomy. The issue could bear further reflection.

16. For an argument that moral appeals to unique features may be more problematical than they at first appear, see Jeffrie G. Murphy, *Evolution, Morality, and the Meaning of Life* (Totowa, N.J.: Rowmand and Littlefield, 1982), 68ff.

17. This view is, of course, not without problems—some of them metaphysical, some of them moral. Some philosophers regard Kant's talk of autonomous rational choice as involving a commitment to a radically antideterminist theory of free will— a theory that these philosophers find just as metaphysically controversial as a doctrine of ensoulment. This raises the important question: Is Kant's moral theory connected to a dubious metaphysical theory and, if it is, can it be detached and defended independently from that metaphysical theory? Also—to consider a moral objection— does Kant's emphasis on the capacity for autonomous rational choice as the respect-conferring human attribute entail that infants, the retarded, the insane, the senile, etc., merit no moral respect? Is this consequence acceptable?

18. See John Rawls, "Justice as Fairness," *Philosophical Review* 57 (1958); and idem, *A Theory of Justice* (Cambridge, Harvard University Press, 1971). This book is a brilliant exposition and defense of a moral view that is Kantian in many ways and that develops in detail the criticism of utilitarianism sketched earlier in the present chapter that utilitarianism mistakenly takes the model of rational choice for one person and transforms it into a model of social rationality—i.e., weighs people the way people weigh their own desires.

19. Ronald Dworkin, *Taking Rights Seriously* (Cambridge: Harvard University Press, 1977, 1978), xi.

20. Nozick, *supra* note 13.

21. In the final section of the present chapter, it will be suggested that the moral options are perhaps richer than would be suggested by this overly rigid (and very likely false) dichotomy. "There must be formal proof of mathematical rigidity or just anything goes" fails to recognize that there are perhaps more ways of being reasonable than simply providing proofs.

22. For a brilliant conceptual analysis of rights, see Wesley Newcomb Hohfeld, *Fundamental Legal Conceptions* (New Haven: Yale University Press, 1919). See also Joel Feinberg, "The Nature and Value of Rights," *Journal of Value Inquiry* 4 (1970).

23. For the reader who wishes to study a detailed introduction to constitutional law, two excellent hornbooks can be recommended: John Nowak et al., *Constitutional Law*, 2nd ed. (St. Paul: West Publishing Company, 1983); and Laurence Tribe, *American Constitutional Law* (Mineola: Foundation Press, 1978). Both are good surveys. The Tribe text, though more difficult than the Nowak, is also an exciting piece of theoretical legal philosophy.

24. *Shelley* v. *Kraemer*, 334 U.S. 1 (1948).

25. *New York Times* v. *Sullivan*, 376 U.S. 254 (1964).

26. By saying that the First Amendment is primarily concerned with cognitive communication, I in no sense mean to suggest that it is exclusively concerned with such communication. It is a matter of considerable controversy whether certain categories of speech (e.g., obscene speech) are denied constitutional protection, whether other categories of speech (e.g., commercial speech) have lesser constitutional protection, and whether symbolic expressive activities (e.g., wearing an American flag on the seat of one's pants as a protest) merit protection as speech. I think that these are all important and complex issues, and thus, simply because limitations of space force me to discuss only a few of the important free speech/free press issues, the reader should in no sense assume that I am presupposing either the triviality of or some solution to the other issues. Indeed, it is my hope that the framework I shall provide might help us to come to terms with some of these other issues. Consider obscenity as an example. If (as I argue) free speech is valuable mainly for its worth to the individual as an element of his or her self-respect, then a case for the protection of obscene speech could be made. If (as others argue) free speech is protected mainly for its social and political value, then obscene speech will not seem worthy of much, if any, protection. For a good discussion of the actual developing constitutional doctrine on obscenity and other categories of speech, see Nowak, *supra* note 23.

27. For a discussion of fundamental rights and the standard of "strict" judicial review (compelling state interest, least restrictive alternative) triggered by the encumberance of fundamental rights, see Nowak, *supra* note 23, 590ff.

28. Alexander Meiklejohn is famous for his defense of the thesis that First Amendment and other constitutional rights exist primarily to serve political purposes—the maintenance of the institutions of constitutional democracy—and that the right to free speech therefore is basically a right to free *political* speech—Alexander Meiklejohn, *Free Speech and Its Relation to Self-Government* (New York: Harper & Row, 1948). But why are these institutions *worth* preserving unless they preserve respect for human beings—their individual rights and choices—and the rights based on such respect?

29. As I now look over my copy of *Anarchy, State and Utopia* (*supra* note 13), I cannot find the phrase "teleology of rights," but at 28ff. find instead (to refer to the same view) the phrase "utilitarianism of rights." I think talk of rights teleology is clearer, for it shows that the view is like utilitarianism in being consequentialist but unlike utilitarianism in having a richer (i.e., nonhedonistic) conception of the relevant consequences.

30. The concept of a *compelling* state interest clearly needs analysis. It must mean an interest or goal that the state, given its basic job, simply *must* pursue. It will be easy to give clear examples of such goals or interests—e.g., national defense or police protection for citizens—but perhaps not so easy to give a theoretical account of what it is that makes these examples clear examples. One thing, however, is evident: for an interest or goal to be compelling, it must involve considerably more than a mere net gain in social utility.

31. There are two reasons for viewing censorship or prior restraint as the most intrusive attack on speech: (1) Censorship, unlike the after-the-fact remedies of criminal punishment or civil damages for publication, does not allow the speech to get out and discussed—the most awful outcome for one who values speech. (2) Censorship or prior restaint typically proceeds through the mechanism of a court injunction. Courts are much more reluctant to overturn or declare invalid one of their own orders than they are to void a criminal statute or an award of civil damages. This is not mere self-protection but is also based on the idea that the rule of law requires that court orders be paid special deference.

32. These matters do not always turn out in fact the way that theory might seem to require. When *The Progressive* magazine sought to publish an article on how to make an atomic bomb, the government sought an injunction to restrain publication. In this case, the court seems to have confused two separate issues: (1) what is the test for justified prior restraint? and (2) what is reasonable to accept as evidence that the test has been satisfied. The court articulated the correct principle—no prior restraint unless there is an immediate threat of serious and irreversible damage to the nation—but then made the mistake of simply taking the word of various government agencies as conclusive evidence of such a threat. Even a very strict test will not restrain the government if courts simply take the government's word for it that the test has been satisfied. See *U.S.* v. *The Progressive*, 486 F. Supp. 5 (1979). (In this case the magazine maintained that all the information in its article had been obtained through public sources and thus had not involved a violation of security or the revelation of any secrets.)

When the United States government kept the press from being present during the invasion of Grenada in 1983, it justified doing so on the ground that the secrecy of its operation—vital to its success—would have been compromised by press presence. Suppose (though this is controversial) that the government here cited the correct principle. Should they still not have a burden of presenting good *evidence* that the principle is satisfied? If not, it would seem that government could stifle the press or speech simply by crying "Threat to national security!" every time it wants to stifle the flow of information.

33. The First Amendement, in addition to linking speech with the press, also links it with religion, petition, and assembly. These other matters—particularly religion—raise complex and special concerns that will not be discussed in this chapter. A few

comments might be in order here, however. It seems reasonably clear that the right of assembly and petition are present primarily to serve political ends—namely, the proper functioning of constitutional democracy. But what about religion? Is it protected because it is part of what it means to respect a person as a person that one not coerce the person in matters as central to one's personality as religious beliefs are sometimes said to be? Or is it rather that religion is believed to have great potential for generating social turmoil and that the rights with respect to religion are granted for the political purpose of trying to keep social peace? Or both?

34. *Gertz* v. *Robert Welch, Inc.*, 418 U.S. 323 (1974). See P. Stewart, "Or of the Press," *Hastings Law Journal* 26 (1975):631.

35. One reason why the phrase "natural rights" is misleading is that some of the rights so designated—e.g., the right to a fair trial—are clearly not natural in the sense that they could exist prior to systems of law and social convention. (What sense could be made of the idea of a *trial* in a presocial or prelegal natural state?) The basic moral point about the right to a fair trial is that this right (like rights to treatment that could exist in nature—e.g., the right not to be killed) cannot be said merely to be an optional matter of social convention, given only to serve certain social policy goals. A society that has trials but makes no effort to insure that those tried will be fairly treated surely shows a *contempt* for at least a portion of its citizens, for it does not accord them the minimum of respect as autonomous persons that would be a condition of citizenship in even a minimally decent society. (The treatment of black rape defendents at rape trials in the South a few decades ago was not merely bad policy, but showed a fundamental lack of respect for blacks as persons.) It is my view that what is best about the natural rights tradition is captured in the idea of respect-based rights—not, of course, that it is going to be all that easy to articulate and defend a complete list of just what those rights will be.

36. For a powerful statement and defense of a generally Kantian view of free speech rights, see T. M. Scanlon, "A Theory of Freedom of Expression," *Philosophy and Public Affairs* 1 (1972).

37. The Meiklejohn thesis (*supra* note 28) maintains that I have this priority ranking wrong. But note the problem stated for that thesis in the note and see further Tribe (*supra* note 23) 576 ff.

38. John Stuart Mill's *On Liberty* (1859) is the classic (and brilliant) statement and defense of this position. See also Joel Feinberg, "Limits to the Free Expression of Opinion," in *Philosophy of Law*, 2nd ed., eds. Joel Feinberg and Hyman Gross (Belmont: Wadsworth, 1980).

The most plausible utilitarian justification for free speech will be provided within the framework of rule-utilitarianism and will proceed by arguing that in the long run human well-being is more likely to be maximized by institutions that have permissive rules concerning speech than by those having repressive rules concerning speech. This kind of argument is consistent with the obvious fact that some particular instances of protected speech (e.g., racist propaganda) are likely to do more harm than good. One thing that makes even the rule-utilitarian case fragile, however, is that we probably lack compelling empirical evidence that it is indeed true that free institutions are more productive of general happiness than are repressive institutions.

Mill lived in an age that saw science and the free discussion that aided in the growth of science as a noncontroversial contributor to human good. An age that realizes the power of certain scientific discoveries to destroy civilized life as we know it, however, will perhaps be a bit more skeptical about the "free discussion leads to science leads to progress leads to happiness" line of Mill's reasoning. If these persons still want to defend a strong right to free speech, the defense will have to be on principle—i.e., will have to take freedom (especially freedom of speech) as a value in itself, a value to be respected and protected even if it fails to advance human happiness.

39. See *Abrams* v. *United States*, 250 U.S. 616 (1919) (Holmes, J., joined by Brandeis, J., dissenting).

40. The intuitive idea behind the connection between speech and press, on the one hand, and fair trials, on the other, is this: It is much less likely that the state will treat

a defendent unfairly in a trial if the proceedings of the trial are open to observation and discussion.

41. See Ronald Dworkin, "The Rights of Myron Farber," *New York Review of Books,* 26 October 1978.

42. *Supra* note 34.

43. *Richmond Newspapers Inc.* v. *Virginia,* 448 U.S. 555 (1980). *Gannett Co.* v. *DePasquale,* 443 U.S. 368 (1979).

44. *Cox Broadcasting Corp.* v. *Cohn,* 420 U.S. 469 (1975).

45. Standards of judicial review have been given their most complex articulation in the area of equal protection analysis. The normal standard of review is sometimes called the "rational basis" test: state action will pass review if it serves a purpose that could be regarded as rational. (This is clearly a weak standard, since a plausible rational defense can be mounted for all but the most outrageously silly state actions.) When fundamental rights are encumbered or when special burdens are placed on members of "suspect classifications" (e.g., racial minorities), "strict judicial scrutiny" is triggered. This involves the "compelling state interest/least restrictive alternative test"—a very tough test for the state to pass. In some cases, however, judges seem to be imploying a test "intermediate" between these two—a test that will uphold the state action if it bears "a substantial relationship to an important interest." This test is triggered by the "quasi-suspect" classification of *gender.* For a good introductory discussion of these matters, see Nowak, *supra* note 23, 590ff.

46. A. R. S. Sec. 12–2237 provides as follows: "A person engaged in newspaper, radio, television, or reportorial work, or connected with or employed by a newspaper, radio or television station shall not be compelled to testify or disclose in a legal proceeding or trial or any proceeding whatever, or before any jury, inquisitorial body or commission, or before any committee of the legislature, or elsewhere, the source of information procured or obtained by him for publication in a newspaper or for broadcasting over a radio or television station with which he was associated or by which he is employed." Constitutional problems could clearly arise in the following kind of case: A newspaper reporter reveals that he has acquired, from a source who desires to remain secret and thus cannot be subpoenaed, information that might clear a defendent in a criminal case. Might not the defendent claim that his right to a fair trial is compromised, if he cannot subpoena this person as a witness?

47. Ronald Dworkin, "Is the Press Losing the First Amendment?" *New York Review of Books,* 4 December 1980. The present section has been much influenced by this article.

48. See the closing pages of Chapter 1 and note 73 for that chapter.

49. See Chapter 1, note 65.

50. If a religion could really do this, perhaps it would not deserve to be called "crackpot." On the other hand, the delusional systems of paranoids can involve total worldviews that are impressive in their coherence; but this does not incline us to doubt that these views are psychotic. Perhaps some simplicity requirement is also involved in certifying worldviews—even highly coherent ones—as rationally acceptable.

51. For the statement and defense of a certain form of ethical skepticism (coupled with an argument that the view, at least in that form, is not as harmful as many take it to be) see Murphy, *Evolution.* See also J. L. Mackie, *Ethics: Inventing Right and Wrong* (New York: Penguin, 1977); and Gilbert Harman, *The Nature of Morality* (Oxford: Oxford University Press, 1977). H. L. A. Hart's review essay of the Mackie and Harman books is also to be recommended: "Morality and Reality," *New York Review of Books,* 9 March 1978. The legal analogue to moral skepticism (perhaps even the legal instantiation of moral skepticism) is the view that there is no rational way successfully to perform fundamental rights analysis in constitutional adjudication. For a provocative and powerful development of such a position, see Paul Brest, "The Fundamental Rights Controversy: The Essential Contradictions of Normative Constitutional Scholarship," *Yale Law Journal* 90 (1981):1063.

52. William Gass, "The Case of the Obliging Stranger," *Philosophical Review* 66 (1957).

53. "Subjectivism" is the name often given to the view that moral judgments simply report personal preferences. (This is also sometimes called "subjective relativism.") "Cultural relativism" is the name given to the view that moral judgments report preferences widely shared in a particular culture. A moral judgment can be objective, then, in the sense that it truly reports a personal or cultural preference. The moral skeptic does not seek to deny this. When the moral skeptic doubts the objectivity of values, the doubt is that ethics can ever attain the kind of objectivity often claimed to be present for scientific judgments—namely, an interpersonal and cross-cultural validity. The moral skeptic (unless also an epistemological skeptic) will very likely claim that the judgment "The DNA molecule has the structure of a double helix" is true regardless of whether all persons or cultures agree on this or not. It is this kind of objectivity for ethics that the moral skeptic doubts. An interesting problem for this outlook is this: The moral skeptic has long traded on a contrast between scientific claims (rational and objective in some strong sense) and moral claims (much more open to doubt). Recent work in the history and philosophy of science, however, suggests that the problems raised for the rational credibility of morality arise for science as well. If so, then at least one of the moral skeptic's fulcrums will be cut from beneath the position. An excellent collection of essays exploring the problem is Martin Hollis and Steven Lukes, eds., *Rationality and Relativism* (Cambridge: MIT Press, 1982). A particularly interesting essay in this collection is Ian Hacking's "Language, Truth, and Reason."

The most impressive attempt to date to try to provide something in the way of a decision procedure for establishing the rational preferability of one moral view over another is to be found in Rawls, *A Theory of Justice*. Rawls has tried out various devices for rational proof over the years, and remnants of all of them are found in his book. The technique developed in Chapter 1 and called "reflective equilibrium" seems to be his present considered view on the matter. It has striking analogies with certain methodologies in science (particularly scientific linguistics) and has both the virtues and shortcomings of those analogies. Whatever one ultimately comes to think of the success of Rawls's own account, one could hardly do better than his Chapter 1 for a profound introduction to the problem of theoretical adequacy in ethics.

54. The study of moral disagreement has led some philosophers to defend an *emotive* theory of ethics—the view that moral judgments have no cognitive content at all (not even as accurate reports of preferences) but simply evince emotions much in the way a cry of pain does when one is kicked in the shin. See C. L. Stevenson, *Ethics and Language* (New Haven: Yale University Press, 1944).

55. On the issue of whether science should be used as a model of rational certainty, see note 53.

56. MacIntyre (*supra*, note 5) is an ethical skeptic in the sense that he believes that it is impossible to provide a rational foundation for ethics that transcends history and culture, and he regards it as the fundamental mistake of the liberal tradition to have pursued this hopeless route. Rationality, according to MacIntyre, is itself a culturally conditioned concept; and, because of this, rational argument—in morals or anywhere else—is possible only in a culture with a shared set of beliefs, values, and commitments. Our only hope of salvaging ethics, then, is to find a way to recapture a world (which the ancient Greeks had) in which there truly is a community of shared standards. The concept of a *community* of shared values is foreign to the tradition of liberal individualism and value pluralism that informs our society and our constitution: thus, if MacIntyre is correct, a real problem arises for those such as Dworkin who want to find an ethical foundation for constitutional law. The problem is this: meaningful ethics is possibly only in a community involving values fundamentally different from those that informed our own constitutional tradition and thus the Dworkin hope is doomed. A conclusion so radical should not be quickly accepted, and I am by no means convinced that MacIntyre has established it. His book *After Virtue* is, however, one of the most profoundly provocative books in ethics written in recent years and thus merits serious study and thought.

57. A thoughtful attempt to overcome moral skepticism, written from the point of view of a scholar concerned with the law, is Michael Moore, "Moral Reality," *Wisconsin Law Review* 1982 (1982):1061.

3

Crime and Punishment

Hangman: Do you have any last
words?

W. C. Fields: Well, this is certainly
going to be a lesson to me.

The core punishments of the criminal law (deprivation of liberty or
life) represent gravely serious assaults on the fundamental rights of
persons, stigmatize and humiliate those persons, and typically cause
those persons great personal unhappiness. Even when punishments
are not actually inflicted on a particular individual, the possibility that
they might be inflicted may be sufficient to generate enough fear in
that individual to cause him to refrain from acting in ways he otherwise
would have found desirable—a coercive curtailment of his liberty.

Because of this radically intrusive nature of criminal punishment,
it is natural that persons committed to the values of individual rights
and a free society would seek for morally and politically acceptable
alternatives to punishment and would regard punishment as justified,
as a last resort, only if no less intrusive alternatives seem reasonable.
Adapting constitutional language from a somewhat different context,
one might seek to discover if criminal punishment, as a mechanism
that encumbers fundamental rights of persons, is indeed the least
restrictive means that could be employed to accomplish whatever
compelling goals or interests the state currently seeks to attain through
punishment. (If one truly values the rights of persons, then surely
one will want to demand that the state not threaten such rights in
the pursuit of goals of a trivial or controversial social importance.)
A thorough examination of this issue would, of course, require careful
consideration of what it means to say of one alternative that it is
indeed more restrictive or intrusive than another and would require
as well an articulate and defensible account of what makes a state

goal compelling. Lovers of liberty should, of course, be willing to take at least this amount of trouble.

A promising way to get into the moral foundations of permissible punishment is to begin, as most philosophers oddly enough do not, with a discussion of criminalization. It seems plausible to maintain that the appropriateness of punishment follows logically from the recognition of certain human acts as violations of the criminal law, which is just that branch of law mandating punishment. And surely no morally coherent theory of punishment would regard punishment as ultimately acceptable if the conduct for which one is punished never should have been criminalized in the first place. So perhaps the basic question with which to begin a discussion of the moral permissibility of punishment is this: When, if ever, is it morally appropriate to make a class of acts criminal in nature?

WHY HAVE THE CRIMINAL LAW AT ALL?

Having raised this question, one must avoid the temptation of thinking that the answer to it is immediate and obvious. One must not simply say, for example, that the criminal law is concerned to prevent seriously harmful conduct and thus it is appropriate to criminalize when and only when such conduct is present or threatened. The range of seriously harmful conduct is considerably wider than the range of conduct that is currently criminalized. Though it would be possible to say that this simply shows that the law needs massive reform (more conduct being made criminal), one would presumably want to think carefully about the implications of this suggestion before adopting a proposal so radical. Consider, for example, defamation (libel and slander). People's rights are violated and their lives are often crippled or destroyed when others maliciously circulate damaging falsehoods about them, yet the remedy the law currently provides for such harm is civil and not criminal in nature—namely, a tort action seeking the award of damages. Even when those additional damages called "punitive" are awarded over and above the compensatory damages, this does not make the matter criminal or quasi-criminal and thus a matter of criminal punishment, as is shown clearly by the fact that constitutional due process requirements surrounding proceedings that are truly criminal do not apply with respect to an award of punitive damages.[1]

Or consider the kind of morally obscene and exploitive behavior that can take place in contract law, such as a powerful and knowledgeable party taking advantage of an ignorant and vulnerable party. Here the doctrine of unconscionability may result in a voiding of such contracts, but there is normally no intervention by the criminal law in spite of the fact that rights are violated, people are harmed, and the exploiters seem sufficiently evil that, if anyone can be said to deserve to suffer, then they are surely good candidates. In short: unless our criminal law is currently radically misconceived, then being an actively evil and hurtful person is not sufficient to make one's evil and hurtful conduct criminal.

Is conduct harmful to a serious degree perhaps then at least a *necessary* condition for criminality? It would seem not, as we can all see from considering (by way of example) certain theft offenses. Has Jones harmed me to any serious degree if he steals my car? Probably not. My loss here will be one primarily of money and convenience, and so long as I am paid off for these injuries (either by an insurance company or by the thief himself if caught and solvent), then it would be hard for me to defend the claim that I had been seriously harmed by the theft. I have, of course, been harmed in that *moral* sense of harm in which I am harmed by the very act of having my rights violated, of being treated without proper moral respect. But the person who steals my car does not do this to any greater degree, surely, than the person who libels or slanders me. Indeed, with respect to libel and slander, the injury I can suffer seems possibly much worse. The value of my car and time can be costed in very literal economic terms—something difficult if not impossible to do for my reputation or self-respect, the values threatened by libel and slander. Thus, in this particular moral framework, the case for criminalizing libel and slander seems much stronger than the case for criminalizing auto theft.

Cases of conduct that is criminalized but (like auto theft) typically causes no serious harm to the victim put heavy strain on the common claim that the sole and unique purpose of the criminal law is to prevent some individuals from mounting major invasions on the rights and interests of other individuals. The common claim is strained perhaps to the breaking point, however, by another class of cases: criminal statutes that deter some persons from conferring *advantages* on other persons. As I have argued elsewhere, blackmail may be such a case.[2] In the typical blackmail scenario, the "criminal" threatens to disclose secret and damaging *true* information about a person unless that person pays him a certain amount of money. (Remember that in a society such as ours with strong constitutional protection of the free dissemination of information, what the blackmailer threatens to do is something he normally has a legal right to do.) As a potential "victim" of blackmail, I might be delighted to have the opportunity to buy the blackmailer's silence on some matter rather than have him publish his information in a public (and perfectly legal) manner. Thus, if there is a criminal statute against blackmail, I might hope that the statute *fails* to deter. If the statute succeeds, I will not view myself as having been protected from harm but will rather see myself as having been deprived of an advantage for which I would have been willing to pay—namely, the continued silence of a person who knows the "dirt" on me. I may view the state here as using the power of the criminal law, not to help me or protect me, but to limit my options and opportunities for a kind of self-help that seems harmless to others and possibly very beneficial to me.

The purpose of the above discussion was not to suggest that all is conceptually and morally acceptable in the criminal law as we now find it—that current divisions between criminal and civil (private) remedies are engraved in stone and beyond challenge and that any correct philosophical account of criminality must thus be consistent with the existing divisions. I do not believe this for a moment and am certain that some radical rethinking here is called for. My point has been much more modest—namely, to suggest that the issue of criminalization just may be too complex to be settled simply by trotting out the common slogans, either utilitarian or Kantian, that one so often hears. In short, such claims as "the criminal law exists to deter persons from engaging in conduct that is seriously harmful to others" or "the criminal law exists to make sure that rights violators get their just deserts" may be considerably less illuminating than they at first appear.

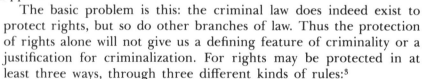

The basic problem is this: the criminal law does indeed exist to protect rights, but so do other branches of law. Thus the protection of rights alone will not give us a defining feature of criminality or a justification for criminalization. For rights may be protected in at least three ways, through three different kinds of rules:[3]

(1) *Property Rule:* My right to X (my auto, say) requires that others bargain or negotiate with me before acquiring X—that they cross the border defined by my right to X only with my consent or permission.[4]

(2) *Liability Rule:* My right to X (my security against being harmed by the reckless driving of others, say) requires that others compensate me (pay me damages) for crossing the border defined by my right to X.

(3) *Inalienability Rule:* My right to X (my life, say) is such that even I may not bargain it away and thus others are prohibited from crossing the border defined by the right even if they obtain my consent or even if they are willing to compensate me fully for any resulting harm.

How does the criminal law figure into all of this? The criminal law functions to *prohibit* and thus to go beyond requirements of mere negotiation and liability. (If you willfully injure me, you may have to pay me compensation, but you are *also* very likely to suffer criminal punishment for what you have done to me.) But prohibition is clearly more intrusive and more limiting of liberty than a requirement of negotiation or compensation. Thus, if we are lovers of liberty and as such prefer the least restrictive means, why do we not seek to respect and protect rights through means less intrusive than a system of criminal prohibition? For example, why not allow all border crossings are rights so long as adequate compensation is paid?

This question has been interestingly discussed by the philosopher Robert Nozick.[5] We cannot, he argues, allow all border crossings so long as compensation will be paid for two reasons: (1) Some injuries that people suffer are *incompensable*—how, for example, are you supposed to compensate me for killing me? If one grants the existence of inalienable rights, it must surely be a feature of them that the harms resulting from their violation are not fully compensable. (2) Some injuries are of such a nature that even the thought that one might suffer them is enough to strike terror into a potential victim, even when that victim knows that he or she will be compensated for them after the fact. How many persons, for example, would negotiate in advance to allow someone to rip off an arm and then pay money, even a great sum, in damages?

Thus we must have a criminal law (that is, a legal mechanism for *preventing* border crossings and the resulting harms) in order to keep some persons from inflicting on others injuries that are either incompensable or that strike fear into potential and actual victims. The state acts as the initiating and enforcing agent in criminal law (this is essentially how it differs from civil or private law) and what more proper role could there be for a state than the role of prohibiting incompensable injuries and reducing a climate of fear?

Nozick's analysis surely gives part of the story, but it still faces a few problems. One problem (particularly painful, I should think, for a libertarian such as Nozick who sees the state's job to be the prevention of force, theft, and fraud between citizens) is that it is unclear on his analysis how criminal laws against *theft* could be justified. Unless I am deeply crazy, I do not live in terror that my car will be stolen, and unless I have a very rare car or one to which I attach great sentimental value, I will not regard the loss of my car as an incompensable injury. Does this then mean that theft should not be a crime? Another problem is this: Nozick's claim that criminal prohibitions function to reduce terror and incompensable injuries leaves out (again, ironically for a libertarian) reasons that many would regard as clearly relevant in favor of criminalizing—namely, that respect for autonomy sometimes demands that a person's moral space not be violated without that person's *consent* (respect for property rules) and that some values are so important that they may not be compromised even with consent (respect for inalienability rules).[6]

But how far do we go with these concerns? Do we become so protective of rights and autonomy that we prohibit *all border crossings* and never allow rights violations even if compensation is paid? This would surely be too extreme. As Nozick correctly points out, we all benefit from living in a society that tolerates *risky* behavior—i.e., behavior that has some chance in resulting in harmful border crossings. Automobile driving is inherently risky, and we could certainly prevent all the harm that comes from automobile accidents by preventing (through effective criminal prohibitions) the very driving of automobiles. But note the social costs and the cost to each one of us in having our activities so radically curtailed. Thus it looks like some risky conduct here must be tolerated—i.e., it seems reasonable to criminalize only the most extreme and irresponsible automotive risk-taking (drunken driving, reckless or grossly negligent driving, intentionally running someone down with a car, etc.) and to allow the level of risk involved in normal driving so long as drivers pay compensation to those they accidentally injure.

The principle "Prohibit all harmful conduct" seems far too strong. The principle "Allow all harmful conduct so long as compensation is paid" seems far too weak. Thus we do not yet have some simple principle that will answer our question of when to protect rights through criminal prohibition and when to protect rights through civil or private legal means.

In addition to the particular insights of his approach, Nozick raises one general issue that may provide us with some help in this area. Nozick has rightly seen that the problem of criminalization and punishment must be located within the context of one of the basic questions of social and political philosophy: why is it justified to have states or governments at all (why not anarchy?) and what *essential* tasks are a part of their justified function? The state is the complaining party in a criminal action (e.g., *U.S.* v. *Jones*, or *Arizona* v. *Smith*) and in a sense views itself as the injured party. Thus unlike the case in private or civil actions (e.g., *Jones* v. *Smith*), the concern of the state is not to address injuries to individuals per se but only to address such injuries to the degree that they also constitute attacks against the state. (This explains why the state will often choose to prosecute crimes in which, as is sometimes the case in treason, there is no personal victim, or in cases where there is a personal victim, as in some instances of child molestation, but the victim would prefer that the prosecution not go forward.) It thus might help in our search for the essence of criminalization if we attempted to understand just what it means to talk of attacking the state or the government over and above attacking an individual. Then we might be able to get a handle on what it means to say that a state interest (perhaps a compelling state interest) dictates the use of criminalization to protect a certain right rather than, say, allowing the right to be protected through the private or civil mechanism of tort liability—e.g., through an award of damages.

We must be careful, in talking about the state as the complaining and injured party in a criminal action, not to allow ourselves to be charmed into the metaphysical weirdness of imagining the state as a kind of abstract entity, a kind of Absolute Person with a personality and values to which the personalities and values of actual persons are merely subordinate. On that road lies Fascism. On the other hand, the idea of harming the state cannot simply mean harming one or several or even many of those who are citizens of the state; if this were the case, we could not account for the fact that (as massive class action tort suits show) the state sometimes allows harm to even great numbers of citizens to be dealt with noncriminally, as a civil or private legal matter. This is why it is useless to intone as many do that the essential function of the criminal law is to express and reinforce a society's moral seriousness about certain public rules of civilized behavior. For there are noncriminal ways of doing that same thing—e.g., enforcing massive damage judgments against those who violate the rule (surely a public rule of civilized life) that condemns the defamation of persons.[7]

What is harm to the state? What is the kind of harm with which it is the job of the criminal law to deal? As a start toward answering this question, let us ask ourselves another question (a familiar one from social contract theory): If a group of persons living in competitive proximity to each other did not have a state or government, what good reasons might they have for *forming* a state or government and accepting the resulting lack of liberty that this would entail?[8] The obvious initial answer seems to be *self-protection*—protection of these persons from outside threats (national defense) and from inside threats from the violent and abusive persons in their midst (police power). These goals, definitive of even a minimal state, will surely strike them as compelling. But remember that they originally enjoyed total liberty and thus, even though they see it is rational to sacrifice some liberty for the protection that a state can offer, they will wish to sacrifice no more than is absolutely necessary—i.e., they will desire that the least restrictive means be employed in pursuit of protection. If we think of the state as an organization we might *hire* to do a certain job for us, the job might well be this: to protect us from external and internal threats to our rights by means that are only as intrusive of our rights to the degree absolutely necessary for the job.[9] We will not want total protection but rather what might be thought of as an *optimal* level of protection—i.e., a level of protection against non-government threats such that, if the government provided a greater level of protection, its own threats to our rights would be greater than those against which we originally sought protection.[10]

What does this excursion into social and political philosophy have so do with criminalization? Simply this: Instead of speaking of crime as harm to the state, it might be better to think of crime as an invasion by an individual into an area of decisionmaking and action that is properly reserved to the state as a part of its necessary job that we, as its "clients," might think of ourselves as "hiring" it to do. We "hire" the state to protect rights and we want our rights protected in the least intrusive way. What this suggests is that the state would initially seek to protect rights through what was earlier referred to as property rules, which require that others cross the borders defined by my rights only by negotiating for my consent. But rights protection through property rules will not always work for this reason: The costs of negotiating with all possible victims of all possible kinds of rights violations would be socially prohibitive and would itself lead to massive rights curtailment. What would my right to drive a car come to if I and all other drivers had to identify all the possible accident victims that might arise from driving and negotiate with each of them in advance what we would have to pay for the privilege of putting them at accident risk? And what would happen if even one of them refused to make a deal or held out through tough negotiating strategy for a prohibitively high price?

Thus, for these reasons, we will have to protect some rights with what was previously called liability rules—rules requiring the payment of adequate compensation if a border crossing results in harm or damage. Thus the state will now lay out liability rules as well as property rules. Will this then be enough? Unfortunately (from the point of view of liberty) the answer to this question is no. Two points are worth making here: (1) as previously noted, we might regard some values as so great (and some threats as so fearful) that we might want a level of protection greater than could be provided by either property or liability rules and (2) even in those cases where we are happy with a system of property and liability rules, how do we guarantee that an individual will not seek to convert a property rule into a liability rule (e.g., steal my car and then see if I am willing to bear the cost and uncertainty and trouble of tracking him down, suing him for damages, and trying to collect my compensation)? Thus the state's job of protecting our rights might require a system of criminal prohibition and punishment in two sorts of cases: (1) cases where private protection of rights (property and liability rules) is inadequate to the rights in question (cases we might protect with inalienability rules), and (2) cases where the established structures and mechanisms of private protection will work only if individuals are given some strong incentive for compliance with those structures over and above the general rational desirability of those structures.

Perceived rational desirability will be enough to guarantee voluntary compliance with the structures on the part of most persons, but if all persons could be counted on in this way, the fears that provoked the need for the state in the first place would never have arisen. Thus some mechanism of coerced or nonvoluntary compliance will be essential to provide the proper incentives. The threat of criminal punishment will be such an incentive. A liberty-protecting state, in short, will always establish a preference for protecting rights through private means; it will adopt criminal prohibition only in those cases where it seems reasonable to believe that private means will be insufficient. On this model, then, the criminal, in addition to the harm he does to an individual victim, attacks the basic structure of society through bypassing its established structures of rights protection (its transaction structures, to use the language of economists) and thus by presuming, as it were, to make his own rules with respect to these matters.[11] It is not so much that he harms or injures the state, then, as that he usurps the legitimate authority of the state.[12] That is why the state sees it as its job to prosecute him regardless of the presence or desires of personal victims.

We perhaps now have at least the beginning of an answer to our earlier puzzle: why are some very serious harms (e.g., defamation) dealt with in the private law and some comparatively trivial harms (e.g., auto theft) dealt with as criminal matters? The answer might be this: Few structures are more important to a complex society than its established mechanisms for economic exchange, for if those mechanisms became unglued, society itself would very likely become unglued. Having established a certain efficient mechanism (negotiated sale) for the exchange of automobiles and other property, the state would be shirking its duty if it allowed persons to attempt to bypass those rules and set their own rules for how property could be transferred. Thus, in criminalizing auto theft, the state is acting to protect its established and efficient mechanism of economic exchange. (In criminalizing murder, it may be acting to protect its established judgment that the value of life lies beyond the domain of economic calculation and that threats and harm to life cannot adequately be dealt with by the after-the-fact remedy of compensation.)

The situation might be different, however, with respect to defamation for three reasons: (1) While our society is perhaps in part held together by an established economic system, it is not (perhaps alas) held together by a system of reputational respect. Assaults on reputations may certainly harm individuals, but—except in certain cases—they probably do little harm to the fabric of society. (2) In the vast majority of cases, the private remedy of a tort suit probably works effectively to protect reputational rights. Even if damage to reputation cannot be compensated in purely economic terms, the very winning of a libel suit functions to vindicate one's reputation, and even if it takes the threat of punishment to deter persons from auto theft, the threat of being sued for defamation might be sufficient to protect reputations against most serious acts of libel and slander. (3) Even in the cases where the threat to reputation may do social harm (e.g., where it affects the reputations of national political leaders) or where the threat of civil damages is insufficient to vindicate a reputation, the state's task of protecting an entire *system* of rights might still condemn criminalization as too drastic a state response. Defamation is, after all, *expression,* and the rights of free speech and publication are clearly among those rights that it is the job of the state (at least "our" state) to protect as fundamental.[13] Accordingly the desire to avoid undue inhibition of the free expression of ideas might well prompt the state to settle for less than fully effective methods of protecting reputation. Nothing comparable, however, seems at stake in the case of auto theft. There is no fundamental right to acquire an automobile and there are powerfully good reasons to inhibit attempts on the part of individuals to set up their own extralegal mechanisms of property exchange. Thus: there are several reasons why the state is much more free to pursue protection of property rights against theft than it is free to pursue protection against expressed threats to reputation. In the area of theft, the state is thus reasonably free to use criminal penalties if that is the only way it can effectively protect those rights it is its job to protect.

This section has only scratched the surface of the extremely complex problems of criminalization and the rationale for specific criminal offenses. More puzzles have been thrown up and more tentative suggestions made than have final solutions been offered, and the reader might well be left with the thought that the decision "to criminalize or not to criminalize" is a decision of staggering uncertainty. I hope this is the result. Many persons—particularly in America—are overly charmed by simplistic slogans (e.g., "the criminal law protects good people from bad people") and thus fail to see the many competing values and considerations at stake in the decision to criminalize. If this section has helped the reader to see that the thought pattern "this conduct is bad so let's pass a criminal law against it" is absurdly simpleminded, then the way to serious thought about crime and punishment may well be opened.

UTILITARIANISM AND DETERRENCE

Criminal punishment may be defined as the infliction by state authority of a consequence normally regarded as an evil (e.g., death or imprisonment) on an individual found to be legally guilty of a crime.[14] So described, it is obvious that punishment describes a state of affairs that stands in need of justification. Given our discussion in the previous section, it seems obvious what the justification must be—namely, that the punishment is necessary in order to prevent rights violations in those cases where private means of enforcement would be ineffective. There is, however, one problem with this: If an individual has been found guilty of a crime, this presumably means that he has *already* invaded someone's rights. So is it not a little late to talk about prevention? One basic question about punishment is (to use the language of H. L. A. Hart) to determine its "general justifying aim" or the reason why we have a practice of punishment at all.[15] And how can such a general justifying aim be prevention, since state punishment waits until a crime has already occurred?

To justify the practice of punishment in terms of the prevention of rights violations (crime control) is to justify punishment in terms of its generally good social consequences. It is thus to give either a traditional utilitarian justification or a teleology of rights justification for punishment. Punishment is justified either to make the majority secure and thus happy or to maximize rights protection or both. (To avoid tedious repetition, the term "utilitarian" will be used to cover both of these in the remainder of this chapter unless the contrary is explicitly noted.) While it is of course true that punishment of Jones for his commission of crime *C* cannot prevent the occurrence of *C* (since *C* has already occurred), punishment of Jones for *C* might prevent *other* crimes in one or more of the following ways: (1) the experience of being punished might affect Jones in such a way that the fear of future punishment will deter him from committing more crimes in the future. This is called *special* deterrence. (2) When others know that Jones has been punished (when he has been used as an example), they might take the threat of state punishment more seriously and thus might be less inclined because of their increased fear to engage in criminal conduct. This is called *general* deterrence.[16] (3) Even if Jones and others will not be deterred by Jones's punishment, certain methods of punishment (e.g., incarceration) will incapacitate Jones and keep him out of circulation so that he will not be free to prey on others again. This justification may strike us as particularly persuasive for highly violent individuals. (4) While punishment itself is unlikely to reform or rehabilitate Jones (unless this simply means special deterrence), certain methods of punishment might provide the state with the opportunity to do reformative or rehabilitative things for Jones while he is in the state's "clutches."[17] If Jones was driven to steal out of poverty bred by unemployment, for example, the state might use a period of incarceration to offer Jones the opportunity to learn a trade and in this way help in his reform or rehabilitation.

While incapacitation and reform may sometimes figure in the justification of punishment, *deterrence* has always been the mainstay of the utilitarian position. Think of a system of punishment, the utilitarian argues, as a kind of price system on conduct.[18] The criminal statutes set price tags on particular kinds of antisocial behavior in the hope that the vast majority of persons will find the price too high to pay. Those persons who do commit crimes and thus show a willingness to pay the price (or, more likely, a failure to calculate in a rational way the risks they were running) must be punished to show, as Justice Holmes said, that "the law keeps its promises." Every time this is done, according to the deterrence theorist, the state reinforces the credibility of its deterrence threat and maintains or even strengthens its "price system" on conduct and the incentives and disincentives built into that system.

This system will not, of course, work perfectly. Some potential criminals do not weigh the costs and benefits of their contemplated conduct in a rational way, others (sometimes correctly, alas) believe that they will be smart enough (or the system will be inefficient enough) that the risk of their detection and conviction will be small, and still others will desire the criminal conduct to such an idiosyncratically high degree that they will be willing to pay a price for it that normal persons would avoid. Such failures can be minimized in certain ways (e.g., through increased police efficiency to increase the probability of detection), but the system will never be perfect. Nor should it be. Society has other important goals besides deterring crime, and the costs in trouble, money, and threats to freedom posed by a perfectly effective crime control apparatus would clearly outweigh the benefits.

(Even the Gestapo was not a perfectly effective crime control apparatus. Would one like a police agency even more costly and intrusive and powerful?)

Also, it is important to remember that crimes differ in their gravity. The utilitarian seeks to accept the great evil of punishment only in those cases where this evil prevents an even greater evil. So what if it should turn out that (because of some psychological quirk) public indecent exposure could be effectively deterred only by a certainty of life imprisonment? Given the trivial social harm caused by indecent exposure, the utilitarian would hardly regard its prevention as important enough to justify inflicting great hardship on the exhibitionist or having society bear the great cost of effective deterrence here. Law enforcement resources could simply be spent in other ways far more likely to maximize the general welfare or far more likely to protect rights more fundamental than the right (if it even is a right) not to be exposed involuntarily to the genitalia of another.[19]

The utilitarian answer on the justification of punishment thus seems simple and persuasive: We criminalize conduct and thus render that conduct liable to punishment in those cases where such action is necessary in order to deter persons from rights violations that either cannot or should not be protected in a purely private way. We make the deterrent as effective as possible (by increasing its severity, its certainty, etc.) in so far as this does not involve taking steps that would themselves be undesirable on utilitarian grounds—e.g., creating totalitarian law enforcement agencies, causing the criminal more harm than his criminality is likely to cause society, etc. Though this system will not be perfectly effective in preventing crime, it will be the most effective system compatible with the kind of general political institutions (e.g., free institutions) that may be defended on utilitarian grounds. Even a deterrence system itself respects freedom, for it exists (in the same way a price system does) by giving the potential criminal a *choice*—the choice of avoiding the criminal sanction by choosing to avoid the commission of the crime.

KANTIANISM AND RETRIBUTION

Deterrence of criminal conduct seems to constitute an excellent justification for punishment and seems to identify, from a generally utilitarian perspective, a state interest in punishing that surely counts as compelling. The matter seems noncontroversial. But is it? Consider the following passage from Immanuel Kant:

Judicial punishment can never be used merely as a means to promote some other good for the criminal himself or for society, but instead it must in all cases be imposed on a person solely on the ground that he has committed a crime; for a human being can never be confused with the objects of the law of things. . . . He must first be found to be deserving of punishment before any consideration can be given to the utility of this punishment for himself or his fellow citizens. . . . The law concerning punishment is a categorical imperative, and woe to him who rummages around in the winding paths of a theory of happiness looking for some advantage to be gained by releasing the criminal from punishment or by reducing the amount of it. . . . Even if civil society were to dissolve itself by common agreement of all its members (for example, if the people inhabiting an island decided to separate and disperse themselves around the world), the last murderer remaining in prison must be executed, so that everyone will duly receive what his actions are worth and so that the bloodguilt thereof will not be fixed on the people because they failed to insist on carrying out the punishment; for if they fail to do so, they may be regarded as accomplices in this public violation of legal justice.[20]

This passage (particularly the part about "bloodguilt") will strike many readers as positively creepy—as some piece of long repressed vindictiveness boiling up from the psychological depths of our Neanderthal past. If one recalls the general structure of Kant's ethical theory, however, one can give an interpretation to the passage that will reveal it as, at the very least, offering a valuable corrective to a totally utilitarian outlook on crime and punishment.

Kant is concerned to defend a theory of punishment that is generally called *retributivism,* and Kant (with all other sensible retributivists) would stress that a commitment to retribution is quite different from a commitment to such unattractive things as revenge or vindictiveness. These latter responses to wrongdoing are *personal* responses to perceived wrongs to oneself and motivated by a concern with one's own self-regard or self-respect. The narrow and personal nature of this concern is revealed in the fact that persons so motivated often seek to take personal and extralegal steps to redress their perceived wrongs. The demand for punishment as retribution is quite different, however, for it grows out of respect for the law (not simply oneself), the demand that attacks against the law (not simply against oneself) be taken seriously, and the belief that the only morally acceptable way to deal with such attacks is in terms of a theory based on *justice* or respect for *rights* (and not utility) as a primary value.

The retributive theory of punishment, then, should be understood as a theory that seeks to justify punishment, not in terms of social utility, but in terms of *this* cluster of moral concepts: rights, desert, merit, moral responsibility, and justice. (Different versions of retributivism differ in which of these concepts they take as primary and the analyses they give for these concepts.) Thus the retributivist seeks, not primarily for the socially useful punishment, but for the *just* punishment, the punishment that the criminal (given his wrongdoing) *deserves* or *merits,* the punishment that the society has a *right* to inflict and the criminal a *right* to demand.

To see that there might be some merit in the retributivist proposal, we might follow Edmund Pincoff's suggestion and ask ourselves this question: How might we justify punishment, not to the bulk of society, but to the *criminal himself*?[21] If we take seriously the Kantian demand that persons (including persons convicted of a crime) are owed basic respect, then surely we owe it to them that our harsh treatment of them can be justified by reasons that they (in so far as they are rational beings) can understand and accept. Here is where the utilitarian theory seems to be in trouble, for it must say this to the criminal: "We are punishing you in order to use you as an example to others and thereby deter crime." But surely the criminal can at this point well ask this question: "What gives you the right to use me in this way?" If he has read some Kant, the criminal might even put the point in this way: "Are you not simply proposing to use me as a means only, as an instrument toward the social good; and do I not have, as a rational being, a right not to be so used?" Since he is now on a roll (and if we are patient enough to allow him to engage in philosophical agumentation), the criminal might even say this: "If the sole reason you have a practice of punishment is to pursue the utilitarian goal of crime control, then why not simply dispense with a guilt requirement and start punishing the innocent, or those who are insane or lack the mental states (e.g., intention) normally required for criminal culpability, or simply use preventive detention for those you think might commit crime? Start scapegoating people. That ought to scare the hell out of potential criminals!"

A portion of this challenge can be met. Even a Kantian, for example, might say that we acquire the right to use the criminal as a means because he has forfeited his right not to be so used through his act of so using others.[22] "You brought this on yourself by your own wrongful choices" certainly is something that we could say to the criminal himself in justification of our punishing him. This line of reasoning would, however, work only for a system of punishment that retained a guilt requirement; for the innocent have certainly done nothing to forfeit their rights in this way. But can the utilitarian successfully justify a guilt requirement? Can the utilitarian justify a prohibition against scapegoating? We know from Chapter 2 how the utilitarian will attempt to meet these challenges. He will have to admit that, in particular cases, deterrence values (particularly general deterrence values) could be served by punishing the innocent. But what would it be like, he will ask, if we adopted such punishment as a general practice—i.e., felt free to use the state's apparatus of criminal law to inflict punishment on a person any time it was believed that a balance of good over bad consequences would flow from so doing? Clearly we would be designing a society of such radical unpredictability that neither freedom nor the general welfare could survive in it. Given a guilt requirement, each citizen can predict with a reasonably high degree of accuracy his or her chances of being punished, for it is reasonable to believe that the safe way to avoid punishment is to avoid crime and therefore not become guilty.

On our other model, however, citizens would have no such basis of prediction; thus it would cause social havoc and would, on such a grand scale, fail even as a general deterrence device. It would be, as John Rawls has argued, like a price system in which persons were never told the price of any commodity until they had already irrevocably purchased it.[23] Just as this kind of price system could not control economic behavior in a rationally predictable way, so would a system allowing the punishment of the innocent fail to control criminal behavior in a rationally predictable way. Thus, on purely rule-ulitarian grounds, a requirement that criminal guilt be a necessary condition for criminal punishment can be defended and, insofar as this is the point being made by Kant, it can be accepted without indulging in a discussion of rights as having primary value.

There is, however, (as we also noted in Chapter 2) a problem with this approach—namely, it will function successfully to condemn the *widespread* punishment of the innocent, but it will not function to condemn such punishment if it is done with sufficient selectivity or with sufficient isolation that the general level of social anxiety or unpredictability does not increase. The Kantian, however, will seek to condemn the punishment of the innocent even in these circumstances (even if done only once!) and will thus argue that the utilitarian has not given the correct reason (or at least the only reason) against punishment of the innocent. Think again, the Kantian retributivist will say, of how we would justify punishment to a particular criminal. Could we say this: "We are justified in punishing you, even though you are innocent, because we have devised a way to insulate the rest of society from concerns that such punishment would otherwise generate"? Or even this: "Our decision not to punish you is not based on any respect for you as a person (any consideration of what you, in justice, deserve) but simply on our belief that everyone else in society would be made terribly twitchy if we did punish you"? Surely, the Kantian retributivist will argue, we must at the very least accept this as an absolute side-constraint on the pursuit of the utilitarian

persons who have already violated our rights but with the question of how to prevent persons from violating our rights in the first place. Thus it would seem that deterrence will always be the dominant general justifying aim of punishment, with retribution—even on a sophisticated theory of retribution—being at most a secondary aim. Where the respect-based theory of retribution will always have a valuable role, however, is as an absolute side-constraint on the pursuit of utilitarian deterrence. As such it will remind us that, in our zeal to pursue the social safety that we hope will flow from an effective system of deterrence, we must not be willing to buy this benefit by treating criminals more harshly than they deserve to be treated. In short, even the criminal is owed the level of respect that is involved in his being a person.

MENTAL STATES, EXCUSES, AND STRICT LIABILITY

If we agree that we shall adopt a practice of punishment for those guilty of crime, we shall still have to decide on criteria for the determination of who shall count as guilty of a crime. That is, we need to supplement our theory of punishment with a theory of *culpability* or *responsibility*. Primitive cultures often take a short course with this issue and regard as guilty anyone who stands in an important causal relation to a resulting injury; for these cultures are willing to hold people responsible for injury in the same sense in which we might say that a slippery road is responsible for an accident—i.e., no sense of agency, choice, or intention is involved at all. Those familiar with Sophocles's drama *Oedipus Rex* have read a description of such a culture. Oedipus kills his father (mistaking him for a robber on the road) and has sexual relations with his mother (not realizing it is his mother). With respect to both actions and the resulting injuries (polluted land and destroyed crops, according to the beliefs of his fellow Thebans), Oedipus acted in an ignorance that was totally not his fault—i.e., in neither case did he have any way of knowing the true nature of what he was doing. This does not matter in the least to his fellow Thebans, however, who brand him as a criminal and banish him from the land.

This is, of course, very different from our own system of criminal responsibility. Most crimes have among their material or defining elements certain mental states or character defects, such as intention or purpose, knowledge, recklessness, or negligence.[27] Murder in the first degree, for example, is not simply the performance of an action that causally results in the death of another human being; it is killing another human being with premeditation or malice aforethought— i.e., with the intention or conscious object of killing that person. Absent this required mental state, the homicide will not be murder but will be of some lesser degree (e.g., manslaughter) for which a lesser punishment is prescribed. Thus, in order to prove murder, the state has the burden of proving, among other things, that the accused acted with the appropriate mental state. Such mental state requirements are usually called *mens rea* (very loosely: "guilty mind") requirements, and they are present in the definition of all but a very few crimes in our system.[28]

In addition to a requirement of certain specified mental states, our system also allows a variety of *excuses*—ways of getting the individual "off the hook" even if the individual performed what would normally be a criminal act with the requisite mental states. Insanity is a good example of such an excuse. Certain kinds of insanity render an individual incapable of having the mental state required for the commission of the offense, and thus the presence of such insanity negates the *mens rea* condition. For example: If Jones is so delusional that he thinks that he is sawing a loaf of bread into slices when he is in fact sawing a person into slices, then Jones is clearly not acting with malice aforethought, and thus, though we would no doubt want to take steps to protect ourselves against Jones (commitment to a mental institution, perhaps) it would be odd to hold him responsible and demand that he be punished. It is not always the case that insanity negates *mens rea*, however. If what some psychiatrists say about klep- tomania is true, then individuals afflicted with this mental disorder steal with the full knowledge that they are stealing; they steal on purpose. However, so the psychiatric claim goes, these persons are *compelled* to steal; they act under the influence of an *irresistible impulse*. (They would steal even if a policeman was standing at their shoulders, perhaps.) This is the nature of their insanity, and it renders their acts of theft not their fault. If such individuals live in a jurisdiction where the formulation of the insanity defense allows, and if a jury believes these claims (often supported by "expert" psychiatric testimony), then these individuals will be excused from responsibility for their acts of theft.[29]

Let us describe the system operative in Thebes during the time of Oedipus as a *strict liability* system. Liability is strict in the sense that it does not depend upon mental states or character defects and does not allow excuses—does not, in short, require that the person who caused the harm by in any sense morally at fault for what was done. (Justice Holmes said that even a dog will draw a distinction between being kicked on purpose and being tripped over accidentally. The strict liability system might draw the same distinction as the dog, but it will not give that distinction any legal significance. Behavior causally resulting in harm is all that matters.) Let us call a system such as our own an *excusing* system. Forgeting for a moment what particular mental states we might want to require or what particular excuses we might want to allow (space does not allow for this anyway), let us explore one general question: Is there any reason for regarding an excusing system as preferable (morally, rationally) to a strict liability system? Most of us are repelled at what we take to be the primitive barbarity of the system described in the Sophocles play and are inclined to regard our own system as clearly the more justified of the two. But can this preference be defended?

If the primary purpose of a system of punishment is deterrence, it might seem that a strict liability system fails simply on this ground. For surely only a responsible person (one thinking about what he is doing, choosing, acting intentionally, etc.) can do the kind of calculating required to make deterrence effective. Thus punishing a person who is not at fault might appear to have no deterrence value. This thought, however, is mistaken. While it might be the case that strict liability could have very little specific deterrence value, it might have con- siderable general deterrence (or general crime control) value.[30] This is so for two reasons: (1) The knowledge that one is living in a strict liability system might tend to make citizens meticulously careful and thereby reduce the frequency of antisocial acts, might cause them to avoid whole areas of action. (Where statutory rape is a strict liability offense, then this might incline adult males to steer clear of sexual encounters with any woman who is not clearly adult.) (2) Every time one allows an excuse into the system or requires another mental state as an element of criminality, one creates another rule to be abused and another element for an already overtaxed prosecution to prove. Thus the probability that truly guilty and dangerous persons will be set free increases in an excusing system. Because of this, advocates of strong crime control and deterrence have reason to believe that strict liability might be a viable option for them. Why else, indeed, would anyone advocate strict liability?

There is, in fact, one other reason sometimes offered in favor of strict criminal liability, not so much a positive reason in its favor but a negative reason against the excusing system. According to one line of thought, our preference for an excusing system rests upon an outdated and prescientific view of human behavior. All the talk about free choice, responsibility, and the importance of mental states fails, according to this view, to reflect what we now know—namely, that causal determinism is true (there is a causal explanation for everything we do) and we are simply complex mechanisms working out our programmed natures. So let us stop all the superstitious talk about fault and responsibility and confine ourselves to the useful task of trying to reduce the harm that some mechanisms do to other mechanisms.

At this point (as usual), H. L. A. Hart makes a valuable contribution to the discussion.[31] Hart seeks to make a case against a system of strict criminal liability (and thus in favor of an excusing system) that (a) does not deny that it could have some general deterrence value, and (b) is compatible with determinism. Hart's point (a generally rule-utilitarian one) is basically this: whatever deterrence value that a system of strict liability might produce, it would be bought at too high a price because it would compromise the ability of the society that employs it to maintain a general scheme of institutions that would promote human welfare.

How might this be so? Hart asks that we grant him three noncontroversial points: (1) Human beings make choices. (2) Human beings value or take satisfaction in making choices. (3) Human beings in general value or take satisfaction in having their destinies be a function of their choices. (Determinism will not affect the truth of these claims; for determinism is the view that everything we do—including making choices—is caused, not the view that we do not make choices or that so doing does not satisfy us.) Now an excuse system, unlike a strict liability system, places a premium on respecting choices. It is, in a sense, a choice system. (Doing wrong by choice is a great part of what we mean by acting with moral fault.) As a choice system, an excuse system gives us great predictability over our lives with respect to the state for it allows us to avoid criminal sanctions and the fear of such sanctions simply by avoiding the choices that would lead to criminal conduct. A strict liability system will punish us even when our harmful conduct is not a result of choice, however, and thus the only way to avoid a serious risk of criminal punishment in such a system would be to live lives so cautious or curtailed that the meaning and satisfactions of liberty (our exercise of other choices) would be lost. How could Oedipus have avoided crime? Only by staying in his home, never traveling, never marrying, never doing any of the things that make human life worth living. Surely this is too big a price to pay simply for a little extra crime control.

Hart has made an important point here, but he has not, as he himself realizes, told the whole story.[32] As we have noted before with rule-utilitarian arguments of this nature, they function well to condemn general or widespread (and thus socially disruptive) injustice, but they seem too weak to condemn selective injustice—something that Kant (and Hart also) wants to condemn. There is simply something unjust or unfair about punishing the innocent, and there is a sense in which a person who lacks all culpable mental states (or has a valid excuse) is innocent. Justice demands individuation—that like cases be treated like and that different cases be treated differently. And it seems elemental that there is a significant moral difference between a person who kills maliciously and one who kills accidentally, a difference brought out if one tries to imagine what one could say to a person who accidentally caused a death to justify treating him as the same as one who killed with malice. It seems unfair not to draw the distinction; for one way to fail to respect persons as persons is to fail to see what makes for individual and morally relevant differences among them.

But do defenders of strict criminal liability deny that it is unfair? I think not. Contemporary defenders of strict liability argue in this way: While it would certainly be socially disturbing to make strict liability our dominant standard for criminal guilt, there are selected areas of conduct where such a standard of liability does serve social utility.[33] For example: Given the great harm that can come to society if persons ship adulterated food in interstate commerce, it is useful to take drastic steps to deter persons who are not positively obsessed with cleanliness from entering this line of work.[34] Knowing that it is an area of work governed by strict liability ought to deter all but the most diligent—the very goal we seek here. Some unfairness may result (even the most conscientious person will sometimes have an accident), but the unfairness is morally tolerable. This is not simply because of the utilitarian values, however, but also because at an ultimate level fairness is served in the process because (1) all persons have fair warning not to enter this line of work unless they are prepared to accept strict liability; they knowingly accept this risk; and (2) not being able to run a food-processing plant is not to be cut off from any fundamental rights, not to be cut off from what makes life meaningful or worth living.

Widespread strict liability would destroy meaningful lives because it would force us to be overly cautious in areas (e.g., travel, pursuing ordinary activities, etc.) where we should not be overly cautious. But this is not true for all areas of social activity. Thus, in order to prevent great harm, what is ultimately the matter with society saying this: "Certain areas of activity (food processing, banking, sexual experimentation with children) have great potential for harm. Since individuals do not have fundamental rights to do these things and since there is no social value in having people casually experiment in these areas (indeed much potential social harm), then what is wrong with making the price for entry into these selected areas a willingness to risk strict liability prosecution? The rule here is not 'You try your very best to prevent harm' but is rather 'You *succeed* in preventing harm.' If you are not a careful and confident enough person to live with this rule, then simply do something else with your life and with your time. Even if one function of the criminal law is to express society's moral condemnation for certain acts and thereby stigmatize the criminal, a person who lacks the wisdom to heed the warning that he stay out of a dangerous area of conduct for which he is unsuited may not be an unfitting object for such ostracism."

This suggestion is fascinating and requires a more complex response than present space limitations allow. One thing can be said, however: To deal with this case for selective strict criminal liability, something more is needed than simply a knee-jerk liberal grumbling about the "unfairness of it all." For the sophisticated defender does not deny that it is unfair but rather argues that it is a morally and socially tolerable unfairness, and that is a more complex claim to assess.

Where are we at this point? I suppose it is safe to say (with Hart) that strict criminal liability is unfair and, if widespread, ultimately buys its deterrence efficacy at the price of the general welfare. Thus we will be rational in adopting an excusing system rather than a strict liability system. We will, however, at least be willing to consider arguments in favor of limited strict criminal liability of the kind outlined above—where strict liability is limited to areas of conduct having the potential for adverse affect on the public welfare and where it at least involves the fairness of advance warning.

Before closing this section, a brief comment on therapy as an alternative to punishment is perhaps in order.[35] Under the influence of psychiatry and the growth of the behavioral sciences—the same influences that expanded *mens rea* requirements and the insanity defense—some have argued that we should drop punishment entirely and replace it with a system of therapy: psychoanalysis, behavior modification, drugs, brain surgery, or whatever else is trendy at the time. "Criminals are sick persons who should be treated," goes the refrain, "not wrongdoers who should be punished. This will be good for them (they will be made well) and good for society (since we will be better protected)."

This has a persuasive ring to it; for it seems scientific (it comes from psychiatry and psychology), humanitarian (who can object to making people well, curing them from illnesses?), and socially hopeful (we shall get social deviants back on the road to social usefulness and away from dangerous acts). It sounds as if everybody will win, and it is not surprising that it spawned a very influential movement in

American criminal law reform. Punishment is a terrible practice, and all sensitive persons will surely want to at least consider alternatives to it.[36]

This movement toward therapy as an alternative to all punishment has tended to dissipate in recent years. This has been in part due to bad reasons: a worry that successful therapy might not be a "quick fix" but might cost more money than we want to spend on such matters and a general attitude of "warehouse the bastards!" characteristic of the right-wing mental climate of the present age. The movement is generally dead even among thoughtful intellectuals of the legal and therapeutic professions, however, and this is no doubt because the following problems with the suggestion have been noted:

(1) There is no such thing as the typical criminal, and it is thus absurd to suppose that all are in some way sick. To be a criminal is simply to be in violation of some criminal statute. Thus such persons as Gandhi and Martin Luther King, Jr., were, as civil disobedients, criminals. Were they sick? Would we presume to rehabilitate them through therapy? To label criminals as "mentally ill" is more often to put an ideological badge on them than it is to do scientific diagnosis.

(2) For all its harshness, the criminal law is surrounded with considerable due process protections. It is an admitted evil, and thus steps are taken to protect individuals against it and its abuses. When we talk of curing illness, however, the benevolent rhetoric may blind us to the fact that our therapy will be coercive, will involve confining people against their wills in institutions. And the mere fact that we call these institutions "hospitals" instead of "prisons" should not blind us to the fact that deprivation of liberty is still involved. Unfortunately, the deprivation of liberty involved in mental hospitalization has been (and still is, though to a lesser degree than in the past) generally unrestrained by due process guarantees. Release is based, not on when you have done your prescribed time, but on whether some behavioral "expert" decides you are well and safe. And things that could never be done to you as punishment can be done as therapy, for we have no constitutional doctrine of cruel and unusual therapy. As the use of state psychiatry in the Soviet Union has shown, the totalitarian implications of such a social movement are enormous and frightening.

(3) All this violation of due process is done in the name of protecting us from dangerous people, but it is unclear that psychiatrists are any better able than the rest of us to predict dangerousness and eliminate it in morally acceptable ways. The claims of behavioral science here may be more hope than fact.

(4) To judge a person as a wrongdoer and to demand his or her punishment is to take that person seriously as a responsible, autonomous

human being. It is, on the other hand, degrading to say of such a person that he or she is sick, not responsible for what was done, and to be pitied and cared for. This is a way of not taking the person or what that person has done seriously, much as we fail to take with moral seriousness the trouble caused by animals, small children, or idiots. We must say this of some social deviants for some of them really are disturbed and nonresponsible for what they do. But to say this of all wrongdoers is to adopt a general attitude toward human beings that might undercut our moral specialness and ultimately our rights. It is thus an attitude we should adopt with considerable reluctance—i.e., only after powerful arguments (not yet forthcoming) and not simply in response to some trendy social movement.[37]

CHOOSING THE PROPER PUNISHMENT: IS DEATH CRUEL AND UNUSUAL?[38]

Excessive bail shall not be required, nor excessive fines imposed, nor cruel and unusual punishments inflicted.

> Eighth Amendment
> Constitution of the United
> States of America

I have no pleasure in the death of the wicked; but that the wicked turn from his way and live.

> Ezekiel XXXII, 11

Let us suppose that we regard the practice of punishment as justified and that we believe that we have adopted justified standards and procedures for judging criminal culpability. This still leaves open the question of what punishment it is proper to select (either by statute or judicial discretion) for particular classes of offenses and particular classes of offenders. We shall here be concerned with both the *kinds* of punishments that we shall employ and—with respect to the kinds of punishments where this makes sense—the *amounts* of those punishments we shall impose. (There are no varying amounts of death, for example.) Our reasons (utilitarian or Kantian) for adopting the practice of punishment and standards of culpability will, of course, largely determine our answer to the questions of kind and amount of punishment; but they will do so in complex and not always obvious ways. Also, in the United States legal system, certain punishments identified as "cruel and unusual" are ruled out in principle. In recent years all these concerns have been brought to a focus in various Supreme Court cases dealing with the death penalty and the question of whether it is cruel and unusual and thus constitutionally impermissible. The moral and legal import of our previous discussions in this chapter can thus perhaps be interestingly brought together in a discussion of this complex and controversial issue.[39]

As was argued in Chapter 2, it is instructive (at least initially and primarily) to view the bans contained in the Bill of Rights as respect-based side-constraints on permissible legislative enactments. In the language of moral theory, one can say that a legitimate constitutional bill of rights is an attempt to formulate deontological restrictions (restrictions of principle) on the pursuit of social utility through the mechanism of majoritarian democracy. These constitutional provisions tell citizens what their rights are, and thus it is wrong in principle (and not just bad policy) to pursue even laudable social goals in violation of such rights. As Ronald Dworkin has suggested, "The Constitution . . . injects an extraordinary amount of our political morality into the issue of whether a law is valid." Thus if one can mount a good argument that to treat a person in a certain way is gravely unjust or shows a lack of respect for him as a person, this is also and necessarily a good (if not always conclusive) argument that his fundamental rights are being encumbered and that it is unconstitutional to treat him in this way. The Constitution is in part a document of moral principle (institutionalized moral philosophy, if Dworkin is right) and it is in this sense antiutilitarian and antidemocratic.

If (as was previously suggested) the primary general justifying aim of punishment is deterrence of crime, then the ban on cruel and unusual punishments must come to this: a principled refusal to adopt certain punishments even if those punishments would serve the primary utilitarian goal. The end does justify the means (how else would one justify means?), but this does not entail that the end justifies *any* means. Some means will be ruled out in principle.

What does it mean to say that the infliction of some punishment *P* is wrong in *principle?* Getting at this question is to get at the core of the Eighth Amendment ban on cruel and unusual punishments. I shall argue that the best way to explicate the concept of a punishment's being wrong in principle is through a *retributive* conception and justification of punishment—i.e., a conception and justification resting upon the concepts of justice, rights and desert (and *not* social utility). Before arguing positively for this, however, let me first briefly suggest why other ways of proceeding (other conceptions of cruel and unusual) will not work.

(1) *Literalism.* The only punishments banned are those that cause great physical suffering and that happen with statistical infrequency—

i.e., punishments that satisfy the literal meaning of the words "cruel" and "unusual."[40]

This analysis, of course, is absurd. Would anyone seriously maintain that radical mutilation or disfigurement will become acceptable as a punishment if we do it under anesthetic and several times a week? Surely not. And does anyone seriously maintain that we can meet all the reasonable objections of those who believe that the death penalty violates the Eighth Amendment by suggesting that we execute painlessly and with great frequency? Physical suffering is a relevant factor and, if severe enough, may even be a sufficient condition for calling a punishment cruel. It is not, however, reasonable to regard it as a *necessary* condition—as the case of anesthetized mutilation demonstrates.

(2) *Historical Authority.* The only punishments banned are those the Founding Fathers regarded as cruel and unusual at the time the Constitution was enacted.[41]

Surely this will not do either. Suppose that the Founding Fathers banned punishment *P1* from a realization that *P1* had horrendous property *Q*. Suppose further that punishment *P2* also has horrendous property *Q* but that the Founding Fathers did not realize this. Are we then to be prohibited from attacking *P2* on constitutional grounds even though we realize that it has the very same property the Founding Fathers most wanted to oppose? This would be a strange kind of historical piety indeed. (For this reason it seems to me incorrect to suppose that the issue of whether the death penalty is cruel and unusual punishment is closed merely because the Founding Fathers did not explicitly ban it.) In my view of constitutional intent, the Founding Fathers should be viewed as intending to formulate reasonable deontological side-constraints or restrictions of principle on the pursuit of majoritarian utilitarianism. Thus, whenever we can mount a good argument for a principled restriction, we are at least not wildly far afield of their intent—as we would clearly be if we tried to interpret the Constitution in terms, not of principle, but of some notion of wise or useful or efficient social policy. The Bill of Rights is not a document of policy; it is a document attempting to give us just or fair ground rules for the pursuit of policy.[42]

(3) *Consensus.* The only punishments to be banned are those that would be rejected as inconsistent with the moral conscience of the citizens of the society at a certain time in history—namely, the time at which the Supreme Court is actually considering the constitutional permissibility of a certain punishment. This is at least part of what it means to claim that the Clause "must draw its meaning from the

evolving standards of decency that mark the progress of a maturing society."[43]

This consensus test is open to two interpretations. On one, it is irrational; on the other, it is redundant. First, let us suppose that the consensus is the sort one could discover by taking a random sample of citizen preferences—e.g., an opinion poll. It is, of course, ludicrous to regard the Constitution as sanctifying this kind of consensus. Probably the best test of what the citizens will find morally tolerable is that which is enacted by their representatives. But to say that a punishment passes the Eighth Amendment test if it has been enacted into law by a legislature is simply to abandon constitutional review of legislative enactments—i.e., to abandon the very point of having a Bill of Rights. One cannot use a right to check majoritarian excess if that right is interpreted in terms of majoritarian preference or tolerance. If tomorrow an opinion poll reveals that Americans are tolerant or even in favor of torture and mutilation, the Eighth Amendment will not have to be reinterpreted in light of that fact. Thus this kind of appeal to consensus is irrational.

A second interpretation of the consensus test is the following: A punishment will be rejected as cruel and unusual if it would be rejected as shocking the conscience, not of a majority of people selected at random, but of those citizens who are truly informed, educated, and morally sensitive.[44] There are two problems with this élitist consensus. First, it is very likely that the characterization of the élite will be circular and question-begging—i.e., we shall count as members of the relevant élite only those persons who hold the view we want to appeal to consensus to defend (opposition to the death penalty, perhaps).[45] Second, and more important, is the following problem: If genuinely enlightened persons all agree that some punishment P is evil and shocking to the conscience, it must be because of some property Q (pain, unfairness, degradation, etc.) that they have found in P. But then P is wrong because of property Q, not because of a consensus of enlightened judges. P is not wrong because there is a consensus against it: there is a consensus against it because it is wrong and can be demonstrated to be so by argument (the showing that P contains Q).[46] This reveals that the consensus is morally redundant. We can go directly to P and condemn it as wrong because we can see that it bears morally obnoxious property Q—i.e., we can be brought to see whatever it is about P that the élite sees that makes them form a consensus against it.[47]

(4) *Utilitarianism.* A punishment is to be banned as cruel and unusual only if it is more extreme than that required for the pursuit of a legitimate state end or goal. As Bentham might put it, the purpose

of punishment is to cause pain to the criminal as a means of deterring him and others from engaging in antisocial conduct, conduct that undermines the general welfare. Any pain inflicted beyond what is required for these goals is simply the gratuitous inflicting of suffering and constitutes cruelty.[48]

In American law, the utilitarian interpretation of the cruel and unusual punishment clause has taken the form of the so-called "least restrictive alternative" test—i.e., a punishment is cruel and unusual (in the sense of being "excessive"—a crucial word in the total language of the Eighth Amendment) if it is more restrictive or intrusive than necessary to accomplish a compelling state purpose.[49] For example: Capital punishment will be cruel and unusual if the same compelling state purpose (deterrence of murder, say) could be accomplished with a less restrictive or intrusive punishment—e.g., long-term imprisonment.

There is insight in this test, and it can be reformulated in retributive language so as to represent a demand of justice rather than utility. For example, I shall later suggest that "excessive" can be interpreted as "lacking a reasonable *proportionality* to the seriousness of the offense"—where the compelling state purpose is conceived to be, not simply deterring murder, but also insuring that the punishment for murder will not exceed a just proportionality to the gravity of murder. And so, too, for other crimes and punishments.[50] When interpreted in a strictly utilitarian manner, however, the test simply will not work as an interpretation of the Eighth Amendment for one very simple reason: It will not account for the paradigms, for the cases of punishments that everyone would agree are cruel and unusual–torture and mutilation. The Eighth Amendment does not tell us that torture and mutilation may be used only when required by a compelling state purpose; it tells us rather that torture and mutilation may never be used *at all*, regardless of the state's purpose. It is this absolute or side-constraint nature of a constitutional ban that no utilitarian outlook can capture.

I wish now to develop a retributive account of the concepts of cruel and unusual punishment that will account for why the ban on such punishments must be regarded as a side-constraint or principled restriction on policy. Recall that a retributive theory of punishment is one that characterizes punishment primarily in terms of the concepts of justice, rights, and desert—i.e., it is concerned with the just punishment, the punishment the criminal deserves, the punishment society has a right to inflict (and the criminal has the right to expect). In this way the theory makes central the special moral status of persons—unique individuals who, because they are autonomous and responsible creatures, must not be used for the benefit of others (as we use objects or animals) but who must be regarded as inviolate. Human persons have that special value that Kant (the most illustrious defender of retributivism) called *dignity*—a value that we respect when we address ourselves to them in terms of their unique characters and acts (i.e., what those characters and acts *deserve*) and not in terms of the general usefulness of treating them in certain ways.[51] The retributivist obviously does not want to ignore such utilitarian matters as deterrence and rehabilitation and incapacitation, but he insists that these values be pursued only *after* the values he regards as primary (rights, justice, and desert) have been secured. The intuitive idea, then, is that a cruel and unusual punishment is among the class of unjust punishments, of undeserved punishments, of punishments we have no right to inflict regardless of utility. A general theory of the *just punishment* is thus what is required.

The basic worry here is not whether punishment of any kind is ever justified; this, though highly controversial, will simply be assumed here.[52] The worry for present purposes is this: Given that we are going to punish in some way, are there certain *kinds* of punishment or certain *amounts* of punishment or certain *procedures* surrounding punishment that are so objectionable as to be banned outright or severely limited for reasons other than utilitarian deterrence? All of these worries—kind, amount, procedure—may plausibly be regarded as covered in the Eighth Amendment, a claim (controversial with respect to procedure) for which I shall argue later in this section. *P* is intrinsically the sort of thing (torture perhaps) that we simply should not do to a person. *P* is not intrinsically evil but this amount of *P* (thirty years in prison for the possession of one marijuana cigarette, perhaps) is too much of *P* for this sort of conduct. *P* is the kind of punishment that is likely to be administered in an arbitrary and capricious way.[53] These are the three primary ways we are inclined to object to a particular punishment on grounds of justice (and thus oppose it in principle) and thus may constitute the primary moral components of the Eighth Amendment ban on cruel and unusual punishments.

Stating all this, of course, is not to solve anything but only to set the problems for discussion. *Why* are certain punishments intrinsically objectionable? *How much* punishment is too much (or too little)? All punishments certainly can be administered in an arbitrary and capricious way, so what is it about certain punishments that makes such administration more likely?

Here traditional retributive theories are not as precisely helpful as one would like, though they do perhaps give us a start in the right direction. Since I have outlined the essentials of the retributive theory in a previous section, I shall not go over this ground again here except to recall three general points in an attempt to counter the bad press the theory usually gets.

(1) The theory is not an attempt to give approval to such barbaric motives as a desire for vengeance or vindictiveness. The only motive behind it is the desire to do justice. Thus retributivism is not an irrational cry for more and nastier punishments. Indeed, if retributivism were followed consistently, we should probably punish less and in more decent ways, for we now treat many criminals in ways harsher than, in justice, they deserve.

(2) Retributivism is built around a rather attractive (if controversial) model of human beings as free or autonomous creatures, as enjoying rights, and responsible for what they do. Surely this is more attractive than the "you are sick and helpless or like a child" model behind a therapeutic response to crime, or the "you can be used and manipulated for the common good" model behind utilitarian deterrence theory.[54]

(3) Even many people who do not like the *name* "retributivist" are persuaded by considerations that are clearly retributive in nature. Suppose it was suggested that we punish negligent vehicular homicide with life imprisonment and first-degree murder with a couple of years in jail, and suppose this suggestion was justified with the following utilitarian reason: Conduct of the first sort is much more common and dangerous than conduct of the latter sort (we are much more likely to be killed by a negligent driver than by someone who kills us with the primary object of killing us), and thus we should use the most severe deterrents against those who are genuinely dangerous. If we object to this suggestion, as most of us would want to, that this would be unjust or unfair because it would not be apportioning punishment to fault or desert, we should be making a retributive argument. Thus even if the label "retributivist" repels most people, many of the actual doctrines of the theory do not.

Let us suppose for the moment, then, that the retributive outlook sketched above can provide a reasonable general justification of punishment in terms of its being unjust or unfair to allow criminals to be free riders or parasites on schemes of social cooperation—something that would occur if they were not made to sacrifice in some way for not having made the required sacrifice of self-restraint. How will this help us in determining the *kinds* or *amounts* of punishment that will be tolerable—i.e., what alternative methods of sacrifice will be allowed, and which ones will be prohibited?

Here the guidance provided by the retributive theory is not as clear as one would like. Some versions of the *jus talionis* ("like for like") principle seems initially tempting; but even Kant—one of its staunchest defenders—cannot consistently maintain it to the end. One immediate problem is that the principle cannot with sense be taken literally in all cases. Hegel observes "It is easy enough . . . to exhibit the retributive character of punishment as an absurdity (theft for theft, robbery for robbery, an eye for an eye, a tooth for a tooth— and then you can go on to suppose that the criminal has only one eye or no teeth)."[55] Kant also sees that there is a problem in applying *jus talionis* to "punishments that do not allow reciprocation because they are either impossible in themselves or would themselves be punishable crimes against humanity in general." With respect to rape, pederasty and bestiality, for example, Kant believes that imprisonment is inadequate as a punishment but that a literal return of like for like would either be immoral (e.g., the rape of the rapist) or impossible (e.g., we cannot by definition commit bestiality upon a human criminal). Thus he proposes castration for the former two offenses and expulsion from society for the latter. He admits, however, that this is not a literal application of *jus talionis* but only in some sense captures the intuitive "spirit" of the principle.

There are serious difficulties here, however, the chief being that, once a literal reading of *jus talionis* is abandoned, its application "in spirit" seems to be largely a matter of intuition unguided by any systematic theory. Kant's favorite example of *jus talionis* is the penalty of death for the crime of murder—this in spite of the fact that the punishment for *almost everything else* is imprisonment, a punishment that can literally satisfy "like for like" only for the offenses of false imprisonment or kidnapping. And speaking explicitly of the death penalty, Kant argues that this punishment must be "kept entirely free from any maltreatment that would make an abomination of the humanity residing in the person suffering it."[56] The criminal's "innate personality," he claims, protects the criminal against any morally indecent treatment.[57] In suggesting that the state should never do anything to a criminal that humiliates and degrades his dignity as a person, Kant seems to be working toward a ban on those punishments that have been described as cruel and unusual—i.e., a principled ban on certain punishments (torture and mutilation?) even when the "like for like" principle would seem to require them. There is insight here, but how the insight is to be squared with his support of castration as a punishment is a mystery to me.

The principle of *jus talionis* has thus produced a bit of a muddle, and the explanation for this is the following: Though a conception of reciprocity may explain why the guilty should be punished, it is not clear that this same principle will explain why like should be returned for like or even that the evil inflicted on the criminal should be of equal gravity with that which the criminal has inflicted on his victim. The criminal has acted unfairly and that is why he must be punished. But unfairness is unfairness, murder being no more *unfair* than robbery. Thus if murder is worse than robbery (and thus deserves a worse punishment) this cannot be shown on the basis of purely formal considerations. Consider, again, the punishment for rape if the "like for like" position is adopted. If it be argued that the position does not entail that we rape the rapist but only do to him something of *equal* evil, it can be replied that the question "What evils *are* equal?" does not admit of a purely formal answer. Thus a retributivism grounded on fairness can at most demand a kind of *proportionality* between crime and punishment—i.e., demand that we rank acceptable punishments on a scale of seriousness, rank criminal offenses on a scale of seriousness, and then guarantee that the most serious punishments will be matched with the most serious crimes, and so on. This ranking must be reasonable, of course, but there is no reason to suppose that it will be determined solely or even primarily by considerations of fairness—i.e., no reason to suppose that seriousness can be totally analyzed in terms of fairness. In particular, considerations of fairness alone will not answer the question of which punishments will be allowed as the most serious. There will be substantive reasons for not allowing certain punishments (e.g., torture) even if these would satisfy a fairness principle of proportionality.

Let me say one other thing at this point about the concept of proportionality as applied to punishment. It can mean either (a) doing to the criminal something of equal gravity to what he has done to his victim or (b) making sure that the most serious punishments are applied to the most serious offenses, etc. So if the most serious punishment in a particular legal system is twenty years in prison and if this punishment is applied to the crime of murder, it could plausibly be argued that the proportionality demand stated in (b) has been satisfied, but not that stated in (a). And my argument thus far has been that (b), but not (a), can reasonably be derived from Kant's theory. At most a constrained variant of (a) might be derivable: (a*) do to the criminal something of equal gravity to what he has done to his victim unless this would require our doing something (e.g., torturing) to which there are serious substantive moral objections. If we allow such substantive restrictions, however, we shall be forced to admit that the decision to allow or not to allow *death* to remain as a system's most severe punishment cannot—contrary to Kant—be based simply on considerations of fairness or proportionality. We must at least reflect upon the possibility that our choice of this as a punishment will be constrained by other morally relevant properties of death.[58]

So far, then, we can get this much from Kant's theory: A punishment will be unjust (and thus banned on principle) if it is of such a nature as to be degrading or dehumanizing (inconsistent with human dignity). The values of justice, rights, and desert make sense, after all, only on the assumption that we are dealing with creatures who are autonomous, responsible, and deserving of the special kind of treatment due that status. This is why animals can be treated wrongly but cannot be wronged, cannot be treated unjustly, cannot have their rights violated. A theory of the just punishment, then, must keep this special status of persons and the respect it deserves at the center of attention. And there are at least two ways suggested by Kant whereby, in punishing, we can fail to do this: First, we can employ a punishment that is in itself degrading, that treats the prisoner as an animal instead of a human being, that perhaps even is an attempt to *reduce* him to an animal or a mere thing. Torture is of this nature. Using Kantian language, one might say that torture is addressed exclusively to the sentient or heteronomous—i.e. *animal*—nature of a person. Sending painful voltage through a man's testicles to which electrodes have been attached, or boiling him in oil, or eviscerating him, or gouging out his eyes—these are not *human* ways of relating to another person. He could not be expected to understand this while it goes on, have a view about it, enter into discourse about it, or conduct any other characteristically human activities during the process—a process whose very point is to reduce him to a terrified, defecating, urinating, screaming animal. We thus seem to have here a paradigm of not treating a person as a person and thus an undermining of that very value (autonomous human personhood) upon which any conception of justice must rest.[59] It is unjust to be tortured, everyone has a right not to be tortured, no has a right to torture, no one deserves torture—all these claims flow from a theory of punishment (such as retributivism) that takes seriously and makes central the special status of persons.

A second way in which punishment can fail to show respect for the status of autonomous persons is through radical lack of proportionality.[60] An autonomous person has a right that his punishment be *addressed* to that status—to those unique features of his individual, responsible conduct that occasion the punishment. A punishment radically disproportionate to the seriousness of the offense is not addressed to that for which he is responsible and blameworthy and deserving of punishment but is necessarily addressed to something else—e.g., society's mere *dislike* of him or his conduct.[61] This, in my view, is how the concept of "excessive" found in the Eighth Amendment should be interpreted.[62] To the degree that a person is being punished out of reasonable proportion to the seriousness of his offense, then to that degree is he being *used*—not being punished as justice would demand.

But is not the amount of punishment prescribed for an offense a criterion for how serious the offense is? That is, is it not almost true by definition that the most serious offenses will carry the most serious punishments—the prescription of the punishment by society being an index of how seriously society deplores the conduct? This challenge, in my judgment, is to be met in the following way: A just society cannot criminalize conduct simply because it deplores that conduct; its grounds for deploring the conduct must be *reasonable*. Conduct such as homosexuality does not cease to be morally trivial and become morally serious simply because a majority of people *think* it is morally serious and deplore it. As the Supreme Court correctly held in the *Robinson* case: if narcotic addiction is a disease, then no reasonable society may criminalize it no matter how much it may represent a status detested and deplored by many persons.[63] In a just society, therefore, punishment must be proportional to the *objective* seriousness of the conduct, not to its subjective seriousness—i.e., the degree to which it is held in disapproval by the society at large.

At present, of course, we lack a coherent theory of objective seriousness. Thus, except in extreme cases, it will be practically difficult if not impossible to guarantee just proportionality in punishing. For one who cares about justice, however, this lack will stimulate research and thinking in order that a reasonable theory on these matters may be developed. The alternative is simply to stop caring about doing justice—hardly an acceptable outcome.[64] As I indicated previously, a theory of justice alone may not be able to tell us which offenses are most serious; it may require supplementation by a consideration of the substantive or intrinsic character of certain kinds of conduct. A theory of justice, however, can at least demand the following: that everyone has the right to have offenses graded in terms of individual fault or blameworthiness (i.e., desert) and not mere social utility, that other even substantive bases for grading be reasonable, that punishments be graded on a comparable basis, and that there be a matching between seriousness of punishment and seriousness of offense. A theory of justice may not be able to supply all the details for ranking, but it can supply the framework.

Thus (by a process of deduction, variation, and free association) I have extracted the following from a generally Kantian account of retributive sentencing: A punishment will be banned in principle if (1) it represents a direct assault on the dignity of persons or (2) it is radically disproportional to the objective seriousness of the conduct criminalized. Consideration (1) is, of course, more basic than (2): certain punishments might pass the proportionality test but would still be rejected because they fail what might be called the "respect for persons" test. Thus the punishment of torture by an act of torture could hardly be faulted on grounds of proportionality, but it would still be rejected as an intrinsically inhuman method of punishment.

Both of the above notions—intrinsic heinousness and radical lack of proportionality—have a secure place in the interpretation of the Eighth Amendment.[65] A ban on the first is clearly a part of the original meaning, and a ban on the second has been prominent in twentieth-century Eighth Amendment cases—including the recent *Coker* case, where it was held that death was too severe a penalty for the crime of rape.[66]

What I wish to do now is to move the general account I have been giving into an area of considerable controversy—namely, the penalty of death. Given the above sketch of the concepts of cruel and unusual punishments, is it reasonable to regard the punishment of death as falling under this description? That is, are there good reasons why, on grounds of justice or respect for rights (rather than utility), we should accept an absolute ban or principled restriction against the death penalty? Does it belong, in other words, in the same camp as torture, mutilation, or punishments of radical disproportionality? We have the right not to be treated as animals or in a dehumanizing way. We have the right to be punished with sanctions proportional to our offenses. Do we also have the right not to be punished with death? If so, is this because death is necessarily a dehumanizing punishment, or because it necessarily lacks proportionality with all possible offenses—or both—or for some new reason entirely?

It should be obvious at the outset that there is no reason to believe that a punishment of death will always fail to satisfy the proportionality requirement. It would, of course, fail to satisfy this requirement for many offenses, but surely not for at least some acts of murder. (Kant's intuition seems correct here.) It is often said that, by making the criminal wait for a long time in terror and uncertainty before execution, we do something worse to him than any murderer does to a victim.[67] But this is just not so. What about the killers of Aldo Moro? Or suppose Patty Hearst's abductors had finally killed her? Are these acts not quite proportional to capital punishment? (It is also perhaps worth noting that much of the waiting is *chosen by the prisoner* while he files appeals.) Or what if the murderer tortured and mutilated his victim before the murder? We think of these activities as so horrible that we shall not even allow them as punishment, so surely their horribleness plus killing could be proportional to capital punishment—if anything, capital punishment might seem disproportionately *little* here. (A query: If torture and mutilation are so terrible that we will not allow them as punishments even when we do allow death, why then do we rank murder as an offense as *more serious* than torture and mutilation?)[68] Thus, if the concept of proportionality can be worked out at all, it seems that it should be possible to work it out for some acts of murder punishable by death.

Even when proportionality is satisfied, however, we shall not use a certain punishment if it is intrinsically degrading to the humanity of the criminal—e.g., we shall not torture the torturer. Is there perhaps, then, something intrinsically degrading, showing lack of respect for persons as persons, in the punishment of death so that it, too, could be banned even in cases where it satisfies the proportionality demand?[69]

'Now it is easy to think that capital punishment is intrinsically degrading if we allow ourselves to be dominated by a certain picture of what capital punishment is like—e.g., the final part of Truman Capote's *In Cold Blood*.[70] But all that this may show is that brutalization may precede and may accompany (as surrounding circumstances) the punishment of death.[71] This would be a reason for objecting to and changing those circumstances. But it would not be an objection to death *simpliciter* as a punishment. For suppose we consider another picture: the final scene of Plato's dialogue *Phaedo*, depicting the execution of Socrates by self-administered painless poison amid discourse with friends and family with all those around, even the jailer, showing great respect. This seems, at least intuitively, to depict a humanized death—a civilized execution. In this way, thus, does death seem to differ from torture. Is it conceptually possible to depict Socrates at a civilized torture session, a humanized case of evisceration of Socrates, a way of sending high voltage through Socrate's testicles which shows respect for him as a person? The answer seems *no*.[72]

In a variety of social contexts (e.g., euthanasia) people are now rallying around the slogan "Death with Dignity." This suggests that they intuitively grasp some distinction between death *simpliciter* (which is surely bad) and circumstances that could surround death that would make it, not just bad, but degrading. But can we imagine anyone, who understands language and knows how to think, suggesting the slogan "Torture with Dignity" as part of a campaign against the excesses of certain political regimes? Death *may* be brought about in a degrading way; torture *must* be brought about in a degrading way. Thus we could imagine devising ways to humanize executions, to design them so that respect for the criminal be shown. We cannot *logically* imagine devising humanized or civilized torture sessions.[73]

Thus it seems to me that it is by no means obvious that execution *in itself* is necessarily, like torture, a way of showing lack of respect for a person, a way of treating him as or reducing him to an animal. Thus death may pass both the proportionality test and the respect for persons test. If so, does this then show that the punishment of death cannot legitimately be opposed in principle, that we have no general right not to be executed by the state, and that opposition to the death penalty on principle is, at best, a kind of well-meaning sentimentality or, at worst, merely an illegitimate attempt to legislate our preferences for policy through the vehicle of constitutional law?[74]

In the remaining part of this section, I shall suggest that there are grounds for answering *no* to this question. I shall suggest that a basic right of citizens in just societies may be compromised by the death penalty and thus that there are possible grounds for a side-constraint or principled restriction against it. My argument will seek to support, in broad outline, a primary portion of the majority reasoning in *Furman* v. *Georgia* and later capital punishment cases.[75]

In what way did the Supreme Court hold capital punishment to be unconstitutional? Many arguments were given, but the one that comes through most clearly is the following: The death penalty is applied in an *arbitrary* and *capricious* way—e.g., it tends to be used upon the poor and blacks and on almost no one else.[76] Thus we are required on constitutional grounds to do *one* of the following (a) devise ways to keep capital punishment from being applied in an arbitrary and capricious manner or (b) ban it outright.[77] Against the general thrust of this argument, two charges are immediately to be made: (1) *All* punishments (including imprisonment) are arbitrary and capricious in the way noted, but it is absurd to say that all punishments are unconstitutional. And yet the Court's decision might seem to commit us to this absurd conclusion.[78] (2) To call capital punishment arbitrary and capricious is to make a *procedural* objection to it, one that could best be expressed by the Fourteenth Amendment "due process of law" or "equal protection" clauses. Why then drag in the Eighth Amendment, as the Court did, in support of its decision? The Eighth Amendment, in banning cruel and unusual punishments, is surely *substantive* and not procedural in nature, and bringing it in simply muddies the waters.[79]

What I should like to do now is the following: Develop a principle relevant to the capital punishment issue that (a) breaks down a sharp substance-procedure distinction and thus renders the Eighth Amendment relevant, and (b) distinguishes death from other punishments—especially imprisonment. That is, I want to meet both of the above objections and thus vindicate the major thrusts of the Court's reasoning.

What will the principle be? Recall that I am concerned with principles
that rest on *rights* (i.e., with principles proper) and not with useful
social policies. And what possible rights could be relevant to the kinds
of punishment permissible other than the ones already mentioned
(right not to be dehumanized; right to proportionality) and tentatively
rejected for the death penalty? I shall suggest the following: *the right
not to be dealt with negligently by one's government,* the right not to have
one's basic interests threatened in casual and irresponsible ways by
the state.[80] But is this not simply a statement of procedure, and, as
such, how can it bridge the substance-procedure gap? To answer this
objection, we can do no better than to turn to the writings of Judge
Learned Hand, whose discussion of negligence in tort law will be
useful for our present purposes:

> The degree of care demanded of a person by an occasion is the resultant
> of three factors: the likelihood that his conduct will injure others, taken
> with the seriousness of the injury if it happens, and balanced against
> the interest which he must sacrifice to avoid the risk.[81]

In other words, there is no such thing as negligence *per se* or in the
abstract. Whether the steps I take to reduce risk (the *procedures* of
my acting) are negligent or not will depend in part on the (*substantive*)
gravity of the harm that might result. Thus what constitutes due care
as a precaution against my hurting your mailbox may not come close
to what constitutes due care as a precaution against hurting your
eyes. And, in the criminal area, what constitutes due process with
respect to a parking fine may not come close to what constitutes due
process for a long jail term.[82]

How does this apply to capital punishment? In the following way:
All trial, conviction, and sentencing procedures are subject to *error*—
to the possibility that they will convict the innocent. And there are
two kinds of innocence at stake here: those totally innocent of any
wrongdoing and those whose conduct, though meriting conviction of
something (e.g., manslaughter), does not merit conviction of an offense
of supreme gravity (e.g., murder in the first degree). Due process is
an attempt to guard against both sorts of error. And what will be
responsible (i.e., nonarbitrary and noncapricious) principles of due
process for various criminal sanctions? How is the state to exercise
due care instead of negligence in dealing with its citizens in terms of
penal sanctions? Obviously, if Hand is correct, this question can be
answered sensibly only if we have a reasonable view of the gravity of
the (substantive) *harm* that might result from the error. Thus we have
broken down the sharp line that supposedly separated substance and
procedure, and the Eighth Amendment at least has a foot in the door.

One objection to the Court's reasoning is thus met. But what about the other objection—that the Court's condemning of capital punishment as cruel and unusual because arbitrary and capricious logically must condemn *all* punishments in our society (even imprisonment) as cruel and unusual? Obviously, the objection can be met in only one way—namely, by showing that death is a *graver harm* than loss of liberty and that, therefore, higher standards of due care ("super" due process) must surround the former sanction.

Can this be shown? Perhaps not in all cases—particularly in the case of life or extremely long-term imprisonment. Studies of the effects of long-term incarceration in "total institutions" indicate that long-term confinement develops in persons an "institutional personality"—i.e., a personality with diminished affect, neurotic dependencies, loss of autonomy and mental competence generally, in short, a kind of death (of personhood).[83] If these studies are correct, then long-term incarceration will be a kind of slow torture and psychic mutilation and *should* no doubt be banned on Eighth Amendment grounds (something the courts may be moving toward in declaring whole prison systems in violation of the Eighth Amendment).[84] This being so, it is a *virtue* of the Court's analysis that its arguments against death also apply to long-term incarceration. If they applied to all incarceration (or even to long-term incarceration if it does not have the above consequence), however, this would indeed be an absurdity. So what is it about death *simpliciter* which makes it a graver harm than loss of liberty *simpliciter*? Is it that people *fear* death more?—surely not, since many people fear death less than loss of liberty ("Give me liberty or give me death!") because they value liberty as a primary good of greater value than life.[85] Is it because death must entail intolerable suffering or degradation? No. As I have previously argued, certain manners of death may have this defect, but not necessarily death itself. What then?

One of the most common claims made in defense of the claim that death is worse than loss of liberty is the claim that death is *irrevocable*. But this will not do. Everything that is past is irrevocable. If I kill you in error, I have indeed done you an irrevocable injury. But so, too, if I imprison you falsely for five years. Margaret Radin, in her excellent discussion of capital punishment, attempts to meet this worry in the following way:

> Of course, even one day in prison is irrevocable in the sense that all past events and their resultant effects on human beings are irrevocable. Yet, although it might be difficult to articulate, most people intuitively recognize a distinction between the irrevocability of everything and the irrevocability of death or mutilation. The latter is the strong sense of

irrevocability referred to here. It encompasses irreversible deprivations
of attributes or capacities essential to, or at least closely connected with,
complete personhood.[86]

This will not work. Radin is trying to show that death is a greater
evil than loss of liberty because death is irrevocable—that is, she is
supposed to be analyzing "grave harm" in terms of "irrevocability."
But she is actually reasoning quite the other way around—i.e. analyzing
irrevocability (in the "strong sense") in terms of grave harm. But if
we already know the harm of death is greater than the harm of loss
of liberty, we do not need the concept of irrevocability at all. One
suspects that her analysis is unhelpfully circular—a suspicion reinforced
when we notice that a synonym for "irrevocable" ("irreversible") is
used in the analysis.

Let me then simply step in at this point and offer my own suggestion:
Death is a greater harm than loss of liberty because it is (a) totally
incompensable and (b) represents *lost opportunity* of a morally crucial
kind. First, the concept of incompensability.[87] This is a concept that
obviously admits of degrees. Some harms that we do to people are
of such a nature—e.g., damage to their property or income—that it
makes sense to speak of totally compensating them for their loss. For
other harms, we cannot totally compensate, but we can at least make
a reasonable attempt. Loss of liberty seems to me of this nature. In
a culture such as ours, we know what it is like—and it intuitively
seems reasonable and acceptable—to set a monetary value on my time
and labor. Indeed, I can reasonably *bargain* these away for money, as
when I work for a living. Thus if I am imprisoned by the state in
error, it is at least not intuitively absurd to suggest that damages be
paid as a way of compensating for the resulting harm. (We cannot
totally compensate, of course, but we can in some sense make a
reasonable stab at it.) But what would it be like to be paid anything
even resembling adequate compensation for being tortured, radically
mutilated, or debased in some other way—for being deprived of my
status of honor or dignity as a person? If these have a price, this
means that in a very real sense I do not have them to begin with—
a man whose honor has a price simply being a man without honor.
Suits in tort law may be brought and won here, of course, but how
many winners would really believe that they had been even close to
adequately compensated? How many would have bargained for this
"price" in advance? Let us now move to death: On a scale of
incompensability, death does indeed seem at the top. It is both logically
and empirically impossible to compensate me if I am executed in
error. (A wrongful death action may pay off someone, but necessarily
not me.) In contract law, we do not even *allow* people to bargain away

for money their life or their personal integrity against torture and mutilation; but we do allow them to bargain away almost totally their personal liberty—e.g., by joining a volunteer army.[88] Should we punish people by doing *S* to them when we shall not even allow them to do *S* to themselves, even for pay?

This question, of course, is rhetorical, and I shall move from it to present the upshot of what I have been saying thus far. I have argued that death is like torture and mutilation (and unlike loss of liberty) in at least one important respect: that when we injure someone by killing him in error, we have done him an injury that is incompensable. Not so with imprisonment in error for this is at least compensable to a significant degree. Thus in at least this one respect death is a graver harm than loss of liberty, and thus it is reasonable to require greater standards of due care or due process to prevent error in its application as a punishment. The Court was thus correct: The procedures that surround the punishment of death may properly be called arbitrary and capricious even if those same procedures are adequate for imprisonment.

But is this all? Is the only reason that death is worse than loss of liberty the fact that the former (when done in error) is totally incompensable and the latter (when done in error) is only partially incompensable? This does not seem correct—not as the *whole* story. Surely death is a worse injury than loss of liberty even when the punishment is *correctly* administered (i.e., not in error)—this being the very point, after all, of having death as the most severe sanction in one's arsenal of responses to crime. What this shows is that the person in favor of the death penalty for the most serious crimes (and reserving imprisonment for lesser crimes) *cannot consistently oppose the Court's reasoning in Furman v. Georgia!* For by that person's own admission, the death penalty *is* more serious than imprisonment, and thus, unless he wants (unreasonably) to quarrel with the claim that standards of due care or due process are in part a function of gravity of harm, he must agree with the Court that higher standards of review are required for the death penalty than for any other.

Why, then, might death reasonably be regarded as substantively more serious than loss of liberty? An answer to this question might help provide an interesting reason for why death is an incompensable injury—i.e., a reason more interesting than "You cannot compensate Jones if Jones is no longer around to be compensated."

Thus I shall now turn to the second point I want to make about death—that it represents *lost opportunity* of a morally crucial kind.[89] What I shall say here will be very brief and may also seem rather old-fashioned and romantically sentimental. Be that as it may, here it is: The most important thing within a human life (something stressed by philosophers from Socrates through Kant and by such other admirable and insightful individuals as Jesus and Tolstoy) is the *development of one's own moral character,* the development of oneself in such a way that one's life can honestly be said to be coherent, meaningful, and perhaps even admirable. To use the language of Plato and Socrates, one might say that what is most important in a human life is not what happens when the *body* is confined but is rather any harm that may come to the *soul*—or, to use less metaphysically provocative language, harm that may come to those crucial attributes of moral character and integrity that are most essential to personhood.

The development of a morally coherent personality is the most crucial task or project of any human life—a project that we all muddle through with various degrees of success or failure for our lifetimes. To block or interrupt this project (or to preclude one's ever having an opportunity to have a change of heart, reflect on one's life, and *start* such a project) is, on this moral view, the gravest harm that one can do to a person. Imprisonment (unless of such a nature or duration as to have profound effects on the inmate's mental health) will not do an individual this kind of harm—witness the number of inmates who in a very real sense have become "new people" while serving prison terms. But death, alas, provides no such opportunities and thus can certainly harm a person in this highly significant (one could say spiritual) way.[90] For death is the *loss* of significant opportunity (the opportunity to accomplish certain things, to treat people differently, to become a new person), and for many persons this must be the most terrifying thing about it.

> His mental sufferings were due to the fact that that night, as he looked at Gerasim's sleepy, good-natured face with its prominent cheekbones, the question suddenly occurred to him: "What if my whole life has been wrong?"
>
> It occurred to him that what had appeared perfectly impossible before, namely that he had not spent his life as he should have done, might after all be true. It occurred to him that his scarcely perceptible attempts to struggle against what was considered good by the most highly placed people, those scarcely noticeable impulses which he had immediately suppressed, might have been the real thing, and all the rest false. . . . 'But if that is so,' he said to himself, 'and I am leaving this life with the consciousness that I have lost all that was given me and it is impossible to rectify it—what then?' (Leo Tolstoy, *The Death of Ivan Ilych*)

Given the exceptional moral gravity of having one's prospects for a morally significant and meaningful life interrupted, one might well want to deny the state any right to do this—i.e., one might adopt a direct absolute ban on the penalty of death. For it is by no means clear that one can show respect for the dignity of a person as a person if one is willing to interrupt and end his most uniquely human capacities and projects. Thus, contrary to initial and plausible impressions of the kind sketched previously, there is perhaps a case to be made that the punishment of death is degrading after all. Even if one does not buy this, however, one must at the very least, given the considerations I have noted, have strong sympathy with the disjunctive position articulated by the Supreme Court—namely, that granting the supreme gravity of the penalty of death, the Constitution requires either (a) significantly more stringent standards of review for this penalty than for any other or (b) an outright ban on the penalty. Recent Court decisions requiring an elaborate consideration of mitigating and aggravating circumstances before a sentence of death may be imposed are an attempt to work with (a).[91] If this attempt fails—i.e., if it turns out that the standards of review surrounding imprisonment are really the best we can do—then we may be led indirectly into an outright ban on the death penalty.[92]

It was earlier argued that the demand of Kantian retributivism— the demand for just punishment or punishment in accord with desert— could not be the primary general justifying aim of punishment. It was, however, suggested that Kant's theory, which is based on respect for persons and the entailed unwillingness merely to use them for social ends, could perhaps provide a subordinate aim and could certainly provide the basis for a principled side-constraint on the pursuit of utilitarian deterrence. The side-constraint is this: Even when deterrence goals would be served, do not impose a punishment in excess of what the particular criminal deserves for his or her particular crime. Such punishments are to be ruled out in principle and social policies are to be constrained accordingly. In the above, I have attempted to make a start (and only a start) toward working out how a Kantian retributivist might assess the permissibility of the death penalty and how those moral worries might in part illuminate the constitutional doctrine of cruel and unusual punishment. Much that I have said is clearly controversial (both morally and legally) and many loose ends remain to be tied up. I hope, however, that I have at least showed that a discussion of capital punishment, like most issues connected with punishment, requires complex thought and thus a transcending of the slogans and conventional wisdom in which much of the public discussion of the issue is currently awash.

NOTES

1. Among the special due process requirements surrounding criminal punishment are these: the right to be represented by counsel, the right against double jeopardy, the right against self-incrimination, the right that illegally acquired evidence not be used against the defendant, the right to a trial by a jury of one's peers, and the right of a defendant to be presumed innocent until the state proves each element of the case against him or her beyond a reasonable doubt. (Only a "preponderance of the evidence" is normally required in civil cases.) In recent years the barrier against the use in trial of evidence against the defendant that was acquired illegally (e.g., after an illegal search or seizure) has been a matter of considerable controversy. Those who support this "exclusionary rule" argue that such a rule is the only way to deter police from conducting illegal searches, etc. Those who oppose the rule argue that it results in persons who are clearly guilty being set free and that there are other ways of disciplining police in the area of illegal searches. One empirical matter relevant to this issue is that of police motivation. If they are mainly motivated by a desire to do a kind of immediate "street justice," then the exclusionary rule will have little effect on their practices. If they are motivated by a desire to secure convictions at trial, then the rule should have motivating power. For an excellent symposium on the exclusionary rule, see *Criminal Justice Ethics*, Vol. 1, No. 2, 1982.

2. Jeffrie G. Murphy, "Blackmail: A Preliminary Inquiry," *The Monist* 63 (1980):156.

3. The following distinctions are drawn from Guido Calabresi and A. Douglas Melamed, "Property Rules, Liability Rules, and Inalienability: One View of the Cathedral," *Harvard Law Review* 85 (1972):1089. See also Chapter 5. For applications of this distinction to the problem of criminalization (applications that have influenced the present discussion), see Alvin Klevorick's "The Economics of Crime" and Jules Coleman's "Crime, Kickers and Transaction Structures," both in *NOMOS XXVII: Criminal Justice*, eds. J. Roland Pennock and John Chapman (New York: New York University Press, 1984).

4. In *Anarchy, State and Utopia* (New York: Basic Books, 1974). Robert Nozick describes our rights as defining an area of "moral space" around each of us and describes rights violations as "border crossings" or "boundary crossings." These are powerful metaphors that give one—at least initially—a good intuitive feel for the nature of rights. For an argument that Nozick's way of thinking of rights ultimately will not work, see Robert Paul Wolff, "Robert Nozick's Derivation of the Minimal State," *Arizona Law Review* 19 (1977):7.

5. *Supra* note 4, 54 ff.

6. It is perhaps easy to see why we might want absolute prohibitions against *others* crossing the borders defined by our right to life. But why are *we* prevented from selling our lives or allowing others to kill us with our consent? Are the reasons here ultimately ones of policy (how would we ever know if consent was really given if the victim was dead?) or are there reasons of principle?

7. It is of course possible that, at least for some crimes, criminal conviction and punishment represent society's way of expressing moral condemnation for the act and reinforcing its own moral code. My point is simply that this cannot be the primary purpose of the criminal law nor is such a purpose limited to the criminal law. (This certainly does seem to be an indirect, costly, and hurtful way to express something!) For a good discussion of these matters, see Joel Feinberg, "The Expressive Function of Punishment," *The Monist* 49 (1965).

8. This "social contract" way of thinking of the formation and legitimacy of government strikes me as a good metaphor for gaining insights on the purposes of government and the reasons we might have for adopting one or giving one our allegiance. Unlike some of its defenders, however, I do not think such a model *proves* either the rationality or the moral legitimacy of government. For an ambitious use of the social contract model, see John Rawls, *A Theory of Justice* (Cambridge: Harvard University Press, 1971).

9. The metaphor of the state as a "dominant protective agency" that we might actually hire to do a job for us (much as we might hire a plumber) is drawn from Nozick, *supra* note 4. This model faces serious problems (see Wolff, *supra* note 4) but it does have the marvelous feature of demythologizing government and the state.

10. From a utilitarian or rights-teleology perspective we must think of the indirect costs of criminalization—costs that can sometimes make criminalization undesirable. Among such costs are the encouragement of intrusive police tactics. Ironically, among such costs can also be a protection of certain criminal interests—a so-called "crime tariff." Criminalizing drug use, for example, might well have the function of encouraging the growth of an underworld subculture to deal in narcotics— something that would not arise if people could get narcotics legally. Thus in such cases we may start with one problem (drug use) and wind up with two: drug use (the same problem we started with) and a criminal subculture doing business in drugs. If a referendum were held tomorrow on the issue of decriminalizing drug use and supply, how do you think the criminal underworld would vote?

11. For a powerful case that criminal law functions to provent persons from bypassing an efficient and established market, see Richard Posner, *Economic Analysis of Law* (Boston: Little, Brown, 1972), chap. 4. This works clearly for property crimes, but it seems counterintuitive for crimes of personal violence, e.g., rape. (What is the rape market that the rapist bypasses?) See Chapter 5 of the present book.

12. This is not, of course, to say that the *intention* of the criminal is usurpation. The criminal is no doubt typically motivated by greed and malice and does not see himself in political terms—i.e., as a revolutionary.

13. See the discussion of free expression and its relation to libel and slander in Chapter 2.

14. For an analysis of the concept of punishment, see "Prolegomenon to the Principles of Punishment," in H. L. A. Hart, *Punishment and Responsibility* (Oxford: Oxford University Press, 1968). For criticism of Hart's analysis, see "Punishment," in Richard Wasserstrom, *Philosophy and Social Issues* (Notre Dame: University of Notre Dame Press, 1980).

15. *Supra* note 14.

16. If the general threat of punishment could be made credible by *faking* punishment, then the utilitarian would have trouble justifying actual punishment on general deterrence grounds. For a classic and powerful utilitarian discussion of crime and punishment, see Jeremy Bentham, *An Introduction to the Principles of Morals and Legislation* (1823).

17. For the development of the idea that the performance of some actions make one "clutchable" by the state, see "Crime, Clutchability, and Individuated Treatment," in Joel Feinberg, *Doing and Deserving* (Princeton: Princeton University Press, 1970).

18. The price system metaphor is used by John Rawls in his "Two Concepts of Rules," *Philosophical Review* 64 (1955):3.

19. Utilitarians have a problem in grading offenses on a scale of seriousness. It seems correct to say that indecent exposure causes too little distress in persons to make it more than a trivial criminal matter. For if one regarded it as a serious crime, one would be inclined to harm the exhibitionist to a degree disproportionate to the harm he does. But is this correct? The exhibitionist certainly does a small harm to each person he offends, but what if he offends a great many people? And suppose others fear (to a small degree) that they might be bothered by exhibitionists. Will all these small distresses at some point add up to a big enough collective distress to justify very harsh treatment of the exhibitionist? Also, will the utilitarian be forced to cater to stupid and irrational prejudices that are the source of unhappiness in those who have them—e.g., the unhappiness that a homophobe experiences through the knowledge that homosexual activities take place in the world?

20. Immanuel Kant, *Metaphysical Elements of Justice*, trans. John Ladd (Indianapolis: Bobbs-Merrill, 1965), 99–106. This selection, as well as many others referred to in this chapter, is reprinted in Jeffrie G. Murphy, ed., *Punishment and Rehabilitation* (Belmont: Wadsworth, 1973).

21. Edmund Pincoffs, *The Rationale of Legal Punishment* (New York: Humanities Press, 1966), 2ff.

22. For an exploration of this and related matters, see Robert Nozick, *Philosophical Explanations* (Cambridge: Harvard University Press, 1981), 363ff.

23. *Supra* note 18.

24. Herbert Morris, "Persons and Punishment," *The Monist* 52 (1968):475; and Jeffrie G. Murphy, *Retribution, Justice and Therapy* (Dordrecht: Reidel, 1979). Both Morris and Murphy draw heavily on the "principle of fair play" articulated by John Rawls in his "Legal Obligation and the Duty of Fair Play," in *Law and Philosophy*, ed. Sidney Hook (New York: New York University Press, 1964).

25. I have pointed out some of these problems in my "Marxism and Retribution" (in *Retribution, Justice and Therapy, supra* note 24)—one of the main ones being that, in an inegalitarian society, many criminals will be drawn from social classes who do not benefit from the rule of law in any clear way. So how can they owe something in return? Also the debt metaphor can be misleading in two ways: (1) criminal "debts," unlike real financial debts, are debts we have an antecedent obligation not to incur, and (2) the payment of a criminal "debt," again unlike the payment of a literal debt, does not make the world exactly the same again (ask any victim of crime). Also, as will be discussed in the final section of this chapter, the retributive theory gives imprecise guidance on the grading of offenses and the matching of appropriate punishments— a problem it shares with the utilitarian theory (*supra* note 19). Perhaps the most serious problem of all, however, is this: the "principle of fair play" has been subjected to powerful and perhaps fatal philosophical attack. See, for example, 90ff. of Robert Nozick's *Anarchy, State and Utopia, supra* note 4. For a general critique of retributivism, see Hugo Bedau, "The New Retributivism," *Journal of Philosophy*, 75 (1978):601; and the Wasserstrom essay, *supra* note 14.

Although I am still inclined to defend the moral desirability of retributivist goals, I have recently become skeptical that they can be compelling *state* goals. For more on this, see my "Retributivism and the State's Interest in Punishment," in *Nomos XXVII: Criminal Justice*, eds. J. Roland Rennock and John Chapman (New York: New York University Press, 1984).

26. Recall that the "profit" or "benefit" is not necessarily something financial or even tangible. It is essentially this: not taking on the burden of self-restraint.

27. Recklessness is acting in the conscious disregard of a risk of harm: negligence is thoughtlessly acting is a risky way in circumstances where one should have been aware. Negligence is thus "faulty" more as a character defect than a mental state (not being aware is hardly a mental state). Is it fair to hold someone responsible for not being aware? Surely the answer is yes if the person had the capacity to keep himself aware in the circumstances and simply failed to do so.

28. Recall that negligence, though a *mens rea* condition for some offenses, is not a mental state.

29. Some jurisdictions have a very *cognitive* test. The so-called M'Naghten rule for legal insanity, for example, excuses only those persons who suffer from a defect or disease of mind or reason such that they do not know what they are doing and do not know it is wrong. Other jurisdictions allow more *volitional* or *affective* tests—e.g., an irresistible impulse test. For a detailed and probing discussion of these matters, see Herbert Fingarette, *The Meaning of Criminal Insanity* (Berkeley: University of California Press, 1972). "Not guilty by reason of insanity" has normally not resulted in release but rather in mandatory confinement in a secure mental hospital for an indeterminate amount of time—a measure designed to protect the public from dangerous persons. Because of the due process problems to be noted shortly in this section, however, such alternative incarceration is no longer always allowed. This is causing enough public nervousness about the insanity defense to prompt movements to abolish it or radically reduce its scope of operation.

30. See "Legal Responsibility and Excuses," in H. L. A. Hart, *Punishment and Responsibility* (Oxford: Oxford University Press, 1968).

31. *Supra* note 30.

32. Hart generally takes a rule-utilitarian approach to legal criticism, but he clearly sees the relevance of appeals to rights, justice, and fairness as independent considerations.

33. For a rich discussion of strict criminal liability, see Richard Wasserstrom, "Strict Liability in the Criminal Law," *Stanford Law Review* 12 (1960):12. As Wasserstrom points out, there can be degrees of strictness in strict liability—e.g., a system could dispense with *mens rea* requirements but still allow some excuses.

34. The main areas where strict criminal liability is employed in American law are with respect to so-called "public welfare offenses" (e.g., shipping adulterated food in interstate commerce) and with respect to the element of *knowledge* in the offense of statutory rape—i.e. reasonable mistake about age is not allowed as a defense.

35. For essays exploring the pros and cons of this issue (e.g., Karl Menninger as a proponent and Thomas Szasz as an opponent), see Jeffrie G. Murphy, ed., *Punishment and Rehabilitation* (Belmont: Wadsworth, 1973).

36. One radical alternative is a scheme of mercy and forgiveness. See Jeffrie G. Murphy, "Forgiveness," in *Midwest Studies in Philosophy VII*, ed. Peter French (Minneapolis: University of Minnesota Press, 1982). See also Alwynne Smart, "Mercy," *Philosophy* (October 1968). A radical alternative of a very different sort is a scheme of preventive detention. On this see Ferdinand Schoeman, "On Incapacitating the Dangerous," *American Philosophical Quarterly* 16 (1979).

37. For a powerful case that a therapeutic response to wrongdoing may be dehumanizing, see Herbert Morris, "Persons and Punishment," *supra* note 24.

38. This section is adapted from Jeffrie G. Murphy, "Cruel and Unusual Punishments," in *Law, Morality and Rights*, ed. M. A. Stewart (Dordrecht: D. Reidel, 1983), © 1979 by D. Reidel and used with permission. Critical comments on my approach occur in the Stewart volume and in a review of my *Retribution, Justice and Therapy* (where the essay also appears) by Anita L. Allen, *Philosophical Review* (July 1981):484–89.

39. The best general treatment of the constitutional issues surrounding an application of the Eighth Amendment—with special focus on the death penalty—will be found in Margaret Jane Radin, "The Jurisprudence of Death: Evolving Standards for the Cruel and Unusual Punishments Clause,' *University of Pennsylvania Law Review* 126 (1977/8):989–1064. My own treatment of the topic has been enormously influenced by her essay.

40. See Chief Justice Burger's discussion (with respect to cruelty) in *Furman* v. *Georgia*, 408 U.S. 238, 392 (1972) (Burger C. J., dissenting).

41. *Furman* v. *Georgia*, 408 U.S. 238, 418 (Powell, J., dissenting).

42. See Ronald Dworkin, *Taking Rights Seriously* (Cambridge, Mass.: Harvard University Press, 1977).

43. *Trop* v. *Dulles*, 356 U.S. 86, 101 (1958) (plurality opinion) (Warren, C. J.).

44. *Furman* v. *Georgia*, 408 U.S. 360 ff. (Marshall J., concurring). Justice Marshall considers and rejects the opinion poll model and adopts a version of an élitist model involving a prediction of what people would deplore if fully informed.

45. One is reminded of John Stuart Mill's "competent judge" test in *Utilitarianism* (Chapter 2). Mill attempts to show that contemplative pleasures are superior to sensual pleasures because persons who have experienced both (competent judges) prefer the former to the latter. Any person who has experienced both and does *not* judge in this way, however, would obviously pose a problem for Mill's test. How does he deal with this? In the following circular way: such persons reveal that they have lost their capacities for finer feelings and thus lose their status of competence.

46. This, of course, is logically similar to Socrates's puzzle in Plato's dialogue *Euthyphro:* Is that which is pious pious because the gods approve of it; or do the gods approve of it because it is pious?

47. The élite, of course, may be *epistemologically* relevant—i.e., they may get us to see or appreciate some morally relevant feature that we otherwise might have missed but for their insight. Their attitude toward the feature is not what *makes* it relevant, however.

48. Jeremy Bentham, *The Principle of Morals and Legislation* (1789), especially Chapter 14.

49. "There is no reason to believe that [capital punishment] serves any penal purpose more effectively than the less severe punishment of imprisonment" (*Furman* v. *Georgia,* 408 U.S. 305) (Brennan J., concurring). The general constitutional notion of the last restrictive alternative is articulated in *Shelton* v. *Tucker,* 364 U.S. 479 (1960). For a more extended discussion of the nature and implications of strict judicial scrutiny (compelling state interest and least restrictive alternative tests), see Chapter 2 of this book. If the ban on cruel and unusual punishments is indeed absolute, this suggests that *no* interest—not even a compelling one—could be used by the state to justify such legal punishments.

50. Consider persons in an "original position" of the kind described by John Rawls. It seems reasonable to suppose that they would choose a system in which penalties were no more severe than necessary to accomplish whatever purpose they set as reasonable. If Rawls is correct in claiming that choices in such a constrained setting yield principles of justice, then we have a nonutilitarian foundation for a least restrictive alternative principle.

51. For more on this, see my "Rights and Borderline Cases," *Arizona Law Review* 19 (1977):228–41, reprinted in my *Retribution, Justice and Therapy.*

52. It is highly doubtful that the state has a moral right to punish at all in a society that is highly unjust. See my "Marxism and Retribution," *Philosophy and Public Affairs* 2 (1972/3):217–243, reprinted in *Retribution, Justice and Therapy.*

53. It has been argued, for example, that capital cases bring out the worst and the most irrational in juries and judges. See Charles L. Black, Jr., *Capital Punishment: The Inevitability of Caprice and Mistake* (New York: Norton, 1974).

54. For an argument that utilitarianism also tends to treat persons as children, see Adrian M. S. Piper, "Utility, Publicity, and Manipulation," *Ethics* 88 (1977/8):189–206.

55. *Hegel's Philosophy of Right,* trans. T. M. Knox (Oxford: Clarendon Press, 1952), 72.

56. Immanuel Kant, *The Metaphysical Elements of Justice,* trans. John Ladd (Indianapolis: Bobbs-Merrill, 1965), 102.

57. *Supra* note 56, 100.

58. As I shall later argue, the mere fact (if it is a fact) that people tend to *believe* that death is horrendous is not a morally relevant property of death. (What people believe about death is surely not a property of death at all.) Such beliefs about death, however, might be relevant in a Rawlsian "original position" in that they might prompt the rational choosers to place special constraints on its intentional causation.

59. For an explanation of this sort of argument (or of a defense for not giving an argument), see my "The Killing of the Innocent," *Monist* 57 (1973):527–50, reprinted in *Retribution, Justice and Therapy.*

60. I say *radical* for the following reason: Any departure from proportionality is less than ideal justice would demand, but it may be impossible to grade these matters in a very fine way. We should still want to condemn, however, cases where the gap in seriousness between punishment and offense is clearly too wide.

61. Obvious examples here are severe punishment for drug use, or consensual homosexual activity among adults, or any other "victimless crimes."

62. See *Lockett* v. *Ohio,* 438 U.S. 586 (1978) (White J., dissenting in part and concurring in part). Justice White articulates both the utilitarian and the retributive analyses of "excessive."

63. *Robinson* v. *California* 370 U.S. 660 (1962).

64. Andrew von Hirsch has made a start toward developing a framework for a theory of objective seriousness. See his *Doing Justice: The Choice of Punishments* (New York: Hill & Wang, 1976). Though von Hirsch believes that such devices as the Sellin-Wolfgang survey technique for measuring degrees of seriousness have a use, he sees clearly that objective criteria for seriousness cannot be ultimately based on popular judgments. Von Hirsch has not (as I believe he would be the first to admit) given us very much, but he has given us a start—and a start in the *right direction* (toward just retribution).

65. For an excellent survey of the history of the Eighth Amendment and its interpretation, see *Furman* v. *Georgia,* 408 U.S. 314 (Marshall J., concurring).

66. *Coker* v. *Georgia,* 433 U.S. 584 (1977). In my judgment, the Court erred in not considering *degrees* of rape and aggravating circumstances that might render a punishment of death proportional—a point well made by Justice Powell in the dissenting part of his judgment.

67. Albert Camus argued in this way in his essay "Reflections on the Guillotine." One other serious problem about long delays is the following: during the delay a prisoner can in a very real sense become a "new person" by morally transforming himself. Is it fair that this new person be executed for a crime committed by a different and previous self? As I shall argue later in the paper, the possibility of self-transformation is a very good reason against the penalty of death.

68. There is, of course, the utilitarian reason: we wish to give the torturer an incentive for not killing his victim after the torture session is over.

69. There are three bad arguments (addressed to me in various public discussions) that the infliction of the death penalty is intrinsically wrong, arguments that—since they may be widely used—are perhaps worth a brief attack. (1) Punishing people by killing them *degrades us*—we are demeaned in the process. But we shall be demeaned by doing this only if doing it is wrong; it cannot be wrong *because* it demeans us. This begs the question. (2) "Two wrongs do not make a right"—a favorite chiché of Americans, particularly undergraduate students. This, of course, begs the question also. The very point at issue is whether capital punishment is a wrong. (3) We must defend the value of the "sanctity of human life"—a value compromised when we execute. This bare slogan is of little help, because it can plausibly cut both ways on the capital punishment issue. Looking at the condemned person, we shall cite sanctity of life as a reason for not killing him. If we look at the *victim* (of murder), however, we could just as well cite sanctity of life as a reason *for* capital punishment—i.e., our use of a punishment this serious is our way of expressing how seriously we take the crime of murder. With analysis, however, this slogan can be turned into an argument—one which I shall develop later in the paper. Even analysed, however, it will rest on a controversial assumption—namely that killing is morally worse than letting die. For a defense of this assumption, see my "The Killing of the Innocent," *supra* note 59.

70. This book (based on a factual murder and execution) was made into a successful Hollywood movie. Both the book and the movie depict two marginal human beings of unclear responsibility who, after being convicted of murder and sentenced to death, arouse our pity and compassion as they reveal both their humanity and animality in touching ways. Their route to death (except for their contact with Capote) is cold and impersonal.

71. For more on the distinction between death and the terrible circumstances that may surround death, see my "Rationality and the Fear of Death," *Monist* 59 (1975/6): 187–203, reprinted in *Retribution, Justice and Therapy.*

72. This is not to say that some persons—e.g., Church martyrs, soldiers who will not betray comrades under torture, etc.—cannot rise above the inherent degradation of what is being done to them. Their animal nature is being addressed, but they hold out for a very long time (perhaps until death) before allowing that nature to answer.

73. We would be much more inclined to regard as insane a person who voluntarily tortured himself than a person who voluntarily took his own life.

74. This is the suspicion expressed by Justice Rehnquist in his dissent in *Furman* v. *Georgia*—a suspicion shared by some of the other dissenting Justices.

75. The major relevant cases, other than *Furman* v. *Georgia,* are: *Gregg* v. *Georgia,* 428 U.S. 153 (1976); *Woodson* v. *North Carolina* 428 U.S. 280 (1976); *Roberts* v. *Louisiana,* 428 U.S. 325 (1976); *Jurek* v. *Texas,* 428 U.S. 276 (1976); *Coker* v. *Georgia, supra* note 66; and *Lockett* v. *Ohio, supra* note 62.

76. This is also the central argument of Charles Black's widely read book on capital punishment, *supra* note 53.

77. The Justices are clearly divided on which alternative is preferable.

78. Again, see Black (*supra* note 53) for a clear statement of and an attempt to meet this objection.

79. "The Eighth Amendment was included in the Bill of Rights to assure that certain types of punishments would never be imposed, not to channelize the sentencing process. The approach of these concurring opinions has no antecedent in the Eighth Amendment cases. It is essentially and exclusively a procedural due process argument [dealt with and dismissed in *McGautha* v. *California*, 402 U.S. 207] . . . and it would be disingenuous to suggest that today's ruling has done anything less than overrule *McGautha* in the guise of an Eighth Amendment adjudication" (*Furman* v. *Georgia*, 408 U.S. 399 and 400) (Burger C. J., dissenting).

80. Again, it is perhaps worth noting (for those who are impressed, as I am, by his theoretical machinery) that Rawls's rational contractors would surely adopt such a principle in the original position.

81. *Conway* v. *O'Brien* (2 Cir. 1940) 111 F. 2d 611, 612. See also *United States* v. *Carroll Towing Co.* (2 Cir. 1947) 159 F. 2d 169.

82. Mr. Justice Harlan wrote: "I do not concede that whatever process is 'due' an offender faced with a fine or a prison sentence necessarily satisfies the requirements of the Constitution in a capital case" (*Reid* v. *Covert*, 354 U.S. 1) (1957).

83. See Erving Goffman, *Asylums* (New York: Doubleday, 1961). See also my "Rationality and the Fear of Death," *supra* note 71.

84. It is not uncommon for federal courts to declare the prison systems of entire states (e.g., Arizona) to be in violation of the Eighth Amendment—the primary reason usually being overcrowding. But what is the matter with overcrowding? Presumably the effects it has on prisoners. But what if long-term incarceration has the same or similar effects?

85. As noted above, attitudes toward death as opposed to other punishments could be relevant in the Rawlsian original position; but, unless these attitudes are absolutely uniform for all persons, it is hard to see how the application of the punishment could be fair—i.e., some will be more hurt by it than others. Again, one needs an objective account.

86. Radin, *supra* note 39, p. 1022. Irrevocability is probably the most frequently cited reason in defense of the claim that death is more serious than loss of liberty. See Black, *supra* note 15. And Justice Marshall: "Death is irrevocable; life imprisonment is not" (*Furman* v. *Georgia*, 408 U.S. 346).

87. For an excellent discussion of the distinction between compensable and incompensable injuries, see Nozick, *Anarchy, State and Utopia*, chap. 4.

88. We do, of course, have the concept of a Faustian contract. But we also take these to be perverse.

89. I have elaborated this point in great detail in my "Rationality and the Fear of Death," *supra* note 71.

90. I say *can* instead of *must* because some persons (e.g., Socrates and other exceptionally rare individuals) seem to have attained personal excellence prior to their execution. The Justices in *Furman* v. *Georgia* who seem to me closest to the view I am here articulating are Marshall and Brennan. Marshall (at 346) writes "Death, of course, makes rehabilitation impossible." And Brennan (at 272, 273) writes: "When we consider why [certain punishments] have been condemned, however, we realize that the pain involved is not the only reason. The true significance of these punishments is that they treat members of the human race as nonhumans, as objects to be toyed with and discarded."

91. *Lockett* v. *Ohio*, *supra* note 62. There is, of course, a social cost of having stricter procedures to prevent error—Hand's third factor in his algebra of negligence. The primary social costs for criminal due process will be expense, court time, and of course the greater possibility that guilty and dangerous persons will be freed to prey again upon innocent victims and that others will be less effectively deterred from crime. I have had little to say about these matters—not because I think they are unimportant but because I wanted to see how far one could go via a different route. On the capital punishment question, however, this issue will not be too central for the following reason: Probably no one would want to grant *less* due process than existed prior to *Furman*. But, even with that amount, executions had become so infrequent as to have (probably)

very insignificant deterrence value. Studies seem to indicate that it is *certainty* of punishment (more than severity), that tends to deter. See Jack P. Gibbs, *Crime, Punishment, and Deterrence* (New York: Elsevier, 1975).

92. Some criminals (e.g., the psychopathic killer) are perhaps best regarded as wild animals or other nonresponsible natural forces of destruction. Such a way of looking at them is not to regard them as persons; but this is all right because, from the moral point of view, *they are not persons.* If drastic steps (e.g., execution) are advocated for them, this cannot coherently be regarded as capital punishment (since they are not responsible and thus not legitimately open to *punishment*) but must be regarded simply as painless extermination—something done in the same spirit in which we destroy a mad dog. I see nothing *intrinsically* wrong about such steps (i.e., see no reason for believing that psychopaths have a moral right to life); but the *practical* dangers of acting in this way (i.e., letting legal authorities—as in Nazi Germany—decide who is and who is not a person) are so grave that it is irresponsible even to consider this as a legal option. For more on this, see my "Moral Death: A Kantian Essay on Psychopathy," *Ethics* 82 (1971/2):284–98, reprinted in *Retribution, Justice and Therapy.*

4

Philosophy and the Private Law

INTRODUCTION

While philosophers have grown considerably more sophisticated in their understanding and treatment of issues in and about the law of crimes, there remains widespread neglect of the philosophic dimensions of areas of the common law, in particular the central areas of private law: torts and contracts. The central purpose of this chapter is to make a start at remedying this situation by providing an accessible framework for students of legal philosophy that will enable each to appreciate the kinds of issues of philosophic interest that arise within the domain of the private law.

This chapter is divided into two sections; the discussion in both follows a similar outline. In the first section I will discuss philosophic issues in tort law; in the second I turn my attention to contract law. Each section begins with a few introductory remarks about the body of law in question. Then, rather than attempting to give an overall philosophic theory of torts or contracts, I will explore particular problems of philosophic interest in each. The goal of this chapter, like the goal of the text itself, is to provide a useful and stimulating introduction to the problems of legal philosophy; in pursuing that goal, no attempt has been made to provide a satisfying general theory of law or of its component parts.

TORT LAW

THE DIFFERENCE BETWEEN TORTS AND CRIMES

Suppose you drive recklessly down the streets of a residential neighborhood. In doing so, you impose unreasonable risks on everyone whose path you cross. Suppose that at some point you lose control of your car, it is propelled through the front door of one of the

houses on the street and comes to rest in its kitchen. One thing is
certain. You're in trouble. What sort of trouble? Very likely, you have
violated several criminal prohibitions. At the very least you may be
charged with criminal negligence or reckless endangerment. When
the police arrive to arrest, book, and put you behind bars, you will
need a good lawyer. But the threat of a stretch behind bars is not
all you have to look forward to. We can assume that you've caused
at least one property owner a good deal of damage. After all, it's
unlikely that your car came to rest in the kitchen peacefully and
without much ado. So, in addition to facing criminal sanctions, you
can anticipate that at least one person will be initiating litigation
against you in an effort to recover his losses. In short, you will be
subject both to a criminal suit and to a civil suit in *torts*.

This little example can be used to illustrate several of the important
differences between the law of crimes and that of torts. First, your
offense in crimes is in some sense against the state; it is prosecuted
by an agent of the state—the relevant municipality's prosecuting
attorney. If you are found liable to criminal sanction, the *state* is
justified in imposing some sort of "harm" or sanction upon you, which
usually consists in your being incarcerated and subject to the loss of
your liberty and assorted legal rights. Your conduct is criminal because
it departs from a special kind of prohibition or requirement imposed
by the state. In this case, your conduct violates the prohibition against
recklessly endangering the lives and property of others. It is not a
necessary condition of criminal conduct that there be an identifiable
victim of it. Some crimes simply have no victims, e.g., unsuccessful
attempts, conspiracy to commit a crime, or possession of a narcotic.
Other crimes involve victims, e.g., assault, murder, rape, fraud and
embezzlement. Whether or not there is a victim depends on the nature
of the crime. In the standard view crimes are offenses against the
state that consist in a failure under certain specifiable conditions to
comply with a class of *legal rules*—i.e., penal statutes.

Because the existence of a victim is not necessary to a conduct's
being criminal, criminal conduct need not result in actual loss or
measurable damage. Unsuccessful attempts to commit a crime may
cause no harm or loss to the intended victim or to anyone else.
Because the existence of damages is only a contingent feature of
crime, present only in some of the cases in which punishment is
appropriate, the general point or justification of punishment cannot
be that punishment rectifies or annuls the victim's loss. Next, even
when there is a victim of criminal mischief who suffers damages,
punishing the criminal does not annul the victim's loss. Nor, indeed,
does punishment annul whatever gains, if any, the criminal may

have secured through his mischief. A bank robber may have buried the loot he stole from the bank. His being put behind bars may leave him with a substantial bounty to look forward to upon his release. Because the act of punishment annuls neither the victim's losses nor the wrongdoer's gains in cases where criminality results in either gain or loss, we need an institutional mechanism other than the law of crimes to concern itself with both the criminal's gain and the victim's loss. Indeed, this institution may legitimately concern itself with gains and losses even when they are not occasioned by criminal misconduct: perhaps not all gains and losses, but not only those which result from criminal conduct. One such mechanism is the law of torts.

Let's take a closer look at those aspects of your conduct that are intricately tied to gains and losses. Here is your car having come to rest in your victim's kitchen. What's to be done about that? Presumably, your victim will initiate litigation against you seeking repair for the damage your mischief has occasioned. Here, then, is one difference between torts and crimes. The suit that is brought against someone in torts is almost always initiated by a *private* party, for damages against him, not for a "harm" against the state. Though he may desire that his injurer suffer some sort of punishment, punishment is *not* the *object* of the victim's suit. The victim's goal is to be reimbursed for those of his losses that are his injurer's responsibility or doing. Should it also happen that the victim's loss exceed or be equal to the injurer's gain, it may be that by holding the injurer liable in damages to him, both his loss and the defendant's gain, will be annulled.

In both torts and crimes, the individual who is subject to liability has failed to measure up to a *standard* of behavior.[1] The standards or duties imposed in torts and in the criminal law are likely to be different, though there is substantial overlap. There is, for example, no crime against blasting *per se*, though harms which result from blasting may be remediable in torts. In contrast, there is no tort called possession of a narcotic, though possession is a criminal offense. Assault and battery, for example, are both torts and crimes. A particularly interesting case is the norm imposing a duty to rescue which is enforced by criminal statute in some states, but not by tort remedy. The difficulty of enforcing such a standard in torts is not due to the absence of a victim—since there is one; instead, the major practical obstacle appears to be the difficulty in assessing the scope of one's liability, that is, the extent of damages for which one could be held liable.

The standards in torts and crimes are different, but what distinguishes them? Which standards trigger criminal sanction for their violation and which tort liability? Is there a principled way to draw this distinction? The standard way of drawing this distinction is to say that duties imposed by tort law cover *private* harms, and those imposed in the criminal law cover *public* harms. I do not find this approach particularly useful. It is more useful, I believe, to think of the difference not in terms of either the kinds of harms the perpetrator causes or the kinds of standard his conduct falls below, but in terms of the kinds of enforcement involved in upholding public norms of behavior. In crimes, we rely upon *public* officials, agents of the state, to enforce the relevant standard; in torts, the standards are enforced *privately*, in the sense that the burdens of detection and initiation of litigation fall on victims.[2] The same standards of behavior may be enforced both publicly and privately, by passing a criminal law prohibiting conduct, and by providing a tort remedy for victims in the event an individual's failure to comply with the relevant norm should occasion another's loss. Other standards of behavior may be enforced only privately, in which case failure to comply may subject someone to tort but not to criminal liability. For example, failures to exercise reasonable care in driving are normally enforced by providing redress in torts for the victims of negligent motoring, not by imposing criminal liability.[3]

Moreover, when we think of the difference between torts and crimes in terms primarily of enforcement devices, we can explore the ways in which the enforcement devices might be differentially manipulated to increase or decrease enforcement and, therefore, to vary the levels of compliance. The policeman and the prosecutor's incentive to enforce public standards is presumably a combination of the conditions of their employment—each is, after all, being paid to do so—and their public spirit. The victim's incentive to enforce public standards is the possibility of his securing compensation. His incentives can be manipulated to encourage or discourage enforcement. Increased damage awards, including punitive damages, increases *private* enforcement.[4] The contingent legal fee also increases enforcement. If we wanted to discourage private enforcement, we might adopt the British rule that the loser in a civil suit must bear the court costs of both parties. Surely, that would discourage suits and not just frivolous ones. All this is important when we think in terms of the overall costs of reducing the level of undesirable, or harmful or harm-threatening conduct. We can imagine certain conditions under which we would be inclined to rely more on private enforcement than on public enforcement, for example, where detection of noncompliance by a third party (e.g., a policeman) is costly or unlikely. And we can imagine other cases where we might be more inclined to rely on public enforcement—e.g., where the conduct though wrongful may lead to low levels of damages, so low perhaps as to discourage victims from initiating what may prove to be costly and not particularly fruitful litigation.

It is interesting to think about the difference between torts and crimes in terms of the difference between *private* and *public enforcement* of *public standards* for another reason as well. The public/private enforcement distinction gives us a way of contrasting both torts and crimes with *contracts*. We will discuss aspects of contract law in more detail in the second section of this chapter, but it is worth noting now that one apparent difference between contracts, on the one hand, and both torts and crimes on the other is that the standards or duties enforced in contracts are *not* public ones; they are self-imposed duties that are binding on the parties because they have agreed to them. Like torts and unlike crimes, these duties are enforced privately. But unlike torts, the duties the state is being asked to enforce are self-imposed (i.e., private ones). Contracts involves enforcing *private* duties *privately*. Not every binding agreement we make is binding in contract law, in part because these agreements are private. What, then, can be the justification for the state's role in enforcing the term of private agreements? This is the question to which we shall return in the discussion of contract law below. For now, it is enough to remind ourselves that there are no torts without victims and their losses, and that, in contrast to the criminal law, tort liability is a private mechanism for enforcing public standards that consists in the victim being awarded damages (when his suit succeeds), and the injurer being held liable to make good the victim's losses. Among the torts you are familiar with—if not as torts—are those which result from automobile accidents, defective products, or toxic waste disposal schemes, as well as those that are incurred at the workplace or involve defamation of character or are the result of pollution and other nuisances.

THE RULES OF TORT LIABILITY

Often when an individual is injured by the doings of another, he suffers measurable damages. The law of torts provides the victim with a possible source of recovery. Were there no remedy, the victim would have to shoulder the costs occasioned by the conduct of others. In torts, we capture this by the expression that *initially* losses shall lie where they have fallen. In short, we begin with the presumption that victims should bear their losses. This is a presumption that can be overriden. Specifying the conditions under which the presumption can be overriden make up the body of tort law.

One reason we might have for thinking that the victims should bear their losses is that it is costly to shift them to others. If there is no good reason for shifting a loss, why incur unnecessary costs? By letting the loss lie where it falls, in effect we hold the victim liable for the costs of harms he suffers, unless he or she is prepared to take steps to have us consider shifting the loss to another—usually, but not always, his injurer. The victim has the burden of coming forward and initiating litigation and the additional burden of persuading a jury that his loss ought to be borne by another.

The courts recognize only some reasons as good ones for shifting losses or, in other words, for overriding the presumption that the victim should bear his own costs. These reasons are captured in *liability rules*. Liability rules set forth the conditions a victim must meet in order to have his losses borne by another. Usually these rules are not conclusive. If the conditions set out by a liability rule are satisfied, the burden is shifted from the victim to the defendant. The plaintiff-victim has met his burden; he has given the court good reason for thinking that he ought not bear his losses, and for thinking that the defendant should. Now the defendant has available to him the opportunity to present an argument to the effect that he ought not shoulder the victim's costs. Not every reason he might offer is a good one. The good ones are captured under the rules of *positive defense*.

We can illustrate the mechanisms involved by reconsidering and embellishing the example from the beginning of this chapter. The home owner will bear the costs your recklessness caused unless he can convince a jury that you should. In an effort to convince someone that the responsibility for these costs lies with you, he initiates litigation. He goes to court and establishes that you were reckless in your driving and that your recklessness caused his damages. He has met the initial burden by showing that you were at fault and that your fault caused the harm. His costs will be your responsibility unless you have a compelling reason why they should not be. Suppose it turns out that you drove haphazardly because earlier that night at a party you both attended the victim without your knowledge had slipped you severely intoxicating beverages. Moreover, the effects of the beverages would be delayed so that you would experience intoxication long after you started driving. The net effect is that you would be unable to reason clearly about what you ought to do in your intoxicated state. All would be beyond your control. In that case, you would have shown that the victim's very own mischief was really responsible for the damage he suffered. In doing so, you have offered a positive defense sufficient to shift the burden back to him. Not every defense you might have tried would have been so successful. Had you argued that you were drunk because you are an alcoholic, you might have received some sympathy from the court, but you could hardly have expected to be freed of the burden of recompense.

In this section, we will focus on liability rules rather than on the rules of positive defense. In other words, we will be concerned with the conditions that must be satisfied in order for a victim to overcome the initial presumption that the losses that have befallen him should remain his responsibility. In general, a distinction is drawn between two kinds of liability rules; these are the rules of fault and of strict liability. If a case is covered by a rule of strict liability, the victim must establish that:

1. The defendant acted.
2. He, the victim, suffered a compensable loss.
3. The defendant's action caused the loss.

Under a rule of fault liability, the plaintiff-victim must establish that each of these three conditions has been satisfied and that the following condition has been satisfied as well.

4. The defendant's conduct was at fault.

Under the rule of strict liability, it is enough that the plaintiff show that the injurer caused the harm for which he seeks recompense. Under the rule of fault liability, he must show both that the injurer is at fault and that his fault is causally responsible for the victim's loss.[5] Certain cases that come before a court are decided on a strict liability basis, others on a fault basis. One question in tort theory is which sorts of cases should be adjudicated under which sort of rule. This question presupposes that we have already determined the relative advantages of each sort of liability rule, and what we are trying to do is to fit the rules to their most appropriate applications. The philosopher of law wants to look more closely at what the traditional analysis takes for granted; he or she wants to know what reasons can be advanced on behalf of either strict or fault liability. The legal philosopher wants to know, in other words, what the relative virtues of the rules are. Does fault liability, for example, promote justice, and strict liability, utility? Or is it the other way around? Indeed, the legal philosopher is troubled by an even more basic question: why rectify gains and losses according to the traditions, customs, and rules developed over the history of tort law? Maybe the whole system of liability rules and positive defence fails to achieve either justice or utility—or maybe it is less successful at promoting justice or utility than alternatives to it might be.

In the law of torts, individuals bring their claims to court on a case-by-case basis. Theoretically, we could deal with their claims in other ways, for example, by lumping together the costs of certain kinds of harms as they accumulate among victims over a period of time, and then compensate the victims as a class through the tax coffers. I don't want to claim that such a plan is preferable to the tort system, but I do want to suggest that we cannot determine if it is unless we first determine what goals we think the law of torts ought to pursue. Only when we have an idea of what it is we want the law of torts to accomplish, will we be able to determine if all cases should be adjudicated on a case-by-case basis. Only then will we be able to determine the relative advantages of the rules of strict and fault liability in securing them.

I want now to explore these issues within the context of a particular issue within the law of torts: namely, the debate over no-fault automobile insurance. No-fault presents a good focal point for this discussion because under a no-fault system, cases are not, in fact, adjudicated individually; indeed, in theory they are not to be adjudicated at all. No-fault, in short, involves abandoning the tort law system as we know it. The costs of accidents under a no-fault scheme are not distributed according to the rule of fault liability, and this seems initially troubling to those who think that justice requires imposing the costs of accidents upon those whose fault occasions them. The intuitive view is that the fault liability rule promotes justice, and that the rule of strict liability abandons justice to promote utility. Abandoning the tort system in general and the rule of fault liability in particular as instruments for rectifying wrongful losses that result from negligent motoring seems to conflict with our ideals of just law, and in what follows I want to see if this initial impression stands up under scrutiny.

JUSTICE AND THE COSTS OF AUTOMOBILE ACCIDENTS.[6]

Which members of the community should bear the costs of automobile accidents?[7] The answer to this question depends first on whether one is to consider traffic accident costs on an individual case basis or as they accumulate over a specified period of time. Should one maintain that those individuals who ought to bear the cumulative costs of traffic accidents are precisely those who are at fault in causing particular ones, the distinction between particular and cumulative costs seems to conflate. This need not be the case, however, since one could maintain that the faulty parties in particular accidents should bear the cumulative costs without committing oneself to the position that each faulty party ought to be responsible for the costs of all and only those accidents that are his fault. After determining that the cumulative costs of accidents should be spread among those at fault in causing particular ones, one could then consult some other criterion to determine what percentage of the total costs, or the costs of which particular accidents, each should bear, for example the criterion of prior capacity to bear loss. What constitutes sufficient reason for shifting the burden of automobile accident costs depends on the goals of accident law. This point is well made by Guido Calabresi in his important and provocative book, *The Costs of Accidents*:

> it is a policy question whether accident costs should be (1) borne by particular victims; (2) paid on a one to one basis by those who injure a particular victim; (3) borne by those broad categories of people who are likely to be victims; (4) paid by those broad categories of people who are likely to be injurers; (5) paid by those who in some sense violate our moral codes (in some sense are *at fault*) according to the degree of their wrongdoing; (6) paid by those who in some actuarial sense are most likely to violate our moral codes; (7) paid from the general coffers of the state or by particular industry groups in accordance with criteria (such as wealth) that may be totally unrelated to accident involvement; or (8) paid by some combination of these methods.[8]

Calabresi suggests that accident law should satisfactorily secure two independent goals. "First [accident law] must be just or fair; second it must reduce the costs of accidents."[9] Thus, whether liability for traffic accident costs ought to be decided on a case-by-case basis in a civil court according to the criterion of fault—as it is in the fault system—depends on whether or not doing so constitutes the most plausible means of *justly* achieving accident cost avoidance. In this section I want to explore briefly some of the ways in which allocating traffic accident costs on a no-fault basis can maximize cost avoidance, and defend the no-fault concept against the charge that it secures cost reduction only at the expense of justice.

Within the goal of cost avoidance, Calabresi includes (1) the reduction in number and severity of accidents, what he calls "primary cost reduction"; (2) the reduction of compensation costs, what he calls "secondary cost reduction"; and (3) the reduction of administrative and legal costs that arise in operating cumbersome judicial machinery and/or in administering an insurance system. This last subgoal of cost avoidance he terms "tertiary cost reduction."

The tertiary costs of the fault system are astronomical. As of 1969, nearly 56¢ of every insurance premium dollar was being devoured by administrative and legal costs! This figure compares unfavorably with the same costs in the Social Security System, Blue Cross, and in most health and accident plans, which are 3¢ per dollar, 7¢ per dollar and 17¢ per dollar respectively.[10] The startling fact is that insurance companies return less than 50 percent of the consumers' premium dollars in the form of liability coverage. A sizeable chunk of the remainder of the consumers' dollar goes into the costly machinery—including lawyers, technicians and law courts—necessary to examine conduct to determine if the criterion of fault has been satisfied. Allocating traffic costs on a no-fault basis seems to guarantee a reduction in insurance premiums if only because it eliminates one of the most costly features of the fault system—the courtroom determination of fault.[11]

One prevalent argument against no-fault is that it does not promote accident deterrence or primary cost avoidance. Underlying this claim is the conviction that faulty conduct is effectively deterred only by penalizing instances of it and, in the case of traffic accidents, only if the penalty takes the form of the injurer being liable for the costs of his victim's injuries. This claim rests on at least two unwarranted assumptions. First, even if faulty driving were deterred only by penalizing instances of it, it would be a mistake to assume that the penalty of liability for accident costs would be the only adequate inducement to safe driving. When the threat of penalty is employed as a deterrent, there is no evidence to suggest that stiff penal fines and the threat of revocation of license are less adequate on that score. Second, vicarious liability statutes and workmen's compensation provisions in the law suggest that in order to secure accident deterrence we need not penalize those at fault (or likely to be at fault) in causing injuries.[12] In the case of workmen's compensation, employers have shown a remarkable facility for improving safety conditions—and thereby reducing the number of accidents—when, regardless of personal culpability, they have been placed in the position of standing to lose in virtue of increased accident costs.

Instead of spreading the risks of an activity among consumers who use a product or employ a service by, for example, having them contract for liability or health insurance, we could distribute the costs among those persons who manufacture products or offer services. According to this extension of traditional products liability law, we might then let the costs of automobile injuries fall on the shoulders of automobile manufacturers. They would presumably purchase costly liability protection for specific automobile-related injuries and then pass the costs of these premiums on to the consumer, probably by increasing the purchase price of automobiles. In addition to being an effective form of secondary cost avoidance—by spreading the costs among all persons who purchase cars—eliminating hidden accident costs may enhance accident deterrence both among consumers and producers by encouraging the production and purchase of safer cars, insofar as their safety is reflected in their lower initial price.[13] A sufficient increase in the cost of automobiles in virtue of the additional "accident costs" would result first in a reduction in the number of cars purchased on a yearly basis. Eventually, fewer automobiles will actuarially come to mean fewer accidents.[14]

In addition, as the cost of the cars increases, there will be a group of consumers on the financial borderline of being able to maintain their automobiles. Members of this group, each of whom stands to lose by faulty driving the convenience of an automobile, have a personal incentive to drive safely and to encourage safe driving generally. Finally, car manufacturers who, in virtue of increased costs, stand to lose the consumer of moderate income are encouraged to produce a safer product. Nothing in this approach requires that traffic victims establish the fault either of their injurer or of the appropriate car manufacturer, and accident deterrence as well as compensatory cost reduction are therefore promoted without regard to the criterion of fault.

In the fault system, insurance plays the traditional role of protecting policy holders against specific losses, thereby promoting secondary cost reduction and helping thereby to maintain an acceptable balance between the burdens and benefits of motoring. One persuasive argument in favor of no-fault is that by abandoning fault as a relevant criterion in compensating traffic victims, we will be able to allocate the costs of accidents in even less burdensome and, perhaps, fairer ways.

Calabresi argues that the most plausible procedures for maximizing secondary cost savings involve distributing costs through either risk-spreading or deep-pocket methods, both of which aim at reducing the relative impact of those losses on individuals. Insurance schemes usually apply the risk-spreading method. That is, within limits determined by the total number of policy holders, liability insurance maximizes the number of persons and, to an extent, the period of time over which costs are spread. Motorists who fall within the same actuarial categories and hold contracts with the same insurance company pay roughly equal premiums for approximately identical coverage. It does not follow from the fact that such policy holders pay equal monetary shares that the burdens of bearing those costs are allocated equally among them. Therefore in contrast with risk-spreading, costs in the deep-pocket method are allocated according to a sliding ratio of assigned shares based on prior capacity to pay. The major theoretical difference between risk-spreading and deep-pocket methods is that, according to the former, losses are presumed to be least burdensome if they are spread thinly while, according to the latter, losses are considered to be least burdensome if they are borne by those most able to bear them.

In the deep-pocket method, the only relevant qualification for status as a risk-bearer is prior capacity to bear loss; one's rank among risk-bearers being determined entirely by how great that capacity is. This feature of the deep-pocket method—its allocating costs without regard to other criteria—has led some to criticize it as unjust in that some persons would seem to be required to pay simply because they could afford to. However, all except the most determined of hermits are engaged in or otherwise benefit from the activity of motoring. Thus, no one contributes *simply* because he or she can afford to. Provided we can clearly distinguish between direct and indirect benefits and degrees thereof, an allocation of losses strictly on a deep-pocket basis may yet be unfair in that it may violate the principle of justice that requires burdens to be commensurate with benefits. As a general principle for distributing losses, the deep-pocket principle could endorse allocating automobile accident costs through highly graduated tax structures, for example, income taxes. Such an alternative could escape certain charges of being unjust if it were part of a comprehensive plan designed to protect citizens against loss resulting from all accidentally caused injuries. What makes this proposal prima facie plausible is the fact that while few individuals would be willing to pay the accident costs of activities they neither engage in nor otherwise benefit from, nearly everyone would be anxious to protect himself against accident losses of one sort or another.[15]

But at what cost? It is unlikely that such a plan could work its way into the hearts of an already heavily taxed citizenry—especially one with free market pretentions. It is even less likely that such a plan would be embraced by powerful insurance and trial lawyer lobbies. Moreover, this form of no-fault coverage, which has obvious compensatory cost-avoidance virtues, could prove counterproductive with respect to the goal of accident deterrence. That is because this no-fault scheme "hides" the accident costs of particular activities by offering blanket coverage for all of them through tax dollars. Shielding these costs eliminates one important opportunity for the consumer to associate an activity with its accident costs, and consequently with its risks.

More modest no-fault plans involve maintaining private insurance, and depend on penal fines and the driver's natural concern for his own well-being to promote accident deterrence. These proposals usually obtain secondary cost avoidance by applying risk-spreading methods. We could alter these traditional approaches to no-fault to incorporate, on a small scale, certain virtues of the deep-pocket principle by having premiums within respective actuarial categories reflect prior capacity to pay. Alternatively we could have everyone pay something through their income tax toward the cost of accidents, and have the remainder of the costs distributed either through the costs of automobiles or the purchase of insurance policies. Thus, those who directly benefit from motoring—those who drive—would pay more than those who benefit indirectly.

Nothing in the previous argument suggests the need to introduce the criterion of fault into accident law as a means of securing any of its economic or utilitarian goals. That should be surprising neither to legal theorists nor to consumers who have borne the high costs of the fault system for too long. But the criterion of fault is not present in accident law to enhance cost reduction. Presumably, consulting it enables us to identify those individuals upon whom the cost of accidents ought to fall if *justice* is to be served, not if money is to be saved. Deciding liability on the basis of fault is, on the accepted view, inextricably linked to justice, which, in turn, is seen as requiring that burdens due to individual fault be allocated according to the criterion of fault, and that those burdens be commensurate with the degree of fault. This conception of justice is seen as supporting a fault system and prohibiting contracting for no-fault liability coverage.

Interestingly enough, if justice were to require that fault-related burdens be distributed exclusively according to the criterion of fault, it would be very hard to imagine how such demands could be met by the fault system, at least as we know it. In the first place, all traditional forms of insurance would be ruled out since they would allocate burdens in part among individuals whose records have been (and may remain) spotless, as well as among past and present tort-feasors.[16] The burdens of the faultless would not reflect their desert and would be objectionable on those grounds. In the absence of insurance, the costs of particular accidents would fall either on individual victims or injurers, with victims being ruled out on the same grounds as the faultless: no fault, no penalty. But if the costs of accidents were to fall entirely on individual wrongdoers, they would often prove disproportionate to the wrongdoing involved—slight errors can result in costly accidents—and this would be objectionable on the grounds that the burden would not reflect the degree of fault.

We might attempt to obviate these difficulties first by altering the fault system, and in the event that fails, by compromising the principle. Suppose that instead of allocating costs on an individual-case basis, we were to lump together the costs of all automobile accidents over a specified period of time and then distribute them among particular injurers by assigning relative weights to the different types of wrong-doing exhibited in the conduct of each. Then each injurer would no longer be responsible for the costs of the damages he caused, but would instead be liable for some portion of the whole: that portion reflecting the degree of shortcoming in his or her conduct. One major flaw in this proposal is that it gives each fault a *market* rather than a moral value, and may therefore fail to satisfy the principle in question. It would, after all, hardly carry the day for the forces of justice if legislators attached a lesser sanction to parking violations than to homicide, but decided on decapitation for the latter, and mere amputation for the former.

Alternatively, we might reintroduce traditional forms of insurance and justify this maneuver as required by the need to resolve a conflict between competing moral principles: one requiring the distribution of costs owing to error to reflect fault, and the other supporting the right to contract voluntarily to protect oneself against losses resulting from future untoward events. Any such form of contract requires that some of the costs of untoward events be absorbed by the faultless, somewhat analogously to the way in which medical expenses covered by health insurance policies are paid for in part through premiums of individuals who themselves may never invoke their policies. Intro-ducing insurance of any sort into accident law—fault or no-fault—necessarily compromises this principle of liability for fault. Compro-mised but not abandoned, it would presumably carry enough weight to require that fault play some role in the allocation of accident costs. This role would perhaps be satisfied by having the costs of particular accidents fall initially on those at fault, as they do in the fault system.

The argument does not yet establish the relevance of this principle of liability for fault to the goals of accident law. And surely it is on the claim of relevance that the argument stands or falls. For if there is nothing to be gained in terms of the aims of accident law—justice and/or cost avoidance—by satisfying the requirement that degree of liability reflect fault, the fact that the fault system with significant alterations meets these demands could not count in its favor. Underlying this claim to relevance is the prevalent view among defenders of the fault system that distributing losses in this way—by having them fall initially on individual injurers—secures the goal of justice, a legitimate aim of accident law, by penalizing the wrongdoing of those at fault. The fault system, by penalizing wrongful conduct, is therefore required by principles of retributive justice. On related grounds, prohibitions against no-fault are supported by principles of compensatory justice, which are said to require that recompense for losses must originate with those at fault. I want to consider both of these arguments in turn.

According to the standard conception of retributive justice, wrongdoing deserves its comeuppance: a measure of pain, suffering, or deprivation should be exacted from wrongdoers, and the deprivation should reflect the nature and magnitude of the wrongdoing. In its most prevalent and, I believe, least acceptable form the retributivist principle is a moral position in a very strong sense that in order for penalization to be deserved, the defective conduct must be morally defective, and the author of it morally at fault. Thus legal fault, insofar as it is based on the moral fault of the actor, ought to be penalized.[17]

One of the most prevalent defenses of a fault system rests on the claim that this principle of retributive justice requires it. The argument usually takes the following form. If an actor's defective conduct is a substantial contributory factor in bringing about harm, we impute the harm to him as his fault. He has, in the legal jargon, satisfied the fault requirement. The fault system, by making those at fault in causing accidents liable for their costs, guarantees that culpable motoring gets its comeuppance and is therefore required by the retributivist principle.

This argument in favor of the fault system does not purport to establish that every time an actor is at fault he is morally blameworthy. It establishes only that he is blameworthy in some sense of the term. And although some faulty driving is morally defective, for example, drunken, reckless driving, most driving faults are not moral shortcomings. If the retributivist principle were to support penalties only for moral wrongdoing, the fault system would justify too much. However, we need not interpret the retributivist principle this narrowly. Perhaps we should understand it as endorsing penalties for nonmoral as well as for moral shortcomings. H. L. A. Hart, for one, has argued persuasively that it is permissible morally to penalize wrongdoing that is an actor's fault—to his genuine discredit—whether or not the flaw in his conduct is a moral one.[18] If Hart is correct, then there exists a moral license to impose penalties on drivers who fail to satisfy the legal standard of due care, provided that failure can be charged against their personal records, that is, is something for which they are to blame. Hart's position does not amount to an endorsement of retributivism since he claims only that genuine wrongdoing may be penalized, while retributivists claim that such penalties are not merely permissible but a matter of right action.

Being at fault, morally or otherwise, has two essential ingredients. One element in fault judgments relates to the character of the act and its relationship to the appropriate standard of conduct, while the other relates to the actor's "state of mind." Most fault judgments are true just in case both the act-regarding and the actor-regarding requirements are satisfied. The essence of these requirements is perhaps best illustrated by the defenses alleged wrongdoers offer to defeat accusations of fault—that is, justifications and excuses. When an actor has a justification for what he has done, he denies that the act, all things considered, fails to satisfy the appropriate norm, or he argues that his conduct is an exception to the rule usually governing that type of conduct, or that it is an exception to the rule that such conduct is wrong. Should he have an excuse for what he has done, he would not be denying that his conduct was substandard, only that it was his fault. The "subjective" or mental element necessary to charge the act against his record, he thus argues, is missing.

If an actor has an excuse for his actions he is not at fault in the sense appropriate to justify imposing penalties against him on the grounds of retributive justice. That is because retributivism licenses penalties for *genuine* wrongdoing only. Insofar as excuses evidence the nonvoluntary character of the conduct, failure to measure up under excusing conditions cannot be considered something for which the actor is to blame. Though the retributivist principle would not endorse penalties for what would ordinarily count as excusable departures from the standard of due care, the system of awarding liability for accident costs on the basis of fault often penalizes those who in Hart's words "could not help doing what they did."

This feature of the fault system is well known among lawyers and has led some legal theorists to question if the courts should apply subjective (internal) or objective (external) standards of fault to determine liability in accident law. In other words, should the law require no more of each member of the community than he is capable of (the subjective test of fault) or should it require each to live up to a standard that may exceed the capacities of some (the objective test). The most famous and perhaps still the most compelling defense of the objective test is articulated in Oliver Wendell Holmes:

> If, for instance, a man is borne hasty and awkward, is always having accidents and hurting himself or his neighbors, no doubt his congenital defects will be allowed for in the courts of Heaven, but his slips are no less troublesome to his neighbors than if they sprang from guilty neglect. His neighbors, accordingly require him, at his proper peril, to come up to their standard, and the courts which they establish decline to take his personal equation into account.[19]

Ascriptions of fault that are verified by applying objective criteria of conduct are not defeasible by excuses. That is their distinctive feature. Thus, if an injurer genuinely could do no better than he did—if, in other words, his conduct was, in a suitably narrow sense, nonvoluntary—this would *not* suffice to free him from the burdens of recompense under the present system of accident law, though the nonvoluntary character of his actions would normally constitute excusing conditions and free him from blame.

We could of course amend the fault system to obviate this sort of difficulty by requiring that it apply only subjective criteria of fault. In this way, the fault system would penalize only those whose failure to exercise due care is to their personal discredit. But even if we recommend the application of the subjective test, the fault system would fail to satisfy the retributivist principle. That is because, in the fault system, only accident-causing wrongful driving receives its due— where the penalty is liability for accident costs—leaving unpenalized the class of dangerous and unnecessarily risky, but not harm-causing, wrongful motoring. From the retributivist point of view, this is unacceptable, since suitably culpable conduct without harmful causal upshots falls within its ambit. Thus, in the criminal law, so-called wrongful attempts are punishable, for example, attempted murder, attempted rape, and so on. From the retributivist point of view, the punishment of wrongful attempts is mandatory. The rough civil law analogue of criminal attempts is conduct that is "at fault," that is, unreasonably risky, harm-threatening, or dangerous. If securing the goal of retributive justice were the only goal of accident law, and if the penalty of liability for accident costs were the only sort of penalty befitting wrongful conduct of this sort, securing that goal would require that liability be spread among those at fault, not merely among those at fault in causing injuries. But even in this system driving faults are rendered market, not moral, values.

Moreover, the retributivist principle requires only that a fitting penalty be administered to wrongdoers. Nothing in the principle specifies that the penalty be liability for accident costs. Indeed, we have seen some of the difficulties inherent in trying to "fit" the penalty of civil liability to driving faults. An accident law in which liability for accident costs is the penalty for wrongful driving conflates two distinguishable issues: those of retribution and recompense. The fault system may be characterized by the fact that it joins these two issues, since in that system, the retribution for wrongdoing is recompense for injuries that are one's fault. The distinguishing feature of no-fault is the separation of these two concerns. By referring to accident law as a no-fault system, we do not mean to imply that there exist no purposes for which conduct should be examined for fault. Indeed, the criterion of fault is perfectly relevant to contriving penal fines or other penalties themselves suggested by the retributivist principle:

penalties more fitting than civil liability in the sense that they are not subject to market fluctuations.[20] All we mean to imply by the label "no-fault" is that the criterion of fault is irrelevant to the issue of recompense. That goal is to be satisfied by ensuring that the traffic victim receives the compensation to which he is entitled. Our notions of retributive justice therefore do not require that compensation, in order to be just, originate with those at fault. Whether or not our notions of corrective justice do is what I now want to consider.

There are a number of statements or ways of characterizing the requirements of corrective justice. I want to begin with the following conception of corrective justice. On this view, corrective or rectificatory justice is concerned with wrongful gains and losses. Rectification is, on this view, a matter of justice when it is necessary to protect a distribution of holdings (or entitlements) from distortions that arise from unjust enrichments or wrongful losses. The principle of corrective justice requires the annulment of both wrongful gains and losses.

In order to invoke the principle of corrective justice to support eliminating or rectifying a distortion in a distribution of holdings or entitlements, the distribution need not itself be just. Corrective justice is a matter of justice on this view *not* because it promotes justice in the distribution of holdings, but rather because it remedies unjust departures from the prevailing distribution of holdings. However, following the requirements of corrective justice is necessary to maintain a just distribution of holdings. Therefore, any theory of distributive justice must make provisions for a theory of corrective justice. Corrective justice is an independent principle of justice precisely because it may be legitimately invoked to protect or reinstate distributions of holdings that would themselves fail the test of distributive justice.

Under the principle of corrective or compensatory justice, the victim of another's fault may have a right to recompense. The principle of corrective justice does not establish the right of victims to recompense for "faultlessly" caused injuries, and though an insurance scheme that protected policy holders against errorless as well as faultily caused injuries might be preferable, the protection such a scheme could offer would extend beyond what injured parties could claim as their *right*.

If compensation for wrongfully inflicted harms is one's right, against whom does the right bearer hold it? Upon whom does the corresponding obligation fall? In an insurance scheme, the injured party's right to recompense may be against his insurance company or against the insurance company of his injurer. That depends on whether the insurance coverage is a "first" or "third" party plan; that is, whether individuals insure themselves against personal loss owing to the conduct of others (or themselves)—first party—or against liability for the injuries they may cause others—third party. According to the most extensive form of no-fault coverage, the victim's right to recompense is a valid claim he holds against his own insurance company: that right being derived from contract. The underlying moral issue is whether or not such contracts and their corresponding rights and obligations are consistent with principles of corrective justice. Is compensation for accidental harms to be analyzed broadly to require only that victims receive the compensation to which they are entitled, or narrowly to require that recompense for victims must originate with respective injurers.[21]

The most compelling arguments for the narrower interpretation emerge from what I have called "state of nature" case. Assume that we were to live in a world without insurance, a state of nature. This state of nature would be a bit less barren than the "historical" one, and considerably less nasty, since persons in it would favor automobiles to dinosaurs as modes of transport. Suppose now that two individuals, X and Y, were involved in an accident that is Y's fault. X's right to compensation creates a corresponding duty to provide recompense that seems to fall on Y, his injurer. It seems, moreover, that justice would require that Y compensate X. If this is so, it suggests the general conclusion that, in order to be just, compensation must come from those at fault.

Why is it that justice requires that Y bear X's costs? Perhaps, if Y does not compensate X, X will go without compensation. One consequence of this would be that X's faultless conduct would be penalized. Certainly that would be unjust.[22] But that justice is avoidable by guaranteeing that X does not have to bear his own costs. That goal is accomplished when anyone other than X, including, but not necessarily, Y shoulders them. Perhaps by Y not bearing X's costs, Y's wrongdoing would go unpenalized. That would presumably constitute a retributive injustice. But the retributive principle requires only that Y's wrongdoing be penalized, and that goal is accomplished not only when Y is made to compensate X, but also when Y is penalized in some other way, for example, through penal channels.

The state of nature case does not yet appear to justify prohibitions against contracting to protect oneself against loss on a no-fault basis, and at one time, I was willing to let the argument for no-fault stop there. But I have come to recognize the possibility that our intuition in the state of nature case may not be grounded in fears that X's innocence will be penalized or that Y's wrongdoing won't, but in something about the nature of compensatory justice itself. Pehaps this example reveals the essential characterisitics of compensatory justice that bar assimilating it with either weaker or stronger principles of retributivism, and that require just compensation for wrongdoing to originate with wrongdoers. I believe, however, that we can distinguish compensation from punishment, and compensatory justice from other principles of justice, while denying that compensatory justice prohibits no-fault accident law.

It is plausible to conceive of punishment as a kind of compensation only if it is reasonable to conceive of society through its penal statutes as the "victim" of criminal conduct. This metaphor has been abused to deny that any crimes are genuinely victimless. But if it remains somewhat unconvincing, the metaphor has nonetheless gathered some respectability through widespread currency. More important, the analysis of punishment as a kind of compensation makes sense only to the extent to which we can interpret penal sanctions as forms of compensation, which they clearly are not. Through penal channels society may seek retribution for harm, not compensation for it. The fact that victims of certain types of criminal activity, such as fraud and assault and battery, are free to seek compensation in *civil court* is evidence for the view that they are *not* compensated by the wrongdoer's suffering a *penal* sanction. Compensation on the other hand, where it is concerned with victims seeks to nullify their losses, to make them "whole" again. And, even the very crude "justification" of punishment, "an eye for an eye," makes no pretense of plugging the gap left by the victim's loss.

Both compensation and punishment are concerned with wrongdoing—wrongful gain, advantage, or benefit. But where punishment involves wrongdoers incurring some evil—usually the loss of assorted legal rights—for their wrongfully obtained (or sought) gains or advantages, compensation aims at annulling, rectifying, or eliminating these undeserved or otherwise unjustifiable gains. Where punishment is concerned with victims only secondarily, the overriding concern of compensation is the nullification of the victim's losses; the reordering of his affairs to make him whole again. James Nickel has simply but insightfully captured this feature of compensatory justice as the elimination of unjustifiable *gains and losses* owing to human action—what he aptly terms "distortions."[23]

If compensation involves the elimination of distortions, surely we must acknowledge that not every means of securing that goal would be endorsed by principles of compensatory justice. However seductive the myth of Robin Hood may be, there is little evidence to suggest that such a method for nullifying unwarranted gains and losses would satisfy the demands of compensatory justice. What further distinguishes compensatory from other principles of justice is that, in order to secure the elimination of distortions, it supports a system of correlative rights and duties between respective victims and wrongdoers. In the typical case of compensation, a finding for the plaintiff amounts to a recognition of his or her (legal) rights to recompense; a right that imposes a correlative duty upon the defendant to provide compensation. In the typical instance of punishment, a verdict of guilty confers upon the state a right to impose some penalty against the defendant. But this right is a moral license, and unlike a claim-right, it does not give rise to a correlative duty; in this case, an obligation on the defendant to be punished or to allow himself to be punished.

But if a distinguishing feature of compensatory justice is this structure of correlative rights and duties, wouldn't principles of compensatory justice therefore prohibit contractual relations that supersede this structure by imposing duties of recompense on the *victim's* insurance company—contractual relations that require the victim's insurance company to discharge what are, in fact, the duties of wrongdoers? Compensation is a kind of repayment, and it is therefore with the category of obligations to repay that we are concerned. In the case of obligations to repay debts or loans, justice does not as a rule require that the repayment originate with the party obligated to repay. Thus, when someone borrows money from the local bank, few protests of injustice are heard above clicking safe locks, provided the money is returned in sufficient quantities and at appropriate intervals, regardless of exactly who is forwarding the payments on whose behalf. My obligation to repay a debt of, say, $100 to you is discharged when my wealthy patron approaches you with that sum, and you accept it as repayment, even if I know nothing of this transaction. Of course some obligations to repay may be described so determinately that they could not justly be discharged by another. Here the requirement that the repayment originate with the obligated party is built into the description of the obligation, and the fact that it cannot justly be discharged by another is a function of the determinacy of the obligation, not of justice.

Though it is a misleading way of talking, we sometimes describe punishment as a kind of repayment. We talk, for example, about criminals as owing "debts to society," which are presumably repaid through incarceration. If there is any merit in viewing punishment as a debt of repayment, then surely it is the sort of debt that in order to be just must be repaid by the "obligated" party, that is, the wrongdoer.[24] Now, is the obligation to provide compensation for accidental torts something that can justly be discharged by intervening parties—in this case, insurance companies—and therefore like obligations to repay debts in this respect, or is it something that can be discharged justly only by wrongdoers—like the purported obligation criminals have to pay back society? If compensation is, in this regard, like punishment, in order to be just, recompense for accidental torts must therefore originate with those at fault and the defense of no-fault would surely be in serious trouble.

It does not make the task any easier to note, at least in one respect, that compensation for accidentally caused harms is akin to punishment. That is, unlike the obligation to repay debts, the obligation to compensate traffic victims is not derived from contractual relation or promise. It is derived from wrongdoing. But wrongdoing plays significantly different roles in punishment and in compensation. In compensation, unlike punishment, wrongdoing is not viewed as something in itself worthy of penalty. Instead compensation is concerned with wrongdoing only insofar as it either involves wrongful gain or benefit at another's expense, or it is evidence of the unjustifiable character of the victim's loss. In the absence of wrongful gain, proof of wrongdoing supports the victim's assertion that his losses have been wrongfully absorbed, and therefore justifies his demanding compensation as a matter of right, rather than requesting it as a matter of benevolence, utility, or welfare.

The distinguishing feature of automobile accidents and of accidental torts generally is that the injurer does not, as a rule, gain from his wrong, nor is it plausible to interpret his conduct as directed at securing some temporary or long-term advantage. It is, after all, the nature of the beast; accidents are unintentional. One does not plan an accident, except as that term may appear in quotation marks. On the contrary, intentional torts such as fraud are undertaken to secure wrongful advantage at another's expense. A no-fault allocation of losses owing to intentional torts involving gain would not nullify the wrongdoer's gain and would be objectionable on those grounds. Nor would punishing him under the criminal law eliminate the gain, since the penal statute requires only that he suffer some evil for his wrong; nothing in it requires that he forfeit his gain. But in the case of accidental torts there is, in general, no gain on the wrongdoer's behalf that needs to be eliminated. That his conduct is wrongful supports the right of the victim to recompense, nothing more. Of course, his conduct may exhibit sufficient fault to merit penalty, but that is a concern of retributive justice and may best be dealt with by penal fine. Thus, it is my contention that principles of compensatory justice would not support a no-fault allocation of losses owing to certain intentional torts—i.e., because of the element of wrongful gain—but would not prohibit no-fault accident law precisely because of the absence of wrongful gain.[25]

This conclusion should be especially comforting to legal reformers such as Guido Calabresi and Jeffrey O'Connell, both of whom have recently urged the separation of accident law from the main body of tort law. Such proposals suggest that accident law govern recompense for harms owing primarily to negligence and defective products, and that they do so on a no-fault, no-defect basis. They are usually recommended to us by dint of their cost-saving features. The arguments I have been considering in this section on compensatory justice suggest still further support for their position. It is hoped that support from these quarters will surprise only those who are wedded to the view that justice and utility cannot be achieved except at one another's expense.

CONTRACT LAW

THE DISTINCTION AMONG CONTRACTS, TORTS, AND PROPERTY

Charles Fried has put the distinction among property, contract, and tort law in a particularly useful way. In his view, property law defines the borders of our legally rightful possessions: the nature and scope of what we can claim legitimate title to. Tort law seeks to secure those borders in a particular way: by making us whole should we suffer damage in virtue of certain "border crossings." In contrast, contract law facilitates our disposing of our rightful possessions "in terms that seem best to us."[26] In short, property defines those of our rights to resources the law recognizes; tort law secures those rights by providing redress in the event our rights are violated or infringed; and contracts entitles us to trade, transfer, or dispose of our resources or our entitlements to them as we see fit. In Fried's view, "the regime of contract law, which respects the dispositions individuals make of their rights, carries to its natural conclusion the liberal premise that individuals have rights."[27] In other words, to have rights means that we are free to dispose as we see fit of the objects of our rights. Presumably, the right to dispose of our rights entails, in this view, the right to call upon the coercive authority of the state, through the law of contracts, to *enforce* and give legal effect to the promises we make to one another.

Both tort and the criminal law, in Fried's view, protect rights: the criminal law by penalizing those who cross the borders defined by a person's rights; the law of torts by providing restitution to the victims of border crossings. To the extent both tort and crimes protect rights, they enforce standards or norms specifying the conditions under which taking what another has a right to or putting him at risk without his consent is impermissible. They differ in terms of the manner of enforcement. Crimes are enforced publicly, torts privately. In contrast, contract law specifies the range of things we can, by our consent, transfer to others, and the conditions under which we are free to do so. Contract law is private law in two senses. The norms or standards of contracts are private ones, binding not because they are imposed by a public body with the authority to do so, but because they are borne of bilateral promise or mutual agreement; they are self-imposed. Moreover, these norms are enforced privately, by one of the parties to the contract who initiates litigation when he feels that the other party has failed to live up to the terms of the agreement. Thus, Fried's view of contracts as involving the private disposition of one's rights according to one's own lights squares nicely with the distinctions we have already drawn between torts and crimes. Torts and crimes enforce public standards but do so differentially. The criminal law enforces standards publicly; tort does so privately. The law of contracts, unlike both torts and criminal law, enforces private standards derived from individual choice or promise; and like torts, it does so privately.

One question this conception of contract law gives rise to concerns the legitimacy of the state's role in enforcing what on Fried's view at least are fundamentally private arrangements. What is the source of the state's claim to authority in the domain of private agreement? Moreover, an argument to the effect that the state has authority to enforce self-imposed responsibilities is necessary, for it is part of this view, not only that contracts free us to commit to one another the resources that are legitimately ours, but that, in doing so, we may avail ourselves of the public power by bringing suit against those who fail to live up to their agreements.

One solution to this problem is to deny that the norms enforced in contracts are essentially private ones. The other solution is to argue that even if the duties of contracts are self-imposed, the state has a legitimate interest in providing the parties with access to the public power in the event one or the other of them fails to live by the terms of the bargain. Arguments of the second sort are of two varieties: the first roots the legitimacy of state intervention in the domain of private contract on utilitarian grounds. Private agreements are necessary for the efficient functioning of markets. Traders in markets might have incentives to defect from their bargains, so everyone who might make a bargain has an interest in having the other party held to the terms of the bargain. It is in everyone's rational self-interest therefore, for a state to provide for the enforcement of agreements. The second approach roots the legitimacy of the state's entering the domain of private arrangements on moral grounds. Fried, for one, takes this tack. His view is that the law ought to enforce what is morally correct. It is right to keep one's promises; wrong to break them. Contracts, in Fried's view, are essentially promises and morally binding because promises are morally binding. Because the law ought to do what is morally required, the state has a legitimate interest in enforcing the terms of private agreements.

The alternative to both of these views is that contract law does not consist entirely or even primarily of self-imposed responsibilities derived from promises. The argument for this view begins by noting that not every promise is legally enforceable. Courts refuse to enforce agreements against public policy or "contracts" that involve criminal conduct. Courts will not generally enforce an agreement between A and B in which in order to repay a debt to B, A promises to turn over to B his wages, if by doing so A is no longer able to provide for his family. That sort of agreement may be objectionable either because it imposes significant adverse third-party effects on A's family, who are not party to the agreement and are therefore unable to voice an objection to it, or because such agreements are contrary to the public interest in protecting the stability of the family.

The law of contracts also imposes duties in some cases where no promise has been made. These are cases in which the doctrine of *promissory estoppel* is involved.[28] A may be under a duty to B when with good reason, B, expects A to perform and in virtue of his legitimate expectations incurs a detriment or cost in justified reliance on A's performance. In such cases, the duty does not arise in virtue of a promise but in virtue of another's legitimate expectations. The "expectation" thesis is more general than the view of contract as promise because explicit promises are only one of the ways in which an individual can induce legitimate expectations in others.

Another reason for objecting to the view of contracts as consisting primarily in self-imposed duties or norms is that courts will not enforce so-called unconscionable contracts: agreements whose terms are blatantly unfair.[29] Suppose all car dealers put a clause in the contract of sale that limits their responsibility to potential buyers. For example, the dealer's contract provides routine maintenance for one year or 12,000 miles in return for which the buyer waives his right to sue in the event he or a passenger in his car is injured in virtue of a defect in the design or construction of the vehicle. The potential buyer gets a bad deal. He waives his right to pursue tort remedies against the dealer or the manufacturer in return for a rather ordinary warranty. The courts might refuse to enforce the terms of such an agreement. The standards of unconscionability are imposed on a contract *externally*. Courts simply won't enforce bargains parties make when the terms are incompatible with an external or objective criterion of fairness.

The contrast between the kinds of views that have been advanced regarding the foundations of contractual duty are clear. Fried's view is that contracts derive from promises, and the duty to enforce contracts derives from the duty to keep one's promises. In this view, because contract is based on and enforces promises, courts are not entitled to use a dispute that arises in contract either to promote an independent ideal of *justice* by refusing to enforce bad or hard deals, or to further the economic or other aims of society as a whole. The alternative view objects that explicit promises are neither necessary nor sufficient for contractual duty. Moreover, external standards of *justice* and *public policy* are imposed in contracts, and these standards are duty imposing even though they do not arise in virtue of an explicit promise.

Philosophers distinguish between corrective and distributive justice. Principles of corrective justice require annulling unwarranted or wrongful gains and losses. Those who argue that in enforcing contracts courts do not enforce promises but seek instead to do justice between the parties usually have in mind the principle of corrective justice. One way to see this is to explore the kinds of remedies courts provide when a contract has been breached. Consider the following example of Fried's:

> II-A. I enter your antique shop on a quiet afternoon and agree in writing to buy an expensive chest I see there, the price being about three times what you paid for it a short time ago. When I get home I repent of my decision, and within half an hour of my visit—before any other customer has come to your store—I telephone to say I no longer want the chest.
>
> II-B. Same as above, except in the meantime you have waxed and polished the chest and had your delivery van bring it to my door.
>
> II-C. Same as above, except I have the use of the chest for six months, while your shop is closed for renovations.[30]

A court can award at least three sorts of damage remedies. It can require that I pay you expectation, reliance, or restitution damages. II-B represents the reliance you undertook in anticipation of my fulfilling my end of the bargain. If the court awards you reliance damages, it seeks to *repair* or *annul* whatever *losses* or *damage* you have incurred in virtue of my reneging. II-C represents the benefit I secure at your expense. If the court awards you restitution damages, it seeks to *annul* whatever *wrongful gain* my deceit brings me. These goals, annulling wrongful gain and loss, are the aims of corrective justice; and to the extent breach of contract occasions either remedy, courts seek to execute corrective justice. But corrective justice falls, by most accounts, within the province of tort law. So the view that contract law seeks to do justice between the parties—in particular, corrective justice—is very closely tied to the view that contract law actually imposes external norms, not unlike those imposed in torts— i.e., the tort prohibition against wrongful gain (which in contract is unjust benefit rectified by restitution damages) and that against imposing wrongful losses (which in contract becomes wrongfully induced reliance rectified by reliance damages.)

Only an award of expectation damages (II-A in the above example) is consistent with the Fried's view of contract as promise. In the deal we struck, I expect the chest and you expect the purchase price. You owe me the chest because that is what you promised me, and I owe you the purchase price because that is what I promised you. If I renege or breach, I owe you the full extent of what I promised to deliver. Thus, only expectation damages square with the view of contract as promise.[31]

The central question in contract theory is, very simply, what is its foundation? Does contract law enforce promises or does it enforce external standards of justice or utility, and is it therefore an appropriate institution by which a state can legitimately seek to promote its conception of the public good? We cannot answer this question here, but we can explore one aspect of it in more detail. In a recent article, Professor Anthony Kronman has argued for the view that contract law not only enforces an ideal of justice, it enforces standards of *distributive justice*.[32] Kronman's argument is especially interesting, for Kronman argues not only for the "public standard" theory of contract law, but for what might seem to be the most implausible version of it.

CONTRACT LAW AND DISTRIBUTIVE JUSTICE

Kronman's Claim

One might think Kronman's view—that contract law enforces principles of distributive justice—constitutes the most implausible version of the thesis that contract law serves the ends of justice simply because, unlike, for example, principles of corrective justice, principles of distributive justice specify what it takes to secure a just distribution of the resources of an entire community *among all of its members*. The scope of distributive justice is too great to serve as a basis for contract law. In contrast, the scope of corrective justice is considerably narrower, for corrective justice aims to rectify the wrongful gains and losses particular persons cause one another. The one-to-one, injurer-to-victim feature of corrective justice makes it a more suitable candidate for the principle of justice involved in contract law—if, in fact, contract law enforces any ideals of justice. Therefore, one would think that critics of Fried, and those who defend the view that contract law has been eclipsed by tort doctrines, would have advanced the thesis that instead of enforcing promises, contract law enforces ideals of corrective justice. Certainly, reliance and restitution damages, regularly awarded in cases of contractual breach, seem closely connected to the requirement of corrective justice that wrongful gains and losses be annulled. Moreover, how can the goal of securing an equitable or just distribution of the entirety of a community's resources be appropriately and adequately pursued in contracts, where issues come before the court on a case-by-case basis, and where courts are further constrained to resolve disputes in terms of the interests of the parties to the disputes rather than in terms of a specific conception of the collective good?

Libertarianism and Liberalism

Kronman maintains not only that courts have the authority to decide cases in terms of the effects of various decisions on the distribution of wealth within a community, but that considerations of distributive justice "must be taken into account if the law of contracts is to have even minimum moral acceptability.[33] His argument for both claims begins by distinguishing between what he calls "libertarian" and "liberal" political philosophies. The libertarian believes that the state does not, in general, have a right to interfere with the exercise of individual liberty. The only grounds upon which political coercion can be justified is in order to prevent someone in the course of exercising his liberty from harming others and thereby reducing the level of their liberty. As a corollary of this tenet, the libertarian believes that the transfer of resources between individuals is legitimate only if it results from free or voluntary choice. Just distributions of resources depend on voluntary behavior, or consensual transfer. Among the practices libertarians object to, therefore, is the progressive income tax, at least to the extent that the proceeds of the tax are used to redistribute wealth. Whereas the libertarian position is that only voluntary transfer is defensible, taxation for the purposes of redistribution involves the involuntary transfer of resources. Because the libertarian rejects the coercive redistribution of resources generally, he denies that contract law is a suitable mechanism for promoting distributive justice in particular. The libertarian view, then, squares with Fried's analysis of contract as promise and, one would think, deeply conflicts with the position that contract law promotes the aims of distributive justice.

Like the libertarian, the liberal is committed to individualism and to the need for the state to justify the use of its coercive powers. Unlike the libertarian who restricts the domain of legitimate state intervention to the prevention of harm, the liberal adopts a somewhat broader conception of the legitimate uses of the public power. The liberal believes, for example, that there are sometimes sufficiently good reasons for redistributing wealth, even though doing so necessarily means appropriating the property of some individuals without their consent.

The liberal and the libertarian are both committed to the importance of individual liberty and to the need for the state to justify the use of its power, especially when doing so restricts the exercise of liberty. The libertarian believes that the state's authority extends only to the prevention of harm; the liberal believes that the state is sometimes justified in redistributing wealth. Because the libertarian denies the legitimacy of nonconsensual transfer generally, he rejects redistribution through contract law in particular. The liberal does not deny the legitimacy of coerced redistribution, but he does deny the appropriateness of redistribution through contract law. For it is part of the liberal position not only that liberty is valuable, but that where liberty must be compromised, the incursion must be minimized. The liberal contends that redistribution through taxation is less intrusive than is redistribution through contract law, and so to the extent redistribution is justified at all, it ought to be secured through taxation—i.e., the least intrusive means.[34]

Voluntariness and Advantage-taking

Kronman begins by considering the libertarian position in part because the libertarian, unlike the liberal, denies that the state, whether through taxation or contract law, could ever be justified in coercing for the purpose of redistributing wealth. Instead, the libertarian holds that only voluntary agreements ought to be enforceable in contracts—or to put roughly the same point in Fried's terms, that all and only promises given voluntarily bind. An agreement into which two parties enter may be voided if the agreement is involuntary on at least one person's part. The circumstances that defeat voluntariness are numerous. In some cases, an individual may seek to be freed of his contractual duties on the grounds that he lacks the cognitive skills necessary to appreciate the consequences of his promise, and that the promise is not voluntarily given and thus not binding. Others seeking to be freed of their contractual commitments might allege fraud or deceit; still others claim physical coercion or ignorance of material (pertinent) fact as the basis for negating an agreement into which they have entered. Generally, as Kronman notes, voluntariness-defeating arguments fall into three categories. The first involve the presence of defects in the promisor: e.g., ignorance, mistake, insanity. The second involve force or fraud imposed by another. The third involve gross disparities in relative bargaining strength usually resulting from one party's being in a monopoly or near monopoly position with respect to a marketable resource.

The problem is to determine whether these categories can be further unified: whether, in other words, there is anything that all involutary agreements have in common. In Kronman's view, all involuntary agreements involve objectionable forms of *advantage-taking*. As he sees it, the problem of giving necessary and sufficient conditions for "involuntariness" is equivalent to determining "which of the many forms of advantage-taking possible in exchange relationships are compatible with the libertarian conception of freedom.[35] For, in each of the cases in which a promisor claims that his promise is not voluntarily given,

> the promisee enjoys an advantage of some sort which he has attempted to exploit for his own benefit. The advantage may consist in his superior information, intellect, or judgment, in the monopoly he enjoys with regard to a particular resource, or in his possession of a powerful instrument of violence or a gift for deception. In each of these cases, the fundamental question is whether the promisee should be permitted to exploit his advantage to the detriment of the other party, or whether permitting him to do so will deprive the other party of the freedom that is necessary, from a libertarian point of view, to make his promise truly voluntary and therefore binding.[36]

In all the cases in which one party seeks to free himself of the obligations his agreement imposes upon him on the grounds that he entered into the agreement involuntarily, the other party has an advantage, and the question always before the court is whether the advantage-taking is sufficiently objectionable to warrant the court's refusal to enforce its terms against the "exploited" party?

In Kronman's view, then, the libertarian's criterion of voluntariness as a condition of binding agreement creates the problem of distinguishing objectionable from permissible advantage-taking. This is the first step in the argument. Involuntariness is to be spelled out in terms of advantage-taking, and enforcing involuntary agreements is wrong because certain kinds of advantage-takings are wrong. The next step in the argument is to spell out the relationship between advantage-takings and distributive justice.

Advantage-taking and Distributive Justice

What one is exploiting in agreements are resources, talents, and certain states of affairs. If Jones deceives Smith into believing that the house he has on the market is structurally sound when it is not, Smith may find himself in court seeking to be freed from his contract. In deciding whether Smith should be relieved of his responsibilities under the contract, the court, in effect, is deciding whether Jones can take advantage of his capacity to deceive or mislead others. But that question is simply whether Jones or others should be permitted to secure gain or wealth in virtue of their capacity to fraud, deceive, or mislead.

To flesh out this idea further, recall Fried's characterization of contracts as that body of the law that governs the individual's right to dispose of his resources or entitlements to them as he sees fit. Contracts redistribute resources among the parties to them: apples for oranges, houses for money, etc. On the view Kronman takes issue with, contracts redistribute wealth or resources according to the desires of the parties, not according to any principle of distributive justice: the desires of the parties being expressed by the *voluntariness* of the promises they give. Kronman's point is that whether an agreement is voluntary is just the question of whether it involves objectionable advantage-taking, and that is the question of the legitimacy of securing wealth through differential patterns of capacities, skills, and resources.

Taking an advantage one has enables one to increase one's wealth relative to those with whom one is negotiating. In effect, when a court upholds a contract, it sanctions or permits the redistribution of wealth between parties according to the patterns of advantage that already exist between them. When it voids or refuses to enforce an agreement, a court objects that a pattern of advantage ought not be decisive in redistributing the resources between the parties. In either case, that is, whether a court upholds or refuses to enforce an agreement, necessarily it is determining whether particular advantages or patterns of advantage should be allowed to determine the redistribution of resources between parties. The court, in essence, is deciding which of a person's resources can be exploited by him (or others) to improve his (or their) relative wealth. The question before a court in every contracts case, then, is whether the parties should be entitled to exploit certain traits, talents, or states of affairs to increase their wealth by contractual relation: contract being the instrument of redistribution by agreement. The voluntariness requirement provides the court with the framework for solving the distributional issue, and to the extent theorists of contract law have seized upon the voluntariness requirement, without regard to its distributional elements, they have obscured the underlying, more fundamental connection between contract law and the distribution of wealth within a community.

It may be useful to summarize the argument that courts inevitably resolve disputes in contracts according to principles of distributive justice:

1. The argument begins by assuming the validity of the strongest argument against the view that principles of distributive justice are relevant to deciding contractual disputes. This is the libertarian principle that all and only *voluntary* agreements are enforceable. In this view, it is the *process* of agreement (whether voluntary on both sides or not) and not its outcome (whether what the parties secure by agreement conforms to the dictates of some distributional ideal) that determines a contract's validity.
2. An agreement is voluntary only if it is not involuntary.
3. An agreement is involuntary if it results from ignorance, mistake of fact, force, fraud, or is compelled by grossly unequal bargaining positions.
4. These conditions of involuntariness each involve objectionable advantage-taking—e.g., fraud involves the exploitation of misinformation.
5. Taking advantage, whether objectionable or not, involves the use of talents, skills, or resources at one's disposal—e.g., fraud involves gaining in virtue of one's capacity to deceive.
6. An unobjectionable advantage-taking allows a person to improve his relative wealth in virtue of the resources at his disposal. Determining that an advantage-taking is objectionable amounts to denying that the person is entitled to enhance his relative wealth in virtue of the resource involved.
7. Contract law therefore is fundamentally about the redistribution of wealth according to talents and resources at one's disposal.
8. The outcomes of contracts necessarily reflect patterns of advantage in talents and resources. To enforce a contract is to sanction the existing distribution of talents and resources as a basis for redistribution by agreement. To refuse to do so is to object to the existing pattern as a basis for redistribution by agreement. To do either requires a standard of distributive justice.

In the view we have just detailed, that courts resolve disputes on the basis of distributive considerations is inevitable. The only question that remains is by which standard of distributive justice courts are to decide upon the enforceability of agreements.

Paretianism and Distributive Justice

If contract law promotes distributive justice, which principle of justice does it enforce? Which advantages does justice entitle us to exploit in exchange relations, and which not? Kronman distinguishes among three alternative criteria by which we can distinguish objectionable from permissible advantage-taking.

1. Natural superiority. According to the principle of natural superiority, some people are more deserving than others—i.e., more beautiful, intelligent, or noble. If they gain in virtue of these advantages, so be it. Unobjectionable advantage-taking involves these natural superiorities or advantages.

2. Utility. According to the utilitarian principle, advantage-taking is acceptable provided it increases utility or welfare of the community as a whole.

3. Paretianism. According to the Pareto Principle, an advantage-taking is legitimate provided it works to the long-run *benefit of the group of persons who are taken advantage of.*[37]

Kronman rejects the first criterion on the grounds that it rests "upon a notion of differential worthiness wholly incompatible with the libertarian conception of individual equality,"[38] and the second on the grounds that utilitarianism fails to take individuals seriously. Natural superiority is inadequately egalitarian; utilitarianism is inadequately individualistic. Both fail, therefore, to distinguish objectionable from permissible advantage-takings in a way that a libertarian might endorse.

Only the Pareto Principle captures the insights of utilitarianism without abandoning the individualism of libertarianism. An advantage is not legitimately taken unless it makes both parties better off. The party who has and takes the advantage does so in order to promote his welfare. The Pareto Principle insures that the welfare of the exploited party is also enhanced. The Pareto Principle is plausible as a candidate for the principle of justice in contract law because satisfying it increases utility, but does not do so at the expense of the party being taken advantage of.

Putting both parts of Kronman's argument together, we get the following: contracts involve distributive justice because in resolving contractual disputes, courts decide upon the legitimacy of various patterns of distributional advantage; and in distinguishing permissible from impermissible advantage-taking, a court ought to apply the Pareto

Principle—i.e., advantage-taking is permissible when it works to the long-term benefit of the "exploited" party. Kronman's argument involves two distinct claims. The first is that contract law necessarily enforces a criterion of distributive justice. The second is that courts ought to apply the Pareto Principle—the principle that advantage-taking is permissible only if it works to the long-term benefit of the exploited party—as the correct principle of distributive justice in contracts.

While the claims are independent of one another—e.g., courts might aim to do distributive justice, but they ought not apply the Pareto Principle in doing so—neither can be sustained. Consider the second claim first, namely, that the appropriate principle of distributive justice in contracts is the Pareto Principle. The argument for the Pareto Principle is that it is both suitably individualistic to satisfy the libertarian and sufficiently welfare increasing to satisfy the utilitarian. Advantage-takings that satisfy the Pareto Principle increase net welfare, though not necessarily as much as would application of an unconstrained principle of utility. The Pareto Principle, unlike the principle of utility, requires that utility be increased by making *both* parties better off. The Pareto Principle expresses a constrained utilitarianism. The constraint that the welfare of both parties be improved is not required by the utilitarian aspect of the Pareto Principle, but by its libertarian element instead. But this is where the Pareto Principle goes astray. To see this, look more closely at what the argument that the Pareto Principle is acceptable to the libertarian really amounts to:

1. The libertarian's concern is that the principle of distributive justice in contracts (if there is one) ought to reflect the fundamental individualism of the libertarian position.
2. The libertarian's concern for individualism is adequately satisfied by the requirement that all advantage-takings work to the benefit of both parties, particularly to the benefit of the exploited party.

The weak link is the second premise. First, whereas the libertarian's concern in contracts as in every other dimension of political and legal experience, is for the individual, his concern is for the individual's *liberty* or his *rights*, not his welfare or utility. For it is part of any libertarian as opposed to utilitarian theory that there are no grounds of justice upon which we might object to an individual's choosing to be made worse off. Jones might freely consent to being exploited by Smith, and if he does, the court is simply not free to decide whether this sort of advantage-taking leads in the long run to a positive increment in Jones's welfare or utility. In this regard, the libertarian is fundamentally nonpaternalistic. As long as someone voluntarily agrees to a course of conduct, he is free to pursue it provided he harms no one else. Now, were Kronman to allege that what is at issue in these cases is precisely whether such agreements are voluntary and that in determining whether they are we must ask whether the course of conduct the individual sets for himself works to his long-run benefit, the libertarian would rightly charge him with begging the question by presuming that one could not willingly act to one's long-term detriment. Surely, we have lots of evidence that people choose to act contrary to their well-being.

Second, the Pareto Principle would be no more amenable to the libertarian if instead of requiring of permissible advantage-takings that they work to the maximum benefit of both parties, it required of permissible advantage-takings that they maximize the *liberty* or *freedom* of both parties. The libertarian would no sooner permit one party to be taken advantage of to promote overall liberty—even if sacrificing one person's liberty could be shown to increase net liberty (whatever that might mean)—than he would endorse a sacrifice in liberty to promote overall utility. In each case, one person's liberty is sacrificed for the good of others or for his long-term good, whether that good is defined in terms of utility or liberty. Under either formulation, the Pareto Principle fails to represent that aspect of individualism the libertarian is committed to.

The problem with Paretianism as a principle of justice in contracts runs deeper still. In Kronman's actual formulation of the principle, an advantage-taking is permissible only if it works to the long-term benefit of *the majority of the individuals in the group to which the exploited party belongs*. As Kronman suggests, this may be the only formulation of the principle of sufficient generality to be applicable by courts. Nevertheless, it is deeply incompatible with the libertarian ideal. For it is no part of this formulation of the principle that a permissible advantage-taking work to the benefit of the exploited party himself in either the short or the long run. Rather, advantage-takings are permissible even if exploitation makes the contracting party worse off, provided it makes members of the group to which he belongs better off in the long run. Surely, this involves precisely the same sort of sacrifice that the unconstrained principle of utility does. Just as the exploited party cannot, in the libertarian theory, be exploited for the benefit of the advantage-taker or the public at large, he cannot legitimately be exploited for the benefit of others in a group to which he happens to belong. Permitting someone to be exploited for the good of the group is incompatible with libertarianism, not only because it involves utilitarian like sacrifice, but because in order to avoid that charge, it involves identifying an individual's interest with that of the group to which he contingently belongs. To do so is once again to misconstrue the individualistic component of libertarianism. Worse, it is to ignore it entirely.

Fourth, these objections might matter less were it not for the fact that we *could* formulate the Pareto Principle in terms of the long-term interests of the exploited party himself. I have elsewhere argued, for example, that one reason for objecting to the All-Volunteer Armed Forces is that, as it is currently formed, the Armed Services take advantage of the limited employment options and the consequently relatively weak bargaining positions of the poor. In spite of this, one could argue, on Pareto Principle grounds, that even though each "voluntary" recruit is taken advantage of, permitting the advantage to be taken works to *the particular recruit's* benefit. After all, refusing to permit that sort of advantage-taking simply makes each potential recruit worse off by further reducing his employment opportunities.[39] Similar issues arise in other contractual circumstances in which a consenting party's weak relative bargaining position makes him especially vulnerable to exploitation, and in agreements by prisoners to be subjects in medical experiments. In these cases, it makes perfectly good sense to decide on the permissibility of an advantage-taking in terms of its effect on the well-being of the exploited party himself, rather than on the well-being of the groups to which he belongs. In short, the Pareto Principle can be meaningfully formulated in terms of the interests of the "exploited" party, not just in terms of the interests of the group to which he belongs. Failure to formulate the principle sufficiently narrowly leads to sacrifices of the liberty of the exploited party of just the sort libertarianism decries.

Lastly, if the libertarian were committed to a principle of distributive justice in contracts, it would be a variant of the Natural Superiority Principle (what we might call the natural advantage principle) that Kronman rejects as inadequately egalitarian. The libertarian could argue that an individual should be entitled to gain in virtue of certain of his natural advantages—e.g., beauty, intelligence, quick wit, humor, height, athletic prowess, etc.—not because he *deserves* to gain in virtue of his possessing these abilities; not, in other words, because these traits make him more *worthy*. Rather, the basic structure of the libertarian's argument for the natural advantage principle, as I understand it, is that any alternative principle will be unjustifiably coercive and incapable of taking individuals seriously. You and I are not much else other than our distinctive traits, and while I may not deserve in any straightforward sense my intelligence, looks, manner, or personality, they are my traits and not yours. Even if neither you nor I *deserve* the fruits our differential talents bring us, it hardly follows that anyone else does. To refuse to permit me whatever gains my talents bring me necessarily entails giving someone else title to them, but on what grounds? Clearly, the talents are not someone else's; what claim can anyone else have on my talents? And if I have no special title to the fruits of my personal traits or characteristics, in what sense can I be thought of as a distinct individual? There are limits to these arguments; they may not even be compelling in the least. I raise them only to show that were a libertarian committed to a principle of redistribution in contracts, there are several reasons for denying that it would be the one Kronman ascribes to him—i.e., the Pareto Principle—and still other reasons for thinking that a libertarian principle would be a suitably formulated variant of the principle of natural superiority that Kronman mistakenly believes the libertarian would reject as inadequately egalitarian.

Contract Law and Distributive Justice Reconsidered

Even if Kronman is mistaken in believing that the Pareto Principle sets forth the correct principle of distributive justice in contracts, it does not follow that he is mistaken in his more fundamental claim that contract law necessarily enforces some principle of distributive justice. This claim may be sustained even if he is forced to abandon the Pareto Principle.

The reader will recall that the argument for the claim that contracts enforce a principle of distributive justice relies on the claim that even a libertarian .must understand the issue before a court in contracts as that of deciding whether a contracting party should be entitled to take advantage of a particular talent or resource he possesses in order to redistribute wealth to his relative advantage. Contracts are just instruments mediating the redistribution of wealth according to existing patterns of advantage.

There are at least two ways of understanding Kronman's claim about the relationship of contracts to distributive justice. The first interpretation makes the claim true but trivially so; the second makes it false. Consider each interpretation in turn. What people do when they contract with one another is transfer resources they have at their disposal. In doing so, the parties create and share "surplus," i.e., the gains from trade. In every case, contracts redistribute wealth, the gains from trade. If that is so—and it is—then contracts necessarily involve distributive justice. Understood in this way, even Fried's view of contract as promise is a redistributive principle: i.e., courts should sanction or permit the redistribution of wealth according to the desires expressed in the promise of the parties. If this is all Kronman means by the claim that contract law is inevitably a matter of distributive justice, the claim is correct but uninteresting.

My view is that Kronman seeks to unearth a more interesting connection between contract law and distributive justice. The deeper argument explains the distributive element in contracts not in terms of the libertarian principle of distribution that courts must enforce promises (and the resulting redistributions), but in terms of the proper analysis of the libertarian's notion of voluntariness. The deeper, more interesting connection between contracts and distributive justice is to be unearthed by giving an analysis of voluntariness in distributive justice terms. To see how the argument goes and where it runs afoul, reconsider the libertarian dictum that all and only voluntary agreements are binding. Involuntary agreements—those made in virtue of mistake, ignorance, duress, force, or fraud—involve objectionable advantage-taking. Once the libertarian sees that involuntariness is just one kind of objectionable advantage-taking, he is on the road to liberalism, in particular, to a distributive justice account of contracts. For once the libertarian agrees that involuntariness is to be analyzed in terms of advantage-taking, the next question concerns the appropriate criterion of advantage-taking: in other words, which of a contracting party's resources may be legitimately taken advantage of in the process of redistribution by agreement?

The libertarian slides down the slippery slope to liberalism, however, only if he agrees that what is wrong about involuntary agreements is that they involve objectionable advantage-taking. But a libertarian is unlikely to object to involuntary agreements on these grounds. In other words, the libertarian may agree that an involuntary agreement involves an objectionable form of advantage-taking, but deny that what makes it wrong to enforce involuntary agreements is that doing so involves unfair advantage-taking. Instead the libertarian might argue that involuntary agreements are wrong because they are coercive. Coercion fails to treat the person with proper respect, as a rational autonomous agent capable of promoting his own ends. Failure to secure someone's consent prior to taking his resources amounts to treating the individual merely as a means to one's own gratification. In the libertarian's view, securing someone's voluntary consent is essential to giving one proper respect; it is necessary to treating someone as an end in himself, rather than as a means to one's gratification. Whether these defenses of the libertarian's insistence on consent as a basis of agreement in contract are ultimately convincing is of no matter here. What matters is that, contrary to Kronman, the libertarian is *not* committed to seeing the fault in involuntary exchanges in terms of their involving objectionable advantage-takings.[40] Because the libertarian is not committed to understanding the morality of voluntariness in terms of the morality of advantage-taking, he is not subject to Kronman's objection—namely, that even he (the libertarian) must see contracts as ultimately an instrument of distributive justice.

One final remark on this score. In Kronman's view, involuntariness involves advantage-taking. Whether an advantage is legitimately taken depends on whether it works to the long-term benefit of the exploited individual's group. But it will always be a *contingent* matter to be decided on a case-by-case basis according to the facts whether an advantage has the desirable effect on the welfare of the exploited party. It follows then in Kronman's view that *whether an involuntary agreement is objectionable is always a contingent matter depending on the consequences in each case of permitting the relevant advantage to be taken.* Surely, the libertarian could never accept Kronman's characterization of the fault in involuntary agreements because the libertarian, whatever else he claims, asserts that involuntary agreements are flat out impermissible, and their impermissibility is *not* a contingent matter to be decided by their fruits on a case-by-case basis.

IF KRONMAN IS WRONG DOES THAT MAKE FRIED RIGHT?

Contract law *may* enforce a principle of distributive justice, but Kronman's arguments fail to demonstrate that it does except as the claim may be given a trivial construal. Unless we understand him to be arguing for the trivial interpretation of his thesis, Kronman is mistaken in thinking that contract law inevitably enforces principles of distributive justice. It does not follow, however, that Fried is correct in thinking that contracts necessarily enforce promises. In order to establish the claim that the core and scope of contractual obligation is the promise, one would have to reexamine the appropriateness of the damage remedies of reliance and restitution as well as the rule of contract that requires a plaintiff to mitigate or help to reduce the damages he suffers in virtue of the defendant's breach. These features of contract law are very closely connected, at least conceptually, to what we think of as basic elements of tort law: recompense for actual wrongful losses caused by another.

I want to close this chapter by advancing the rather radical suggestion that not only are aspects of contract law very much like those of torts, but that we can think of breaches of contracts as torts. In other words, let's consider the possibility not just that many remedies for breach of contract have the same structure and purpose as tort remedies, but that breach of contract itself may be analyzed as a tort. In this analysis, to contract is to use the *public language* in a particular way. There are well-established conventions regarding the ways in which language is used among individuals to convey ideas, intentions, beliefs, and to create expectations. When Jim promises Slim to purchase Slim's automobile at an agreed upon price, Jim uses the language of promising and is subject to the conventions regarding its use. In virtue of certain of these conventions, Jim's promise creates expectations in Slim. If Jim breaches, he has failed in some significant way to abide by the public standards of linguistic usage. He has failed either through negligence—as would be the case if he did not seek to understand fully the conventions of promising—or through wrongful intent—to abide by the rules of promise-making, and he has harmed Slim in so doing. Why shouldn't the failure to abide by certain conventional rules of linguistic usage constitute a tort for which victims may receive recompense. Then, even if contracts enforce promises, contract law may be reduced to tort law because promise-breaking may be analyzed as a tort: i.e., the wrongful use of the linguistic conventions surrounding "promising."[41]

Not all failures to abide by linguistic conventions are likely to frustrate protected expectations and so not every failure to comply with linguistic practices is tortious. Moreover, the "reduction" does not go in the other direction—from torts to contracts—since not all torts can be analyzed as involving a breach of promise except in the very attenuated sense that as members of civil society we have already promised to abide by all public standards of behavior, whether criminal, tortious, contractual, or linguistic. But even in this view, it is not that individual torts are breaches of particular promises; instead, it is that the promise is the fundamental *source* of all political and legal obligations, whatever the actual nature or scope of a particular obligation may be. So we have a potentially interesting thesis worthy of further exploration.

In short, the view that contract law is not merely an instrument of distributive justice does not entail that a contract is a promise, for it remains a very open and important question in legal theory whether remedies for breach of contract and breach of contract itself can be usefully analyzed as tort remedies and as torts respectively. There is probably no more interesting and important, yet inadequately developed area in the philosophy of the private law than that defined by the set of issues regarding the analytic and normative foundations of tort and contract, and the relationships, if any, between them.[42]

NOTES

1. By a public standard, I mean one imposed on parties either by public morality, convention or legitimate civil authority. It is not, in contrast, a self-imposed standard, binding because one has agreed to abide by it.

2. When I use the term "private enforcement," I do not mean to suggest vigilantism or the absence of state mechanisms that enable judgments to be reached and carried out. Rather, my point in this: *detection* of an alleged failure of compliance with a standard depends on private persons initiating litigation. For example, suppose there is a prohibition against negligent motoring, but it turns out that no victims of another's negligence ever brought suit to seek damages. In that case—in the absence of a corresponding criminal standard against negligent motoring—the standard simply would be unenforced.

3. In general simple negligence does not constitute a criminal offense; so-called "criminal negligence" that borders on what we think of as recklessness does.

4. The existence of punitive damages in torts might suggest to some that the distinctions I draw between torts and crimes is not nearly so sharp as I suggest they are. One cannot, of course, assume that the distinctions are as clear cut in reality as one would like them to be. Still, punitive damages are not really punishments. Were they, one would suspect that the same kinds of due process guarantees that alleged offenders in the criminal law can avail themselves of would be open to them in torts. In fact, they are not. It's best to see punitive damages in torts simply as an award in excess of actual damages which is sometimes necessary to induce private parties who are victims to take the risks of initiating litigation in certain kinds of cases. It is a further matter to determine the range of cases for which punitive damages are an appropriate and desirable inducement to litigation.

5. A person is at fault in torts if his conduct is either negligent, reckless, or is the result of a wrongful intent to injure. A negligent person is one who simply fails to exercise the care of a reasonable man or woman of ordinary prudence.

6. The following section is a slightly revised version of my paper, "Justice and the Argument for No-Fault," *Social Theory and Practice* 3 (1974).

7. It is the legislator's task to decide not only how and among whom accident costs ought to be allocated, but also to determine which costs of accidents fall within the ambit of accidental law. Thus, in no-fault plans, we invariably find provisions limiting recompense for so-called "pain and suffering."

8. Guido Calabresi, *The Costs of Accidents* (New Haven: Yale University Press, 1970), 22.

9. Ibid., 24.

10. These figures come from Jeffrey O'Connell, "Expanding No-Fault Beyond Auto Insurance: Some Proposals," *University of Virginia Law Review* 59 (May 1973):749–56. To my knowledge this essay contains the best discussion of the implications of no-fault automobile accident law for accident law generally.

11. Evidence for this claim was not long in coming. The *New York Times* of 3 October 1972, reported that: "The Massachusetts law has resulted in substantial savings in bodily injury premiums as well as an unexpected decline in claims for damages."

12. An example of vicarious liability in the law is the doctrine of Legal Agency. Thus, if in the course of activity as Y's legal agent, X is at fault in causing harm to Z, the burden of recompense may fall on Y, not X.

13. Compensatory (or secondary) cost avoidance is meant to include the reduction both in cumulative and individual costs. Thus it involves both absolute and relative cost reduction and is therefore somewhat confusing. Secondary cost reduction is achieved either when the absolute number of dollars going to compensate traffic victims decreases drastically or when the relative burdens of bearing those costs on individuals decreases.

14. There is at least one obvious flaw in this sort of argument. An increase in new car prices is as likely to keep older, outdated cars on the road as it is to result in fewer cars on our highways. If this were so, and if older equipment were less safe than newer

automobiles would be, then it is possible that the result of market deterrence would be an increase in accidents.

15. Precisely this sort of program has recently gone into effect in New Zealand.

16. Alternatively, one may view third-party insurance schemes as requiring a modest fee that is part of the cash reserve collected to indemnify someone against losses caused by his fault. However, the fee one contributes to the reserve may help to pay for the cost of accidents that are the fault of others, and may on the view I am considering be subject to the moral criticism that it is unfair to require someone to help discharge the compensatory obligations of others.

17. My arguments in this section of the essay draw from a discussion of the fault system in my essay "On the Moral Argument for the Fault System," *Journal of Philosophy* 71 (August 14, 1974):473–90.

18. Cf. H. L. A. Hart, "Legal Responsibility and Excuses," in *Punishment and Responsibility* (New York: Oxford, 1968), 39.

19. O. W. Holmes, *The Common Law* (Boston: Little, Brown and Company, 1963), 86.

20. Though such penalties are not affected by market values, they may be subject to considerations other than moral fault, e.g., deterrent value.

21. For reasons of relevance and manageability, I am confining the discussion of compensation and compensatory justice to recompense for losses owing to the wrongful conduct of another, though I am inclined to believe that the exposition of compensatory justice presented here would be enlightening in analyzing and resolving issues of "compensatory" benefits for historically disadvantaged groups.

22. We might consider the principle that a victim's innocence should not be penalized as stating the demands of *weak* retributive justice.

23. James Nickel, "What Is Compensatory Justice?" *William and Mary Law Review*, Vol. 3.

24. Imagine the effects on our notions of responsibility of an insurance scheme for criminal liability!

25. What I want to claim here is not that we can't imagine any situations in which accidents are beneficial to wrongdoers, but only that accidents in general are not beneficial to them, and, moreover, that accidents in general do not discriminate between victims and injurers in terms of likelihood of harm or gain. In other words, a priori, there is no reason to think that injurers more than victims will gain from accidents, just as there is no reason to assume that victims more than injurers will lose from them.

26. Charles Fried, *Contract as Promise* (Harvard University Press: Cambridge) 1981.

27. Ibid., 2.

28. For a lucid discussion of the doctrine of promissory estoppel, see Friederich Kessler and Grant Gilmore, *Contracts: Cases and Materials*, 2nd ed. (Boston: Little, Brown and Company, 1974), 226–28.

29. The Uniform Commercial Code defines an unconscionable contract or clause as follows:

§2-302. *Unconscionable Contract or Clause.* (1) If the court as a matter of law finds the contract or any clause of the contract to have been unconscionable at the time it was made the court may refuse to enforce the contract, or it may enforce the remainder of the contract without the unconscionable clause, or it may so limit the application of any unconscionable clause as to avoid any unconscionable result.

When it is claimed or appears to the court that the contract or any clause thereof may be unconscionable the parties shall be afforded a reasonable opportunity to present evidence as to its commercial setting, purpose and effect to aid the court in making the determination.

30. Fried, *supra* note 29, 18–19.

31. But as we will see in the next chapter the economic analysis also specifies expectation damages as necessary for *efficiency*.

32. Anthony T. Kronman, "Contract Law and Distributive Justice," *The Yale Law Journal* 89 (1980):473.

33. Ibid., 474.

34. Kronman also argues against the view that taxation is a less intrusive vehicle of redistribution than is contract law, *ibid.*, 498–511.

35. Ibid., 480.

36. Ibid.

37. Ibid., 487.

38. Ibid., 485.

39. Jules L. Coleman, "Liberalism, Unfair Advantage, and the Volunteer Armed Forces," in *Conscripts and Volunteers: Military Requirements, Social Values, and the All-Volunteer Force*, ed. Robert K. Fullinwider (Totowa, N.J.: Rowman and Allanheld, 1983).

40. Cats are animals. Suppose you object to cats and to animals both. You may object to cats either because you object to animals generally or because you have a special dislike for cats; they can be diffident. It just so happens that you object to both cats and animals, but if you could be persuaded no longer to dislike animals generally you might yet object to cats. Now think about the involuntariness/objectionable advantage-taking argument. One can agree that involuntariness involves objectionable advantage-taking, but have independent grounds for objecting to involuntary agreements such that even if one could be persuaded that objectionable advantage-takings in general should not be sufficient grounds for voiding a contract, involuntariness should.

41. The view that breach of contract can be a tort takes linguistic conventions as primitive or basic. According to at least one distinguished philosopher of language, linguistic conventions are not primitives and should be analyzed in quasi-contractual terms, i.e., as involving agreements. Cf., John Pollock, *Language and Thought* (Princeton, N.J.; Princeton University Press) If Pollock is right, is it possible still to analyze breach of contract as a "linguistic tort" without being led to an infinite regress?

42. Space limitations prevent me from considering other philosophic problems in the private law—for example, in property. If I had the opportunity, I would have discusssed the following problem. The Fifth Amendment to the U.S. Constitution prohibits the state from taking an individual's private property and putting it to a public use without rendering just compensation. But what is to count as a taking of property? Consider two cases. The state condemns your house and takes title to it so that it can construct another leg on its freeway system. That's clearly a taking that requires that you be compensated. Now suppose that you own a parcel of land in a developing area of town which at the time you purchased it was zoned for commercial use. As the town grows up around you, the value of your property escalates. Suppose you bought it at $100,000 and that it is now worth $1,000,000. Local environmentalists discover that migrating geese stop year after year on your property on their way south in the fall and north in the spring. They bring this to the attention of the local zoning commission, seeking to change the zoning of your land to prohibit any industrial, commercial, or residential use that might adversely affect the migration patterns of the geese. They win a zoning change. Your property is now, in effect, a wildlife reserve. You retain title, but the value of the land is virtually nothing: it is not a marketable resource. Is the rezoning of your property a taking of it? This is not a trivial question since if it is, the government must repair your loss; if it is not, if instead it is a *regulation of property* (not a taking) under the state's police powers, you are left without remedy. Can we determine in a nonquestion-begging way what constitutes a taking? If so, what does the analysis of "taking" mean for our analysis of "property?"

5

Law and Economics

The previous four chapters have explored several of the central issues in the philosophy of law. It should be clear by now both that there is a good deal about the law of interest to philosophers and that recent work in legal philosophy has greatly extended its frontiers. Nevertheless, there have been no attempts by philosophers to develop a unified, comprehensive moral or philosophic theory of law. No philosopher has claimed that the substance of such diverse areas of the law as crimes, torts, property, contracts, civil procedure, corporations, and family law could possibly derive from any one moral principle or set of consistent moral principles. There are several reasons for this. First, the claim that one could derive the substance of such complex and diverse bodies of law strikes the cautious intellect as a bit preposterous on its face. Second, most philosophers lack the requisite knowledge of law to attempt such a broad sweep. Third, it is highly unlikely that philosophers could ever agree upon one principle or set of principles as the one or ones the law seeks to enforce. To the extent there is widespread agreement among philosophers, we converge on method (on ways of framing issues and pursuing solutions to them) rather than on substance (on a particular principle that systematically ought to be employed to solve problems). Philosophy of law has no "research program" as such.

While there is nothing we can refer to as a research program in legal philosophy, such a program has emerged in the field of law and economics. Over the last several decades economists and lawyers trained in or enamored of economics have sought to explore the extent to which virtually all areas of the law could be understood as the institutional embodiment of the principle of economic efficiency. It

This is an expanded version of an article which will appear in a forthcoming volume of *Ethics*, July 1984, University of Chicago Press.

is strange that economists do not find the claim that all of the law could derive from a single principle at all preposterous. The work in law and economics has had both analytic and normative dimensions. The analytic work has aimed at demonstrating that large areas of law could be explained by seeing them as concerned not so much with matters of justice but with the efficient allocation of resources. The normative work in the field is concerned to give legislators and judges a framework for legislating and adjudicating cases so as to promote the goal of efficiency.

This chapter explains the economic analysis of law. It requires absolutely no prior knowledge of economics, nor does it presuppose any familiarity (by the student or the instructor) with the law and economics literature. Consequently, I have broken the chapter into three general sections. In the first section, I give definitions of the key concepts in the analysis and present the basic models that the analysis uses. In the second section, I show how the economic analysis can be used to elucidate various areas of the common law. In this section, I demonstrate how the economic analysis can be applied to problems of pollution, automobile accidents, and breach of contract. I also discuss briefly the results of the seminal piece of the economics of crime, and show how one can use game theory to characterize when it is rational for a litigant in a civil suit to pursue litigation or to accept (or offer) a pretrial settlement. In the third section, I consider several objections—some good; some popular, but not so good—to various features of the economic analysis of law.

BASIC CONCEPTS AND MODELS

UNDERSTANDING EFFICIENCY

One reason philosophers of law should take economic analysis seriously is because the most basic notion in the analysis—efficiency or Pareto optimality—was originally introduced to help solve a serious objection to the widely held moral theory, utilitarianism. Utilitarians hold that the principle of utility is the criterion of right conduct. Whether one advances total or average utilitarianism, applying the principle requires interpersonal comparisons of utility.[1] How can we evaluate policies in virtue of their effect on individual welfare or utility, if one persons' utility cannot be compared with that of another? The claim that we can compare utilities is quite controversial. The Pareto criteria were first introduced to obviate the problem of interpersonal comparability. There are two Pareto criteria: *Pareto optimality* and *Pareto superiority*.

Pareto superiority ranks or orders social states according to the following conditions:

> *Definition$_1$*: One state of the world, S_1, is Pareto superior to another, S, if and only if no one is worse off in S_1 than in S, and at least one person is better off in S_1 than in S.

Whether or not a person is better off in one state or another usually depends on his relative welfare, and each person is presumed to be the judge of his relative well-being. Pareto superiority is sometimes characterized in the following way as well:

> *Definition$_2$*: S_1 is Pareto superior to S if and only if no one prefers S to S_1 and at least one person prefers S_1 to S.

The Pareto superiority criterion obviates the interpersonal comparability problem of classical utilitarianism. Because no one is made worse off, there are no losers in Pareto improvements whose losses are to be subtracted from, i.e., compared to, the winner's gains. If at least one person is better off, i.e., has a greater utility in S_1 than in S, and no one is worse off in S_1 than in S, then in going from S to S_1, there is a net gain in total utility.

We can now introduce the derivative concept of Pareto optimality:

> *Definition$_3$*: S_i is Pareto optimal if and only if there exists no S_n such that S_n is Pareto superior to S_i.

A Pareto optimal state has no states Pareto superior to it. When resources are distributed in a Pareto optimal fashion, there is no way of making anyone better off without making someone else worse off. Pareto optimal states are the eventual outcome of a sequence of Pareto superior moves, though one can reach a Pareto optimal state through a sequence of non-Pareto superior moves. Consider the following simple example. Suppose there is only one commodity, C; and ten units of it; two persons, X and Y, both of whom prefer more C to less. Imagine the following two distributions of resources between X and Y.

S_2: X has 10 units of C; Y has 0 units of C.
S_1: X has 0 units of C; Y has 10 units of C.

Both S_2 and S_1 are Pareto optimal. Any change from S_2, for example to S_1, can enhance Y's well-being only by diminishing X's. Just the same, though in reverse, obtains in any move from S_1 to S_2. In going from S_2 to S_1 or from S_1 to S_2 we secure an optimal outcome through a non-Pareto superior change. Suppose the initial distribution is represented as S_0:

S_0:   *X* has 5 units of *C; Y* has 5 units of *C*.

Here the initial distribution is Pareto optimal as well. It is easy to see that there are a large number of Pareto optimal states that can be attained from a given initial distribution of resources. Some of these involve a sequence of Pareto superior moves; some involve no Pareto superior moves; others involve a mixture of Pareto superior and non-Pareto superior moves.

With respect to one another, Pareto optimal states are Pareto noncomparable; that is, they cannot be compared by the Pareto superiority criterion. Look at S_0, S_1, and S_2. Each is optimal, but none is Pareto superior to either of the others.

The set of Pareto optimal states attainable from an initial distribution of resources is represented as points on the so-called utility/possibility, or Pareto, frontier. Consider Figure 5.1.

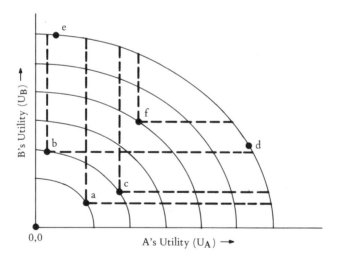

Figure 5.1   Utility/Possibility Frontier

In Figure 5.1 the origin represents the initial distribution of resources. Every move to the northeast of the origin represents a Pareto improvement. A move to the north represents a gain for B; a move east represents a gain for A; a move northeast is a gain for both, or at least a gain for one at no one's expense. The points *a*, *b*, *c*, *d*, *e*, and *f* represent improvements from the origin for both A and B. Compare *a* and *b* and *a* and *c*. In going from *a* to *c* the lot of both A and B is improved. In going from *a* to *b*, however, B's utility is increased, but A's is not.[2] Now compare the moves from *a* to *d* and *a* to *e*. Both *d* and *e* are Pareto optimal, and Pareto noncomparable with respect to one another. In going from *a* to *d*, A and B attain an optimal state through a Pareto superior move.[3] In going from *a* to *e*, A and B attain an optimal outcome through a non-Pareto superior move. So if A and B attain *d* first by moving to *a*, then *c*, they follow a Pareto superior path. If, however, they reach *e* first by going to *a*, then *b*, they secure a Pareto optimal outcome through a mixture of Pareto superior and non-Pareto superior steps.[4]

The graph of the utility/possibility frontier enables us to illustrate and explain a point economists make about the relationship between economics and political morality. The economist sees himself as trying to frame policies or rules that insure that a society reaches the Pareto frontier. Having done that, he is satisfied that the relevant rules, policies, or institutions are *efficient*—that is, no one can then secure a gain except at another's expense. But there are a large number of places on the frontier. Each is optimal, and each therefore satisfies the economist's efficiency requirement. They differ from one another *distributionally*, from the point of view of who has what. Recall our original example: S_0, S_1, and S_2 are all optimal; they differ in regards to the distribution of C between X and Y. For the economist, once we attain the frontier, it is the job of the social theorist/philosopher to determine which efficient outcome is "best." To use what turns out to be a somewhat inaccurate dichotomy, the economist sees the domain of efficiency as the size of the "pie," and the domain of justice or morality as the shape and distribution of its pieces. In the economist's view, efficiency is prior to justice; first make the pie as large as possible, then slice it as "fairly" as possible.

This may be as good a time as any to discuss briefly one objection to this way of putting the relationship between efficiency and justice. Suppose that a point within the frontier is more "just" than any point on the frontier. Then in order to do justice one must forgo efficiency. Justice is therefore prior to efficiency. The economist's response is that for every point within the frontier, there exists a point on the frontier that makes neither of the parties worse off and enhances the welfare of at least one of them. The parties could trade with one another from that or any other point within the frontier to the frontier.[5] In the absence of adverse third-party effects,[6] what grounds could we have for preferring the point within the frontier to the point on the frontier, i.e., an outcome that starts from a just distribution and involves only voluntary exchange. The same argument could be made with respect to all points within the frontier; i.e., for every point within the frontier that is desirable for its "justness" there exists at least one point on the frontier attainable by voluntary transfer. If a point within the frontier is just, we can describe a process that increases efficiency and preserves justice.

Pareto superior policy changes increase net utility, thus obviating the interpersonal comparability problem of classical utilitarianism. What is the relationship between Pareto optimality and utility? A move to a Pareto optimal state need not increase net utility. That is easy to see, since what makes a state Pareto optimal depends on whether there are any Pareto superior moves that can be made *from* it, not whether the move *to* it is itself Pareto superior. In our graph, the move from *f* to *e* is a move to a Pareto optimal state from a nonoptimal one, yet there is no reason to believe that in making such a move overall utility is increased: B is made worse off, A better off. Because the move is not to the northeast of the origin, it is not a Pareto superior one. We cannot know then whether there has been a gain in utility unless we can compare A's and B's utility.

It also does not follow that a point on the frontier represents a utility maximum. This is a somewhat more difficult point. To say that a state of the world is Pareto optimal is just to say that there are no Pareto improvements in store. Pareto improvements are one way of *validating* whether a change in policy is utility maximizing, a way that does not require interpersonal comparability. It does not follow that a move from one social state to another cannot be utility maximizing even if it is not Pareto superior. It is just that in *determining* whether a non-Pareto superior move is utility maximizing we need to compare utilities. And if we cannot compare utilities we cannot *know* if such a move increases utility. (Of course, if we could compare utilities there would be considerably less need for the Pareto superiority criterion.) In short, from the fact that a social state is Pareto optimal nothing follows about whether the move to it is a utility-maximizing one, nor does anything follow about whether any further utility-maximizing moves can be made. What does follow is that no utility-maximizing move that increases net utility in virtue of its satisfying the Pareto superior criterion is possible. So it is the Pareto superior criterion only that entails any judgments at all regarding total utility.

The Pareto superiority criterion is limited, however, in a very basic way. It enables us to order or rank social states and thus to evaluate policies only when there are no losers. Policies can prevent losers in one of two ways: straightaway or by compensation *ex post*. If you and I exchange goods that makes us both better off, we satisfy the Pareto superior criterion in a straightforward fashion. Suppose, however, you engage in a risky activity—e.g., blasting—because even if you had to compensate me for damages should an occasional blast cause me property damage, you would still be better off than if you did not engage in the activity at all. Now you blast, gain a $100 thereby, and cause me $20 in property damage. The move from the state in which you forego blasting to the state in which you blast and cause me damage is *not* Pareto superior because I am worse off. If, however, you compensate me fully for my loss, the move to the state wherein you blast, damage, and compensate from the state in which you do not engage in blasting is a Pareto improvement. Compensation *ex post* is often a key step in making Pareto improvements.

The *possibility* of compensation is important in a different way. The Pareto superiority standard applies only where there are no losers. Most social policies and legal rules produce losers as well as winners. The Pareto test is therefore nearly useless in regard to the evaluation of most activity of concern to the social, political, or legal theorist. The Kaldor-Hicks test, based on the *possibility of compensation*, was introduced to obviate this problem and to extend the usefulness of the Pareto rankings:

> *Definition$_4$*: S_1 is Kaldor-Hicks efficient to S if and only if in going from S to S_1 the winners *could compensate* the losers so that no one would be worse than he or she was in S and at least one person would be better off than he or she was in S.

Another way to put this is to say that S_1 is Kaldor-Hicks efficient to S provided that were compensation paid no one would prefer S to S_1 and at least one person would prefer S_1 to S. The Kaldor-Hicks criterion enables us to evaluate social policies that produce winners *and* losers. The difference between Pareto superiority and Kaldor-Hicks efficiency is just the difference between *actual* and *hypothetical* compensation. If compensation were paid to losers a Kaldor-Hicks efficient move would become a Pareto superior one. Therefore, the Kaldor-Hicks criterion is often called the Potential Pareto superiority test.

If compensation could be paid, why isn't it? That is not as hard a question as it would seem. The reasons are usually of two sorts: First, some losers deserve to lose—for example, when policies are implemented to break up inefficient monopolies. There is no reason to render monopolists no worse off after breaking up their monopolies than they were while engaged in monopolistic behavior. Second, it is often very costly actually to compensate losers. Compensation is a transaction and has associated with it certain costs: transaction costs.

Suppose Jones gains $8 in the move from S to S_1, and Smith loses $6. The move from S to S_1 is therefore a Kaldor-Hicks improvement, because Jones could compensate Smith $6 and still be ahead $2. Now suppose that Jones and Smith are unknown to one another. The search costs alone are likely to exceed $2. If they do, then actually requiring Jones to compensate Smith would make Jones worse off than he was at S. Actually compensating Smith would not be Pareto superior. This brings us to a general point. When the Kaldor-Hicks criterion is employed, the "hypothetical compensation" condition assumes that compensation is to be *costlessly* rendered. Actual compensation is not costless, however, and that is primarily why it is not paid.

Let us conclude this subsection by reviewing the definitions of the key efficiency criteria in terms of the analytic relationships among them:

1. S_1 is Pareto superior to S provided no one prefers S to S_1 and at least one person prefers S_1 to S.
2. S_1 is Pareto optimal provided there is no S_n Pareto superior to S_1.
3. S_1 is Kaldor-Hicks (K-H) efficient to S provided that the winners at S_1, *could* compensate the losers so that no one would then prefer S to S_1 and at least one person would prefer S_1 to S. S_1 is K-H efficient to S provided S_1 is Potential Pareto superior (P-P-S) to S.

When economists talk about efficiency they almost invariably mean Pareto optimality. When lawyers who advocate economic analysis talk about efficient legal decisions, rules, or policies it is considerably less clear whether they have Pareto optimality, superiority, or Kaldor-Hicks efficiency in mind. The differences, as we shall see below are by no means trivial.

THE COASE THEOREM

Much of the economic analysis of law grows up around the line of argument presented in Ronald Coase's "The Problem of Social Cost."[7] Suppose Jones the rancher lives adjacent to Smith the farmer; Jones raises cows, Smith raises corn. There is no fencing separating their property. Jones's cows wander and destroy Smith's corn crop. For every additional cow Jones raises there is an associated reduction in Smith's corn crop. Each cow Jones raises imposes a *private cost* (the cost to Jones of raising it) and a *social cost* (the cost to Smith in damages). *Social costs* are external effects: effects of one person's conduct or consumption on the welfare of others. Some external effects are

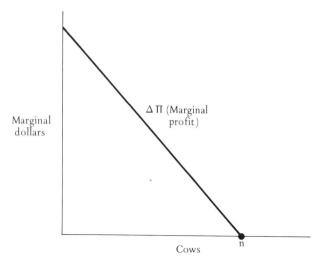

Figure 5.2   Marginal profit without internalized social costs

positive; i.e., they increase another's well-being. Others are *negative;* i.e., they decrease another's welfare. *Externalities* are *inefficient* external effects: i.e., non-Pareto optimal, external effects of one person's activity on another's welfare or utility.

If Jones were *not* liable for the damage each of his cows imposes on Smith's corn crop, Jones would raise cattle until that point at which his marginal private costs equaled his marginal benefit (see Figure 5.2).

The economist distinguishes among total, average, and marginal benefit (or loss). If Jones profits $50 from his first cow, $40 from his second, $30 from his third, $20 from his fourth, $10 from his fifth, and $0 from his sixth, his *total* profit is $50 + $40 + $30 + $20 + $10 + $0 or $150; his *average* profit is 150 ÷ 6 or $25; his *marginal* profit is $50 for the first, $40 for the second, and so on. Marginal benefit (loss) is that corresponding to each additional unit of production (consumption). Economic analysis of law is concerned primarily with the concept of marginal gain/profit/loss/welfare, and when we talk about economic gain (loss) we should be understood to mean marginal gain or loss, unless we explicitly state otherwise.

It is plausible to assume that the number of cows Jones would raise were he responsible for his private costs exceeds the number he would raise were he liable for the damage his cows cause. That is because Jones ceases to raise cows when his marginal cost equals his marginal benefit, and imposing liability upon him for Smith's losses increases his marginal cost while holding his marginal benefit constant. On the other hand, in the absence of Jones's liability, Smith not only has to shoulder the private costs of farming corn, but the social costs of Jones's ranching as well. So were Jones liable in damages to him, Smith would grow more corn. The amount, and therefore the price of both beef and corn is directly affected by the question of who bears the social costs of Jones's ranching activity. Who should bear the social costs of ranching on farming? First we must determine how much corn and how many cows ought to be ranched. Then we can determine if the external effects of Jones's cows cause an inefficient number of cows to be raised and corn to be farmed. But how can we figure out whether the amount of cows and corn is efficient without first knowing who is to bear the social costs of ranching and farming? We can, and here's how.

Instead of rancher Jones and farmer Smith on adjacent plots of land, imagine there is only Jones-Smith who is both a rancher and a farmer and owns both plots. The question for Jones-Smith is how much of each activity to engage in. Posing the problem this way makes the costs of ranching on farming part of Jones-Smith's *private* cost calculation. The very idea of a social cost is thereby eliminated. The process by which external or social costs are made part of one's private cost accounting is called "internalizing externalities."

At each stage in his decisionmaking Jones-Smith asks himself the following question: Will I secure more profit by raising the next cow (where my profit is equal to the benefit minus the cost of raising the cow *and* the cost of foregone corn crop profits) than I would secure from foregoing the cow for the corn? As long as he answers in the affirmative, he raises cows; when his answer is in the negative, he stops raising cows in favor of corn. He stops where his marginal benefit and cost curves intersect. Notice, he might have gone through the same process starting with corn. He would have asked himself: When does the marginal cost of farming corn exceed its marginal benefit? Here the costs are the sum of the standard farming costs *plus* the costs of foregone cattle. Again, Jones-Smith stops where his cost and benefit curves intersect (see Figure 5.3).

One gets the same result whether one begins with corn or cows. This is important as we shall see below. Moreover, the point at which the curves intersect marks the Pareto optimal allocation of Jones-Smith's resources since at that point any further cattle can make Jones-Smith the *rancher* better off only by making Jones-Smith the *rancher-farmer* worse off.[8] The same holds in reverse. There we have it. A fail-safe way of determining how much corn and cattle to raise without first determining who should bear the social costs of ranching on farming.

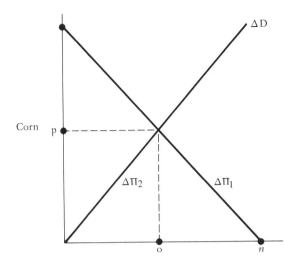

Figure 5.3 Marginal profit with internalized social costs

Back to the example in which Jones and Smith are two distinct persons who own adjacent properties. How do we duplicate the result of this illustration? We could follow Pigou. Pigou argued that in order to internalize externalities a civil authority should impose a marginal tax on the offending party set equal to the marginal damage imposed by the offense. (Pigou also thought that subsidies should be awarded to encourage *positive* externalities.) To make our example concrete, assume the following schedule of profits and damages:

	Marginal Profit to Rancher	*Marginal Damage to Farmer*
Cow 1	$50	$10
Cow 2	$40	$20
Cow 3	$30	$29
Cow 4	$20	$40
Cow 5	$10	$49
Cow 6	$0	$57

If we impose a Pigouvian tax, Jones will raise the first cow and pay $10 in taxes; the second and pay $20; the third and pay $29. He will not raise a fourth cow. This is the same result that would have been obtained given these figures were Jones and Smith one person. Thus, the Pigouvian tax secures the efficient outcome by getting Jones to internalize the relevant externalities.

In the Pigouvian tax approach to externalities, the state must identify one of the parties as the *cause* of the externality and impose and collect a marginal tax set equal to actual marginal damages. In

"The Problem of the Social Cost," Ronald Coase presents an alternative to the Pigouvian approach that denies the necessity of both causation and taxation to efficiency. Indeed, Coase goes further than denying the relevance of causation to the goal of efficiency; he denies the existence of nonreciprocal causal relations. His argument, which economists by and large take seriously but which they ought not to, is as follows. The rancher's cows cause the farmer a loss. But if the state restricts the rancher from raising cows because cows trample corn, it causes the rancher a loss. There is, then, a reciprocity in the causation of harm; either we cause the farmer harm by permitting the rancher's cows to graze or we cause the rancher harm by prohibiting his cows from trampling the corn. The central question is not which activity causes harm—they both do. The question is which harm (and how much of it) should we permit.[9]

Of course Coase is wrong. He treats the harm the rancher's cows cause the corn as if it were the same sort of harm the state does by reducing the level of the rancher's activity. Surely, whether the state interferes or not, cows destroy crops. That is the very plain sense in which causal relations are not reciprocal.

This blunder aside, Coase can be read sympathetically not as denying the existence of causal relations, but as denying the relevance of causal relations to the pursuit of efficiency. The argument is this: Assume that the rancher and the farmer act cooperatively and that transactions between them are costless. The state might assign the rancher the right to raise as many cows as he would like or it might give the farmer the right absolutely to prohibit cows.

Consider first the case in which the rancher has the absolute right to raise cattle. The value to him of the fifth cow is $10, but the cost to the farmer is $49. The farmer will suffer $49 in damage if the rancher raises the fifth cow. The farmer and the rancher have incentives to strike a deal. The rancher wants at least $10 to forego the fifth cow, and the farmer is prepared to pay him up to $48 to forego it. At a price somewhere between $10 and $48 a deal between them will be struck and there will be no fifth cow. Similar reasoning leads to the rancher foregoing a fourth cow. The fourth cow nets him $20, but costs the farmer $40. Again a deal will be struck. The farmer will pay the rancher something between $20 and $40 in exchange for which the rancher will forego a fourth cow. The third cow nets the rancher $30 and causes the farmer $29 in damage. No deal will be struck since to forego a third cow the rancher will not accept less than $30 and the farmer will not offer more than $29. The same holds for the first and second cows. The result is that the rancher raises three cows even if he is assigned the right to raise as many as he would like to.

Consider now the case in which the farmer is given the right to prohibit all cows. The first cow causes the farmer $10 in damage but is worth $50 to the rancher. The rancher stands prepared to offer the farmer more than $10 and less than $50 for the right to ranch that first cow. A deal will be struck that will enable the rancher to raise that cow but that provides at least full compensation to the farmer. The same argument holds for the second and third cows, but not for the fourth or fifth. In the latter two cases the damage exceeds the benefit to the rancher. The farmer is unprepared to take less than full reimbursement for damages, but the rancher is unprepared to pay that much since it exceeds the value of each cow to him. Once again, the rancher will raise three cows even though we began by assuming that the farmer had the right to prohibit all cows.[10]

We secure the same result regardless of the assignment of rights with which we begin. The result duplicates the result of the Pigouvian tax, which duplicates the result we obtain when we imagine only one person, rancher-farmer, who aims to maximize his profits by finding the optimal levels of ranching and farming. Coase has given us a way of internalizing externalities through *private exchange*. Indeed, there is a sense in which, when transactions are costless and people behave cooperatively, there are no externalities. In effect, the rancher and farmer are just like rancher-farmer. Just as he aims to maximize the joint profits of ranching and farming, the upshot of their negotiations is to do the same.

We can summarize Coase as follows. Where exchange is costless: (1) identifying one party as the cause of the externality is unnecessary to achieve efficiency; (2) there is no need for a state to impose a tax on one or the other party because the efficiency results from private exchange; (3) no matter who we assume has the relevant right, the efficient distribution of resources will result since the rights only define initial bargaining positions; (4) the assignment of legal rights therefore is otiose to efficiency; and (5) the assignment of rights can effect the relative wealth of the parties.

All of these points but (5) have already been illustrated; (5) is easy to show. If we give the farmer the right to prohibit cows, there will be three cows, but in order to obtain the right to raise them the rancher would have had to pay the farmer, thereby increasing the farmer's wealth. On the other hand, if the rancher is assigned the right to raise cattle he will end up raising three, but the farmer would have had to buy him down, thus increasing the rancher's wealth.

What is usually called the Coase Theorem can be put as follows:

> *Definition₅*: When transactions are costless and individuals act cooperatively, any assignment of legal rights will be efficient.[11]

Compare now the Pigouvian and Coasian approaches to externalities.[12] We have specified the conditions under which the Coasian approach is efficient: costless transactions and cooperative behavior. What are the conditions under which the Pigouvian approach is efficient?

When the Pigouvian tax is imposed the parties might be foreclosed from further negotiations or continued negotiations might remain an option.[13] Consider the case in which the parties remain free to negotiate. There are two options regarding the tax revenue. It can be given to the damaged party in the form of compensation for marginal damage or as a lump sum transfer, or it can be put in the general coffers. The Pigouvian tax is efficient only if compensation is paid, not otherwise. This may seem counterintuitive since the point of the tax is to force the injurer to take the social costs of his activity into account, which it succeeds in doing in either case. What accounts for the difference in efficiency? The tax transfer is necessary to induce the correct behavior *in the victim*. The following abbreviated benefit/damage schedule of the rancher-farmer negotiations illustrates this:

	Marginal Benefit (Before Tax)	Marginal Damage
Cow 1	50	10
Cow 2	40	20
Cow 3	30	29

We determined before that three cattle would be optimal. When the rancher pays the tax into the general coffers the schedule for the third cow looks like this:

	Marginal Benefit	Marginal Damage
Cow 3	$1 (30–29 tax)	29

A third cow is worth only $1 after taxes to the rancher, but that cow will still bring about $29 damage to the farmer. The farmer will pay the rancher to forego a third cow, leading to an inefficient outcome. They both gain by acting inefficiently.

In contrast, if the tax revenue is awarded to the farmer on an actual damage basis he is *always* indifferent between a cow and there not being one. That is precisely what full compensation means. Because he is in general indifferent for all levels of ranching, he is indifferent regarding the third cow. The rancher, however, is not indifferent; he wants a third cow because there is a marginal gain of $1 ($30 minus $29) in it for him. Thus, it is to his advantage to raise the third cow.[14]

Now consider the efficiency of the tax when further negotiations between injurer and victim are impossible. There are two other relevant variables. The first is whether the tax revenue is transferred to the damaged party or or placed in the general tax coffer. Again, there are two ways in which the tax revenues can be transferred. The first is on a marginal damage basis; the second is by a lump sum transfer, the basic condition of which is that the amount of transfer not be set to reflect damages, marginal or total. The second variable is whether the behavior of the injured party can affect net damages. That is, can the injured party take precautions that will reduce total costs?

The general problem can be set out as follows:

Let's begin with case 4. If no negotiations are possible and the tax revenue is not transferred to the damaged party and the damaged party's behavior cannot affect efficiency, the tax will be efficient. The reason is obvious. The only person's behavior that can affect damages is the offending party and his behavior is being taxed to reflect its damages. The tax leads him to engage in his activity at the efficient level and only his behavior counts. Provided negotiations are impossible, this line of argument implies that whenever the damaged party's behavior cannot affect net damages, the Pigouvian tax will be efficient whether or not the tax revenues are transferred to the injured party. The tax is therefore efficient in case 2 as well.

What happens when the injured party's behavior can affect net damages as in cases 1 and 3? Where there is no transfer the tax will be efficient. The tax leads the offending party to efficient behavior and the absence of compensation leads the injured party to adopt optimal precautions. By not being reimbursed for his losses, the injured party has an incentive to take precautions to reduce them. Holding the offending party's behavior constant, the victim will take just those precautions the cost of which are less than or equal to the gain to him in reduced damages—i.e., the optimal precautionary behavior. On the other hand, if the tax revenue is transferred to the injured party in the form of marginal damages equal to the damages he suffers, he is indifferent for all levels of damages. He has no incentive therefore to reduce them. If a change in his behavior is required to accomplish optimal cost reduction, a transfer set equal to marginal damage will lead to inefficiency since he has no incentive to reduce damages.

In summary, the optimality of the Pigouvian tax depends on three factors: (1) the possibility of further negotiations; (2) the scope and nature of any transfer of the tax revenue to the damaged party; and (3) the contribution of the relevant parties to the level of damages. Where further negotiations are possible the optimality of the tax depends on its revenue being given on marginal damage basis to the injured party, otherwise both parties will perceive a joint advantage in reducing the offending activity to inefficient levels. Where negotiations are not possible, the Pigouvian tax is optimal whenever *only* the behavior of the taxed party contributes to the level of damages. The tax is also optimal when the absence of a transfer acts as if it were a tax on the damaged party whose behavior effects net damages and who is thereby given sufficient incentive to take optimal precautions. Finally, where a transfer equal to marginal damages does occur, the damaged party whose behavior does affect net damages has no incentive to take the necessary precautions and the tax is inefficient.

ASSIGNING ENTITLEMENTS: LAW AS MARKET MIMICKER

A central difference between the Coasian and Pigouvian approaches to externalities concerns the role of the state. While the Pigouvian approach does not require the state to assign rights to the damaged party that would preclude various levels of the harmful activity, it does require that the state or its agents identify one of the parties as the *cause* of the damage, impose and collect a tax from that party, and decide how to distribute its revenues.

In contrast, when transaction costs are trivial or nonexistent, the state need only secure the integrity of the bargaining process by enforcing the resource allocations to which individuals negotiate. Because either assignment of property rights will prove efficient, there is no party on whom the state is required to confer the relevant property right. It is natural then to associate the Coasian property right approach with minimal government.

The Coasian approach entails minimal government only when transaction costs are trivial, since only then are negotiations efficient. When transaction costs are nontrivial, efficient negotiations may not occur. For example, if the value of a third cow to the rancher is $30, and the value to the farmer of prohibiting it is $29 (his damages), then there will be a third cow (which is efficient) only if the rancher is initially assigned a property right to ranch that cow or if transaction costs are less than $1. If, however, the farmer is entitled to prohibit a third cow, the rancher will not purchase the right to raise that cow whenever the *costs* of the transaction exceed $1. The rancher will not pay more than $30 (which he would have to when transaction costs exceed $1) to obtain an entitlement that is worth only $30 to him. The farmer maintains the right to prohibit a third cow—a right he exercises—thus reducing the number of cows to two, which, *ex hypothesi*, is inefficient.

It follows that when transaction costs are not trivial, it matters how property rights are assigned. Because the assignment of rights can make a difference in the efficiency of resource allocations, we need a principle to guide the assignment of property rights. It is at this juncture that the law and economics literature which derives from the Coasian property rights alternative to Pigouvian taxes begins to focus on the work of Richard Posner.

Posner's most basic contribution is the following. Where the conditions of the Coase Theorem—zero transaction costs and cooperative behavior—are satisfied, the law need not assign property rights in any particular way. Market exchange will always insure efficiency. When these conditions are not met, the law should promote efficiency by mimicking the market. By "mimicking the market," Posner means that the relevant legal authorities ought to assign property rights to those parties who would have secured them through market exchange.[15] If the rancher would have secured the right to a third cow via negotiations regardless of the initial property right assignment, mimicking the market requires the courts to give the rancher that right straightaway.

Posner's Principle for assigning legal rights—the principle that law should mimic the market—is a simple directive to courts to allocate resources as the market would have. The market would have allocated resources efficiently. When the market breaks down, the law should produce the result the market would have. There are two ambiguities in the "mimicking the market" slogan. The first concerns whether the law should mimic or replicate the rational autonomous feature of market behavior, or the efficiency of market outcomes.[16] This becomes important when we inquire into the *normative* basis of economic analysis.

The second concerns which exchange market the law ought to mimic. There are two choices. The first is the market in which the parties are in fact negotiating with its particular structures, costs of transactions, individual endowments, etc. The alternative is the Coasian market of costless exchange taking place between cooperative, fully informed, perfectly rational individuals.[17]

For now we will assume both that the feature of markets the law ought to replicate is the efficiency of exchange *outcomes* and that the market the law ought to mimic is the Coasian market of rational, fully informed individuals completely cooperating with one another in an effort to maximize joint welfare (or profits) through mutually beneficial exchange.

Once assigned, property rights need to be secured and enforced. In one of the most important papers in the literature, Guido Calabresi and Douglas Malamed distinguish among three ways of protecting entitlements: by (1) property rules, (2) liability rules, and (3) inalienability rules.[18]

Property rules protect entitlements by enabling the right bearer to enjoin others from reducing the level of protection the entitlement affords him except as he may be willing to forego it at a mutually acceptable price. If a right is protected by a *liability rule,* a nonentitled party may reduce the value of the entitlement without regard to the right holder's desires provided he compensates *ex post* for the reduction in value. The value of the reduction, i.e., damages, is set by a collective body, usually a court, and need not coincide with what the entitled party would have been willing to accept for a reduction in the value of his entitlement. Liability rules give nonentitled parties the license to purchase on a pay-as-you-damage basis at objectively set prices part or all of an entitlement held by another. Property rules prohibit such transfers of entitlements in the absence of an *ex ante* between the relevant parties.

An example might illustrate this difference. Suppose the right to my cabin in the mountains is protected by a property rule only. In that case, if you wanted my cabin or any part of it then you would have to seek me out and convince me that I should transfer a part of my right to you, otherwise you have no claim or liberty with respect to my house. In contrast, if the right to my cabin were protected by a liability rule only then you need not secure my consent in order to avail yourself of it. Instead, you would be subject to liability for your use of it and for whatever damages I might incur. On the other hand,

I have no basis for prohibiting you from action contrary to my right. Instead, the structure of our relationship is as follows. The right is mine, but my having it does not entail that you must first seek to negotiate with me over its use. You may do as you please provided you pay a "user fee," the proceeds of which are transferred to me. The same property right may be protected by either a property rule, a liability rule, or both. If my cabin is protected by a property rule only, I have no redress if you are not adequately induced to avoid reducing its value to me without my consent.[19] That is one good reason for protecting a right with both a property rule and a liability rule. Sometimes property rules may suffice if there are insufficient incentives to impose damage without consent, or if there are sufficient incentives not to, if, for example, the criminal sanction is employed successfully as a secondary means of enforcement.

In contrast, it is sometimes necessary to forego property rules as vehicles for protecting entitlements in favor of liability rules. This occurs most often when transaction costs are high. If transaction costs are high, a property rule is likely to prove inefficient since transfer to more valued use requires negotiations. If negotiations are costly, property rules may lead to entitlements being held by individuals who value them less. Liability rules may therefore be substituted for property rules where transaction costs are high. Under a liability rule regime, individuals who value entitlements more than the individuals upon whom the rights are initially conferred are induced to secure the entitlements without transaction and to pay damages. In such cases, the party who values the entitlement most secures it, which duplicates the outcome of the market exchange process. If damages under liability rule set by a court are equal to or greater than the decrease in the value of the entitlement to the injured party, the optimal outcome is secured through a Pareto superior *forced transfer*. If damages are set below the value of the entitlement to the injured party, the forced transfer is not Pareto superior. Property rules induce optimal transfers through Pareto improvements. Whether liability rules involve Pareto improvements depends on the level of compensation.

Liability rules and property rules differ from inalienability rules in that when a right is protected by an inalienability rule transfers of any sort are *prohibited*. Inalienable rights are not transferable. Rights protected by inalienability rules are not transferable. The right to one's freedom from servitude and the right to vote are examples of rights protected by inalienability rules. Protecting a right by an inalienability rule may amount to a decision to forego efficiency in favor of promoting or protecting some other social good. Some people might well be induced to exchange their rights. Doing so might be efficient; blocking such transfers might then be inefficient. On the other hand, if there is a reason to believe that a willingness to exchange a right like that to freedom from servitude for monetary gain indicates a lack either of full information or rationality, protecting rights by inalienability rules might be justified on the grounds that such transfers would not occur in a costless market populated by fully informed rational persons. So there is an argument from efficiency, albeit a somewhat attenuated one, against permitting certain exchanges by the use of an inalienability rule.

Considerations of efficiency can generate a principle for allocating initial entitlements—e.g., Posner's mimicking the market principle— as well as various vehicles for protecting entitlements once assigned— e.g., the Calabresi-Malamed property rule/liability rule/inalienability rule distinction. It is time to turn our attention to the application of this framework to central problems in law.

APPLYING ECONOMICS TO LAW

NUISANCE

Imagine a typical nuisance, a polluting feedlot, whose level of pollution increases with its output.[20] The damages incurred by its neighbors also depends on output. Let us make the example concrete by the use of the following schedule of benefits and damages.

Output in 25 unit intervals	Marginal profit (marginal benefit − marginal private cost)	Marginal damage
25	200,000	10,000
50	100,000	20,000
75	75,000	30,000
100	50,000	40,000
125	30,000	50,000

Suppose a case initiated by the neighbors comes before a court. They seek compensatory damages or an injunction against the pollutor. What would be the efficient thing for the court to do? How should it rule?

Ignoring the unlikely use of an inalienability rule strategy, there are at least four things (following the Calabresi-Malamed distinctions) a court might do: (1) it could assign to the neighbors the right to be free from pollution and secure that right by a property rule; (2) it could assign the neighbors the right to be free from pollution, but protect it by a liability rule; (3) it could assign to the manufacturer the right to pollute and protect it by property rule; or (4) it could assign to the manufacturer the right to pollute and protect it by a liability rule.

If the neighbors' right to be free from pollution is protected by a property rule, then the manufacturer has to purchase from them the right to impose any pollution-related damages. If that right is protected by a liability rule, the manufacturer is in effect free to pollute provided it pays damages to its neighbors. If the court assigns to the manufacturer the right to pollute and protects that right by a property rule, then the neighbors must negotiate with the manufacturer to induce it to reduce the level of pollution. If the court assigns to the manufacturer the right to pollute but protects it by a liability rule only, then the neighbors are free to force a reduction in the level of output provided they pay damages. Here damages would be measured by foregone profits.

Which, if any, of these combinations is efficient? If transaction costs are zero (or trivial) all approaches can be efficient depending on the level of compensatory damages set by the court. In other words, if the court has full information and transactions between the manufacturer and its neighbors are free, then all four combinations are efficient.

Consider first the cases in which rights are protected by property rules. In effect, this amounts in the one case to the neighbors securing an injunction against the polluting manufacturer; in the other it amounts to the manufacturer securing an injunction against any efforts its neighbors might make to reduce the level of its output without its consent. The table indicates that 100 units of output is efficient.[21] Where transaction costs are zero, the property right assignment backed by a property rule simply follows the argument for the Coase Theorem. If the right is assigned to the neighbors, the manufacturer will purchase from them the right to 100 levels of output by paying them damages for each 25 unit increment to 100. To produce 125 units the manufacturer would have to pay its neighbors at least $50,000 whereas the marginal value of him to that additional 25 units is only $30,000.

If the right to pollute protected by a property rule is assigned the manufacturer, then the neighbors will purchase a reduction from 125 units of output to 100 units by offering him at least $30,000 but less than $50,000. They will be unwilling to negotiate further reductions since the value of the additional reductions (measured as avoided damages) is less than the value to the manufacturer of the liberty to pollute.

The liability rule approach is efficient only if compensatory damages are set equal to actual marginal damages. Consider first the case in which the neighbors are assigned the right to be free from pollution protected by the liability rule. If compensation under the liability rule equals actual damages, the neighbors will be indifferent among all levels of output. The pollutor will produce only if the dollar value of benefits net damages is positive. Once again that occurs at all intervals until 100 units are manufactured. Thereafter the corresponding figure is negative.

The same line of argument applies in the seemingly odd case of the manufacturer's right to pollute being secured by a liability rule. If damages are set equal to foregone marginal benefits, the neighbors have incentive to force a transfer that reduces output to 100 units, but no incentive to force additional reduction. Because compensation is set equal to damages, i.e., foregone benefits, the manufacturer this time is indifferent among all levels of output. The incentive structure for the neighbors is all we need to be concerned about. Where they would have to pay more in damages than they would secure in pollution avoidance costs, no forced transfer will ensue. Once again, 100 units of output will result: the efficient outcome.

What happens when the conditions of the Coase Theorem are not satisfied, in particular, when the court has incomplete information, when transaction costs are high, and when the parties engage in strategic behavior? What effect, in other words, do information costs, transaction costs, and strategic behavior have on the efficiency of our various alternatives.

Consider strategic behavior first. Behavior is strategic when what one individual is prepared to do depends on his assessment of what others are likely to do. The main source of inefficiency from strategic behavior is "hold out" behavior—a refusal to make a deal either because an actor thinks he can induce the other party to accept terms even more favorable to him or because he wants to establish a reputation as a "hard bargainer." Hold out behavior has its greatest negative impact on efficiency whenever negotiations are required to promote efficiency. Negotiations are required only when rights are protected by property rules. The possibility of strategic behavior is an argument for dealing with nuisance cases by liability rules. However rights are initially assigned, transfers to more valued uses under the liability rule regime do not require negotiations and agreement. Only the behavior of the injuring party needs to be affected to secure efficiency, and that result depends entirely on the level at which damages are set.

Roughly the same argument for liability rules in nuisance cases can be extended to cover other transaction costs as well. If the costs of transaction are sufficiently high to threaten trade to efficient outcomes, simply protect rights by rules that allow nonnegotiated transfers to more valued uses—i.e., through liability rules.

There is, however, *one* case in which the possibility of strategic behavior and the existence of high transaction costs are not incompatible with the property rule approach to nuisance law: that is where the court is able to assign to the manufacturer the right to *exactly* the efficient level of pollution. In our example that amounts to giving the manufacturer the right to 100 units of output. Strategic behavior and other transaction costs may make further negotiated trade impossible, but then, further trade is not needed. The assignment, as it stands, is efficient.

Let's look at what sort of information a court must have at its disposal to secure efficiency under the conditions we have imagined. To apply the property rule approach under the threat of strategic behavior the court must know the efficient level of production. It can determine that only if it knows both the manufacturer's schedule of benefits and the neighbor's schedule of damages. In effect, it has to have access to the information contained in our table. As an exercise, hold your hand over either the benefit or the damage column while reading the figures in the other. Can you determine which level of output is efficient?

Playing the same "game," determine what information you would need to apply the liability approach efficiently. If the court assigns to the neighbors the right to be free from pollution, then the liability rule will be efficient only if the court knows the neighbors' schedule of damages. If the court assigns damages correctly, compensation will make the neighbors indifferent among all levels of output. The manufacturer then reveals his benefit schedule by his behavior. The same argument works in reverse when the right to pollute backed by a liability rule is assigned to the manufacturer. There a court that is to set compensatory damages must know the actual benefit schedule of the manufacturer to insure that the liability rule approach will be efficient.

When a court has none of the relevant information there is no guarantee that either approach will be efficient. Where transaction costs are low and the chance of strategic behavior minimal, a court lacking information about benefit and damage schedules may do well to use a property rule, thereby forcing both parties to reveal their schedules through exchange. Where transaction costs are high or the threat of strategic behavior substantial, the property rule approach is unlikely to be efficient. The liability rule then seems more promising. But the efficiency of the liability approach requires very specific information about damages. It will fail to be efficient whenever damages are set too high or too low. A court does not always need a lot of information in order to induce efficient behavior. It does need some of the "right" sort, however.

ACCIDENT LAW

Recall the Coase Theorem for a moment. When the conditions of its application are met, two parties acting cooperatively act as if they were *one*. That, after all, is the power of illustration in which we determine what is efficient for them to do by considering what would be efficient for one person engaged in both activities to do. What is efficient for one person to do is to maximize benefits net costs. When the conditions of the Coase Theorem are satisfied, then efficiency amounts to maximizing *joint* benefits minus *joint* costs. The *distribution* of that sum is not the concern of efficiency. Taking these two points together, it is easy to see why economists sometimes draw the distinction between efficiency and justice as follows: efficiency concerns the size of the pie; justice its distribution. The efficiency the law wants to replicate is the maximization of joint benefits minus joint costs. The question before us is which set of legal rules for accident law are efficient in this sense.

Using the apparatus developed in the discussion of nuisance law, we have four alternatives: (1) the right to injure protected by a property rule; (2) the right to injure protected by a liability rule; (3) the right to be free from injury protected by a property rule; and (4) the right to be free from injury protected by a liability rule.

It is inconceivable that in automobile accident law efficiency could result from any right assignment backed by property rules. In automobile cases the costs of *ex ante* transaction would be so high that negotiations would be impossible. (Can you identify in advance all the drivers and pedestrians you might injure and with whom you should now be entered in negotiations?) In other accident contexts, especially employment-related injuries, negotiations are more likely and a property rule approach might be more tenable. Let us confine the discussion then to accidents between what in the literature are called "strangers"— i.e., parties who are not otherwise involved in contractual relations with one another, and to automobile accidents more particularly.

Though we could conceivably begin by assigning the relevant right either to those who are likely injurers or to those who are potential victims, we will confine the discussion to that case in which victims are entitled to freedom from injury. Because protecting that right by a property rule will almost never be efficient, the only alternative is to secure it by a liability rule. Liability rules are of at least two sorts: strict liability and fault liability.

Under the rule of fault liability an injurer is not obligated to compensate the victim of his conduct unless he is at fault. Conduct is at fault if it is negligent, reckless or intentionally and unjustifiably harmful. In accidents most conduct that is at fault is negligently so; some is recklessly mischievous; by definition, none is intentionally at fault. To simplify matters we will focus entirely on negligent misconduct. Therefore, in this discussion of accident law, the rule of fault liability is a rule of negligence. An injurer who is not negligent will not be liable in damages to his victim. In terms of a level of care, negligence is defined as the lack of reasonable care.

Strict liability is liability imposed without regard to injurer fault. Thus, under the rule of strict liability an injurer must make his victim whole regardless of the care he takes to avoid injury. While the potential victim's right to freedom from injury is to be protected by a liability rule rather than by a property rule, there is an important difference in the level of protection the liability rule affords him depending on whether the rule is one of strict or fault liability. It might be useful to distinguish between levels of protection afforded by fault and strict liability rules by referring to the former as an *incomplete* form of protection and the latter as a *complete* form of protection.[22]

In addition to rules that impose liability for damages, courts can apply rules that defeat liability—for example, the rule of assumption of risk or that of contributory fault. An injurer who is at fault or strictly liable to his victim may nevertheless be freed from the responsibility of making his victim whole if, for example, the victim assumed the risk or if his negligence contributes to the damages. There are at least the following combinations of liability rules:

1. Strict liability
2. Strict liability with the defense of victim negligence
3. Fault (negligence) liability
4. Fault (negligence) liability with the defense of victim negligence[23]

Which of these strategies is efficient—that is, which rule or combinations of rules maximizes joint benefits net joint losses of injurer and victims? To explore the efficiency of these various strategies consider the following example. Imagine two drivers, Jones and Smith. Assume that the level of damages and benefits is determined only by driving speed. The greater the speed, the greater the risk of harm, the greater the expected damages. Let us distinguish further among five levels of speed: slow, moderately slow, moderate, moderately fast, and fast. We can construct the following table of benefits and expected damages on the further assumptions that Smith's driving injures Jones—that Jones is the victim—and that Jones's conduct is not negligent. There is, in other words, no contributory negligence. Only Smith's conduct can affect damages, and the extent of damages depends entirely on how fast he drives.

Speeding options for Smith	Benefits to Smith	Expected damage	Joint expected gain (Benefits net-Expected Damage)
Fast	1000	800	200
Moderately fast	800	500	300
Moderate	600	200	400
Moderately slow	400	150	250
Slow	200	50	150

The efficient outcome, maximum net gain, results when Smith drives moderately. Under the strict liability rule Smith will compensate Jones *whenever* he injures him, regardless of the speed at which he drives. Because Jones is compensated in all cases, he is indifferent among the various levels of care that Smith exercises. For all Jones cares, Smith can drive as fast as he would like. Smith will drive moderately. If he drives moderately he nets $400 (after compensation), whereas his payoff is less if he drives at any other speed. In what economists call "one party accidents," where only the injurer's conduct contributes to the probability of damage, a rule of strict liability will be efficient.

How about negligence rule? Under a negligence rule Jones will *not* be indifferent among all speeds at which Smith might drive since he will be compensated for damages only if Smith's driving is excessively fast. Assume Smith's driving moderately corresponds to the standard of reasonable care. If Smith drives too fast he will be liable to Jones, otherwise not. If he drives very fast he would net $200, that is, $1,000 minus $800; if he drives moderately fast he nets $300, that is, $800 minus $500. If he drives moderately he nets $600, that is, $600 minus $0, because his compliance frees him of the burden of liability. His reward is less at lesser speeds as well, $400 and $200 respectively. His greatest payoff results from compliance with the standard of due care. In contrast, suppose a court mistakenly takes driving very fast as the standard of reasonable care. Then, Smith's greatest payoff comes from driving very fast since compliance frees him from liability and his expected payoff would be $1,000. The negligence standard would not then induce efficient driving. A negligence rule therefore can induce efficient accidents *only* when the court sets the negligence standard to correspond to the efficient level of care. In other words, if the court knows in advance that moderate driving by Smith is efficient, then a negligence standard will be efficient if the court sets the standard of care at driving at moderate speed. Generally, for a negligence rule to be efficient in a one-party accident, reasonable care must just mean efficient care. Thus, economists argue not only for an efficiency approach to accident law, but for an economic analysis of fault or negligence. To be at fault—i.e., negligent—is to act inefficiently.[24]

In a two-party accident, where the behavior of both parties can contribute to the efficient outcome, a rule of strict liability is inadequate to induce efficient behavior. *Ex hypothesi*, the victim's behavior contributes to the efficient outcome. But because a rule of strict liability provides full compensation in all cases, it makes the victim indifferent between injury and freedom from it. No victim then has an incentive to take accident-avoidance measures. Because victim-avoidance measures are necessary to achieve efficiency, the rule of strict liability will be inefficient in two-party accidents.

Though a rule of strict liability is not efficient for two-party accidents, a rule of strict liability with the defense of contributory negligence is. If the *victim* drives negligently, *he* bears the full loss no matter what the injurer does. To avoid those losses he drives efficiently. We continue to assume that driving moderately is efficient, so the contributory negligence standard induces victims to drive moderately. Once the victim drives efficiently, the rule of strict liability is applicable for the injurer's decision. The situation then collapses into the one-party accident case in which we assume the victim drives at the appropriate speed. The greatest gain for the injurer is $400, which he secures only when he drives at the efficient level. Strict liability with contributory negligence is efficient.

Provided the court is capable of correctly setting the negligence standard, the rule of negligence liability is efficient, as is the rule of negligence with the defense of contributory negligence. Demonstrating the efficiency of the latter is trivial. In order to avoid having to bear the entirety of his losses should he be injured by another, the victim will drive nonnegligently. Only then does he stand a chance at reimbursement for his losses. Indeed, the victim's behavior tends toward efficiency whenever the injurer has available to him the defense of contributory fault, quite apart from whether the rule governing the injurer's conduct is one of fault or strict liability. Assuming victim compliance, the case then collapses into the one-party accident example in which we hold the victim's conduct constant and assume it to be efficient. Under those conditions, as we have already shown, the negligence rule is efficient.

The interesting case is when the injurer's liability is determined by a negligence standard and he does not have available to him the defense of contributory negligence. Can such a rule provide optimal incentives for both parties in two-party accident? The answer is yes. The injurer will be free from liability only when he acts efficiently, i.e., drives moderately. His optimal strategy is to drive reasonably no matter what victim does. The victim's negligence will not bar him from recovering, so what incentive does the victim have to drive nonnegligently (efficiently)? Because the negligence rule induces the injurer to moderate driving, the victim must assume that under the negligence rule an injurer's conduct will tend toward reasonableness. In that case the victim must assume that he will *always* bear his losses. He wants therefore to minimize them. To do that he will have to compare the gain to him by increasing his speed with the expected loss of increased velocity. The latter figure will always be greater, since otherwise it would be efficient for him to drive faster and faster, and we are assuming that it is not the case. So while there is a gain in driving faster (savings in time), there is an increase in expected costs (damages) attributable entirely to the victim's increased velocity. The expected damages will always exceed the expected benefits if we assume that driving faster than driving at moderate speeds is inefficient. Comparing these figures, the victim who must bear his own losses will act efficiently by not driving in excess of the reasonable rate. Injurer negligence, then, absent any defense of contributory negligence is an efficient liability rule—even in the case of two-party accidents.

These last remarks provide us with the basis of another easy demonstration of the inefficiency of strict liability in the two-party accident case. Because the victim's losses will always be borne by his injurer, he ignores the expected increase in damages that result from his driving faster than what is optimal. He doesn't, however, ignore the additional benefits. Instead, he tends to drive faster because of those additional benefits. The benefits of inefficiency are all his, its costs are his injurer's. Strict liability does not induce adequate precautions by victims in two-party accidents.

To sum up: In one-party accidents only the injurer's conduct affects efficiency. In that case a rule either of negligence or strict liability would be efficient. A negligence rule will be efficient, however, only if the court correctly sets the level of due care. In the absence of pertinent information, a court may be wise to impose a rule of strict liability.

In two-party accidents, the rule of strict injurer liability will not be efficient. The rules of strict injurer liability with the defense of contributory negligence, injurer negligence with a similar defense, and injurer negligence with no such defense, are *all* efficient. In each case a court must be able to determine correctly the efficient level of due care. No liability rule strategy has an advantage over the others on that account. Whereas all the rules are efficient, they differ with respect to the question of who bears the costs of accidents when neither injurers nor victims are negligent. Under both versions of the negligence rule, the victim bears the loss when neither party is negligent. Under the strict liability rule with the defense of victim negligence, the injurer bears the loss when neither party is at fault. The decision among the various rules cannot be made on efficiency grounds, but can be made on distributive grounds, provided we have reason to believe that potential victims or potential injurers—to the extent we can reasonably distinguish these groups—ought in general to bear the costs of accidents that result in spite of both parties reasonable efforts to avoid them.

CONTRACTS

Unlike records, contracts are not made to be broken. Nevertheless some are. One question for the economist is which rules for damages induce efficient breach. The problem of efficient breach is different in significant ways from the problems of nuisance and accidents we have already discussed. One key difference concerns the role of negotiations in formulating and resolving the problem. In the nuisance cases, property rules are efficient (on the zero transaction cost assumption) just because they *encourage negotiations.* In the accident case, high transaction costs make prior negotiation inconceivable and future negotiations unlikely. Efficiency can only be secured through rules that provide for the transfer of resources to higher valued uses in the absence of negotiations—i.e., liability rules. In automobile accidents, negotiations are assumed to be very unlikely; in nuisance cases, the negotiations are often possible; in breach of contract cases, *negotiations have already taken place!*

A contract is breached only when its terms are not fully specified. A fully specified contract leaves absolutely nothing out. Provisions are made for every possible contingency. A fully specified contract leaves no room for "surprises." A fully specified contract is also always efficient, for it is the outcome of costless negotiations and, as Coase demonstrated, costless negotiations between rational, cooperative, fully informed individuals are efficient. In short, if negotiations are in fact costless, there is nothing to lose in specifying the rights and duties of contracting parties under any possible set of feasible conditions.

It follows that one reason contracts are not fully specified is that it is too costly to negotiate terms over all possible contingencies. Where the costs of negotiations are too high, contract terms may be left unspecified. Contracting parties in effect decide to leave it up to the court to specify their responsibilities and liberties in the event an unanticipated contingency arises. Suppose I am a builder and you and I agree that I will construct a house for you for $100,000. Neither of us anticipates that the legislature will pass any laws that will materially affect our arrangement at least during the period of time it takes for me to complete construction. We are wrong, though. Suppose the state triples the minimum wage for members of the construction trades, thereby driving my costs skyward. It now would cost me $175,000 to build a house for which I can expect to receive only $100,000. Alternatively, suppose that state decides to make me the state's official and only licenced builder, in effect making me a monopoly. As a monopolist I could charge others significantly more than I'm charging you. In both cases I have an incentive to breach. I breach and we go to court to determine what our claims are against one another. What should the court do?

One convenient way of thinking about the problem is as follows. The court is trying to replicate the terms we would have agreed to had we negotiated over this contingency. If we had a fully specified contract, how would we have resolved this contingency? The terms of the fully specified contract are efficient. To say they are efficient is to say that they maximize joint benefits net joint costs. The terms we would have agreed to would have been efficient. Therefore the court ought to decide the breach action to promote efficiency. They would promote efficiency by reproducing the results of a fully specified contract between us. The general process then requires first producing a fully specified contract. Let's explore the process through a concrete example.[25]

Begin then by fully specifying a contract for sale.[26] Jones is the seller; Smith is the buyer; Brown is another possible buyer lurking in the wings. Jones is one of the few makers of high quality electronic crossover networks for use in audio loudspeakers. Smith makes loudspeakers. His are not particularly outstanding speakers, but they're not bad either. He wants Jones's crossovers because of their reliability. Brown is thinking about getting into the audio business. He will do so, however, only if he can either get in cheaply or if he can be certain to produce a very high quality loudspeaker that will command a good price.

Jones and Smith work out a deal with the following terms: crossovers are sold by the dozen only. Jones needs the money from Smith upfront, otherwise he is unable to produce crossover networks in sufficient quantities. For one carton of twelve crossovers, Smith pays Jones $75 upfront. The production costs to Jones are $50. The value to Smith of the crossovers is $110. (Suppose that represents what he would have to pay someone else to get what he sees as an equally reliable crossover.) When Smith and Jones exchange money for the crossovers, their net gain is $60—i.e., $35 for Smith, ($110 minus $75) plus $25 for Jones ($75 minus $50).[27]

They both know, however, that Brown is in the wings, and because theirs is a fully specified contract they have to negotiate terms regarding Brown as a possible buyer of Jones's crossover networks. They don't know what particular decision Brown will make, but they know he is contemplating one of three options. If he does not enter the business, they know the value of the crossovers to him will be $0. If he can enter at the high end, then because of their sonic characteristics, he will value these particular crossovers very highly, say at $150 per dozen. If he can get in cheaply then these crossovers are perhaps no more valuable to him than are many other ones and he values these at only $83, the going rate. He is also unclear, if he gets in the market at all, whether he prefers to get in at the bottom or the high end.

Jones and Smith have to decide what to do about Brown. Suppose they decide as follows:

(1) If Brown does not enter the market, he values Jones's crossovers at $0; in that case Jones delivers to Smith per the terms of their agreement.

(2) If Brown enters at the low end and values the crossover at $83, then Jones still delivers to Smith.

The first clause needs no explanation. It is easy to see the rationale for the second. Suppose transactions were costless and Jones delivers to Brown. Brown would sell to Smith. Whether Jones sells to Smith or to Brown, Smith will end up with it. Smith's having the crossover package is efficient. Another way to put this point is as follows. As we demonstrated above, when Jones delivers to Smith the net gain is $60 between them. Suppose now that Jones produces for the network $50, and sells it to Brown for $83. If he sells to Brown his gain is $33. Brown values it at $83 which equals his purchasing price so he has no gain. Their net gain is $33. The gain when Jones sells to Smith is $60. Maximizing net gain would lead to a clause like (2).

(3) If Brown values the crossover at $150, Jones will deliver to Brown, but compensate Smith $125.

The argument for this clause is easy enough. If Brown is willing to pay more than Smith for the crossovers, Jones wants to be free to make the better deal. Smith does not want to be a stumbling block to Jones's gain provided it is not at his expense. So he wants to make sure that Jones makes him *at least* as well off as he would have been had Jones delivered to him. In order for Smith to be at least as well off as he would have been in the event of delivery, Jones will have to compensate him his expected value ($110) plus whatever reliance Smith undertook in anticipation of the exchange being effectuated. Let's set Smith's reliance costs at $7. Smith will not permit Jones the option of selling to Brown unless the contract has a clause like (3) according to which Smith is to be compensated at least $117 in the event Jones decides to sell to Brown. Clause (3) gives Smith $125. Thus, clause (3) provides Smith with a net gain of $125 minus ($7 plus $75)—reliance plus the purchase price—or $43. If, on the other hand, Jones and Smith go through with the $75 deal, Smith's net gain is only $28: $110 minus ($75 plus $7). Thus, Smith is $15 better off when Jones sells to Brown under the conditions set forth in clause (3), so he is willing to accept a clause like (3).

Whether Jones will accept such a clause depends on whether he'll be better off selling to Brown even after he compensates Smith than he would be otherwise. If he sells to Smith he receives a $25 gain ($75 selling price minus $50 production cost). If he sells to Brown, Jones's profit is the $75 he gets from Smith less this $50 production cost plus the $150 he gets from Brown minus the $125 he has to pay Smith, or $50. Jones would accept such a clause. The joint gain to Jones and Smith in virtue of Jones's decision to invoke clause (3) would be Jones's $50 plus Smith's $43, or $93. Because the third clause produces a gain of $93, whereas the contract itself called for a sale with a surplus of $60—actually $53 if we include Smith's reliance—clause (3) maximizes net gain and is therefore efficient.[28]

One problem in contracts is which damage remedy, if any, will induce efficient breaches? Which damage remedy, in other words, would duplicate the effect of clauses (1) to (3) of the fully specified contract?

We can distinguish first among the following damage remedies: (1) specific performance; (2) expectation damages; (3) reliance damages; and (4) restitution damages.

Under the rule of *specific performance*, the breaching party is required to perform. Under *an expectation damage* remedy, the breaching party must pay the victim of his breach the expected value of the contract to him so that the victim would be indifferent between the contract's completion and breach plus remedy. Under a *reliance* remedy the breaching party must compensate the victim the full cost of his reliance, so that from the victim's point of view it's as if no contract had ever been made.[29] Under the *restitution* remedy the victim is awarded damages sufficient to nullify whatever gain the breaching party may have secured at his expense.

Specific performance "completes" the contract. Expectation damages make the breached-against party as well off as he would have been had the contract been completed. Both reliance and restitution damages aim to put one or the other party in the position he would have been in had the contract never been made. In reliance damages, that party is the victim of the breach. In restitution damages, that party is the individual who breaches.

Specific performance, as in our example, would be efficient if transactions were costless. If Jones is required to sell to Smith then if Brown values the crossover at $150, *Smith*, upon completing the contract with Jones, will turn around and sell to Brown. Same result in terms of net gains as in the fully specified contract though the distribution of the gain is different. Of course, where transactions are costless any remedy will be efficient. But then if transactions were costless, every contract would be a fully specified one.

Assume that the contract has no provision regarding a potential second buyer (Brown) of Jones's sophisticated crossover networks. As luck would have it Brown emerges from the shadows and offers to buy Jones's crossover networks. It would be efficient—as we determined from the fully specified contract—for Jones to sell to Brown if he offers $150, but not otherwise. Which, if any, damage remedy would lead Jones to breach with Smith and sell to Brown only when Brown values the crossovers at $150? Consider the expectation damage remedy first.

If the court awards expectation damages, Jones will not sell to Brown if Brown offers him $83. To accept Brown's $83, he would have to pay Smith the expected value of the contract, i.e., $110. Smith already gave him $75, $50 of which was spent on production costs. So he is already up $25. Add Brown's $83 and he is up $108. But he has to pay Smith $110. So to receive $108, he would have to pay $110, a trade he is very unlikely to make.

When Brown offers him $150, he is already up $25 from the $75 he got from Smith net his production costs of $50. Brown's offer makes him $175 better off. If Jones has to pay expectation damages, he will still be up $65 ($175 minus $110) and Smith will be up $28 ($110 minus $75 plus 7) for a net gain of $93. Jones will breach then only when Brown values the networks at $150, which is the efficient thing for him to do; expectation damages encourage efficient breach.

What about reliance damages? If the reliance remedy is in force, then the contract price is more likely to be $70 than $75.[30] In no case would it be lower than $50 (the price of production), or higher than $103 (the expected value to Smith net his reliance costs). To keep the example simple, let's continue to suppose that it is $75. When the reliance remedy is imposed, Jones will breach if Brown offers him $83. Smith pays Jones $75. Jones spends $50 of this on production. He's now up $25. Adding Brown's $83 puts him up $108. The reliance remedy requires him to pay back the contract price ($75) plus other reliance ($7), or $82, to Smith. After all is said and done he is up $26 ($108 minus $82) or $1 more than he would have been had he not breached. He breaches, then, even though the expected value of the crossover to Smith ($110) is higher than it is to Brown ($83). Reliance remedies may induce inefficient breaches.

Restitution damages are also likely to induce inefficient breach. Because Smith has paid Jones in advance, the only benefit he has bestowed upon Jones is the contract price, say $75. Therefore, all he has to do when he breaches under the restitution remedy is pay Smith $75. So if Brown values the network at $83, Jones breaches, though such a result is for the reasons already discussed inefficient.

Only expectation damages are efficient. And it is easy to see why. Whenever expectation damages are awarded, the seller has no incentive to sell to a party who values his goods less than does the contracting buyer. Other remedies sometimes induce breach to sell to a party who values the goods less than does the breached against party. Such breaches are necessarily inefficient. Moreover, if the seller will still be better off after paying expectation damages, then failure to breach would be inefficient. In some cases breaching then paying expectation damages is Pareto superior to not breaching.

ECONOMICS AND CRIMES

The economic analysis of crime usually falls into three categories. The subject matter of the first category is the potential criminal. Here economic analysis involves applying principles of rational choice under uncertainty in order to model criminal behavior. The analysis focuses on the extent to which variations in the probability of detection and severity of sanction can induce conduct in conformity to the dictates of the criminal law.

The second category is concerned primarily with society's decision regarding the distribution of resources spent on law enforcement. There is only so much money at a government's disposal. Some of it goes to national defense, some to public health, social programs, education, etc. Some of it goes to law enforcement. There are two subcategories here. The first is determining the general level of appropriate expenditures on crime; the second assumes a given expenditure and is concerned to distribute it optimally.

In both the first and second categories of economic analysis of crime, some characterization of conduct as criminal is taken as given. Given a characterization of conduct as criminal, the first type of analysis asks how we might use economic theory to induce compliance. The second form of analysis asks both how much should be spent on enforcement generally and how should the funds be optimally distributed. In contrast, the third kind of economic analysis of crime is concerned to give an economic analysis of the conditions of criminality. Here again, there are several questions. For example, is there an economic argument ever for making some conduct criminal rather than reducing its incidence in some other way? If there is an economic justification for the criminal category as such, are there special kinds of economic reasons for making certain types of conduct subject to the criminal sanction? Is there, in other words, an economic criterion of criminality?[31]

In this section I can only discuss some very basic problems in the economic analysis of crime. In particular, I want to focus on the basic result of Gary Becker's seminal piece on the economics of crime, "Crime and Punishment: An Economic Approach."[32] My exposition of the problem does not follow Becker's, but the general line of argument is the same in both cases.

One thing economists assume is that the criminal sanction, however complex and rich we philosophers might think it is, can be given a dollar equivalent. Instead of a criminal sanction, we will find it more convenient, then, to talk about a criminal fine or simply a fine. Suppose the fine for jaywalking is $5—at least that's what it used to cost me to jaywalk in Wisconsin. That figure makes no sense in the abstract: what does it represent? We must suppose that the $5 fine is like the optimal Pigouvian tax; it represents the total marginal "damage" to the victims of jaywalking. In other words, we begin by assuming that the fine for jaywalking is itself *optimal;* it is set equal to the total cost of the disruption in the flow of traffic and other inconveniences that result from each occurrence of it.

We assume that the fine is optimal; that it functions like the Pigouvian tax, or as a liability rule would in a nuisance case. If it is optimally set, then potential jaywalkers are led only to efficient jaywalking. Jaywalking is efficient only when the benefits to the jaywalker exceed the costs of jaywalking (i.e., $5). Recall from the argument developed in the discussion of the Coase Theorem that if the potential jaywalker could get together with everyone who might be adversely affected by his jaywalking, he would make a deal with them that would permit him to jaywalk whenever the benefit to him of doing so exceeded the costs to them of his doing so. In other words, if "victims" had the right to foreclose jaywalking, he would buy them off whenever his gain exceeded $5.

The fine is set to induce individuals who value jaywalking under $5 not to jaywalk, but to permit those who value jaywalking more than $5 to jaywalk. Does it follow that we will get efficient jaywalking from the fact that the fine is optimally set at $5? The answer is no. We have left out something that distinguishes the criminal fine from the liability rule in the nuisance case, and that is *enforcement.* Liability rules in nuisance and torts generally are *privately* enforced. You injure me: *I* go to court to seek an injunction or a damage remedy. Criminal statutes are *publicly* enforced. (It is a serious question in the economic analysis of law what the optimal mix of public and private enforcement should be.)

The state must hire someone (i.e., spend money) to enforce the fine. Though the fine is optimally set to induce efficient compliance, it will do so only if the probability of enforcement is 1.0. But the probability of enforcement will approach 1.0 only if people turn themselves in, or if there is a great expenditure on enforcement. It is not inconceivable that an expenditure great enough to induce perfectly efficient compliance would more than exceed the actual benefits of compliance. The question is one of optimal compliance, and that always includes the costs of securing compliance.

We see straightaway the manner in which the first two categories of economic analysis of crime interact. The nature and scope of various inducements to efficient conduct depends on the costs of enforcement. If a society is unable to spend much on enforcement, that will certainly affect the ways in which it seeks to induce efficient compliance.

Let's specify more precisely the relationship between enforcement costs and efficient compliance. The $5 fine equals the actual damage done by jaywalking. If the probability of detection is equal to 1.0, then we secure perfect compliance. Suppose, however, it costs the state $1,000,000/year to guarantee 100 percent detection. Suppose now that the state could spend $100,000/year to catch one out of ten violators, or it could spend $10,000/year to catch one out of one hundred, or it could spend $1,000/year to catch one out of every one thousand jaywalkers. What ought it to do?

Believe it or not, it can spend whatever it wants on enforcement (i.e., either of these options) provided two other conditions are satisfied:

(1) it must raise the fine to offset the reduction in detection rates, and (2) it cannot impose a fine greater than the average wealth of its citizens. All this is easy to demonstrate. If the probability of detection drops by a factor of ten, the *expected fine* remains the same provided the fine itself is increased by a factor of ten. So if the state wants to spend $100,000 on enforcement, it must raise the fine to $50. If it is willing to spend $10,000, the fine for jaywalking should go up to $500; if its enforcement expenditure is to be $1,000, the fine for jaywalking will be $5,000. Indeed, if it wanted almost costless enforcement, $1/year, it need only fine each instance of jaywalking at $5,000,000. A fine that high should have everyone crossing streets at the corner.

The general point is that as long as individuals are assumed to be risk-neutral they are concerned only with *expected outcomes*. The expected outcome for each potential jaywalker is $5. On these assumptions rational enforcement would be set equal to the least enforcement cost compatible with the constraint that no fine can exceed the average wealth of the citizen.[33]

GAME THEORY AND LITIGATION

In applying economics to legal problems we have thus far confined the discussion to the role of individual rational choice under conditions of uncertainty in guiding the choice of optimal legal rules in both common and criminal law contexts. Now for something completely (sort of) different.[34]

The application of game theoretic models in an overall economic analysis of law has pretty much been confined to modeling decisions by litigants to file suit and to pursue litigation. Two basic models of the decision to litigate have been advanced, both of which have elements of strategic interaction. According to one analysis, a plaintiff makes two separate decisions. First he decides whether to file suit. Then the defendant decides whether to offer a settlement. If he offers a settlement, the plaintiff then must decide whether to accept it. If he accepts the settlement, the case does not go to court. If he does not accept then the case is litigated in court.

In the other model, a plaintiff makes a decision to file. The defendant then decides whether to offer a settlement. Suppose the defendant offers a settlement. The plaintiff may either accept the settlement or not. If he does the game ends without litigation. If the plaintiff does not accept the offer, he goes to trial. Suppose the defendant does *not* offer a settlement. According to this model, the plaintiff has a choice.

He can either go to trial or *drop out.* It is the possibility of dropping out that distinguishes the two models.

The possibility of a litigant's filing, then dropping out after a defendant decides not to settle is a plausible one, especially if we consider that litigants may file suit on the off chance that a defendant might want to settle rather than pursue litigation. Once the defendant decides not to be taken in, however, the plaintiff may back off. The second model is therefore the richer of the two. Let's take a look at how it would operate to model behavior in a simple tort case.

As in our previous discussions of the economic approach to law we assume that litigants are risk-neutral. They are interested in the expected outcomes of "the litigation game." The model of the game can be more or less complicated depending on, for example, the likelihood that the court will render the correct decision, the knowledge of each litigant of what that decision is, as well as their assessment of the court's capacity to reach it.

The simpler models in microtheory usually assume that decision-makers have full information (recall the Coase Theorem); the basic models in game theory do not. Indeed one feature of strategic interaction in the game situation is the extent to which various strategies might be developed to exploit disparities in information. In the model I want to explore, to my knowledge first set out by I. P. L. P'ng,[35] there is *an inequality in information.* In particular, the defendant knows whether or not his conduct is in compliance with the relevant legal standard. The plaintiff is uncertain of the legal status of the defendant's conduct. The defendant knows whether or not he is at fault; the plaintiff does not.

The idea of a game tree is familiar to some of you. In any case, it is not a difficult notion. The game tree maps all the possible paths the various players might take. Fig. 5.4 is the basic game tree for *all* two-party litigation games in which the defendant has information the plaintiff does not regarding the legal status of his conduct and in which the plaintiff might file suit *only* in order to extract a settlement offer.[36]

One difference between the plaintiff and defendant is that the strategies the defendant adopts can always be affected by his knowledge of whether or not he is at fault, whereas the plaintiff's cannot. Therefore, whenever the plaintiff makes a choice, he cannot make that choice based on the fault of the defendant. So the branches represent distinct strategies for the defendant, but not for the plaintiff. Whatever decision he makes in one branch at a particular point in the litigation must be the same in the other branch (see Figure 5.4).

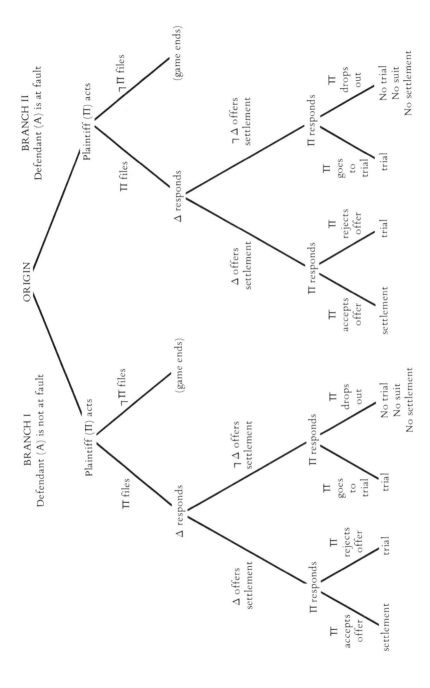

Figure 5.4 Game Tree

We can trace the various strategies through the tree's branches. The plaintiff has available to him the following strategies:

(1) He can choose *not to file* an action.
(2) He can *file* a suit, then *accept* a settlement if the defendant offers one, or to go *trial* if he does not.
(3) He can *file* a suit, then *accept* a settlement if the defendant offers one, or *drop* the suit if he does not.
(4) He can *file* a suit, then *refuse* a settlement if the defendant offers one, and go to trial.
(5) He can *file* a suit, then go to *trial* if the defendant offers to settle, or *drop* the suit if the defendant makes no offer.

Following P'ng we abbreviate these as:

(1) do not sue
(2) sue, settle, try
(3) sue, settle, drop
(4) sue, try, try
(5) sue, try, drop

The defendant has four possible strategies depending on whether or not he is at fault.

(1) Whether or not he is at fault he might offer to settle.
(2) Whether or not he is at fault he will be prepared to go to trial.
(3) If he is at fault he might settle, but go to trial if he is not.
(4) If he is at fault he might go to trial, but offer to settle if he is not.

Again, following P'ng, let's abbreviate these as:

(1) settle, settle
(2) try, try
(3) settle, try
(4) try, settle

Where the first strategy in each pair expresses the defendant's game plan if he is at fault, the second his strategy if he is not.

It seems odd that a plaintiff would file suit, then go to trial if the defendant offers a settlement, but drop litigation entirely if he does not (sue, try, drop). The strategy makes sense, however, if the plaintiff has reason to believe that the defendant will not make an offer to settle if he is innocent. If the plaintiff takes the defendant's refusal to offer a settlement as a sign of his innocence, then if the defendant does tender an offer, the plaintiff will seek the higher award by going to trial; but if he fails to tender an offer, the plaintiff backs down.

Now suppose the defendant figures that the plaintiff will take the defendant's decision about possible settlements as the best evidence of his (the defendant's) culpability. The defendant might then try to confound the plaintiff by giving reverse signals, that is, by adopting the fourth strategy (try, settle). He does not offer a settlement if he is at fault, otherwise he offers to settle. In the event the defendant adopts such a strategy, he will be a big winner if the plaintiff adopts the "sue, settle, drop" strategy.

The point of the game model is in part to figure out which strategies are most likely to be pursued over the long term: the behavior we can expect from litigants regarding settlements and trials generally. In the language of game theory, we are looking for strategies in equilibrium. One well-known game theoretic notion of equilibrium is the Nash equilibrium. A strategy pair is in a Nash equilibrium when each strategy is the utility-maximizing one for a player to adopt no matter what strategy the other player adopts.

The most well-known illustration of (a nonoptimal) Nash equilibrium is the single-instance Prisoner's Dilemma. In the Prisoner's Dilemma matrix illustrated below the best strategy for player 1 is alternative a_1. If Player 2 chooses b_1, then Player 1 receives 1, rather than 0 which he would have received had he chosen to play a_2. If Player 2 chooses b_2 then Player 1 recieves 10 rather than 9 he would have received had he played a_2. Similar considerations lead Player 2 to play b_1. The pair $a_1 b_1$ is a Nash equilibrium. It is not an optimal equilibrium because both would do better off at $a_2 b_2$.

Player 2

		b_1	b_2
Player 1	a_1	(1, 1)	(10, 0)
	a_2	(0, 10)	(9, 9)

Figure 5.5 Payoff structure for single-play Prisoner's Dilemma

Back to the litigation game.[37] What are dominant strategies for the litigants? What sort of behavior would be expected from them in the long run? To determine the set of possible Nash equilibria, we have to construct a payoff matrix. The values of the particular plays depends on five factors:

(1) the settlement
(2) the damage award
(3) the plaintiff's legal fees

(4) the defendant's legal fees
(5) the probability (p) that the defendant is at fault.

The structure of the game matrix is as follows:

Let S = Settlement
    A = Litigated award
    L_1 = Plaintiff legal fees
    L_2 = Defendant legal fees
    P = Probability of Defendant fault

Defendant's Strategies

		settle, settle	try, try	settle, try	try, settle
	No Action	0, (0,0)	0, (0,0)	0 (0,0)	0 (0,0)
	Sue Settle Try	S, (-S, -S)	$P(A)$-L_1) $((-A$-$L_2)$, L_2	$P(S)$-$(1$-$P)L_1$ $(-S,$-$L_2)$	$P(A$-$L_1)$ + $(1 - P)S$ $((-A$-$L_2)$,-$L_2)$
Plaintiff Strategies	Sue Try Try	$P(A)$-L_1 $((-A$-$L_2)$, -$L_2)$	$P(A)$-L_1 $((-A$-$L_2)$, -$L_2)$	$P(A)$-L_1, $((-A$-$L_2)$-$L_2)$	$P(A)$-L_1, $(-A$-$L_2)$,-L_2
	Sue Try Drop	$P(A)$-L_1 $((-A$-$L_2)$,-$L_2)$	0, (0,0)	$P(A$-$L_1)$, $(-A$-$L_2)$,0	$-(1$-$P)L_1$ 0, -L_2
	Sue Settle Drop	S (-S,-S)	0 0,0	$P(S)$ $(-S,0)$	$(1$-$P)$ (S), $0,$-S

Figure 5.6 Payoff matrix in "Litigation-Settlement Game"

Each box (or cell) has two payoffs. The first represents the payoff to the plaintiff, the second to the defendant.

To make the example concrete, let's assign values to the various parameters and then determine the payoffs for one plaintiff's strategy against all the defendant's possible strategies. Let the award be $1,000,000, the settlement $750,000, legal fees $100,000 each for defendant and plaintiff, and the probability of the defendant's negligence .5. Let's spell out the fourth row of the matrix in which the plaintiff files suit, goes to trial if the defendant offers a settlement, drops otherwise.

An explanation of the computation for each entry follows in Figure 5.7.

| | | | Δ Strategy | | |
		settle, settle	try, try	settle, try	try, settle
Π Strategy	Π Payoff	.5(1,000,000− 100,000)	0	.5(1,000,000− 1,000,000)	−(1−.5)1000,000
Sue Try Drop	Δ Payoff	(a) −1,000,000 +(−100,000)	(a) 0	(a) −1,000,000 +(−100,000)	(a) 0
		(b) −100,000	(b) 0	(b) 0	(b) −100,000

Figure 5.7 Payoff computation

Each payoff pair is to be read as follows: the top payoff represents the expected payoff to the plaintiff. The bottom two, (a) and (b), represent the likely payoffs to the defendant depending on whether he is at fault. In (a) he is at fault; in (b) he is not. When the plaintiff adopts the strategy of filing, then pursuing a trial if the defendant offers to settle, and dropping otherwise, he never settles. He either goes to trial or he drops out. If he goes to trial his expected payoff is equal to the award ($1,000,000) discounted by the probability of the defendant's being at fault, i.e., .5 minus his legal fees. So in box 1 his expected payoff is .5 ($1,000,000) minus $100,000 or $400,000. The defendant always offers to settle in box 1 so the case will go to trial, because the plaintiff goes to trial whenever the defendant offers to settle. The defendant's expected payoffs depend on his guilt or innocence. If he is guilty, he loses $1,000,000 plus his court costs of $100,000. If he is innocent he loses his legal fees of $100,000.

In cell 2 the defendant makes no offer to settle and goes to trial come what may. If the defendant makes no offer to settle the plaintiff drops out; so his expected payoff is zero. Because the plaintiff drops out before trial, the defendant incurs no costs, whether or not he is at fault.

In 3, the defendant responds to the plaintiff's move by offering to settle if he is at fault (the plaintiff does not know whether or not he is, only the probability of his being so), but by not offering to settle otherwise. If the defendant does not offer to settle, the plaintiff backs down. The defendant does not offer to settle if he is innocent. The probability that he is innocent is (1 minus the probability he is not, which is .5) or .5. So the plaintiff backs down 50 percent of the time and that outcome can be anticipated 50 percent of the time. He can expect a pay off 50 percent of the time. The defendant offers to settle when he *is* at fault, i.e., 50 percent of the time. So the plaintiff can expect a payoff equal to his award, $1,000,000, minus legal fees, $100,000, or $900,000, 50 percent of the time. His expected outcome then is $450,000: .5 ($1,000,000 minus $100,000). If the defendant is at fault, he offers to settle, and goes to court. There he loses the award and his legal fees $1,000,000 plus $100,000. If he is innocent, he does not offer a settlement and the plaintiff drops out thereby imposing no costs on the defendant.

In box 4, the defendant offers to settle only if he is innocent. (The plaintiff's expected payoff again depends only on the probability that he is.) If the defendant offers, the plaintiff takes him to court, where he can expect to lose his court costs discounted by the probability that the defendant is at fault, $100,000 multiplied by .5 or $50,000. The defendant offers to settle only if he is innocent. The plaintiff responds by pursuing a trial. The defendant wins but must pay his court costs. If he refuses to settle when he is at fault, the plaintiff drops out, in which case he incurs no costs.

The numerical example illustrates at least one of the potential Nash equilibria for this game. If the plaintiff adopts the strategy of sue, try, drop, then whether or not he is at fault the defendant does best by adopting the strategy "try, try." No other outcome is as good for "both" defendants. To show that the pair of strategies are together in Nash equilibrium would require filling out more of the matrix to demonstrate that when the defendant plays, try, try, the plaintiff's dominant strategy is to play sue, try, drop. Of course whether or not sue, try, drop is the plaintiff's dominant strategy depends on the values assigned to the relevant variables.

If the reader examines the algebraic characterization of the game, it is easy to see that depending on the values assigned there are six possible Nash solutions. For example sue, settle, try, and settle, settle are a Nash equilibrium[1] if the settlement is greater than the expected outcome of trial for the plaintiff and the settlement is less costly to the defendant than are the total costs of litigation. In that case if the defendant plays settle, settle, the plaintiff does best by sue, settle, try. And if the plaintiff chooses sue, settle, try, the defendant does best by settle, settle. On the other hand, if both the expected outcome of trial exceeds the settlement, and the settlement exceeds the costs of litigation, the following outcomes are Nash solutions: sue, settle, try, and try, try[2]; sue, try, try, and settle, settle[3]; and sue, try, try, and try, try[4]. And if the expected outcome is less than zero, both sue, try, drop, and try, try[5]; and sue, settle, drop, and try, try[6] are Nash equilibria.

In the various equilibria the case is either settled (1), goes to trial (2–4), or is dropped by the plaintiff (5,6). The general question is what values must the key parameters have to make these differences? In the first equilibrium, the case is settled because both parties are best off by adopting the strategy of settlement if the other makes such an offer. The plaintiff would not accept an offer unless the settlement were equal to or greater than his expected return from trial, and the defendant would not allow a settlement to be greater than his expected total costs from trial. If these conditions are not satisfied, litigation ensues except when the plaintiff drops out.

There is nothing counterintuitive in these results. There is no reason to think there ought to be. The power of the game theoretic model of litigation is not in its capacity to startle or confound. Rather, its force consists first in its providing a formal apparatus that supports our intuitions about litigation. Next, if the apparatus is itself basically sound, and it appears to be, it might be usefully extended to far more complicated litigation "games"—e.g., where both litigants have imperfect information; where there are more than two litigants; where initiating litigation is not costless; and more important, where courts are imperfect. These are the kinds of cases where we are unlikely to have intuitions about which cases in general go to trial and which are settled or withdrawn. Here the model might increase rather than merely reinforce our understanding of the litigation process. Perhaps the results of extended models might inform an enlightened legislature of the effects of various parameters on litigation that legislature might use, for example, to discourage frivolous litigation or to encourage litigation that is currently being hastily withdrawn or settled.

OBJECTIONS TO THE ECONOMIC ANALYSIS OF LAW

THE IDEOLOGY OF THE ECONOMIC ANALYSIS OF LAW

Despite its obvious power as a tool to model and evaluate legal arrangements and institutions, philosophers have, with rare exceptions, remained unimpressed by the economic analysis of law. That is because to the extent philosophers are familiar with economic analysis it is through essays by individuals unsympathetic to it, who have advanced questionable interpretations of economic analysis and misguided ob-

jections to it. The objection that has secured the greatest currency—
and is therefore most responsible for the prevailing attitude toward
the whole enterprise—is that the economic of law involves an insidious,
unpalatable ideology.

Roughly, the objection that economic efficiency is not normatively
neutral turns on the fact that what is efficient depends on what people
are willing to pay, and what people are willing to pay in turn depends
on what they are capable of paying. In short, the greater one's wealth,
the more likely one is to increase it. And it is not just that economic
analysis lends itself to this pattern of distribution; rather it is that
economic analysis requires and sanctions such patterns of distribution
under the guise of pursuing the presumably desirable goal of efficiency.

The argument has a certain initial plausibility which is easy enough
to sketch. Recall Richard Posner's suggestion that in order for courts
to promote efficiency they should assign entitlements by mimicking
the market. For Posner, mimicking the market in this regard involves
assigning rights to resources to those parties who would have purchased
them in an exchange market. This just means to assign the right to
the party who would have paid more for it.

Therein lies the connection between efficiency and willingness to
pay. One's willingness to pay surely depends on what one can pay,
thus the connection is extended from efficiency to actual wealth. This
connection makes economic analysis unsavory enough, but it gets
worse. If rights are assigned this way, the richer not only get richer,
but because their newly acquired entitlements increase their wealth
further, they are in an ever better position to increase their wealth
again by securing more rights on the grounds that their doing so is
required by efficiency. Thus, efficiency not only depends on prior
wealth inequities; pursing efficiency leads inevitably to further inequities.

It is undeniable that "auctioning" certain extremely scarce goods—
e.g., the only glass of water in the desert to the high bidder among
a group of weary and bone-dry travelers—would constitute a moral
outrage, even if doing so would be efficient in Posner sense. Since in
such cases, each person would bid to the limit of his wealth, efficient
resource allocation would be tantamount to giving resources to the
wealthiest individual. But absolutely no defender of economic analysis
claims that the analysis is supposed to cover such cases. The notion
of efficiency is intended to be useful in genuine *market settings*, or in
contexts that are sufficiently similar to exchange markets to render
efforts to mimic the market plausible. There is no sense in which the
desert example can be construed as involving an exchange market

for water. To say that the *scope* of economic analysis is limited in some ways is not to deny its power within its domain.

We can all agree that sometimes assigning resources to the highest bidder is undesirable even if efficient. Economists do not deny this. But assigning rights to those willing to pay more for them does not in fact always amount to assigning rights to those most able to pay. Reconsider the nuisance example. Suppose the manufacturer is considerably more well-off than are its neighbors. Presumably it could outbid them and pollute to its content. But it does not do so simply because doing so would be irrational. If it gains only so much by polluting, it bids only so much for the right to continue polluting, regardless of its capacity to pay. On the other hand, the neighbors, regardless of their wealth, bid at least the value of their damages to force a reduction in pollution. After all, they are already bearing those costs as damages. Their bids are determined by the value of the damages they suffer, not by their relative wealth. The manufacturer accepts bids according to the value of the gain it would forego, not in virtue of its relative wealth. So it goes in all the examples discussed in that section and in the application of economics to the resolution of legal disputes generally; capacity to pay is not always nor is it often the relevant parameter.

The claim here is not that one's relative wealth *never* is determinate in deciding upon the allocation of resources. Of course it can be. In general, however, the connection between efficiency and relative wealth is a good deal less important than the advocates of the ideology objection would have us believe. For we would not be inclined to speak of an unsavory or insidious ideology embedded in economic analysis if it turned out that all we could show was that for some resources all the time (tragically scarce ones, as in the desert example), and other resources some of the time, one's ability to secure them depended largely on one's wealth.

In fact, this last assertion seems no more true of economic analysis than it is of markets generally. For there are things in virtue of my relative wealth I can purchase in a market that others cannot, and there are things others can purchase that I cannot. And we recognize, I trust, that there is in general nothing wrong with these sorts of differences, though we might all agree therefore that not everything should be distributed in a market—e.g., access to scarce life-saving medical treatment. In short just as we recognize the existence of cases in which, in spite of their efficiency, markets are inappropriate allocation mechanisms, proponents of economic analysis recognize that *mimicking markets* is sometimes inappropriate for the very same reasons.

In short, the ideology argument is no more nor less an objection to economic analysis than it is to markets generally.

Economic analysis is closely connected to the idea of a market; we can see this most clearly in Posner's dictum that for law to promote efficiency it ought to mimic the market. Like the market, economic analysis does not rely on, require, or endorse any particular distribution of wealth or of property rights. We can talk meaningfully about the efficient outcome of exchange that takes place within a market in which people are given absolutely equal shares of the wealth just as meaningfully as we can talk about the efficiency of exchange in markets where wealth is unequally distributed.

One might object that even if the notion of an efficient market outcome makes sense when individuals given equal shares of the initial entitlements, once resources are reallocated through trade or the political process, disputes will arise in which continuing to promote efficiency will serve only to redistribute wealth further in the direction of the already well-to-do. But this is just wrong. In markets, rational exchanges are made only when they are to the advantage of both parties. When rights are assigned to high bidders along the lines Posner suggests, the wealth of one of the litigants increases—though as we pointed out, that person or group need not be the *ex ante* wealthier one; it might simply be the person or group that has the most to gain by securing the resource. Still, there is nothing in economic analysis that precludes making lump-sum transfer payments from those who gain entitlements to those who have lost out. So the gain in efficiency need not create a snowball effect in favor of those who obtain rights on efficiency grounds. In theory at least *ex post* lump-sum transfer or compensation may rectify efficiency related inequalities of wealth while in no way inhibiting the pursuit of efficiency. In short, there is no bias in favor of any economic group in the economic analysis of law. Efficiency analysis works—if it works at all— regardless of the initial distribution of wealth; and the wealth effects of assigning rights on efficiency grounds can be rectified by lump-sum wealth transfers. I want now to focus on more powerful objections to economic analysis.

COASE AND STRATEGIC BEHAVIOR

Time and again where the economic approach to law calls upon the courts to promote efficiency by replicating the outcome of market exchange, it has in mind the efficiency of exchange under the conditions of the Coase Theorem. These conditions are zero transaction costs and cooperation. But there is reason to think that these conditions are inadequate to assure efficient exchange.

Exchange in a market is a bargain and involves bargaining. Bargaining can be viewed as a kind of closed-ended game. It takes time; it has a beginning and an end. The end is successful or not depending on whether an exchange occurs. The length of the game may vary, depending on the patience of the parties, the cost of negotiations, alternatives open to each, incentives to reconcile differences, etc. The Coase Theorem is based on exchange. Exchange is a bargain. Bargaining is a game. Simple private exchange can be modeled within game theory as a bargaining game. The Coase Theorem is just the claim that bargaining games with zero transaction costs have optimal equilibria.

The standard interpretation of the Coase Theorem locates it within traditional microeconomic theory, rather than in game theory. In both micro and game theory, agents (players) are presumed to be rational maximizers of their expected utilities. The difference is that in micro theory the model is that of individual rational choice where the behavior of other agents is taken as part of the background of individual choice. While this model may capture aspects of rational choice, it does not capture rational interaction among agents. In game theory, the analysis of expectations seeks to capture their essential interdependence. What the rancher expects the farmer will offer him to forego the next cow depends in part on what the farmer expects the rancher will accept, and so on. Game theory talks of interdependent strategies rather than of choices against a given static backdrop.

In the standard interpretation of the Coase Theorem, it is simply assumed that negotiations will be fruitful as long as they are costless. In part, that is because the standard interpretation fails to capture the elements of negotiations that may threaten their success. To illustrate this, it will be helpful more precisely to characterize bargaining games.

In general we can distinguish between games that reallocate stakes, those that produce advantage, and those that do both. In a reallocation game, players vie for shares of a given pot. Their actions neither create nor destroy; they merely redistribute the stakes. Games of reallocation are more likely to be familiar to you as "zero-sum" games: my gain is your loss, and *vice versa*. Other games require cooperation or coordination to secure common objectives. Successful coordination assures victory or gain for all; inadequate coordination may be to everyone's disadvantage. Team sports are cooperative games. A market exchange is a bargaining game that has elements of both productive and reallocative games. Recall the example in the breach of contracts section. Jones has the stereo crossover network Smith wants. Smith has the cash. If they agree on a sale at $75 (the contract price), they have redistributed the stakes: the stakes being the combination "electronics plus cash." By successfully redistributing the stakes, Jones and Smith manage as well to produce a *surplus*. It cost Jones $50 to produce the electronic devices so he secures a surplus of $25. Smith values the equipment at $110, so at the contract price he nets a surplus of $35. Their joint surplus benefit is $60. The market exchange, if successful, is a bargaining game that is both redistributive and productive. It is productive, however, only if it is successfully redistributive. If agreement over shares of the stakes can not be secured there is no surplus. The "pie" is not enlarged. Efficiency, in other words, is threatened by an inability to settle on a distribution of the fruits of cooperation.

Coase is credited with having established that private exchange can circumvent inefficient liability decisions whenever transactions are costless. Such a view expresses an enormous amount of confidence in the ability of negotiating parties to agree on a division of the stakes. For failure to do so blocks exchange and thus inhibits efficiency. This roadblock to efficiency, moreover, is not a function of high transaction costs. Indeed, as we shall see, it may be more likely to occur the lower the costs of transaction.[38]

Once one conceives of exchange as a bargaining game, it is not at all clear that confidence in its success is warranted. Bargaining is a process of offers and counteroffers. It sometimes involves rounds of negotiations and can go on for some time. Given this characterization of bargaining, consider the effect of transaction costs on the efficiency of exchange. Suppose that overall transaction costs are not so high as to render exchange unprofitable from the outset. If transactions are costly, continued rounds of negotiation will reduce the size of the surplus. At each stage of negotiations, parties will be contesting for decreasing stakes. Higher transaction costs may induce successful negotiations by encouraging parties to lessen their demands and to reconcile their differences for fear that continued negotiations may lead to a vanishing surplus. In contrast, if continued negotiations are costless in every way (time and opportunity as well as money), then the process of making demands and entertaining offers may proceed without success as no external inducement to reconciliation manifests itself. Without an external push, costless private exchange may prove anything but efficient. This feature of strategic behavior, of threats and bluffs, of proposals and counterproposals, is simply glossed over in the nongame theoretic reading of Coase.

One might meet this odd sounding objection—that zero transaction costs are as likely to block exchange as to facilitate it—in one of three ways. The first response is that strategic behavior is itself a transaction cost, so inefficiency that results from it is ruled out by the zero transaction cost assumption. Economists criticize philosophers for using terms like "justice," "fairness," and "causation" as too imprecise and murky for their taste. No term in the philosopher's lexicon is more imprecisely defined than is the economist's term "transaction costs." Almost anything counts as a transaction cost. But if we are to count every failure to reach agreement on the division of surplus as necessarily resulting from transaction costs (I have no doubt that *sometimes* it does), then by transaction cost we must mean literally anything that threatens the efficiency of market exchange. In that case, it could hardly come as a surprise that in the absence of transaction costs, market exchange is efficient.

Another line of response that I am unable to explore in detail here is that a failure to reach accord over the division of stakes is irrational. Rational cooperation entails agreement whenever there are gains from trade to be had. If we fail to reach an accord, that may be unfortunate, regrettable, an unhappy event, the cause of which we should try to work through next time around, but not necessarily irrational. Am I irrational if I am stubborn? Sometimes I am if, for example, I turn down your offer to give me all the surplus. What else could I be negotiating for? Recall that in the Coase Theorem we are negotiating in lieu of going to trial; we are trying to settle, for example, on cows and corn, rather than have a court impose an arrangement on us. In that case what settlements are rational for us to accept will certainly depend on our personal assessments of the likely outcome of litigation. One's subjective evaluation may be mistaken; one's failure to accept a division of the stakes based therefore on miscalculation. But miscalculation does not entail irrationality. The possibility of gains from trade provides the incentive for rational cooperation, but in the absence of a mechanism for cooperation, it cannot insure its success.

Finally, one might respond that strategic behavior is a failure to cooperate. Cooperation is a background condition of the Coase Theorem. Strategic behavior is therefore ruled out by the assumption that the parties cooperate with one another. In this view, cooperation entails the success of negotiations: cooperation entails agreement. This, too, is an odd use of the term "cooperate." We would normally distinguish cooperating from noncooperating parties by their wilingness to negotiate, not by the success of their negotiations. There is no contradiction involved in the report that two parties came to the bargaining table, tried to iron out their differences, fully cooperated with one another, but were unable to reach an accord, thereby forcing the matter to arbitration.

On the other hand, we could *define* cooperation so that it would entail successful bargaining. But then the Coase Theorem would be an even less informative proposition than it is normally taken to be. For the claim that when transactions are costless and parties cooperate market exchanges circumvent inefficient rules just means that when transactions are costless agreement is necessary. Private exchange can only fail to be efficient if agreement is not reached. Agreement is not reached only if parties are unable to agree on a division of the stakes, or if transaction costs make negotiations unprofitable. If transaction costs make negotiations unprofitable, no effort at exchange is made. But when transaction costs are low, our experience is that rational people still sometimes fail to reach agreement. But if we ascribe all such failures to a breakdown in cooperation, then we have simply trivialized the theorem, for we have identified all the conditions that could ever lead to its falsifiability and have assumed their absence in the statement of the theorem's initial conditions. Understood this way, Coase does not offer an alternative approach to externalities. The Coase Theorem is simply a stipulative *definition* of rational cooperation in the absence of transaction costs.[39]

POSNER, EFFICIENCY AND UTILITY

The standard interpretation of the Coase Theorem presumes that costless negotiations will result in agreement. The game theoretic interpretation of it makes no such assumption. The Coase Theorem holds in the bargaining theory interpretation only if cooperation precludes strategic behavior. If cooperation does not preclude the possibility of strategic behavior, the Coase Theorem may simply be a mistaken hypothesis.

Assume for the sake of argument that Coase was right: that costless transactions inevitably result in agreement, and that private agreements can circumvent inefficient legal decisions. Costless negotiations are successful and their outcome is efficient.

Because so much emphasis has been placed on the zero transaction cost condition of the Coase Theorem, the central question in the law and economics literature has been, "What should a court (or legislature) do when transaction costs are high?" The general principle, first advanced by Posner, is that law should "mimic the market," that is, replicate the outcome of costless exchange. In the case of assigning property rights, mimicking the market means allocating rights or resources to those individuals who would have purchased them in the costless exchange market.

In what sense is Posner's principle for assigning rights an extension of Coase? In Coase, rational, fully informed individuals negotiate to optimal outcomes by the process of mutual gain *via* trade. The picture Coase presents is of (small numbers of) persons reaching Pareto optimal outcomes through Pareto superior exchange: efficiency through mutually advantageous trade. Part of what makes the picture Coase paints so attractive is that is suggests harmony between the pursuit of efficiency and the exercise of autonomy. This harmony is illusory, however.

If courts could apply Posner's principle, their doing so would produce Pareto optimal allocations. A court could apply Posner successfully only if it had adequate information regarding which party valued the relevant entitlement at the greater price. In some instances the information it needs is *not* easy to come by. For example, as we determined in the nuisance section, as assignment of a legal right secured by a property rule can be efficient only if the court knows the manufacturer's profit and its neighbor's damage schedules. In general, the court usually does not have sufficient information adequately to apply Posner's principle. For now, assume that sufficient information regarding the litigants' hypothetical behavior in costless markets is available to the court. Then the decisions of courts would be Pareto optimal, thus duplicating the optimality of exchange in Coase.

By assigning the right to the party who would have purchased it in a costless exchange market, the court allocates resources to individuals *who could have compensated* nonvictorious parties and still have secured a net gain in welfare. Suppose, for example, that the polluting manufcturer, already at 75 units of output, values the next 25 units at $50,000, and that its neighbors value the manufacturer foregoing those 25 units at $40,000; and that negotiations between them are too costly, thus resulting in litigation. Following Posner, the court ought to assign the right to the 100 units to the manufacturer since, had those units been initially assigned to its neighbors, it would have purchased the right to them, and had the units been assigned to it, the manufacturer would not have parted with them at any price the neighbors would have been prepared to offer. Once in possession of the right to the next 25 units, the manufacturer could have compensated its neighbors and still have been better off than when it was producing only 75 units of output. Because individuals who secure entitlements under its directive could render compensation and still be better off, Posner's rule satisfies the Kaldor-Hicks criterion.

In Coase, the party who values the entitlement most also eventually possesses it, but often it has to purchase it from the party who values the entitlement less. That party is fully compensated *ex ante* for whatever damages the other party's having the entitlement might ultimately impose on it. In Posner, assigning the entitlement straightaway to (in this case) the polluting manufacturer, makes its neighbors *worse off*. So, even if the allocation is optimal and Kaldor-Hicks efficient, it does not constitute a Pareto improvement. The importance of this departure from the Coasian paradigm of Pareto superior exchange leading to Pareto optimal outcomes emerges as soon as one asks why courts in particular or political institutions generally ought one assign entitlements by mimicking the market.

Two answers are normally given to this question: the first is that mimicking the market promotes efficiency; the second is that it promotes utility. The first answer is unsatisfactory because it is incomplete, since it is natural to ask why legal institutions ought to promote efficiency. What after all is the normative basis of efficiency? The second answer is simply unsatisfactory because mimicking the market need not result in gains in utility. Consider the second answer first—i.e., that mimicking the market produces increments in net utility.

There are two reasons for thinking that following Posner's principle would maximize utility. The first is that the assignment of rights on the market model involves a net gain in utility because it is *Pareto optimal*. The second is that such an assignment involves a net gain in utility because it satisfies the *Kaldor-Hicks criterion*. Neither claim can be sustained, however.

Consider first the relationship between Pareto optimality and utility. It does not follow that a move to a Pareto optimal state is itself utility-maximizing. Not every more to a Pareto optimal state involves a Pareto improvement. Of course, not every utility-maximizing move is Pareto superior. However, to determine if moves other than Pareto superior ones increase utility requires interpersonal comparability. So we cannot know whether assigning rights according to Posner's principle is utility-maximizing simply in virtue of its being Pareto optimal to do so. Consequently, we can not with confidence claim that the justification for promoting efficient outcomes in accord with the prescription that the law should mimic the market is that doing so promotes utility.

Now consider the claim that even if adhering to Posner's principle need not increase utility, doing so necessarily moves the "economy" from an inefficient state to an efficient one, and is therefore preferable or defensible on grounds of efficiency if not utility. The fact is, however, that we cannot make good even this weak claim—i.e., that judicial decisionmaking along the lines of Posner's principle is justified on the grounds that adhering to it promotes efficiency: this in spite of the fact that following the assignment principle will produce Pareto optimal, i.e., efficient outcomes. This has an odd ring to it, but the problem with the efficiency defense of Posner's principle emerges upon reinspection of the relationship of points on the frontier to those within it. Every point on the frontier is Pareto optimal.[40] Following Posner presumably guarantees that we attain the frontier. But it is a well-known fact of microeconomic theory that not every point on the frontier is preferable in economic terms to every point within the frontier. Though for every point within the frontier there exists a point on the frontier preferable to it, the reverse does not hold. Only points to the northeast are preferable on efficiency grounds. Because we do not know exactly where on the frontier we land after applying Posner's principle nor where we are within the frontier before we apply it, we simply cannot assert with confidence that applying his principle promotes efficiency in the same sense economists find desirable—quite apart from the more fundamental question of whether promoting efficiency in the economist's sense is itself desirable. From the fact that assigning rights according to Posner's principle leads to Pareto optimal outcomes, no conclusions about the desirability of those outcomes from the point of view of *efficient or utility* are warranted.

Now consider the relationship between efficiency and utility on the one hand and the Kaldor-Hicks criterion on the other. In addition to securing optimal outcomes, Posner's principle insures that legal rights will be assigned in conformity with the Kaldor-Hicks criterion. Is a Kaldor-Hicks improvement desirable from either an efficiency or a utility standpoint? That depends in part on whether Kaldor-Hicks actually extends the Pareto rankings in a way which would enable us to rank or order social states as being more or less desirable in virtue of their satisfying the criterion. That depends in turn on whether Kaldor-Hicks specifies a transitive ordering relationship. Unfortunately, Kaldor-Hicks is subject to the Scitovsky Paradox: S can be Kaldor-Hicks efficient to S_1 even though S_1 is Kaldor-Hicks efficient to S. Because S and S_1 can be Kaldor-Hicks efficient to one another, the Kaldor-Hicks criterion fails to specify a transitive ordering relationship. For that reason it can not provide us with an adequate efficienty related reason for preferring one state of affairs to antoher. So the fact that Posner's principle leads a court to make Kaldor-Hicks improvements cannot count as an argument in its favor. A brief illustration of the Scitovsky Paradox follows in Figure 5.8.[41]

Imagine two states of the world, S and S_1; two persons, X and Y; and two commodities, a and b, and distributed in S and S_1 between X and Y according to the following matrix.

	S		S_1	
	a	b	a	b
X	2	0	1	0
Y	0	1	0	2

Figure 5.8   Illustrations of Scitovsky Paradox

Assume the following ordering of preferences for a and b by X and Y respectively:

X: 1,1; 2,0; 1,0
Y: 1,1; 0,2; 0,1

It is easy to show that given these preference orderings S and S_1 are Kaldor-Hicks efficient to one another.

S is Kaldor-Hicks efficient to S_1. In going from S to S_1, X is made worse off, Y better off. At S_1, Y could compensate X one unit of b. Then X would have one of both a and b, thus attaining his most preferred state, whereas Y would have no units of a and one of b, which would put him no worse off than he is at S. Because compensation could take place at S_1 that would make at least one person prefer S_1 to S and no one prefer S to S_1, the move from S to S_1 is Kaldor-Hicks efficient.

S is Kaldor-Hicks efficient to S_1 as well. In going from S_1 to S, X is made better off and Y worse off. Once at S, X could compensate Y one unit of a. Having done so, Y would be in his most preferred state, and X, now possessing one unit of a and none of b, would be no worse off than at S_1. Once again, compensation if rendered, would make the move from S_1 to S Pareto superior; so the move from S_1 to S is Kaldor-Hicks efficient.

The relationship between Kaldor-Hicks and utility is now easy to specify. It cannot follow from the fact that S_1 is Kaldor-Hicks efficient to S that in going from S to S_1 there has been a net gain in *utility*. While S and S_1 may be Kaldor-Hicks efficient to one another, it cannot be the case that S and S_1 have more total utility than one another. Kaldor-Hicks therefore cannot be justified on grounds either of efficiency or utility.

The convergence between autonomy and utility in Coase breaks down in just those cases in which Posner's principle is supposed to be applied. Indeed, whereas one could with some plausibility defend Coase on grounds either of efficiency, utility, or liberty, no defense from any of these quarters can be offered on behalf of Posner's principle. In following Posner, we duplicate the outcome of exchange, but not exchange itself and therefore not the rational autonomous behavior of informed individuals. Moreover, in doing so we may produce efficient outcomes—i.e., attain the frontier—but we have no reason for thinking that in doing so we have promoted the ends of efficiency or utility. It does not follow from the fact that we have attained the frontier through a Kaldor-Hicks efficient assignment of rights that we have promoted efficiency or increased utility.[42]

PARETO SUPERIORITY, KALDOR-HICKS AND CONSENT

There are serious problems then in finding a utilitarian or purely economic foundation for the pursuit of either Pareto optimal states or Kaldor-Hicks improvements. The normative defensibility of the enterprise of law and economics might then rest on finding a defense for the *Pareto superiority* criterion. One argument for *Pareto superiority* is that Pareto improvements increase net utility. This attempts to root one dimension of economic analysis in utilitarian moral theory. For two very different sorts of reasons, few advocates of economic analysis have been drawn to this defense of economic analysis. First, Richard Posner, who to my knowledge is the only advocate of economic analysis to have self-consciously attempted to ground economic analysis in moral theory, explicitly rejects utilitarianism as a moral theory. If utilitarianism is the only moral theory upon which economic analysis can rest, it cannot rest comfortably—at least if Posner is correct. The second is that by and large, little, if any, economic analysis actually employs the Pareto superiority criterion. Most economic analysis involves Kaldor-Hicks and Pareto optimality. Neither of these can be grounded in utilitarian moral theory. So even if one embraces utilitarianism, it will not follow that much of economic analysis can thereby be morally grounded, since only Pareto superiority bears a direct relation to utilitarian moral theory, and Pareto superiority is nearly useless in actual applications of economics to law in particular, and to public policy in general.

Kaldor-Hicks and Pareto optimality are not utilitarian criteria of efficiency. Pareto superiority is. If one rejects utilitarianism as a moral theory, as Posner does, what other arguments, if any, can be offered on behalf of Pareto superiority? Because utilitarianism—whatever its ultimate merits—cannot be offered in defense of Kaldor-Hicks, what kinds of arguments can? More generally, are there nonutilitarian arguments for *any* of the relevant efficiency notions?

In an early paper, Kaldor himself suggested that one could justify both the Pareto superiority and the Kaldor-Hicks criteria by appealing to arguments based on the consent of the parties affected by either Pareto or Kaldor-Hicks improvements. Such a defense would be especially attractive for the same reasons the Coase Theorem is: it would demonstrate the ultimate compatibility of economics and liberty—the fundamental convergence of utility and rational autonomous choice.

Kaldor's argument is contained in the following little-known passage:

> This principle [Kaldor-Hicks], as the reader will observe, simply amounts to saying that there is no interpersonal comparison of satisfactions involved in judging any policy designed to increase the sum total of wealth just because any such policy *could* be carried out in a way as to secure unanimous consent.[43]

The argument appears to be this:

1. A Pareto superior move involves the unanimous consent of relevant parties.
2. A Pareto superior move is therefore justified on grounds of consent.
3. A Kaldor-Hicks move is a Potential Pareto one; that is, compensation *could* be paid.
4. Any Kaldor-Hicks move could be a Pareto superior one.
5. Therefore, we could secure unanimous consent for a Kaldor-Hicks improvement.
6. Therefore, Kaldor-Hicks is justified in grounds of consent, and so its justification does not depend on our capacity to make interpersonal utility comparisons.

There are several places in the argument with which one could take issue. Even if we accepted the first four steps in the argument, the conclusion would not follow. There is all the difference in the world between actual and hypothetical compensation. Even if a winner could have secured a loser's consent by compensating him, in a Kaldor-Hicks move winners do *not* in fact compensate losers, and so they do not in fact secure the loser's consent. The argument that attempts to justify Kaldor-Hicks by treating the consent involved in Kaldor-Hicks as tantamount to that involved in Pareto superiority fails.

There is an alternative consent argument for Kaldor-Hicks that I have previously explored.[44] Begin by assuming what we will ultimately reject—that compensation constitutes consent. In Pareto superior moves, consent is secured through either exchange or compensation *ex post*. The question is what sort of compensation is involved in making Kaldor-Hicks improvements?

The central difference between Kaldor-Hicks and Pareto superiority concerns the nature of compensation. Losers are compensated *ex post* under the Pareto criterion but not under Kaldor-Hicks. Compensation has associated with it certain transaction costs—the costs of rendering compensation. Making Kaldor-Hicks gains is less costly than securing Pareto superior ones because Kaldor-Hicks involves no *ex post* compensation. This reduction in cost is a savings; the savings is a kind of *ex ante* compensation that all participants secure when the Kaldor-Hicks criterion is employed.

An example might be useful. In automobile accident law, we could adopt a rule either of strict or negligence liability. One difference between the two is that under the rule of strict liability, victims are often more compensated than they would be under a rule of negligence. The negligence system requires less compensation and would prove less costly on those grounds. If that is so, then liability insurance costs would be lower under a negligence system, but fewer victims would be compensated. For ease of exposition, let us suppose that the strict liability system involves Pareto superiority (i.e., injurers would only harm if they gained even after compensating fully their victims) and that the negligence system involves the Kaldor-Hicks criterion (i.e., injurers could, but do not in general have to, compensate their victims). Under the negligence (Kaldor-Hicks) system, the reduction in liability insurance costs constitutes *ex ante* compensation for the losses victims suffer that are not compensated for *ex post*, but that would have been compensated for *ex post* under the strict liability (Pareto superiority) criterion.[45]

The general argument then is that Pareto improvements are justified because they are consented to *ex post* and that Kaldor-Hicks efficient moves are justified because they are consented to *ex ante*. In both cases, consent is given by one's accepting the relevant form of compensation. But accepting compensation, whether it be *ex post* or *ex ante*, fails to constitute consent. So even if consent were sufficient to justify Pareto superiority or Kaldor-Hicks, accepting compensation would not be.

Consider first the case of accepting compensation *ex post*. Suppose you injure me in an automobile accident. I sue and win a damage award against you. I have a choice. I can either accept or refuse compensation. Suppose I accept full compensation. If you gain in virtue of injuring then compensating me, your injuring and compensating me constitutes a Pareto improvement. You are better off having done me wrong and I am no worse off once I have accepted compensation. But does my accepting compensation in the form of a damage award constitute my giving consent to what you have done? Think of it this way. If I accept compensation, I give my consent. I can refuse to give my consent to your misbehavior only if I turn down compensation. Surely this must be wrong. I not only wish to accept compensation; I demand it from you as my *due.* Compenstion is owed me for what you have done to me—as a means of protecting or securing my entitlement to bodily security, not as a way of securing my consent to your mischief.

On the other hand suppose I refuse your compensation on the grounds that my refusal to accept compensation is the only way I can withhold my consent. But wouldn't we rightly infer that my failure to accept compensation indicates that I did not feel compensation was my due, that I had waived my right not to be injured by you, or that I had consented to or assumed the risk. *Ex post* compensation as consent fails to provide an adequate basis for justifying the Pareto superiority criterion.

Now consider the argument that *ex ante* compensation constitutes consent, in the light of an example I have used elsewhere.[46] Imagine that you are choosing between purchasing homes in two neighborhoods: one in a high-crime, low-cost neighborhood; the other in a low-crime, higher-priced neighborhood. Suppose the difference in housing costs is attributable only to a difference in crime rates; the higher price reflects a lower crime rate; the lower housing cost reflects a higher crime rate—nothing else. You choose the lower-priced house. The price differential constitutes *ex ante* compensation for the increased risk of crime. Suppose your house is burgled. It hardly follows that you have consented to the burglary. That is, while we might think it fair that your insurance rates reflect the higher crime rate, we do not believe that in purchasing the house you have in effect given your consent to whatever criminal mischief might befall you. *Ex ante* compensation does not constitute consent. Compensation, whether *ex post* or *ex ante*, will not suffice to justify either Pareto superiority or Kaldor-Hicks on consensual grounds.

Arguments from consent are of two sets: actual and hypothetical. They may apply to particular actions or policies, or to institutions. There are then at least four categories of consent arguments: (1) arguments from actual consent applied to individual actions or institutional events; (2) arguments from actual consent applied to the choice of institutions or to the principles in the light of which such institutions are to be framed; (3) hypothetical consent arguments applied to individual events; and (4) hypothetical consent applied at the level of institutional choice. We have so far rejected actual consent arguments advanced to support individual applications of both the Pareto superiority and Kaldor-Hicks criterion—i.e., arguments of the first sort. Arguments from actual (explicit) consent for the application of their Kaldor-Hicks or Pareto efficiency at the institutional level— that is, arguments of the second sort—are not *a priori* arguments at all. Whether either standard of efficiency would be chosen at the institutional level is an empirical question. We would have to wait and see. So arguments of the second sort cannot be fruitfully discussed here. I have elsewhere explored the possibility of defending both Kaldor-Hicks and Pareto at the level of social choice by the use of hypothetical consent arguments.[47] In the context of this chapter I cannot do justice to the arguments on either side of that claim, and so will refrain from rehearsing even a summary of those arguments here. Instead I want to explore the argument from hypothetical consent for individual instances of the Pareto superiority criterion— arguments of the third sort—largely because there is reason to believe that this is the sort of argument advocates of economic analysis have in mind.

The general argument is developed by considering an example. Suppose A injures B. Suppose that the value to A of the activity that causes B's injury is 100, and that the value of the damage to B is 50. We can imagine three social states. In one, A foregoes engaging in the activity to avoid imposing a 50 loss on B. Label this S. In the next, A engages in the activity and causes B to suffer a 50 loss so that he might secure a 100 gain. Label this S_1. Finally, imagine A engages in the activity, gains 100 thereby, causes B a 50 loss, then compensates B 60, thus bringing his final gain to 40 and B's to 10. Label this S_2. A ranks these states: S_1, S_2, S. B ranks them S_2, S, S_1. S_2 is a Pareto superior to S, since both A and B are better off in S_2. Both A and B therefore prefer S_2 to S; that is, if asked in advance which between S and S_2 each prefers, both A and B would presumably prefer S_2. But if S_2 is preferred to S, then both A and B would have chosen S_2; they *would have consented* to S_2. Thus, S_2, the Pareto superior state, is justified on hypothetical consent grounds.

All arguments of this sort proceed by deducing an individual's hypothetical consent from his preference ranking. An individual's consent is built into the *definition* of what it is for him to have a preference. Then it is logically inconsistent to prefer one state of the world to another but to withhold one's consent to the preferred state. The problem is that when it is analyzed entirely in terms of what it is to have a preference, a person's consent plays no independent justificatory role. One adds nothing of justificatory import by claiming that S_2 is justified on hypothetical consent grounds that is not already contained in the claim that going from S to S_2 is in both A's and B's interest—i.e., S_2 is Pareto efficient.

In order to carry independent justificatory force, arguments from hypothetical consent must not be entirely deducible from an analysis of what it means for a social state to be in one's self-interest. The difference can be put as follows. One's ordering of preferences is independent of paths (how one gets from one social state to another); what one is prepared to consent to is not. I may always prefer the state of the world in which I am wealthy and famous to that in which I am not, but I might withhold my consent to that state if the only way I can attain wealth and fame is through criminal mischief. What a person is prepared to consent to cannot be inferred from his preference ranking.

This objection might be met by building the path taken to a social state into a fuller description of it; so that it is not true that I prefer being rich and famous to my current relative anonymity and middle class existence. Instead I prefer the former to the latter if I attain the former through hard work—for example, by publishing scholarly works—but I do *not* prefer the former to the latter if I attain the former through fraud or mischief.

The problem with this approach is that it greatly reduces the *scope* of arguments from hypothetical consent. To see this, reconsider the original example. A and B may both prefer S_2 to S, but if the path is to figure in the description of S_2, then B might prefer S_2 only if he in fact agrees in advance to A's injuring then compensating him. B will have none of A's injuring him without first securing his consent, then compensating him for damages done. The need for actual consent as a basis of hypothetical consent greatly reduces the scope of the latter. For it is not the fact that the move to the more preferred state is Pareto superior that warrants the inference to the relevant parties' hypothetical consent; rather it is the fact that the more preferred state is attainable by *actual ex ante consent* that warrants the inference.

To sum up, there is no argument for Kaldor-Hicks from either utility or consent. There is an argument for Pareto superiority from utility, but not from consent—either actual or hypothetical—at least not the one its proponents have advanced. There has been a reluctance to wed Pareto superiority to utilitarianism especially among economists and lawyers who have been impressed by the standard textbook objections to utilitarianism. More important, perhaps, the vast majority of economic analysis does not rely on the Pareto superiority criterion. So even if Pareto superiority could be justified on utilitarian grounds, it would not follow that much of economic analysis would be.

INSTITUTIONAL FRAMEWORKS AND THE
JURISPRUDENCE OF ECONOMIC ANALYSIS

I want to close by discussing briefly three lines of objection to economic
analysis that warrant further consideration. These are all essentially
jurisprudential in nature. First, the economic analysis of law is apparently committed to legal realism as a jurisprudential thesis. For it
is essential to the enterprise that judges be free to decide cases in
accordance with the dictates of efficiency, rather than in accordance
with any set of preexisting claims litigants might have against one
another. In addition, the economic analysis is an instrumentalist theory
of law, since it views litigation in terms of the opportunities claimants
give courts to promote global or collective interests. Whether economic
analysis is ultimately instrumentalist and realist requires further inquiry;
whether, if it is both instrumentalist and realist, this should count
against economic analysis requires more thought as well.

Secondly, on the pure economic analysis of law advocated by Posner
among lawyers and Mitchell Polinsky, for example, among economists,
the aim of the court in resolving disputes is to promote efficiency.[48]
In Polinsky's case, and perhaps less so in Posner's, when efficiency is
contrasted with justice the contrast is between the size of the pie and
its distribution. It is the difference between efficiency and distributive
justice, or between efficiency and equity. This, as philosophers will
note, is not a rich conception of the range of issues within the ambit
of justice. The central point, however, is that on the economist's view,
the comparative advantage of courts is promoting efficiency, while
the comparative advantage of legislatures is doing justice, which
amounts to redistributing wealth to promote an ill-defined conception
of equity. This seems to constitute an odd reversal of institutional
roles. Promoting social goals like efficiency requires gathering a good
deal of empirical information, and we tend therefore to think of
courts as lacking the tools let alone the proper authority necessary
to act as advocates of efficiency. In contrast, the prevalent pretheoretical
intuition is that courts, in part because they are essentially unac-
countable, nondemocratic institutions that do not seek out issues or
goals to promote or advance, are best left to adjudicate claims brought
to them by particular litigants and framed in terms of the interests
of the litigants alone. In short, our intuitions regarding the comparative
advantages of courts and legislatures are exactly the opposite of what
the economic analysis claims they are. For, unlike the economist, the
common view is that promoting human welfare is the comparative
advantage of legislatures, while doing justice between persons is the
comparative advantage of courts.

Finally, I want to draw attention to a line of argument against economic analysis that emphasizes that market exchange is always relative to a framework for trade. Versions of this objection have been developed by both James Buchanan and myself, but I believe his came first.[49] I will try to explain the source of our concern.

The standard move in economic analysis is to imagine trade under the conditions of the Coase Theorem, then to define the outcome of trade under those conditions as efficient. Then when courts are asked to promote efficiency, they are being asked in effect to replicate that outcome. Buchanan's point is that the outcome of free trade under the conditions of the Coase Theorem is efficient *given the particular institutional framework defined by those initial conditions.* The conditions of the Coase Theorem; however, constitute only one possible framework for trade. We can therefore define efficiency more generally as the outcome of free exchange relative to a particular institutional framework. So we could refer to the outcome of trade within a framework of trade that is restricted by transaction costs as efficient in the same sense as trade under the Coase Theorem is efficient. In Buchanan's view, the standard economic analyst is committed to efficiency as an ideal, as the outcome of exchange under idealized circumstances. Not only don't those circumstances exist; if they did, they would at best constitute only one of many possible frameworks for trade. For Buchanan what makes a state efficient is that given the existing framework for trade, no further voluntary trades can be made that would benefit both parties.

It is easy to see how radically different Buchanan's economics, what he calls constitutional economics, is from traditional economic analysis of law. Its implications for the whole line of analysis explained in the second section of this chapter are enormous, for time and again in applying traditional economic analysis we have shown how courts, when asked to promote efficiency, would first determine what is efficient by imagining what trades would have occurred when the conditions of the Coase Theorem were satisfied. But if Buchanan is right, what grounds justify giving priority to efficiency under the conditions of the Coase Theorem as that which courts seeking to mimic the market should strive to replicate? My version of this objection is a bit less radical, but I think Buchanan has a fundamentally sound point. When we talk of efficiency in terms of trade or transfer, we assume a framework—a set of rules, conventions, and practices, that govern trade, exchange, and transfer. And a good deal of what the traditional economic analysis of law treats as a mere transaction cost is in fact part of the framework for trade. In imagining trade in the absence of those costs, often we are in fact imagining trade under different rules—within a different framework for trade. And what is efficient under those conditions may have little or no bearing on what is or what would be efficient within the existing market framework.

These are only three of several areas of inquiry not yet adequately addressed by either advocates or critics of the economic analysis of law. I hope that by offering several objections to it I have not given the reader the impression that I find the economic analysis of law thoroughly useless. Quite the contrary. Economic analysis is far more sophisticated and powerful than are the vast majority of the objections against it. My goal has not been to undermine economic analysis; rather my purpose has been to explain it, to give the reader an appreciation of its methodology and scope and to explore some doubts I and others have had about it.

NOTES

1. We can distinguish between ordinal and cardinal rankings. In a sample *ordinal* ranking, *Jones* prefers outcome S_4 first, S_3 second, S_2 third, while S_1 is his least favored alternative. But the ordinal ranking doesn't tell us just how much more Jones prefers S_4 to S_3 to S_2 to S_1. A sample *cardinal* ranking might be that Jones prefers S_4 twice as much as he prefers S_3, which he prefers four times as much as S_2, which in turn he prefers six times as much as S_1. Cardinality reflects the *intensity* of one's desires or preferences as well as their order. The problem of interpersonal comparability arises when *Smith* as well as *Jones* has a cardinal ranking over outcomes, and we adopt a policy that makes Jones better off and Smith worse off. Whether that policy increases utility on balance depends on whether the gain to Jones exceeds Smith's loss. Determining whether Jones's gain exceeds Smith's loss, however, requires that we have some *common* ground that allows us to put the intensity of Jones's desire on the same scale as Smith's. All we have is Jones's *relative desire* and Smith's *relative desire.* And we may have no way of bringing these scales of relative desire in accord with one another.
2. The move from *a* to *b* is a move to the north—to B's advantage—but to the west which brings A closer to the origin, and thus is to his disadvantage.
3. Again, A is made worse off.
4. For A, the move from *a* to *b* is not an improvement, but the move from *b* to *e* is; thus, the claim that the move from *a* to *e* through *b* mixes Pareto superior with non-Pareto superior moves.
5. This assumes that trade is both possible (i.e., there are no rules prohibiting it) and costless.
6. The point here is that the negotiations between A and B do not have any impact on anyone else. What this means for economists is that everyone other than the two of them is indifferent between the distribution of goods between A and B before and after their negotiations.
7. Ronald Coase, "The Problem of Social Cost," *Journal of Law and Economics* 3 (1960):1, $\Delta\pi$ and ΔD curves marginal profit exceeds marginal damage.
8. That is, any more corn can makes Jones-Smith the *farmer* better off only by making Jones-Smith the *rancher-farmer* worse off. An additional cow after the nth cow would mean that his marginal private costs would exceed the benefit he could accrue by raising it, and it would be irrational for him so to act. The key notions here are marginal benefit and marginal cost.
9. Coase, "The Problem of Social Cost," 1–2.

10. For some doubts about the success of negotiations, see discussion below in pp. 258–62.

11. There are at least two other ways of stating the basic point of the Coase Theorem. These are:

(1) If individuals are cooperative and free to negotiate, there exists a private, market solution to all externality problems.

(2) Under the conditions set out in (1) market exchange can always circumvent an inefficient legal rule.

12. The discussion here moves quickly into subtle distinctions between the two approaches. The reader might be content simply to skim this discussion for the sake of getting a rough idea of the differences. The conclusions are summarized at the end of the section.

13. In other words, the state may impose a tax on A whose conduct is harmful to B and then say: "Look, no negotiations between you two. The prevention of harm is a matter for the public power"; or once the tax has been imposed it might impose no prohibition on what goes on between A and B, thereby leaving it up to them to negotiate further if they choose to do so.

14. The general point is this: if the person harmed is not awarded the tax revenue, he still experiences his loss. If, even after paying taxes, A gains by engaging in a harmful activity he will continue to engage in it provided he is not bought off. But the person who is harmed will buy him off whenever the harm he suffers exceeds the "after tax benefit to A." Therefore, when tax revenues are not distributed to the damaged party, negotiations may lead to too much reduction in harmful activities. On the other hand, if B is given revenue exactly equal to his damages, he just doesn't care how much damage he suffers, thereby leaving everything up to A; and A will respond to the tax so that he will stop harming B when it costs him more to harm B than he stands to gain by doing so.

15. Richard Posner, *Economic Analysis of Law* (Boston: Little, Brown and Co., 1977).

16. Advocates of markets are equally likely to laud markets for their efficiency as for the fact that in markets individuals are free to express their rational autonomous nature. So one finds libertarian defenses of the free market as well as economic defenses of it. And when the conditions of the Coase Theorem are satisfied, no conflict between the libertarian and economic defenses of markets arises: optimal outcomes are secured through free trade. As we shall see, interesting conflicts emerge when the conditions of the Coase Theorem are not satisfied.

17. In other words, suppose A and B go to court to resolve a dispute. The judge has read Posner and he wants to resolve the dispute as it would be resolved by the market. Which market? A and B are acting in a particular market or framework for trade. That market is bound by certain social and institutional facts and their negotiations reflect those constraints as much as they reflect their attributes, opportunities and information. Should the judge try to figure out what outcome A and B would negotiate to in *that* market, or should the judge abstract further and imagine which trades A and B would have made had the market in which their trading were to take place satisfied the conditions of the Coase Theorem? For a fuller discussion of this problem see pp. 273–75.

18. Guido Calabresi and Douglas Malamed, "Property Rules, Liability Rules and Inalienability: One View of the Cathedral," *Harvard Law Review* 85 (1972):1089.

19. That is not to say that you are free to ignore my right. For we might impose a criminal sanction for your misconduct. Indeed, on the standard economic theory of criminal law, that is precisely why we have a criminal law: to induce individuals to seek out market alternatives when they are available.

20. In this section, all the examples assume that the agents are risk-neutral. A risk-neutral person is defined as indifferent among a set of bets of the following sort: a certainty of receiving $10; a 50 percent chance of winning $20; a 25 percent chance of winning $40; a 1 percent chance of winning $1,000. Another way to put this is to say that a risk-neutral person cares only about *expected* outcomes. The expected outcome

is determined by the *value* of the outcome discounted (multiplied) by the probability of its occurrence. In the set of bets described above, the expected outcome is the same in all cases, i.e., $10.00. For a more detailed discussion of the application of economics to law which does not assume risk neutrality, includes the possibility of insurance against risk, and which considers more applications see A. Mitchell Polinsky's outstanding introduction to economic analysis, *An Introduction to Law and Economics* (Boston: Little, Brown and Co., 1983).

21. Here the efficient result is for the manufacturer to produce 100 units of output. At 125 units of production marginal costs exceed gains.

22. A more detailed discussion of fault and strict liability in terms primarily of the justice or fairness of each is presented in Chapter 4.

23. To keep things relatively simple, I will not here discuss other alternatives, for example the defense of *comparative*, rather than contributory negligence.

24. See Learned Hand's characterization of negligence in *United States* v. *Carroll Towing Co.*, 159 F. 2d 169 (2d Circuit 1947).

25. What is at issue is a determination of the damage remedy that would replicate the outcome of our negotiations regarding the effect of my liability to you in the event I were to breach or find another buyer.

26. This example closely follows Polinsky's.

27. Again, Jones produces the networks for $50 and Smith pays him $75 for them. That deal nets Jones $25. Smith values them at $110, but pays Jones only $75. Smith gains $35. Their joint gain is $60.

28. We said at the outset that efficiency in the contract setting is equivalent to maximizing net gain. The net gain in the sale to Brown is $33; $33 for Jones, $0 for Brown. The net gain in the sale to Smith is $60. Thus the efficient outcome is that whenever Brown values the crossover at the going rate—i.e., $83—Jones should deliver to Smith.

But this argument requires modification. If Brown knows that Smith values the networks at $110, he will sell to Smith, so his net gain (if we suppose he gets Smith to pay the full freight) is $110 minus $83 or $27. His $27 gain and Jones's $33 gain results in a net gain of $60; the very same net gain results then whether Jones delivers to Smith or to Brown. Indeed, Jones might be inclined to sell to Brown since by doing so he stands to secure a greater share of the gains from trade: $33 versus $25. (What we have working here is the insight of the Coase Theorem. No matter what terms the parties initially agree to, if everyone is fully informed and transactions *among them* are costless all outcomes will be efficient.) The fact that he (Jones) could sell to Brown at a greater personal gain with no consequent loss in social optimality might encourage him to bargain harder with Smith. He might up his asking price from $75 to $83. For his part Smith could counter that he pays Jones $75 upfront and is unwilling to pay him $83 upfront. Jones might be satisfied that having the money upfront—which we assumed was necessary for him to produce the crossovers—is worth foregoing $7 of possible gains, especially if the cost of borrowing from a third source the money necessary to begin production exceeds $7.

The net gain in both cases is $60 only if transactions are costless and all the relevant parties have full information regarding one another's preferences. In a real contract situation these conditions are unlikely to be satisfied and so any additional transactions may involve costs that will reduce the net gain. So even if the net gain can, under certain ideal circumstances, be set equal to that secured by a direct trade between Jones and Smith, it is unlikely that either party would prefer that Jones sell to Brown then leave it to Brown to sell to Smith when Brown values the crossover less than Smith does.

29. Reliance costs are those one assumes in legitimate anticipation of securing what one has bargained for. If Smith expected to receive the crossover, he might have purchased a storage facility for them in which they could be safely kept until he could find someone to sell him woofers and tweeters of sufficiently high quality.

30. I only mention this point in passing. If B is contracting with A, then what B is willing to pay A (regardless of the value of the product he is trying to secure) is in

part a function of the damage remedy he has at his disposal in the event A were to breach. Reliance damages are in general worth less than expectation damages and so from B's point of view there is a greater risk involved in a deal secured only by the reliance remedy. He is less than certain he will secure from the agreement what he had hoped to gain from it, and this will be reflected in the price he will be prepared to pay. Because the reliance remedy would be the only remedy every potential trader had at his disposal in negotiations with A, A could not expect to receive a higher price from someone other than B (other things being equal). Another way to think of this is that expectation damages provide a kind of insurance against risk to purchasers, thus driving prices up a bit from what they would be under a reliance remedy.

31. For a more extensive discussion of the economics of the criminal category, see Alvin Klevorick, "On the Economic Theory of Crime," and Jules Coleman, "Crime, Kickers and Transaction Structures," in *Nomos XXVII: Criminal Justice,* eds. J. Roland Pennock and John W. Chapman (New York: New York University Press, forthcoming).

32. Gary Becker, "Crime and Punishment: An Economic Approach," *Journal of Political Economy* 76 (1968):169, 209.

33. This constraint is important since it is not feasible to fine people more money than they have.

34. This section may be the most difficult to follow, and the instructor may simply want to summarize its main points for the student. Still, the basic ideas are intuitive enough and there is no harm in introducing philosophy students to elements of game and decision theory, in particular, to the idea of an equilibrium.

35. I. P. L. P'ng, "A Model of Suit, Settlement and Trial in the United States Legal System," Working Paper No. 5, *Stanford Law School Working Paper Series,* in the Law and Economics Program.

36. That is, in this game the defendant knows whether or not he is at fault; the plaintiff does not. In some cases, the defendant may also be uncertain of his guilt.

37. The analysis gets difficult quickly. Though it may take a little extra work to get through, I am convinced it's worth the effort. In any case, don't give up entirely. If all this pains you too much, I can provide solutions at an additional price. Actually, if it gets too difficult, just move on to the last section.

38. For a fuller discussion of this point, see Robert Cooter, "The Cost of Coase," *Journal of Legal Studies.*

39. For a discussion of rational cooperation: in particular, whether there is a unique solution to every bargaining game, cf. Jules L. Coleman, *The Market Paradigm* (manuscript).

40. See p. 214.

41. Tibor Scitovsky, "A Note on Welfare Propositions in Economics," *Review of Economic Studies* 9 (1941):77.

42. For a fuller discussion of this argument, see Jules L. Coleman, "The Economic Analysis of Law," in *Nomos XXVI: Ethics, Economics and Law,* eds. J. Roland Pennock and John W. Chapman (New York: New York University Press, 1982).

43. Nicholas Kaldor, "Welfare Propositions of Economics and Interpersonal Comparisons of Utility," *Economic Journal* 49 (1939):549.

44. For a more complete discussion, see Jules L. Coleman, "The Normative Basis of the Economic Analysis: A Critical Review of Richard Posner's The Economics of Justice," *Stanford Law Review* 34 (1982).

45. The negligence system is not really a Kaldor-Hicks system because victims are sometimes compensated—i.e., if they can prove fault. Under a true Kaldor-Hicks system victims would not be. Therefore, the negligence system only approximates a true Kaldor-Hicks system. The important point, however, is the contrast with the system of strict liability in which victims are compensated regardless of their injurer's fault.

46. Coleman, "The Normative Basis of the Economic Analysis," 1122–23.

47. Ibid., 1123–31.

48. Polinsky, *Introduction,* 7–10, 106–13.

49. James Buchanan, "Positive Economics, Welfare Economics, and Political Economy," and Jules L. Coleman, "The Foundations of Constitutional Economics," in *Constitutional Economics: Containing the Economic Powers of Government,* ed. Richard McKenzie (Lexington, Mass: D.C. Heath and Co., 1984).

Suggestions for Further Reading

An extensive bibliography of further readings may be developed by consulting the footnotes for each chapter. The selections listed here are those judged by the authors to be the best initial readings for the person who wishes to get a more detailed understanding of the issues explored in the book.

CHAPTER 1: THE NATURE OF LAW

Benditt, Theodore. *Law as Rule and Principle.* Stanford: Stanford University Press, 1978.
    A discussion of the debate between H. L. A. Hart and Ronald Dworkin on the question of whether law should be viewed as a system of rules or in terms of legal principles.

Cohen, Marshall, ed. *Ronald Dworkin and Contemporary Jurisprudence.* Totowa, N.J.: Rowman & Allanheld, 1984.
    Critical essays by Rolf Sartorious, Jules Coleman, Joseph Raz, and others on Dworkin's work. Contains Dworkin's reply to his critics.

Coleman, Jules L. "Negative and Positive Positivism." *Journal of Legal Studies* 11 (January 1982).
    An attempt to assess the degree to which the views of H. L. A. Hart and Ronald Dworkin can be rendered consistent. Involves a detailed analysis of varieties of legal positivism.

Dworkin, Ronald. *Taking Rights Seriously.* Cambridge: Harvard University Press, 1978.
    An attack on legal positivism and the presentation of a stimulating defense of the theses that there is a right answer to every legal dispute and that such an answer is in part to be determined by a moral theory of rights assignment. The focus of this book is upon the problem of judicial decision. The paperback edition is preferable because it contains an Appendix that is a reply to some of Dworkin's critics.

Hacker, P. M. S., and J. Raz, eds. *Law, Morality and Society: Essays in Honour of H.L.A. Hart.* Oxford: Clarendon Press, 1977.

A series of essays by Ronald Dworkin, Joseph Raz, Joel Feinberg, and others dealing with problems upon which Hart has written.

Hart, H. L. A. *The Concept of Law.* Oxford: Oxford University Press, 1961.

This book is probably the finest contribution to jurisprudence of this century. It contains an analytical discussion and criticism of various legal theories and presents a sophisticated defense of legal positivism.

MacCormick, Neil. *Legal Reasoning and Legal Theory.* Oxford: Clarendon Press, 1978.

An attempt to assess the relative merits of Hart's positivism and Dworkin's rights thesis through an extensive examination of legal cases.

Raz, Joseph. *The Concept of a Legal System.* Oxford: Clarendon Press, 1970.

An attempt to defend a generally positivistic analysis of law against such critics as Dworkin.

CHAPTER 2: MORAL THEORY AND ITS APPLICATION TO LAW

Baker, C. Edwin. "Scope of the First Amendment Freedom of Speech." *UCLA Law Review* 25 (1978).

————— . "Press Rights and Government Power to Structure the Press." *University of Miami Law Review* 34 (1980).

Baker's work on the First Amendment is both informative and provocative.

Brest, Paul. "The Fundamental Rights Controversy: The Essential Contradictions of Normative Constitutional Scholarship." *Yale Law Journal* 90 (1981).

Skepticism directed toward those who think that a correct moral or political theory will produce systematic unity for constitutional doctrine. The works discussed by Brest merit study by the reader interested in normative constitutional jurisprudence. Particularly valuable is John H. Ely, *Democracy and Distrust: A Theory of Judicial Review.* Cambridge, Mass.: Harvard University Press, 1981.

Feinberg, Joel. "Limits to the Free Expression of Opinion." In *Philosophy of Law*, 2nd ed., edited by Joel Feinberg. Belmont: Wadsworth, 1980.

A careful exploration of the issue of the circumstances under which it is justified to use state coercion to inhibit free expression. Feinberg's *Doing and Deserving*. Princeton: Princeton University Press, 1970, and *Rights, Justice, and the Bounds of Liberty*. Princeton: Princeton University Press, 1980, are also worth exploring. The essays reprinted in these books cover a wide range of topics and are valuable studies by one of America's most important moral and legal philosophers.

MacIntyre, Alasdair. *After Virtue*. Notre Dame: University of Notre Dame Press, 1981.

A sustained critique of liberalism (e.g., Rawls and Dworkin) and libertarianism (e.g., Nozick) in moral and political philosophy. Argues that the models of rational proof offered in contemporary ethics are illusions and that ethics requires a community of shared values that is missing in the modern world.

Nozick, Robert. *Anarchy, State and Utopia*. New York: Basic Books, 1974.

A stimulating statement and defense of a libertarian moral and political outlook.

Rawls, John. *A Theory of Justice*. Cambridge: Harvard University Press, 1971.

A masterpiece of twentieth-century moral philosophy that defends a generally liberal moral and political outlook. Wide-ranging in scope and detailed in argument, it sets the standard against which other systematic works in ethics must be judged. Even those highly critical of it (e.g., Nozick) recognize its central importance.

Richards, David A. J. *Sex, Drugs, Death and the Law*. Totowa, N.J.: Rowman and Littlefield, 1982.

Philosopher and law professor Richards discusses both moral theory and constitutional doctrine in defense of a generally liberal view of freedom and state coercion in private matters.

Scanlon, T. M. "A Theory of Freedom of Expression." *Philosophy and Public Affairs* 1 (1972).

A generally Kantian analysis and defense of free expression.

Schauer, Frederick. *Free Speech: A Philosophical Inquiry*. Cambridge: Cambridge University Press, 1983.

Wolff, Robert Paul. "Robert Nozick's Derivation of the Minimal State." *Arizona Law Review* 19 (1977).

Though specifically directed against Nozick, this article provides a generally radical or Marxist basis for a critique of both libertarian and liberal moral and political theories. Critical of economic analysis of law.

CHAPTER 3: CRIME AND PUNISHMENT

Feinberg, Joel. *Harm to Others.* New York: Oxford University Press, 1984.
This is the first volume in Feinberg's projected four volume study entitled *The Moral Limits of Criminal Law.*

Fingarette, Herbert. *The Meaning of Criminal Insanity.* Berkeley: University of California Press, 1972.
The best general philosophical treatment of the insanity defense and other issues in law and psychiatry.

Fletcher, George P. *Rethinking Criminal Law.* Boston: Little, Brown, and Company, 1978.
A rich and complex theoretical review of the criminal law. Influenced by studies on comparative law, it offers original perspectives on a variety of topics. Difficult reading, but very provocative and stimulating.

Gross, Hyman. *A Theory of Criminal Justice.* Oxford: Oxford University Press, 1979.
A good introductory level presentation of the criminal law and the philosophical problems raised by it.

Hart, H. L. A. *Punishment and Responsibility.* Oxford: Oxford University Press, 1968.
A collection of Hart's important essays on the criminal law.

Kadish, Sanford, et al., eds. *Criminal Law and Its Processes,* 4th ed. Boston: Little, Brown, and Company, 1983.
Legal cases and scholarly materials on central issues in the criminal law. Organized in a very philosophically sensitive manner.

Murphy, Jeffrie G., ed. *Punishment and Rehabilitation.* Belmont: Wadsworth, 1973.
An anthology of readings from classical and contemporary sources on the philosophy of punishment. A new edition will appear soon.
———. *Retribution, Justice, and Therapy: Essays in the Philosophy of Law.* Dordrecht and Boston: D. Reidel, 1979.
Essays defending the retributive theory of punishment and exploring the suggestion that therapy might be used as an alternative to punishment.

_____ . "Blackmail: A Preliminary Inquiry." *The Monist* 63 (1980):156.
An attempt to show how difficult and complex the decision to criminalize can be by using the crime of blackmail as an example.

Radin, Margaret Jane. "The Jurisprudence of Death: Evolving Standards for the Cruel and Unusual Punishments Clause." *University of Pennsylvania Law Review* 126 (1978):989.
_____ . "Cruel Punishment and Respect for Persons: Super Due Process for Death." *Southern California Law Review* 53 (1980):1143.
Radin's articles are legally informative and philosophically sophisticated explorations of the death penalty in the light of the Eighth Amendment ban on cruel and unusual punishments.

Wasserstrom, Richard. "Punishment." In *Philosophy and Social Issues.* Notre Dame: University of Notre Dame Press, 1980.
A typically lucid and valuable discussion by Wasserstrom of a variety of philosophical issues with respect to punishment. A good initial follow-up reading for the material in this chapter.

CHAPTER 4: PHILOSOPHY AND THE PRIVATE LAW

A. TORT LAW

Calabresi, Guido. *The Costs of Accidents.* New Haven: Yale University Press, 1971.
Calabresi asks whether the current tort system provides the best approach to reducing justly the costs of accidents. The classic work on the normative economic approach to torts.

Coleman, Jules L. "Moral Theories of Torts: Their Scope and Limits." Parts 1, 2. *Law and Philosophy* 1 (1982); 2 (1983).
Coleman considers and rejects several arguments that tort law enforces ideals of justice. He then advances the view that there are central features of torts that can be explained by appeal to the principle of corrective justice but that other even more basic features of torts may require a nonmoral justification, i.e., an efficiency defense.
_____ . "Corrective Justice and Wrongful Gain." *Journal of Legal Studies* 11 (1982):421.
Coleman responds to Posner's charge that even corrective justice is analyzable in terms of efficiency.

Epstein, Richard. "A Theory of Strict Liability." Journal of Legal Studies 2 (1973):151.

Epstein defends the view that the moral basis of tort law is to be found in the requirement of liability that the defendant's conduct *causes* the victim's loss. Causation, not fault, is the key to the moral defense of torts.

Fletcher, George. "Fairness and Utility in Tort Theory." *Harvard Law Review* 85 (1972):537.

Fletcher defends the view that tort law can be thought of either as promoting a utilitarian (efficiency) end or as promoting justice, in particular, reciprocity of risk. Fletcher and Epstein are the most important philosophically inclined lawyers thinking about the relationship between justice and tort liability.

Posner, Richard. "A Theory of Negligence." *Journal of Legal Studies* 1 (1972):29.

Posner defends the claim that when courts impose liability on the basis of fault they are appealing to an economic analysis of negligence. Posner is the most articulate defender of the economic approach to tort law—indeed, to all law.

————. "The Concept of Corrective Justice in Recent Theories of Tort Law." *Journal of Legal Studies* 10 (1981):187.

Posner tries to capture the insights of his "corrective justice" critics—Coleman, Epstein, and Fletcher—by trying to derive their claims about tort law from the principle of efficiency.

B. CONTRACTS

Epstein, Richard. "Unconscionability: A Critical Reappraisal." *Jounal of Law and Economics* 18 (1975):293.

Epstein considers whether the doctrine of unconscionability in contracts can be defended on grounds consistent with libertarian principles of political philosophy.

Kennedy, Duncan. "Form and Substance in Private Law Adjudication." *Harvard Law Review* 89 (1976):1685.

Kennedy contrasts individualism with altruism and considers the role of the law of contracts in furthering individualistic ends at the expense of community or altruistic ideals.

Kronman, Anthony T. "Specific Performance." *University of Chicago Law Review* 45 (1978):351.

Kronman explores the viability of specific performance as an award in a breach of contracts case, especially in conjunction with the liability rule/property rule distinction explored in Chapter 5 of this book.

Posner, Richard. "Gratuitous Promises in Economics and Law." *Journal of Legal Studies* 1 (1977):411.

Posner explores the economic basis for individuals making promises without securing something of value in return and the economic justifiability of enforcing such promises in contracts.

CHAPTER 5: LAW AND ECONOMICS

Ackerman, Bruce. "The Economic Foundations of Property Law." Boston: Little, Brown & Co., (1975).

A valuable collection of essays exploring efficiency arguments for various aspects of property law. Several of the classic essays are included, for example, Michelman's piece on the Takings question and Hardin's "The Tragedy of the Commons."

Coase, Ronald. "The Problem of Social Cost." *Journal of Law and Economics* 3 (1960):1.

The seminal piece in the field. Coase shows how, under certain constraints, individuals will negotiate around efficient legal rules to promote efficient outcomes.

Coleman, Jules L. "Efficiency, Auction and Exchange: Philosophic Aspects of the Economic Approach to Law." *California Law Review* 68 (1980):221.

Coleman distinguishes among various efficiency notions and explores the ways in which the economic approach to law confuses them.

———. "Efficiency, Utility and Wealth Maximization." *Hofstra Law Review* 8 (1980):509.

Coleman explores the relationship of efficiency to utilitarian moral theory and the relationship of both to Posner's conception of wealth maximization.

———. "Crime, Kickers and Transaction Structures." In *Nomos, Vol. XXVII: Criminal Justice*, edited by J. Roland Pennock and John W. Chapman. New York: New York University Press, 1984.

Author considers and rejects several versions of the economic approach to crime focusing especially on the economic argument for the existence of a criminal category.

Dworkin, Ronald. "Why Efficiency?" *Hofstra Law Review* 8 (1980):563.

Dworkin rejects all arguments for economic efficiency that claim that efficiency is worth pursuing for some reason other than doing so may in some contexts promote justice.

Kennedy, Duncan, and Frank Michelman. "Are Property and Contract Efficient?" *Hofstra Law Review* 8 (1980):711.

Kennedy and Michelman consider various economic efficiency-related arguments for the institution of private property and for the legal enforcement of contractual arrangements.

Klevoric, Alvin. "The Economics of Crime." In *NOMOS, Vol. XXVII: Criminal Justice*, edited by J. Roland Pennock and John W. Chapman. New York: New York University Press, 1984.

The best discussion of the most difficult issue in the economic theory of crime: Why make conduct criminal? Like almost everything else in the economic analysis of law, Klevoric's piece draws heavily upon the distinction between property and liability rules first advanced by Calabresi and Malamed.

Kronman, Anthony T., and Richard Posner. *The Economics of Contract Law.* Boston: Little, Brown and Company, 1979.

A collection of essays by and large supportive of the economic approach to contract law which discuss every facet of contracts, from the general justifying aim of the institution to the variety of remedies for breach. Includes the Posner, Kronman, Epstein, and Kennedy pieces referred to in the bibliography for Chapter 4.

Polinsky, A. Mitchell. *An Introduction to Law and Economics.* Boston: Little, Brown and Company, 1983.

The absolute *best* introduction to law and economics, especially for the mathematically unsophisticated. A perfect companion for the Posner book. Philosophers are likely to find the treatment of issues of justice and institutional competence a bit unsophisticated. Ignore this fault and appreciate the clarity and conciseness of the exposition.

Posner, Richard. *The Economic Analysis of Law.* Boston: Little, Brown and Company, 1973.

The most comprehensive effort to apply economic analysis to every aspect of legal experience. Extremely impressive, but not for beginners.

Table of Cases Cited

Index

Index